THE AMERICAN JUDAISM READER

E. SCHACHNER

edited by PAUL KRESH

The
American Judaism
Reader

essays,
fiction
and poetry
from the
pages of
American Judaism

Union of American
Hebrew Congregations

NEW YORK, N. Y.

American Judaism has been the official publication of the Union of American Hebrew Congregations and its affiliates: National Federation of Temple Sisterhoods, National Federation of Temple Brotherhoods, National Federation of Temple Youth, National Association of Temple Administrators, and National Association of Temple Educators.

London	*New York*	*Toronto*
Abelard-Schuman	Abelard-Schuman	Abelard-Schuman
Limited	Limited	Canada Limited
8 King St. WC2	6 West 57th St.	896 Queen St. W.

Printed in the United States of America

To Rabbi Maurice N. Eisendrath
who encourages courage

ACKNOWLEDGMENTS

The editor wishes to thank the many authors, artists and their representatives who so generously made it possible for us to reprint the written material and illustrations in this volume which first appeared in the pages of *American Judaism*.

A special vote of thanks is due to the editorial board of the magazine, to our previous chairman of the board, Rabbi James Heller, and to our current chairman, Mr. Roger W. Straus, Jr.

I also wish to thank Miss Myra Miller, former Associate Editor of the magazine; her successor, Mr. Bernard Evslin; Miss Rayanna Simons, Editorial Assistant; Mrs. Dorothy Bodkin and Mrs. Annette Jackson for the weeks and months of gruelling work which went into preparing the manuscript for publication.

A special debt of gratitude has also been earned many times over by Mr. Ralph Davis, Production Manager, and Mr. Manny Kurtz, Art Director; of *American Judaism*.

Acknowledgment also should be made of the wise, sympathetic counsel and stimulating interest in the publication on the part of the various directors and staff members of the Union of American Hebrew Congregations and its affiliates, and especially to our Director of Program, Mr. Albert Vorspan.

Contents

[VII]

[VIII]

[IX]

[x]

Introduction

At this time, when overt anti-Semitism seems to be on the wane and supposedly it is "in" to be a Jew, Jewish subject matter is encountered everywhere — on the marquees of Broadway theatres, on the covers and in the pages of popular weeklies, in the columns of newspapers, in the grooves of phonograph records, on radio and television — everywhere. Everybody seems to know at least a couple of Yiddish words, and while the Jewish image is far from flattering these days in places like Harlem, it is much admired in less embittered circles. A foothold of security has been achieved, providing a climate for a kind of self-examination by our writers which would have been unthinkable a generation ago. The commissioning of flattering portraits of Jews and the Jewish milieu is left more and more to our institutions of defense, while the independent writer feels free to report what he sees and hears and experiences with a genuineness never before possible. This new freedom and determination to probe and question, to report on reality plain and whole, without self-conscious retouching, and with honesty — sometimes to a point of rudeness — is reflected in the pages of this book. We have grown weary of self-flattery and nostalgia, of a Jewishness identified only by way of the bagel and sentimental recollections of

Grandma with her tart tongue and gold-plated heart. We have found, too, that it is possible to make a clear-eyed inspection of the underpinnings of our faith in terms of modern science and philosophy with no fear whatever that the structure will collapse on examination.

Judaism, which has survived all these thousands of years, is much stronger, much more resilient, much more amenable to inspection and introspection than the cautious guardians of a sometimes airless past could have dared to believe. These attitudes, too, are reflected in *American Judaism*. The stories about *buba* and her benevolent despotic sway, the boastful polemics, the inspirational hymns of self-praise by the self-congratulatory, the self-conscious essays about boring historical figures too noble to be true, are still written, but you will not find them in this collection.

All is not solemn either. It seems to us that publications that take themselves too seriously are in danger of floating off at last on clouds of their own inflated pomposity; the Lord preserves the simple.

As of Fall of 1967, *American Judaism* is undergoing another metamorphosis, which it is hoped will result in further growth and maturity. The publication is merging with the UAHC's journal of adult Jewish education, *Dimension*, and will appear as a quarterly under the title *Dimensions in American Judaism*. The new journal will combine the symposia, articles and essays that have been appearing in *Dimension* with the high literary approach of *American Judaism*. News will be published in a separate newspaper, *The Voice*. In this book we present a distillation of the best offered in the past six years in the short story, religious writing, political action, travel, poetry and humor. That elusive quality, "a Jewish theme," is the strand that binds these pieces together. Whatever in them delighted, moved, disturbed or instructed us we can only hope will do the same for you.

Paul Kresh

About
American Judaism

What is the function of a religious periodical? Should it preach? Should it propagate the faith? Should it operate as a sober news medium? Should it report mainly on developments in the institution that supports it? Should it be literary? Should it be political? Should it offer practical guidance to those who administer houses of worship? Should it address itself to the clergy, to the lay adherents of its own sector, to the world at large? In short, should it be a house organ preoccupied with the affairs of its sponsors or an independent organ of opinion projecting the philosophy of the religion with which it is associated in ways more subtle and indirect than the outright assertion of credal positions?

In the spring of 1960 I was offered the exciting opportunity to edit *American Judaism*. Here was a magazine published for many decades and circulated to a quarter of a million families belonging to the Reform synagogues and temples of America. It was called the "official publication" of the Union of American Hebrew Congregations, which is the central congregational body of Reform Judaism in the Western Hemisphere, representing almost a million people. Yet for years this publication existed as a kind of institutional house organ. Would it be possible to break through narrow parochial patterns and create a magazine that might awaken widespread interest among readers grown apathetic over its contents without losing the special character of the publication which gave it its reason for being in the first place?

The UAHC is an organization renowned for its farsightedness. Its president is the outspoken and courageous Maurice N. Eisendrath. The editorial board of *American Judaism* was headed at the time by Rabbi James Heller and now by Roger Straus.

I asked the members of that board to let us open our windows to the world, to call in the most talented writers of fiction and essayists and poets we could find. We didn't have much money, but we could still do things on a professional basis. Every writer, every artist, would be paid something. Of course, some diehards couldn't see the point. What did a short story by Philip Roth about a grocer who drops dead in his bathroom have to do with the management of a temple concerned with the problem of Friday night synagogue attendance? And why should an article by Karl Shapiro about the techniques of modern prose take up space that might go to a discussion of the proper pronounciation of Hebrew in a Jewish religious school? One board member blanched the first time it was proposed to publish a five-part poem by Muriel Rukeyser — the first section of which was to take up two printed pages.

"What? Two pages for poetry?" Did I realize what two pages cost to print? Besides he had asked his wife, his mother-in-law and his college-educated daughter to explain the poem to him and none of them could. Had it not been for an alert member who sprang to her feet to remind this man that scholars are still quarrelling over the meaning of the Song of Songs, the superb long poem, "Akiba," reprinted here, might never have appeared in the magazine at all. As it happened, both readers and board members began soon enough to catch on to what we were doing — honoring the intelligence, perception and taste of our subscribers on the assumption that so educated and cultivated a membership could find the kernel of wisdom in a poem or a short story without having to see the message spelled out as in a sermon.

We wrote to the best authors. We invited the best artists to illustrate what they wrote. It was reassuring to find out that many a writer was willing to waive the alluring fees of commercial publications in order to speak to the special audience he wanted to reach, and could reach, through *American Judaism.*

We have tried to offer in each issue a varied menu of fiction, essays, poetry, religious thought, critical and political comment held together by the thread of themes directly concerned with Jewish life and Judaism. When illustrations have seemed appropriate, we have called on the finest artists we could find. In this way, rather than through propaganda or preaching, we have tried to convey the spirit and viewpoint of a vibrant, enlightened, progressive faith.

Although we could not compete with commercial rates and our size and frequency of publication were severely limited, we were amazingly successful from the first in attracting talent of the highest order to the pages of *American Judaism.* We have been able to offer articles of a challenging nature on matters of theology, politics and plain human interest and to balance these with fiction, criticism, poetry and that *sine qua non* of Jewish life — the element of humor. By our decision to transcend narrow interests and speak to the world, we have had the satisfaction of seeing our articles reprinted and discussed in many countries, and in such publications as *The New York Times, Time* magazine, the Scripps-Howard newspapers and a variety of others.

What, after all, is an "official" publication? We live in the age of the Foregone Conclusion, when much of what is written is simply a process of rationalizing a preconceived idea. But good writing is concerned more with the pursuit of truth wherever it leads than with the justification of a conventional position. Because Reform Judaism is concerned more with man's deeds than with the rigid observance of traditional ritual and taboos, we publish in an atmosphere of relative flexibility. In addition, *American Judaism* points out on its masthead that "the opinions of authors whose manuscripts are published are their own and do not necessarily reflect the viewpoint of the UAHC, its departments, regions or affiliates." Yet the spirit of our contents and the outlook of our movement are, for the most part, compatible.

When a Jew goes to synagogue or opens the "official publication" of a religious movement to which he belongs, he doesn't suddenly leave his mind outside — or lose it. Judaism has never been an isolated creed but has always been a way of life, a culture. Our readers — the members of our temples — are the

[xv]

same people who buy the books, attend the concerts, support the theatre, admire and demand the best in writing and in the arts. They will not be patronized. The greatest mistake any editor could make would be to underestimate them. There was some reluctance to publish an article "Toward a New Jewish Theology" by Rabbi Jack Bemporad because there was some concern that the language and ideas in it might prove too abstruse. However, it was printed anyway — and the piece resulted in the biggest outpouring of letters from readers ever received: hundreds of thoughtful responses to that one essay.

Meanwhile, unsolicited manuscripts continue to pour in. We find ourselves wading through endless pages written in that morose vocabulary peculiar to the prose of religionists, or verses in the doggerel style of bad old hymns, or grubby stories about grubby people whose only claim to attention rests on the fact that the characters bear Jewish names and eat Jewish food. Yet every such manuscript must be read because once in a while there gleams, amid the dross, the pure metal of good writing — the immediate sign of talent recounting an experience freshly perceived. An editor is thrilled when he receives a first-rate manuscript from a famous author, but the real adventure of editing is to discover promising new voices, almost drowned out by the shrill clamor of the bad writers who can be oh so angry but so inarticulate.

Few magazines spring full-blown into being. It takes time to achieve excellence. A publication evolves—or rather grows—like a living child, and *American Judaism* is still young, still growing, still suffering from growing pains. But we are fortunate to be coming of age in a time when Jewish subject matter has attained a tremendous prestige.

BEN SHAHN

SAUL FIELD

Articles
of
Faith

"*Canst thou by searching find out God?*"

Job X:21

Religious writing has become so specialized that some of it resembles technological prose with its private vocabulary and shorthand frames of references rather than the language of common speech. Theologians seem to be writing for each other. Rabbis and ministers tend to compose sermons, and many religionists easily fall into the homiletical tone, the pious cliché, the reiteration of the obvious. With all of the Bible and its commentaries to choose from, they repeat a dozen or so favored quotations, to the neglect of unmined biblical riches. Another weakness of religious writing is the indulgence in a rather heavy-handed type of fantasy. Since fantasy is one of the most difficult forms of literature, such writing gets bogged down all too frequently in the sandtraps of sententious dialogue or whimsy. It's rare, indeed, when attempts of this sort suceed in their aspiration of getting off the ground.

With religious writing swinging from the tense, turgid prose of philosophy to the childlike homilies of those who patronize their flock, it is especially refreshing to discover from time to time a piece of writing that is lucid, challenging, inspiring and attests to the respect of its author for his own craft.

The essays in this section struck us as direct and expert in tone as well as exceptionally provocative in content.

Rabbi Maurice N. Eisendrath

WILL SUCCESS SPOIL
THE SYNAGOGUE?

Rabbi Eisendrath, an acknowledged leader of Reform
Jewry, is president for life of the Union of American
Hebrew Congregations. He is the recipient of the first
Four Freedoms Award, the Gandhi Peace Award and the
Clergyman of the Year Award as a fearless defender of
justice. He has been a vigorous champion of civil rights.
His book *Can Faith Survive?* was a work of extraordinary
moral vision. In "Will Success Spoil the Synagogue?"
Rabbi Eisendrath deplores the substitution in our houses
of worship of shallow values for the timeless values of
Judaism.

The grievous failings of American culture—the worship of money,
power, status—have inevitably permeated the spirit of the synagogue in America. We have only to be honest with ourselves and
examine ourselves with unclouded eye. Our synagogues have become middle-class institutions. In order to maintain a large plant
and a growing staff, dues must necessarily be set so high that
Jews of lesser means are unable to belong. To be sure, most congregations loudly boast that "no Jew is turned away" from their
doors (unless he doesn't have a ticket on the High Holy Days),
that there is plenty of room for the poorest of the poor at every
Sabbath service (especially Sabbath mornings when attendance
is sluggish), and that no child will be refused admission to the
religious school, regardless of his parents' financial condition in
life.

But exalted as all such talk and policy admittedly are, candor
compels the confession that there is a golden curtain drawn
between the financially disadvantaged and the synagogue, unless they are willing to subject themselves to some—however
subtle and gentle—demeaning "means test," unless they are prepared to face the indignity of pleading poverty. Some congregations—though not enough of them yet—have moved in the
direction of a flexible dues system in which each family pays in

proportion to its ability to pay. This I regard as a healthy trend, worthy of greater emulation.

Notwithstanding this general "bowing the head and bending the knee" before the altar of mammon, rabbis are generally accorded a free pulpit. But the leaders of not a few temples have a low tolerance for political and economic dissent. In many congregations, particularly in the South, certain topics are definitely taboo, like "trefe" (non-kosher) food in a strictly Orthodox home.

Social action is repugnant to many trustees who cannot see what race relations and civil liberties have to do with religion and who, in any event, regard controversy as the ultimate heresy in the synagogue. Thus, even when a social action committee is finally and, after prodigious effort authorized by the Board, it is more than likely that any strong proposal for public action on a controversial issue will be laundered and bleached into vapidity before it emerges from the wringer of the board of trustees. It is no wonder that there is a rapid turnover of social action chairmen in most synagogues. Characteristically, the idealistic and socially sensitive social action chairmen and the members of the board of trustees function on two different conceptual planes. Social action is, by its nature, an uphill struggle in the contemporary American synagogue. A popular social action committee is probably doing nothing important.

In the face of such general apathy, and even of active opposition, I am especially proud of the role of resolute leadership played by the Union of American Hebrew Congregations. From its very founding, it sought to relate religion to life and to apply Judaism's prophetic teaching to the social, political, economic, national and international problems of the day.

The social action program of Reform Judaism has made good and rather impressive progress. Our national Commission on Social Action has become the social conscience of the Reform Movement, and most Reform synagogues now have social action or community affairs committees. But this progress has been made despite considerable apathy and even resistance which mounts formidably whenever decisive forward steps are contemplated.

In the effort to apply Judaism to life, the rabbis, on the whole, have played vital roles. As a matter of fact, there was a time when the rabbis enjoyed a virtual monopoly in this realm, when almost every rabbi was himself a veritable social action committee. And while most rabbis have long lamented the absence of laymen in the genuinely Jewish enterprise, there are others who would like matters to remain that way "forever and ever, Amen," who appear to resent the "intrusion" of the laymen into their once sacrosanct precincts. But this is to perpetuate a newly risen evil in Jewish life: the altogether un-Jewish distinction between layman and rabbi.

As a consequence, what is happening to the American rabbi? He is allowing himself to be shaped in accordance with the laymen's conception of what a rabbi should be—preacher, counsellor, ambassador to the Christians, community relations expert, public speaker, temple bulletin editor, administrator, and fund-raiser. The rabbi is becoming all things to all men. His salary, in many instances, is commensurately high; his effectiveness is, too frequently, low. His public status is relatively high; his level of scholarship is lower than it should be and than it used to be. The rabbi is a busy, frustrated, harassed public figure who has almost ceased to be the teacher of Torah. Rare is the rabbi who has the time to achieve scholarship. He has become too easily assimilated to the anti-intellectual atmosphere of our day, to the climate in which irrationalism has been enthroned and the egghead has become the butt of every snide and sniveling sneer.

The peculiar merit of the rabbis of the past was their resolute resistance to the bread and circuses, the gladiatorial spectaculars, and the popular pastimes (there was card playing in their day, too—read the denunciations of this long-favorite pastime among Jews by the rabbis of the Middle Ages) which were part and parcel of the culture of those centuries. While the masses of Jews invariably, then as now, followed the multitude and slavishly adopted the ways of the gentile, Jewish leadership consistently repudiated such imitation which deprived the rabbi of his birthright of scholarship.

It is unhappily not generally so today. Too frequently the hankering after a superficial, first-name popularity—on the golf course, at the bridge table, or the cocktail party—is filching from the contemporary religious leader the time that he might otherwise spend in the learning which, certainly to Judaism, is the title deed to his lofty designation as rabbi (teacher). The criteria of pulpit committees—rotund voice, graceful gestures, affable manner, pleased countenance, safe on politics, soft on social action, and not too exacting of his flock—give a clue to what too many laymen seek in their so-called spiritual leaders and to which I fear some of our rabbis too cravenly capitulate.

Especially revealing of this distressing portrait was the report of the Executive Vice-President of the Central Conference of American Rabbis, Rabbi Sidney Regner, growing out of his years of experience in pulpit placement. He tartly observed that ". . . the image of the rabbi today, in the eyes of some people, has something of the Madison Avenue tint and the Organization Man touch. Rabbis, full of vim, vigor and vitality who, in popular parlance, will 'sell' themselves and their personalities, neither too meek nor too aggressive, who by all means should not be too far out of step—those are the desiderata most frequently stressed. . . . I have never yet had a congregation tell me that they wanted a scholarly rabbi."

Surely the committed rabbi must rouse himself to rebel against such an incongruous denouement to so noble a calling. We cannot permit this stultification of the descendants of Hillel and Akiba, of Jochanon Ben Zaccai and that long line of teachers whose title the rabbi proudly bears.

As the desire and demand for learning are thus being diluted, so is the voice of social action being muffled. By every canon of our Jewish tradition the rabbi is called upon not only "to learn and to teach," but perhaps even more persistently "to observe and to do." Familiar to even the most superficial student of Judaism is the stubborn insistence that "Not study is the chief ingredient, but action." And did not Rabbi Eliezer in Pirke Aboth warn that "He whose wisdom exceeds his works, to what is he likened? To a tree whose branches are many but whose roots are few and the wind comes and plucks it up and overturns it on its face." Still further did one of our sages go when he dared to assert that "He who occupies himself with study alone is as if he had denied God Himself."

There are too many of us who thus deny God today, who are victims of this creeping, even leaping, indifferentism of our time. The same infection is seizing our theological students as well. William Whyte, in *The Organization Man*, bemoaned the fact that American college students, in striking contrast to the radical revolt of youth characteristic of the thirties, in contrast also to the still flaming youth in Africa, in Asia, in South America, and in Israel, find their outlets too frequently in panty pilfering, in destructive games and riots, crowding into telephone booths, and bed-pushing antics. "No cause seizes them, they seem fed up with all this political jazz . . . this applies to theological students as well. Without exception, those heads of seminaries I have interviewed find the present generation less inquiring of mind, more ready to accept authority, and indeed most anxious to have it laid on the line."

Here, too, Jewish life absorbs the worst in its surroundings, rather than the best. As with American youth in general, so is it with Jewish youths, according to an intensive survey conducted by then one of our leaders of the Reform Jewish youth movement, Rabbi Jerome Davidson. No rebellion or discontinuity takes hold of them. No cry for ideals in any way foreign to typical American middle-class America rouses them. The majority interviewed are not really bothered by the problems of poverty or segregation. "The people wouldn't live in slums if they didn't want to," they superficially assert as they smugly conclude that the prophets would indeed approve the conditions of twentieth century America.

And as it thus seems to be with the average run of American Jewish youth, so too does it appear to be tragically true in our seminaries. It was not so in the now long, long ago when I sat in the classroom. Not only were we constantly inspired and challenged by the vivid presentation and contemporary application of the prophets, but the then-popular social gospel of Christendom also wielded its potent influence upon us. Today the pages of Rauschenbusch and John Haynes Holmes are unread and unheeded, while the habit of accommodation to things as they are becomes contagious. Pastoral counseling rather than prophetic preaching is de rigeur now. I am not against pastoral counseling. But I am opposed to the altogether un-Jewish, distinctively Christian overemphasis on the salvation of the individual—which in our time often salves the conscience through the confession of one's sins on one's knees, or the outflow of free associations on the couch—rather than the galvanizing of the individual's resources for the redemption of society.

It was not so when the founders of our theological schools brought them into being. Isaac Mayer Wise constantly urged his "boys," as he affectionately called them, to "break asunder wherever we can the chains of the bondsman, the fetters of the slave, the iron rod of despotism, the oppressive yoke of tyranny.

Let us banish strife, discord, hatred, injustice, oppression from the domain of man," was his rallying cry. And Stephen S. Wise, the founder of the Jewish Institute for Religion in New York City, pleaded with his students to help transform our synagogues into "forces of righteousness rather than farces of respectability in the community."

To be sure, the picture is not altogether black; although I still insist the situation is indubitably foreboding, there are, of course, nevertheless, many elements of promise in the contemporary synagogue. In the first place, a majority of American Jews now identify themselves with the sanctuary. Regardless of the diverse motivations which bring them to the temple, the fact that they belong presents an unparalleled opportunity to strengthen their Jewish commitments and to deepen their knowledge. Moreover, the frank dissatisfaction which rabbis and sensitive lay leaders feel in the quality of the contemporary American synagogue, touching off a wave of self-searching which sometimes amounts to self-flagellation, is itself a healthy augury. This restlessness is resulting in new emphasis on adult education, rising standards for religious school instruction, creative ventures in a religious camp experience for adults as well as youth, an awakening interest in social action, a fresh approach to the teaching of Hebrew, a budding taste for the ultilization of the arts and the best of Jewish and world literature within the synagogue. In addition, the status of the synagogue, despite all its shortcomings, has risen sharply in the Jewish consciousness.

A generation ago, the American Jewish community consisted of the Zionist groups, the lodges, the philanthropic and welfare funds, the civil defense bodies, the Yiddish cultural agencies, plus the synagogue. Today the American Jewish community consists of the synagogue, plus the others. Debates as to whether or not the synagogue should receive primacy or centrality in the American Jewish community still break out from time to time, but such debates deal with sterile abstractions. The reality is that the synagogue *is* becoming central and will be even more so in the future as Christians identify Jews—and as Jews identify themselves—as, primarily, a religious community. Beyond any other Jewish institution, the synagogue is the embodiment of the total Jewish way of life. And this great promise makes it all the more incumbent upon us to examine ourselves with the utmost frankness.

[8]

We have got to cease our preoccupation with numbers. Our current predilection toward the counting of noses is no more healthy than the tendency of a past generation to change their noses, to "cut their nose to spite their race," as the great Rabbi of Temple Sinai, Chicago, Emil G. Hirsch, once phrased it. It is not important that we have 1,000 or 500 or 200 families in our respective synagogues, or that we have 1 million or 2 million persons in our Reform Movement as a whole. What *is* important is what the synagogue does for them and to them, how it affects the quality of their lives and their dynamic urge to transform the lives of others, the very life—or death—of mankind. We need to rise above the lowest common denominator—a standard so low it is almost invisible—to aim at standards of excellence. To be a lay leader of a synagogue, one should be required to undertake a regimen of Jewish learning, to live an ethical Jewish life in business and community alike, and to participate in the religious as well as the fiscal tasks of the congregation. It seems to me we do not expect enough from our people; we settle too easily. We aim too low. We are too afraid to fail. Such timidity, such short-selling of synagogue membership and especially of its leadership is, according to a well-known Midrash, a gross transgression. "Just as it is forbidden to utter the name of God in vain, so should you not assume a public office if you are not worthy of it."

At the same time, the potential of what we could achieve is almost limitless. We are free in America to fashion whatever Jewish life we will. The financial resources are here. So are the human resources—a Jewish community of 5 million persons, almost all of them eager to identify themselves as Jews, many of them hungry for moral and spiritual guidance of a meaningful kind. Our three-faith culture has invested the synagogue with an unparalleled prestige. The existence of the State of Israel can be a fructifying force for American Jewry. Our camps and youth programs offer hope for a new and committed generation.

But this much I think remains crystal clear: the future of American Jewish life depends on what the synagogue becomes. If the synagogue can shape itself into an effective vehicle to carry the timeless values of Judaism, Jewish life in the year 2000 will be vigorous and distinctive in America, and Judaism will be a faith by which men live. But if—as present trends portend—the American synagogue becomes a blend of Jewish country club and Protestant church, if we continue to reward leadership on the basis of un-Jewish criteria, if we confuse busyness in the synagogue with the true business of Judaism, if we allow the synagogue to become a comfort station in a world of challenge and change, then the synagogue may nevertheless survive, but only as a forsaken shrine of a forgotten past. But the fires of faith which warmed a hundred generations of the covenant people will become ashes, cold and dead on the free soil of America.

We must be vigilant to make certain that the American synagogue does not meet the fate portended in an ancient rabbinic story. We are told that in the old temple at Jerusalem there was a flute fashioned out of reeds, an old flute dating back to the time of Moses. Its sound was sonorous and sweet, exalting the hearts of all worshippers who heard it. One day the priests of the temple decided to decorate the flute—after what was, no doubt, a high-pressure, card-calling, fund-raising campaign among the status-seeking populace. The appeal was evidently successful for the flute was overlaid with heavy and costly gold. Its appearance was superb. But its once mellow resonance was now metallic and jarring. Gold had debased its former ravishing tone.

God grant that this will not be the destiny of the American synagogue—that we will not be spoiled by success.

Philip Roth

THE NEW JEWISH
STEREOTYPES

Philip Roth is not only one of America's best fiction writers but writes nonfiction that always threatens the complacency of his readers.

"The New Jewish Stereotypes," which gave rise to a stream of controversy after it appeared in *American Judaism,* was adapted from a lecture delivered at a symposium on "The Images and Minds of Man" sponsored by the Anti-Defamation League of B'nai B'rith and Loyola University.

I find myself living in a country and in a time in which the Jew has come to be—or is allowed to think he is—a cultural hero. I once heard on the radio a disc-jockey introducing the theme song from the movie, *Exodus.* The words were to be sung by Pat Boone. The disc-jockey made it clear that this was "the only authorized version of the song." Authorized by what? For whom? Why? No further word from the radio. Only a silence drenched in piety, and then Mr. Boone, singing out of something less than a whirlwind—

> This land is mine,
> God gave this land to me!

I do not know whether I am moving up or down the cultural ladder, or simply sideways, when I recall that there has been the song "Exodus," preceded by the movie, *Exodus,* preceded by the novel, *Exodus.* There does not seem to be much doubt that the image of the Jew as patriot, warrior, and hero is rather satisfying to a large segment of the American public.

In an interview in the *New York Post,* Leon Uris, the author of the novel, claims that his image of the Jewish fighter is a good deal closer to the truth about the Jew than the image presented of him by other Jewish writers. I take it, by the way, that I am one of those writers to whom Mr. Uris is referring—the *Post* clipping was mailed to me by a woman demanding some explanation or apology for "the anti-Semitism and self-hatred" that she saw revealed in a collection of short fiction of mine that had just been published. What Uris told his interviewer, Joseph Wershba, was this:

There is a whole school of Jewish American writers, who spend their time damning their fathers, hating their mothers, wringing their hands and wondering why they were born. This isn't art or literature. It's psychiatry. These writers are professional apologists. Every year you find one of their (sic!) works on the best seller lists. . . . Their work is obnoxious and makes me sick to my stomach.

I wrote *Exodus* because I was just sick of apologizing—or feeling that it was necessary to apologize. The Jewish community of this country has contributed far more greatly than its numbers—in art, medicine, and especially literature.

I set out to tell a story of Israel. I am definitely biased. I am definitely pro-Jewish.

An author goes through everything his readers do. It was a revelation to me, too, when I was researching *Exodus* in Europe and in Israel. And the revelation was this: that we Jews are not what we have been portrayed to be. In truth, we have been fighters.

"In truth, we have been fighters." So bald and stupid and uninformed is the statement that it is not even worthy of dispute. One has the feeling that, single-handed, Mr. Uris has set out to counter with his new image of the Jew, an older one that makes him nervous and mad—the one that comes down to us in those several stories, the punch line of which is, "Play nice, Jakie—don't fight." However, there is really not much value in setting oneself the task of swapping one stereotype for another. What I should hope Mr. Uris will do, when he does not happen to be having revelations by way of "researching" novels, is to read a new book called *Dawn*, by Eli Wiesel. Mr. Wiesel is not an American-Jewish writer; he is a Hungarian, now living in New York, and his first book, *Night*, was an autobiographical account of his experiences as a fifteen-year-old boy in Auschwitz and

[12]

Buchenwald, those concentration camps, he writes, which "consumed my faith forever . . . murdered my God and my soul and turned my dreams to dust." *Dawn*, the second book, has for a background the Jewish terrorist activities in Palestine before the establishment of the State of Israel. The hero of the book is assigned the task of executing a British major who has been taken hostage by the Jewish terrorists; the novel deals with the hours the hero spends just prior to the execution. . . . I should like to tell Mr. Uris that Wiesel's hero is not so proud to discover himself in the role of a fighter, nor is he able to find justification for himself in some traditional Jewish association with pugnacity or bloodletting. But actually however, it turns out that there is really no need for me to tell Mr. Uris anything; if we can believe a news item that we find in *Time* magazine, Mr. Uris apparently knows a good deal more than he lets on to the *New York Post*.

In Manhattan (*Time* reports):

> . . . Captain Yehiel Aranowicz, 37, . . . one-time master of the blockade-running Israeli refugee ship "Exodus," reported some reservations back home about the best selling (4,000,000 copies to date) novel inspired by his 1947 heroics. "Israelis," he said, "were pretty disappointed in the book, to put it lightly. The types that are described in it never existed in Israel. The novel is neither history nor literature." . . . In Encino, California, *Exodus'* author Leon Uris rebutted: "You may quote me as saying, 'Captain who?' and that's all I have to say. I'm not going to pick on a lightweight. Just look at my sales figures."

Certainly, it is unsafe to indict a man on the basis of what *Time* quotes him as having said; it may even be *Time's* pleasure to titillate its readers with still another Jewish stereotype, the Fagan, the Shylock, who will sell anything, his people, their history, anything, for a price. There was a time when this image was very helpful to certain Gentiles as a tool in dealing with the Jew. Now, however, there is another way of dealing with him— there is the image that Mr. Uris has sold, the image millions have read about and other millions have seen flickering on the screen, the image which is able to make the Jew and Jewishness acceptable and appealing and even attractive.

There is Leon Uris to make our image over again, and there is that famous optimist and cracker-barrel philosopher, Harry

Golden. The image of the Jew that Harry Golden presents has, to my mind, been thoroughly and brilliantly analyzed in thoroughly and brilliantly analyzed in Theodore Solotaroff's essay in *Commentary,* "Harry Golden and the American Audi‑ ence." Mr. Solotaroff points out that in Golden's three books, *For 2¢ Plain, Only in America,* and *Enjoy, Enjoy!* he "satisfied both Jewish nostalgia and Gentile curiosity," that "he presents with depressing clarity certain very real problems and conditions of our society in the past decade—a society characterized by its well-intentioned but soft, sloppy, equivocal thinking about it‑ self. . . . Garnished with a little Manischewitz horse-radish the perplexed banalities of the middle class come back to [the reader] as the wisdom of the ages."

Mr. Solotaroff thinks of horse-radish; in considering matters Goldenian, I am a *shmaltz* man myself. It is interesting to note that Mr. Golden, in replying to Solotaroff's comments, manages himself to lay on the shmaltz with one hand while at the same time trying to wipe it off with the other; as any housewife will tell you, the end of such monkey business is very sticky fingers. In the columns of his newspaper, *The Carolina Israelite,* Golden writes that Solotaroff is dead wrong in accusing him of glam‑ orizing the life in the New York ghetto. With characteristic re‑ straint and logic, Golden explains, "We Jews . . . not only had a society, but, quite frankly, a Jewish city, and this sense of com‑ munity is what lends memories of the old East Side its glamour, and it is for this reason that the bulk of American Jewry up in the middle class, lick their fingers over everything I write about the Lower East Side of New York. Sentiment alone could never sustain such amazingly wide-spread interest." The word of course is spelled sentimentality, and if *it* can't produce wide-spread interest, what can? Truth?

Popular Jewish interest in Golden, and in Uris, isn't very hard to understand. For one thing there is the pleasure of recognition, not of truth necessarily as of verisimilitude, the plain and simple kick that comes of seeing the words *kugel* and *latkes* in print. Then there is the romance of oneself: The Hebrew Hero on the one hand, the Immigrant Success on the other. Harry Golden, a self-confessed Horatio Alger, furnishes us with the names of the judges, movie stars, scientists, and comedians who have risen from the Jewish Lower East Side to fame and fortune. But what of the Gentile interest? Four million people have bought copies of *Exodus;* two million, copies of *Only in America;* surely they have not all been Jews. Why this flowering of Gentile interest in Jewish characters, history, manners, and morals? How does Pat Boone come to be singing "the only authorized version" anyway? Why not Moishe Oysher or Eddie Fisher?

One of Mr. Solotaroff's suggestions for Golden's appeal, is that among other things, Golden presents to his readers a world characterized by "vividness, energy, aspiration, discipline, and finally the warmth of its life—that is, precisely those qualities which are said to be declining in the modern middle-class family and suburb." Surely there does seem to be a fascination these days in the idea of Jewish emotionalism. People who have more sense and anxiety than to go up to Negroes and engage them in conversation about "rhythm," have come up to me and engaged me in conversation about "warmth." They think it is flattering—and they think it is true.

I do not believe that they think it is complicated: that warmth, when it does appear, does not just radiate itself—at the center there is generally a fire. There were several Jewish graduate students in a class I taught at the Writing Workshop of the State University of Iowa, and during one semester three of them wrote stories about their childhood, or at least about a Jewish childhood; and in all three there was allusion to the emotionalism in Jewish family life. Curiously enough, all of the stories had similar situations and similar characters. The hero in each was a young Jewish boy, somewhere between ten and fifteen, who gets excellent grades in school and is always combed and courteous. The stories are told in the first person and have to do with a friendship that grows up between the hero and a Gentile neighbor or schoolmate. The Gentile is from the lower class—in one instance his background is Italian-American—and he leads the Jewish boy, who is of the middle class, into the mysteries of the flesh. The Gentile boy has already had some kind of sexual experience himself. Not that he is much older than his Jewish companion—he has the chance for adventure because his parents pay hardly any attention to him at all; they are divorced, or they drink, or they say "God damn" all the time, or they are uneducated and don't care; or in one stupendous notion of Gentileness, they combine all these attributes. This leaves their offspring with plenty of time to hunt for girls. The Jewish boy, on the other hand, is watched—he is watched at bedtime, at study-

[15]

time, and especially at mealtime. Who he is watched by is his mother; the father we rarely see, and between him and the boy there seems to be hardly more than a nodding acquaintance. The old man is either working or sleeping or across the table, silently stowing it away. Still there is a great deal of warmth in these families—especially as compared to the Gentile families—and almost all of it is generated by the mother. And interestingly enough, it does not strike the young hero in quite the same way as it strikes Harry Golden and his audience. The fire that warms also burns and smothers: what the hero *envies* the Gentile boy is his parental indifference—because ultimately he envies the Gentile his sexual adventure. Religion is understood not as the key to the mysteries of God, but to the mysteries of sex; it is not without historical precedent, of course, for religion to have to do with the quest for animal heat and passionate spontaneity. The warmth these Jewish storytellers want then is the warmth the Gentiles seem to have, just as the warmth that Harry Golden's Gentiles envy him for is the warmth he tells them the Jews have.

I must hasten to point out that in these stories the girls to whom their Gentile comrades lead the heroes are never Jewish girls. The Jewish women in the stories are mothers and sisters. The sexual dream—for whatever primal reason one cares to entertain—is for The Other. The dream of the *shiksa*. The dream of the Jewess. Though there may well be biographical fact at the bottom of these stories, as there is doubtless biographical fact at the bottom of Golden's anecdotes, the satisfactions that are derived through the manipulation and interpretation of the real events are the satisfactions of one's fantasies, one's dreams. I do not mean to denigrate the talent of these students, by the way, in comparing them to Golden; what the heroes of their stories learn at the end—as their Gentile comrades disappear into other neighborhoods and into maturity—is the burden of their own reality.

Golden and Uris, of course, burden no one with anything. Indeed, much of their appeal lies in the fact that they help to dissipate guilt, real and imagined. It turns out that the Jews are not poor innocent victims after all—all the time they were supposed to be being persecuted, humiliated, and mocked, they were having a good time being warm to one another and having their wonderful family lives. What they were developing—as Mr. Solotaroff quotes one reviewer as saying of Golden—is their "lovely Jewish slant on the world." Ah, this lovely Jewish slant—its existence surely can soothe consciences: if the victim is not a victim, then the victimizer is not a victimizer either. Along with the other things that Harry Golden offers, there is a kind of trap door for those Gentiles who, if they have not been anti-Semites, have at any rate been visited with suspicious, distrustful, or merely uncomfortable feelings about Jews and Jewishness, feelings which they are told they should not have. Golden assures them (as he assures the Jews) that we are really a happy, optimistic people—is he himself not living proof that bigotry does not exist in the American heart? There he is, a Jew—and one who speaks up, mind you—a respected citizen in a Southern city. Wonderful! And not in Sweden either, or in Italy, or in the Philippines. Only—Golden tells them—in America!

This may finally be good therapy for certain anxious and well-meaning Gentiles, in that they do not have to continue feeling guilty for crimes of which they are not in fact guilty; it may even unburden some half-hearted anti-Semites, who don't like Jews because they don't like themselves for not liking Jews. I do not know that it is very respectful, however, to the Jews themselves, to the facts of their history, realities of their suffering, humiliation, and pessimism. Or even to the validity of the Gentile suspiciousness. For why *shouldn't* the Gentiles have suspicions? The fact is that if you are committed to being a Jew, you believe that in those matters most crucial to man's survival and humanity—what the past was, what the future will be, who and what man's God is—that you are right and the Christians are wrong. You believe that one cannot understand the breakdown of order and values in the western world without considering the inadequacies of Christianity as a moral force in the lives of men. . . . However, who wants to admit to all this, out loud? What we witness daily in American life is "the socialization of the anti-social . . . the acculturation of the anti-cultural . . . the legitimization of the subversive." These are phrases of Lionel Trilling's; he has used them to describe the responses of certain of his students to modern literature. They have for me an even broader cultural reference: that is, to the swallowing up of difference that goes on around us, the deadly tolerance that robs—that is designed to rob—those who differ, who diverge, who rebel, of their powers. Instead of being taken seriously as a threat or a madman or a prophet, a man is silenced by being made popular.

[17]

They are presently holding beatnik parties in the suburbs—which does not convince me, however, that all men are brothers. On the contrary, they are strangers; that fact is made clear to me every day when I read the newspapers. They are strangers, and often they are enemies, and it is because *that* is our condition, that it is incumbent upon us not to love one another—which is to deny the truth about ourselves — but to practice no violence and no treachery upon one another, which is to struggle with the darkest forces within ourselves.

But, of course, the Jews *have* done violence. It is the story of their violence that Leon Uris is so proud to tell America. Its appeal to American Jews is not difficult to understand—but once again, what of the Gentiles? Why all the piety about "the only authorized version" of a popular song? Why is the song even popular? Why is the movie so popular, the book? So strong, in fact, is the appeal of this story, that for myself, I am inclined to wonder if a burden has not been removed from the nation's consciousness, the burden of contemplating the murder of six million Jews, of contemplating it in all its raw, senseless, unavenged, and unavengeable horror. It is almost as though a popular song or movie had come along that would enable us to cease contemplating that other unsolved moral riddle of our time: the murder of the citizens of Hiroshima. With Hiroshima it might be possible that we be told a story about the beautiful, modern city that has risen from the ashes, about the prosperous, healthy, and more enterprising life that is lived in the new city as opposed to the old one. But be that as it may—and who is to guarantee that it may not be—now there is Golden on the one hand to assure us that Jews are really happy, optimistic, successful, and warm (as opposed to grieved, pessimistic, dissatisfied, and xenophobic), and then there is Uris to say that you don't have to worry about the Jews after all, they can take care of themselves. *They have* taken care of themselves. One week *Life* magazine presents on its cover a picture of Adolph Eichmann; some weeks later, a picture of Sal Mineo, as a Jewish freedom fighter. The most horrendous crime in the world's history—a crime to which there is no adequate human response, no compassion, no vengeance to which a mere man is equal—seems, in part, to have been avenged. When the scales appear at last to be balanced, there cannot help but be a sigh of relief. At long last the Jew is no longer the spectator on the violence of our age,

[18]

nor is he the victim of that violence; now he is a participant. Fine then. Welcome aboard. A man with a gun and a hand grenade, a man who kills for his God-given rights (in this case, as the song tells us, his land) cannot sit so easily in judgment, or in horror, of another man when he kills for *his* God-given rights, as he chooses to define them.

Mr. Uris' discovery that the Jews are fighters fills him with pride; it fills many of his Jewish readers with pride too, and his Gentile readers with pride perhaps—in man's indomitable spirit —but surely with relief as well. It fills the hero of *Dawn*, however, the novel of the Palestinian terror, by the Hungarian Eli Wiesel, with less satisfying and buoyant emotions. He is filled with shame and confusion. No matter how just he tells himself are the rights for which he murders, he is not able to deny the blight of murder. Nothing in his past, nor in the past of his people, seems finally to remove him from the tragic nature of the act. He has seen and suffered so much, in Buchenwald and Auschwitz, that it is with a final sense of the death of what he thought he was, that he pulls the trigger on the British officer and becomes another of the executioners in our violent century. He is one of those Jews, like Job, who wonder why they were born.

There are people who have told me and who have written to tell me that Harry Golden and Leon Uris have made many friends for the Jewish people; they have told me that it is a long time since the Jew has been so respected and honored as he is today in America. I nod my head, for I am no enemy of honor and respect, and I enjoy friends. I enjoy them so much that I know there are times when we are even led to make them at the expense of our sense of ourselves, of our character, and of our fate. That is why at this point in human history, when power seems the ultimate end of government, and "success" the goal of individual lives; when the value of humility is in doubt, and the nerve to fail hardly to be seen at all; when a wilful blindness to man's condition can only precipitate further anguishes and miseries—at this point, with the murder of six million people fixed forever in our imaginations, I cannot help but believe that there is a higher moral purpose for the Jewish writer, and the Jewish people, than the improvement of public relations.

[19]

Norman Cousins

THE JEWISHNESS
OF JESUS

Norman Cousins, editor of *Saturday Review,* believes that editors should get out and experience directly the ideas and events treated in their magazines. This conviction has prompted him to visit every state in the Union, make eleven trips to the Far East and circle the world several times. His books reflect the range of his interests: *In Place of Folly,* which outlines the alternatives to nuclear destruction, *Dr. Schweitzer of Lambarene, In God We Trust,* and half a dozen others.

Always a controversial figure, Mr. Cousins took on a new controversy when he wrote this article urging Jews to acknowledge the greatness of Jesus, and Christians to acknowledge his Jewishness. The result was a torrent of mail defending and attacking the author's viewpoint. Yet Mr. Cousins didn't write the article deliberately to stir up controversy. He wanted to put down as carefully and thoughtfully as he could his own ideas on how to achieve "a sense of spiritual community between Christians and Jews."

Christianity and Judaism share one of the great reluctances of history. Both are reluctant to live openly and fully with the fact that Jesus was a Jew. Christian theology is incomplete; it has never been able to explain to itself why Jesus should have come out of Judaism. And Judaism has tended to dwell outside the full significance of the Jewishness of Jesus and his vast spiritual role in human history.

The reasons behind the reluctance are, of course, different. So are the effects. In any case, it seems reasonable to suggest that the reluctance be re-examined and restudied. For if the question is subjected to the full play of creative inquiry, it is conceivable that a new relationship between Christian and Jew could

[20]

emerge. *Not* a common faith, but an important new amity and concurrence; possibly even a sense of spiritual community.

We proceed, therefore, to the re-examination.

The earliest Christians knew neither awkwardness nor reticence over the fact that Jesus was a Jew. Most, if not all, were Jews themselves. Christianity to them was not a faith apart from Judaism but an assertion of it. They never claimed to be the originators of a new religion; they were summoning man to Jesus' vision of spiritual and moral excellence. They called for a return to the great simplicities of essential Judaism, for an awareness of the reality of biblical prophecy, and for a response to the sense of God that lay deep within man. They were critical of the nature of the existing Temple and of temple worship. They turned away from sacrifice and from the exercise of the religious spirit through elaborate ritual. And they reaffirmed the fundamentals of Judaism: the oneness of God, the omniscience of God, the justness of God, and the reality of God's total command of the universe and history, now and forevermore. The purpose they saw in Jesus was to reawaken and strengthen this faith and not to replace it.

To these Jews, the Jewishness of Jesus was not incidental or extraneous but inevitable. His coming, they believed, had been foretold in the Hebrew Scriptures; it awakened the dictates of faith that were natural to the Prophecy. Messianism was in the air; the idea of salvation was powerful and dominant.

The Jews who carried this message of Jesus carried it primarily to their own people, for it was only natural that the fulfilment of Hebrew prophecy should be recognized by members of the Hebrew faith. Moreover, the idea of Messianism was an important article of faith among Jews at the time; almost all expected salvation in one form or another. Even so, the actual confrontation in living history with the fact of a Messiah found many Jews resistant. The idea that the greatest of all religious prophecies could occur during one's own lifetime was as difficult then to accept for many people, however religiously impelled, as it would be now. If, for example, there would appear in our own time a figure of the same character and dimensions as Jesus, would it be easy to find a church that would accept him? Events of this magnitude do not easily fit into a contemporary frame.

The Apostles were Jewish. The historical record is skimpy on this subject but there has been speculation that the first Pope may also have been Jewish. And the religious ideas in the New Testament are preponderantly and authentically Jewish in accent and outlook. Indeed, there is a consistent progression from the Torah, with its revelation of the word of God, and its spiritual poetry, to the New Testament which is based not alone on the reality of the fulfilment, but on the nature of God—His presence, His words, His acts on earth, and His direct teachings for man. These were the Witness Chronicles; they told and retold the signs of the birth and the story of the birth, the growing up and the coming of age, the natural wisdom and the natural power, and the circumstances of death and resurrection. The narrative is not of a piece with what Christians call the Old Testament; neither, for that matter, are the books of the Old Testament themselves of a single piece. But the line of development between Old and New is visible and real; there is a direct kinship in purpose and values.

If the impact of Jesus' followers on their fellow Jews was not immediate and sweeping, it must be recalled that Judaism at the time was subject to many calls for reassertion and renewal and to the cross-currents and impulses for change. There was no paucity of proclaimers about the imminent end of the world and the doom of man. Jesus' own vision about world's end was viewed by many against this general background.

Still another barrier to the recognition of Jesus as Messiah was the view held by some religious scholars at the time that Jesus was born in Nazareth of Galilee, and grew up in Galilee. The New Testament is specific on the point that Jesus was a Galilean. Yet the Biblical prophecy had clearly stated that the Messiah would be born in Bethlehem. Was it unreasonable to raise the question of a disparity in what was literally the most important matter in the history of man? In any case, Jesus grew up in Galilee; the difference between the religious environments of Galilee and Bethlehem had considerable importance. Bethlehem was traditional, Orthodox, secure. Galilee was deeply religious, too, but it was surrounded by non-believers and Gentiles. The contrasting winds were many; they produced a gale of ideas. People were in a mood for reappraisal and self-examination. The atmosphere, if not cosmopolitan, was at least mixed.

The spread of the Christian Gospel by Gentiles created something of a paradox when they attempted to convert Jews. It seemed strange that non-Jews should have to tell Jews what their own Bible meant, and to pass judgments concerning the fulfilment of Hebrew prophecy.

The response of non-Jewish Christians—and also of what might be called "Jewish Christians"—to this argument was that while God revealed Himself to the Jews He was a universal God, as Judaism itself declared. "God is One." Therefore, the Old Testament was not the book of Judaism alone but the spiritual fund of all mankind. Anyone who felt its truth should feel free to listen to the voice of the Deity through it and also to speak to the Deity through it in prayer. Moreover, the early Christians reiterated they were not trying to start a new religion but to act on the new revelations that Judaism had been awaiting for many centuries. In this sense, what they were espousing was a "reformed" or a "Christian" Judaism. In any event, a branch was breaking away and was finding its deep and powerful root.

The most dramatic and significant aspect of the break, of course, was represented by the crucifixion. Though the Romans sentenced and nailed Jesus to the cross, the Jews had rejected him and had entered the complaint. The Christians' cry, "They killed our Lord!" has no historical substance but in back of it was their conviction that if the Jews had accepted Jesus as their king, Jesus would not have been killed.

And here we come to what is perhaps the greatest single paradox in the history of Western religion. Christianity could not exist without the crucifixion. That one event and the witnessed resurrection that proceeded out of it form the specific and vital crystallizing element of Christian faith. The virgin birth and the miracles lead in a straight line to the culminating symbol of Christ on the cross. "He died for our sins" is the cry that keeps the cross alive in the Christian soul, and makes the resurrection possible. The suffering gives depth to the identification.

Yet these two cries—"They killed our Lord!" and "He died for our sins!" are basically at war with each other. The first assumes an act of human free will. The second assumes an act of divine determination. If Jesus died on the cross in order to purge man, then every act that leads up to it is essential, explicable, predetermined. In the same sense, if Christianity could not have come about without the Crucifixion, and if it was the will of God that Christianity should have been born in this way, then all the circumstances of the Crucifixion are part of a design, and the

[23]

people who figured in the event, whatever their role, were carrying out the parts divinely assigned to them. The idea of the all-powerful God makes explicit the fact that God cannot be killed. Therefore, the incident of Calvary takes on a symbolism independent of those who were essential to it.

Can Christians believe that God had no power or purpose in the circumstances attending the death on the cross?

Is it reasonable for Christians to believe that God, who arranged a virgin birth for His manifestation on earth, did not also have a divine plan for His departure? And if divine determinism did exist, is it not sacrilegious to assail anyone who belonged to that final Plan? Can Jews or Romans be condemned for the cross without bringing into question the divinity of Jesus?

Christianity has not fully faced up to these questions or the paradox involved in the accusation that, though Jesus died in order to make people aware of their sins, Jews are to be held responsible for his death.

The world, two thousand years ago, like the world of today, was a world of many peoples. There were Chinese, Japanese, Africans, fair-skinned northern Europeans, dark-skinned Near Easterners, red-skinned Westerners (later known as American Indians), Eskimos, and Icelanders—many of them with their own gods and religions. The contacts among these peoples were either slight or incomplete, yet they were all God's children. Why did God choose to be born a Jew? The "Christian" Jews said that this was the way God wanted it, or He would not have revealed His coming to them in the Holy Scriptures. Other Jews, with a feeling perhaps for a universal design, wondered why He would have appeared on earth as a member of a particular sect.

But the essence of faith is the appearance of truth to the individual, whatever its form, whatever its circumstances, whatever the challenge, whatever the array of contrasting evidence. And Christians rest their faith on the reality of Old Testament prophecy and its fulfilment in Jesus. And they therefore do not question the fact that Jesus chose to be born a Jew. Yet should it not also follow, in the same terms, that Christians must not allow themselves to become separated from Jesus' own religion? There is not a single word in John or Mark or Matthew or Luke in which Jesus repudiates Judaism. He practiced Judaism scrupulously. He gave constant expression to the religious and ethical requirements of Judaism. He observed all the Jewish Holy

Days. It is widely believed that the Last Supper was a Passover ceremony.

The question growing out of all this for Christians is whether they can detach themselves from the allegiances and observances of Jesus. Can a Christian, believing in revelation through Jesus, accept him as Messiah but reject his own religion? And if it is contended that Jesus did not believe in Judaism, why did he choose to be born a Jew? In the same sense, are not acts against Jews, solely because they are Jews, a direct repudiation of Jesus? Should not the fact of Jesus as Jew serve as the holiest of bonds between Christian and Jew? Should not Christianity regard itself actually as a kind of "Christian" Judaism—that is, a religion accepting the mission of Jesus as he himself defined it—namely, to simplify, purify, and rekindle the Hebrew faith into which he was born? So long as the New Testament rests on the base of the Old Testament, so long as it stands as fulfilment of Biblical prophecy, the essentials of the Old Testament that Jesus himself held sacred cannot be set aside by Christians. For the reforms of Jesus were not directed to the elimination of the essentials but to the recognition of their full significance. These essentials most assuredly embraced moral excellence, restraint, and humility in the daily affairs of men. The statement of these ethics, magnificent though they were, did not burst upon Judaism as totally new concepts; the strain of gentleness, purity, charity, simplicity, and selflessness had been present in the works of Hillel and other Jewish moralists who were influential only a few decades before Christ.

Moreover, terms like "The Kingdom of God," "Messiah," "salvation," "Judgment Day," "repentance," and "blessed"—important words in the vocabulary of Jesus—were in the mainstream of the Jewish tradition.

If all this be true, how and why did Christianity veer away from Judaism? How account for the substantial differences that were to give Christianity its distinct character? The historical answer is that though Christianity is Jewish in origin, it is Greek and Roman in its principal early influences. The need to define and codify, the sense of eternal mystery, the mythological habit— all these inevitably helped to mold the emergent new faith. What was most nteresting about the total mixture, Jewish, Greek, and Roman, was that it was to bring together the worlds of East and West. Jesus was not European but Asian, yet Christianity took its strongest root not in Palestine but in Greece and Rome, with a consequent change in accent.

This turning to the West was an important factor in the subordination of the fact of the Jewishness of Jesus. The Jewishness of Jesus was explicable, in the light of Biblical prophecy, but it was not a congenial fact to Christians. Indeed, it could be an uncomfortable fact. It created connections and obligations many Christians were to find awkward to recognize or even acknowledge. But recognized or not, it is the presiding fact; Christian theology, worship, and practice can never be whole until it accepts it and acts on it, not out of reluctance, but out of genuine and essential conviction.

Is it extreme to suggest that it might be salutary if the members of the first Christian family were referred to in terms of their origins, i.e., "The Jewess, Mary," or "Joseph, the Jew," or "Jesus, the Jew"? Isn't it likely that the absurdity of anti-Semitism might become more visible and audible through such reminders? This emphasis might now be unnecessary were it not for the fact that for two thousand years it has been subdued or overlooked or its implications shunned.

It is by setting aside the reluctance to see Jesus as a Jew that a creative and compassionate basis can be found for Christianity's new approach to Judaism.

The same is equally true of Judaism in its approach to Christianity.

Judaism's reluctance has been fortified by long centuries of adverse symbolism. The cross for millions of Jews has been identified with cruelty, heartbreak, prejudice. The cross to them has not become a sign of mercy or peace or charity or justice. Christians spoke and acted in the name of Christ; it was difficult to separate their acts from their faith. A new image of Jesus took shape for Jews, one that had no sanction either in the reality of Jesus or the ideas of Jesus. The image was not spiritually fulfilling; the new image meant pain and despair; the new image was resisted.

Over the centuries, this resistance has hardened to the point where the name Jesus almost produces a conditioned reflex among Jews. If Jesus' name is invoked in a company of Jews, the effect on many of them is one of profound uneasiness, as though their inner citadels were suddenly being challenged. Their reaction makes it seem as though a social contract were being violated. This condition has been more severe among the Orthodox than the other branches of the Jewish faith, but even among many Reform Jews a reticence exists toward the fact of Jesus. Most of the Reform congregations will discuss, occasionally, aspects of Jesus in pulpit or Sunday school, but most of the members themselves seem possessed by the historical rigidity. The New Testament as such is not studied in most Reform schools. However, Hebrew Union College now has a chair in New Testament studies so that graduating Reform rabbis may be in a position to institute the new studies.

There is every reason for Judaism to lose its reluctance toward Jesus. His own towering spiritual presence is a projection of Judaism, not a repudiation of it. Jesus is not to be taxed for the un-Christian ideas and acts of those who have spoken in his name, Jesus never repudiated Judaism. He was proud to be a Jew, yet he did not confine himself to Judaism. He did not believe in spiritual exclusivity for either Jew or Gentile. He asserted the Jewish heritage and sought to preserve and exalt its values, but he did it within a universal context. No other figure—spiritual, philosophical, political, or intellectual—has had a greater impact on human history. To belong to a people that produced Jesus is to share in a distinction of vast dimension and meaning.

Jesus' own teachings are a high point in the Jewish tradition. A sense of inspired recognition must run through the Jew who knows his Torah, the poetry of the Psalms, or the gentle aphorisms of great Jewish teachers and philosophers like Hillel. Jewish teachings are based on the idea of a natural goodness in man; it is to this goodness that Jesus the Jew has spoken.

The modern synagogue can live openly and fully with Jesus. It can do more than take pride in the fact of his being and in his existence and his ideas and his claim on history. And the rediscovery of Jesus can help Jews in the most vital respect of all; he can help them to forgive their tormentors—including those who have done evil to them in Jesus' name.

If it will help the Christian to come to terms with the fact of Jesus as Jew, so it may help Judaism to give weight to the same fact of Jesus' Jewishness—openly, fully, freely, proudly.

For twenty centuries two branches of the same religion have lived without harmony and understanding. Both have a common origin and can come together in a new attitude toward the figure of Jesus, the Jew. The common reluctances can give way to common knowledge and respect based on the reality of the connecting figure of Jesus. Such an amity speaks to the spiritual condition of both Christian and Jew. And out of this amity can come the nourishment of reconciliation.

Rabbi Roland B. Gittelsohn

NOT SO SIMPLE, MR. COUSINS

> Shortly after Norman Cousins' article, "The Jewishness of Jesus," appeared, scores of manuscripts started coming in purporting to answer the points made in the piece. Most of them were distinguished more for their sound and fury than for their sense, but one reply did seem to us to merit publication.
>
> The author, Rabbi Roland B. Gittelsohn, is spiritual leader of Temple Israel, in Boston, and chairman of the Commission on Jewish Education of the Union of American Hebrew Congregations and the Central Conference of American Rabbis. Rabbi Gittelsohn is author of *Little Lower Than the Angels, Modern Jewish Problems,* and *Consecrated Unto Me* — a book for teenagers offering a Jewish view of love and marriage.
>
> Here is Rabbi Gittelsohn's reply to Norman Cousins' "The Jewishness of Jesus"— and a comment by Mr. Cousins.

Norman Cousins makes a persuasive case for the acceptance by both Christians and Jews of Jesus as a Jew. For at least two reasons his argument deserves more than a page of cursory reaction in the form of correspondence. First, he himself is so spiritually sensitive and ethically dedicated a person that his views require analysis in depth. Second, too many Jews know only the side of Jesus disclosed by Mr. Cousins. We should not lose so fine an opportunity to educate them further.

There can be no disagreement with much of what Mr. Cousins

[28]

has written. It is true that Jesus in large part taught doctrines which were essentially Jewish. It is also true that Christians need sorely to understand this and to recognize the core-inconsistency in their own teaching concerning the Crucifixion. If, as they profess to believe, Jesus was crucified according to a divinely predestined plan, then at worst Jews must not be blamed for their alleged complicity in that plan; at best they should be congratulated for having served to that point at least as instruments of the divine will. In either event, it becomes incumbent upon Christians to acknowledge that Jesus was born, lived, and died as a Jew and that the most precious ethical and spiritual insights of Christianity are inextricably rooted in Judaism. To quote Mr. Cousins directly, "It is by setting aside the reluctance to see Jesus as a Jew that a creative and compassionate basis can be found for Christianity's new approach to Judaism." Thus far I would have no inclination to disagree.

It is when Mr. Cousins calls upon his fellow Jews to open their hearts and minds to Jesus that I begin to feel discomfort. The question is: to which Jesus? Mr. Cousins writes as if there were only one. The ineluctable historic fact is: there were three. The first, as we have already seen, was Jesus the Jew, or perhaps more accurately, Jesus the Reform Jew of nearly two millennia ago. The ethical imperatives of this Jesus were, of course, Jewish in origin. The God of Love concerning whom he preached so eloquently was recognized and acknowledged eight hundred years earlier by the Prophet Hosea. The Golden Rule which he pronounced in affirmative form was issued negatively a generation before him by Hillel. When this Jesus was asked, "What is the first of all the commandments?"—he answered, "Hear, O Israel, the Lord our God, the Lord is One: and thou shalt love the Lord thy God with all thy heart and with all thy soul . . . this is the first commandment, and the second is like unto it: Thou shalt love thy neighbor as thyself. There is no commandment greater than these." In answering thus, Jesus was consciously quoting these words from the Hebrew Torah, a tradition which antedated his own career by many centuries.

If this is the Jesus Mr. Cousins has in mind, his plea for Jews to accept him is, to say the least, superfluous. It amounts to urging that Jews should accept a carbon copy of Judaism when the original is already in their possession. Granted that Jesus was a particularly attractive personality and a most imaginative and effective teacher of these Jewish doctrines. The fact remains, however, that he originated none of them, that all of them were evolved and taught by the authentic teachers of Judaism long before he had even been born. What have we to gain, then, by accepting them in the particular form enunciated by Jesus? How does the injunction to love our neighbors, as voiced by Jesus in the gospels, add anything to the original of that lofty challenge, as expressed earlier in Leviticus?

Let me reinforce my point additionally by way of analogy. Frederick Chopin, in his "Butterfly Etude," composed a melody line of exceptional beauty. A hundred years later a composer whose name isn't even worth remembering took the exact notes of Chopin and made of them a popular song called "I'm Always Chasing Rainbows." Who deserves credit for this melody—Chopin or his imitator? To whom does it really belong? What kind of sense would it make to urge that a man who knows and appreciates Chopin should buy a recording of the popular song in order to hear his favorite melody?

I don't mean to suggest for a moment that Jesus was a cheap imitator like the man who musically chased rainbows. What I do mean is that he taught values and ideals which he learned from Judaism. Why, then, should Judaism go back to him to recapture that which it already possesses?

So much for the first Jesus, the one on whom Mr. Cousins concentrates. The second Jesus spoke in accents irreconcilably foreign to Judaism. He recommended celibacy, for example, as the noblest goal of human sexual conduct, specifically praising those who "make themselves eunuchs for the kingdom of heaven's sake." Judaism urges not sexual frustration but legitimate sexual fulfilment in marriage as God's purpose for human life.

The second Jesus, in effect, taught that morality has nothing to do with politics, that the two are in altogether separate categories of experience. He said, "Give unto Caesar that which is Caesar's and unto God that which is God's." Judaism insists that morality enters into every area of life, including that of politics; that nothing belongs to Caesar unless first it has been consecrated by the values we associate with God.

The second Jesus castigated the rich purely because they were rich. In the parable of the rich man and Lazarus, the former inherits hell not because he has committed any evil but plainly and simply because he possesses wealth. This Jesus said, "Woe unto you that are rich, for ye have received your consolation; and woe unto you that are filled, for ye shall hunger." He also said, "It is easier for a camel to go through the eye of a needle than for a rich man to enter the kingdom of heaven." Judaism teaches that we must show prejudice against or favoritism for neither the poor nor the rich but treat all men justly. Judaism implied that what counts is not whether a man has wealth, but (a) how did he obtain his wealth and (b) for what purposes does he use it?

Perhaps the most frequently quoted precept of the second Jesus is this: "Whosoever smiteth thee on thy right cheek, turn to him the other also. And if any . . . would take away thy coat, let him have thy cloak also." Thus did Jesus articulate his doctrine of non-resistance to evil, another emphasis completely contradictory to Judaism, which teaches that evil must always be resisted and justice always pursued. In the words of the late Dr. Joseph Klausner, perhaps the greatest Jewish interpreter of Jesus, "What room is there in the world for justice if we must extend both cheeks to our assailants and give the thief both cloak and coat?"

The second Jesus urged his followers to love their enemies. Judaism is far too realistic and sober a faith to endorse so psychologically impossible a precept as that. Judaism orders its adherents to help their enemies when they are in trouble, to rescue the animal of an enemy when it lies helplessly under a heavy burden. Judaism proclaims: "If thine enemy be hungry, give him bread to eat, and if he be thirsty, give him water to drink." But never would Judaism torture its adherents with guilt by expecting them to *love* their enemies!

The temptation is to go on and on. It would be easy to do so; the evidence in the form of direct quotation from Jesus is plentiful. But isn't this enough to identify the second Jesus? And to establish the utter inconsonance between his teachings and those of Judaism? Or, for that matter, the inconsistency between these precepts and his own when he speaks as the first Jesus? Which Jesus is it, then, which Mr. Cousins would want Jews to accept? If, as I strongly suspect, it's only the first, would he then, for the sake of the spiritual bridge he so yearningly seeks, ask Christians to relinquish the second? And if he did, is there any realistic probability they would do so? These are questions which come close to the essential heart of the matter.

The usual explanation for the antipathy of most Jews to the very name of Jesus is that they and their ancestors have been subjected to such inhuman suffering in his name. Perhaps there is another reason in addition to this. Perhaps the generations of Jews were perceptive enough, even if only by intuition, to recognize that so much of the teaching attributed to Jesus is the very opposite of Judaism, the direct negation of what Judaism pronounced as valid. Obviously, the problem is considerably more complicated than Mr. Cousins makes it out to be.

It becomes still more complicated when we remember that there is yet a third Jesus—the Christ. Though I devote only a passing paragraph to this Jesus, let it not be forgotten that for the overwhelming preponderance of Christians this Jesus outweighs by far both the first and the second. This is the Jesus alleged to be God incarnate, born of a virgin, the fulfilment of Hebrew prophecy, the Messiah ordained by God, the second partner to the Trinity. This is the Jesus without whom, for all practical purposes, Christianity disintegrates, for without him, Christianity becomes simply a branch of Judaism. I hesitate to be flippant on a matter so sacred to millions of my fellow men, but I feel almost compelled to quote here the comment of Heine: "Christianity without Christ is like turtle soup without turtle." It's all very well to say that this third Jesus is not the real one, not the historic one, that this one is a product of what later enthusiasts did to Jesus the Jew. But saying so doesn't alter the fact that for all but a very small fringe of Christians this is the Jesus who counts, the central figure of their faith.

I think I know Norman Cousins well enough to feel sure that he isn't asking us to accept the third Jesus. I'm not absolutely sure whether or not he would have us accept the second, though I suspect not. If, then, we agree to accept the first—would this lead to "the nourishment of reconciliation" for which Mr. Cousins pleads? I think not. In a paradoxical, almost a perverse way, it might in fact have the opposite effect. For this in reality would mean to ask that Christians "water down" Jesus to what many of them would consider a least-common-denominator. This would come perilously close to making the whole development of Christianity a superfluity based on distortion. I suspect that this —far from bringing Jews and Christians closer together in amity— might well exacerbate whatever enmity there is, fanning it into aggravated warfare.

[32]

Mr. Cousins' motives are beyond reproach. His spirit is that of unbounded love for humanity, all humanity. He wants brotherhood and peace so passionately that I'm afraid he has used the materials of history and of fact too selectively to be valid. The real road to interreligious harmony—a long, hard, often discouraging road, but one nonetheless worthy of our most intense effort —is for Jews to be the most devoted kind of Jews they can be and for Christians to strive toward understanding who Jesus really was and what he truly taught.

Can Jews accept Jesus? Only the first Jesus. Only the one who learned Judaism from his parents and rabbis and who preached it as he understood it, when he understood it. We can and do accept Jesus as a Jewish teacher, one among many teachers—as a magnetic personality, as an expert in the use of parables—one among many such experts whose words are recorded both in Bible and Talmud.

As for the amity Mr. Cousins so properly seeks, Rabbi Milton Steinberg pointed the only realistically hopeful way to achieve it. He asked, "Will the gap be filled? Will the two religions, mother and daughter, ever be reconciled?" And he answered, "Many . . . in both camps see no reason why the two faiths need coalesce. Let each be as pure and strong in its own character as it can. For the rest, there is need not for filling in gaps but for bridging them with mutual candor and understanding."

*A Comment
by Norman Cousins*

Dear Rabbi Gittelsohn:

Let me say at once that your commentary was by far the most valuable and searching of any that I have seen, whether in AJ or elsewhere. It provides sharp, serious focus on the subject. I have learned from it and thank you for it.

I differ with it in this respect: The pivotal point in your commentary has to do with your assumption that I am asking Jews to "accept" Jesus. You then go on to consider different roles of Jesus in his relationship to Jews. If I had asked Jews to "accept'

Jesus, everything you say in this part of your discussion would be valid. But my purpose in writing the article was not to persuade Jews to "accept" Jesus or Christianity or any other religion. I wanted Jews to be objective about Jesus, to free him of stigma for the persecution carried on in his name, to take pride in him as one of the two or three greatest spiritual figures in human history, and to evaluate his ideas outside of the context of religious orthodoxies or competitions. At the very least, I wanted my fellow Jews to get over the feeling that too many of them have — a feeling of uneasiness or discomfort when the name Jesus is mentioned. In short, I wanted them, as I said in my article, to live openly with the fact of Jesus and to give full weight to the fact that he was a Jew.

The word "accept," in the religious contest, has connotations of conversion or theological surrender or replacement. This was not what I meant to suggest. I would be opposed to any such attempt at conversion or replacement. Your commentary would seem to indicate that I failed to make my purpose clear. I therefore thank you for the privilege of your analysis; I welcome the chance to make my meaning clear.

Sincerely,
Norman Cousins
Editor, *Saturday Review*

Rabbi Maurice N. Eisendrath

A DECALOGUE OF DECENCY
FOR OUR AGE

A firm tenet of Reform Judaism is that the traditions of the past must be interpreted in the light of the needs of the living. Here Rabbi Eisendrath takes a new look at the Ten Commandments and proposes a contemporary Decalogue for ethical action.

His remarks were part of his address when he accepted the "First Spiritual Freedom Citation" from the Chapel of the Four Chaplains in Philadelphia on February 7, 1960.

What we require today more desperately than ought else besides is in my judgment a decalogue of decency for the relationship between man and his brother-man which might read something like this:

I. I AM THE LORD THY GOD who brought not alone the Hebrews out of Egypt but the Ethiopians from Caphtor and the Arameans from Kir, which means quite simply, as both Moses and Amos would have understood it, that I am the Lord not merely of those Americans who believe today that He is their sole possession but I am the Lord likewise of those hundreds of thousands, even hundreds of millions of humble children of the Divine, behind even the Iron and the Bamboo Curtains. I am the Lord not only of the proud and supercilious whites but I am the Lord also of the colored. I am the Lord who cannot be confined into any structure of stone, be it cathedral or church or synagogue, but I am the Lord of the Heaven and of the Earth, one and indivisible.

II. THOU SHALT HAVE NO OTHER GODS BESIDE ME neither of status nor of success before which men so grovelingly

[35]

bow down today, nor of Mammon nor of Mars, both of which claim man's seemingly undeviating allegiance in our time.

III. THOU SHALT NOT TAKE THE NAME OF THE LORD THY GOD IN VAIN by stamping "In God We Trust" upon your coins and postage stamps and trusting almost exclusively not in Him but in your proud accoutrements of war.

IV. REMEMBER THE SABBATH DAY, TO KEEP IT HOLY in order that through decent leisure men may feel again their dignity as children of the Divine, that they may no longer feel, as increasing numbers are coming to believe themselves today, to be mere machines and tools, motes of dust on a vast conveyor belt, slots in an IBM calculator.

V. HONOR THY FATHER AND THY MOTHER that thou might safeguard the security and the decency of the home, that there might be peace again between the generations.

VI. THOU SHALT NOT MURDER either the one or the many, either singly or in the mass, either thy contemporaries in impending incineration or the generations still unborn by polluting the atmosphere with the noxious, noisome, nauseating poisons of nuclear fall-out.

VII. THOU SHALT NOT COMMIT ADULTERY not merely in person but as a society, by adulterating the ether-waves, by the cheapening tawdriness that makes the whole of life seem to the younger generation cheap and leads them into the dens of juvenile delinquency.

VIII. THOU SHALT NOT STEAL either outrightly or more subtly by stealing a man's birthright, by making it impossible for him either because of color or creed or station in life to pursue his education or his employment or to live where he chooses rather than in the imposed ghettos of our vigilantly guarded neighborhoods of the North as well as the South.

IX. THOU SHALT NOT BEAR FALSE WITNESS by misleading innuendoes and rumors and gossip against thy neighbor's faith, precluding every opportunity for advancement even to the highest places in our land to a man because supposedly he pursues some other faith.

X.   THOU SHALT NOT COVET not only thy next-door neighbor's house, nor his ox, nor his ass, but thou shalt not covet the distant nation's missiles to the moon but covet instead thine own divinely decreed mission unto mankind.

This is the decalogue of decency which I would have our time, our nation, our people pursue, so that bound together in life as those four Chaplains were in their courageous and comradely death, we might in truth usher in God's Kingdom in our time.

JACOB LANDAU

[37]

Rabbi Jack Bemporad

TOWARD A NEW
JEWISH THEOLOGY

When Rabbi Jack Bemporad became director of worship
of the Union of American Hebrew Congregations, his first
concern was the neglect of the theological foundations of
Judaism. In "Toward A New Jewish Theology" he tried
to present as plainly as possible the need of a theology
appropriate for contemporary Judaism.

Rabbi Bemporad has taught philosophy at the University of Rome, the Hebrew Union College-Jewish Institute
of Religion and the New School for Social Research. In
addition to his affiliation with the UAHC, he is chaplain
and director of religious activities at the Hawthorne Cedar
Knolls School in Hawthorne, New York.

There are three major Jewish theological positions prevalent today: religious *naturalism,* religious *existentialism* and, for the lack
of a better name, what may be called *traditionalism.* Each
presents insurmountable difficulties but, when carefully examined, indicates the great need of a new theology for contemporary Judaism.

Traditional theology is a diluted version of medieval Jewish
philosophy. It is implicit in our prayer books, it underlies the
theology of our religious school texts, and is the generally
accepted view of God, man, and the universe for most present-
day Jews. Concern here, therefore, will be with those areas in
which this view is especially vulnerable to criticism. Existentialism and naturalism will be mentioned only briefly, since I hope to
deal wth these latter positions in separate articles.

Traditional Jewish theology is vulnerable because of its in-
dissoluble connection with the presently discarded Aristotelian
philosophy.

Aristotle's philosophy emphasizes the static, self-contained

[38]

character of substance at the expense of *process, temporality,* and *relativity,* which typifies modern thought. Moreover, the theology of traditional Judaism is full of numerous ambiguities of its own which make it religiously suspect. Two major ambiguities stand out glaringly:

There is the problem of man's freedom in terms of his relation to God.

There is the problem of evil in relation to God's creation.

It is my view that the traditional position on these two points is deficient. If the modern Jew clings to this view, he will be confused about his Judaism—if not, indeed, alienated from it.

The problem of freedom concerns itself with an attempt to reconcile God's *omnipotence* with *human responsibility.* To say that God is omnipotent—in the traditional sense—means that God has all possible power. But if God has all possible power, and all possible knowledge, then God must not only *direct* all that happens but must *know* all that has happened, is happening, or ever will happen.

Such a view of God makes it impossible for man to have any genuine freedom or capacity to create. For how can he affect the process of creation at all—either positively or negatively—if God has all power?

God determines all. God knows all. God does all. If all that I am to do is already determined in God's mind, if the entire process of history is pre-written there, then how am I free?

To state this argument technically:

If God is all-powerful, then there can be no power other than God's.

If there is no power other than God's, then man can have no power.

If man has no power, then man can have no responsibility.

Traditionalists have affirmed that man has freedom in spite of the omnipotent character of God. Surely this is based on a confusion, which readily can be seen. *It stems from the belief that responsibility can be divided between God and man without, at the same time, dividing power between God and man.*

To have genuine responsibility, man must have genuine power. For traditional theology this means an intolerable assault on God's omnipotence. It is a mistake to believe, however, that this demand for man's power does detract from God's omnipotence. Such a belief is based on a misunderstanding. Omnipotence means the greatest possible power for any single being. It does not and cannot mean all possible power in general.

The root of this difficulty lies in the confusion between what can be asserted by logical definition and what can be asserted ontologically. One could develop a perfectly logical system that would be in no sense real. It would not pass the test of ontology, which implies reality and existence. God's omnipotence is not to be understood only in terms of what is logically meaningful but by what is ontologically meaningful: by reference to what exists.

Let me illustrate what I mean. Medieval philosophy generally recognized logical limits to God's power. For instance, it affirmed that God could not do what is logically impossible, like square a circle, or create a stone so heavy that He could not lift it. What has not been seen clearly is that there are certain limits in terms of real being to God's omnipotence. These do not detract from that omnipotence. On the contrary, they render it intelligible. The ontological limit of God's omnipotence is the reality of man and creation. Once God creates the world, a real element is introduced which has being and power and which demands its due. God then has maximum power, but He cannot have all possible power if His creation *really* is to exist.

It is important to note here that though the confusion over omnipotence and man's freedom is characteristic of most medieval as well as modern theological thinking, it is not true of Maimonides' thought.

Maimonides' doctrine of negative attributes makes it unnecessary to define God's omnipotence since one can only speak of God in terms of what He is not and not in terms of what He is. Maimonides also makes a distinction between His relational attributes (goodness, power, etc.) and His essential attributes (infinitude, unity) which further resolves this dilemma. But the extent to which this contribution can be meaningful in a modern Jewish theology deserves profound investigation.

If God is defined as omnipotent and omniscient in the traditional sense, then man's freedom is limited to a re-enacting of a pattern already in God's mind. This means that man does not genuinely create or decide anything. Creativity and freedom mean the capacity to decide what is really undecided. They imply an open future with real alternative possibilities; the real determination of what is essentially indeterminate.

[40]

Judaism affirms that man has a real choice and is responsible for that choice; it affirms that his choice makes a difference for good or for ill to man himself and to the universe in which man lives. Therefore, a new theology, in order to vindicate the power and creativity of man, must endeavor to show that omnipotence cannot mean all possible power. In short, it must be recognized that there are limitations to God's power other than purely logical ones. There are limits in terms of *what exists.*

The second major difficulty deals with the problem of evil. This problem is usually stated as follows: If God is all powerful and all good then how can He allow evil? If God is omnipotent then God by definition has the power to prevent any possible evil. If He is all good—absolute goodness—then He could not possibly desire any evil. Now, if God does not desire evil and has all the power necessary to prevent it, then why is there evil in the world?

It would follow from this argument that God is either *deficient in power* or *deficient in goodness,* otherwise the evil in the world has to be explained away as not really being evil at all. Most Jewish thinking on this question has denied the reality of evil. Medieval Jewish theology generally maintained that evil was merely the "absence of good." Some philosophers made evil necessary so that it could be overcome by the good.

If God is all powerful and all good then the world can have no power or goodness. All power and goodness are His alone. But for the universe to contain evil it must have sufficient power to produce the good that evil destroyed. For evil to be real there must have been the possibility of genuine good in the world, but if we admit the possibility of genuine good in the world then the world must possess sufficient power and goodness to bring it into being. In effect, it is impossible for the world to contain evil without it having at the same time the possibility of achieving good, yet in order for it to achieve good it must have power and goodness. It is, therefore, wrong to say that God is all power-ful and all good since, then, the world would have no power, goodness, or being.

What we must affirm is that God has the *most* power and goodness but *not all possible* power and goodness. The world must have *some* power and goodness in addition to God's power and goodness for the world to contain evil. And so, as tradition-ally stated, the question will not stand. If God has all power and goodness (all *possible* power and goodness) then creation cannot have *enough* power and goodness even to allow for the reality of evil.

It may seem at first as if this were a variation on the traditional solution with respect to man's freedom; that is, that man has freedom to choose evil. But this is not the case since, as we have shown above, the traditional view can in no way explain genuine choice and hence in no way can explain man's freedom. The solution lies in redefining God's attributes of *omnipotence, omniscience,* and *goodness* to mean that God is in *no sense* deficient in power, knowledge, and goodness. God is the most powerful being but not the being with all power, the most good but not the being with all goodness.

All the confusions in traditional theology, and the essence of the confusion concerning the problem of evil, stem from the Aristotelian dogma that God is to be identified with substance and that substance needs nothing but Itself in order to exist; that It contains everything, is complete, immutable, and in splendid isolation. Once God is identified with the Aristotelian substance then the fullness of being, goodness, and power is complete in God, and the world and man can add nothing to God. This means that God is exactly the same with or without creation. But here is the basic problem. If creation really *is*, then God cannot be the same and have the same attributes and existence as if creation *were not.* By affirming that God is the sole being and sole reality then traditional theology denies the possibility of a multiplicity of real beings. In denying a genuine multiplicity of real beings it speaks in one context as if the world has being and thus, in some way or other, is additional to God, and in another context as if it has no genuine being and God is the sole reality.

In order to resolve these ambiguities a new theology must affirm that there is a genuine difference before and after creation. After creation man and nature have being and power, and all the attributes of God have to be redefined so as to account for the being and power of creation. Once we affirm that not only God but creation also has being, power, and goodness, then one major consequence follows. God is not the sole cause of the continuing process of the world. He is the major cause in sustaining, ordering, and actualizing the world but not the *only* cause, and hence cannot be *solely responsible* for actuality. Other beings make a genuine difference in this process. This allows for a genuine freedom. It vindicates both man's power and man's responsibility.

What I have suggested in these pages is that we need a new theology which will attempt to unravel the ambiguities and contradictions of traditional theology through a rational re-appraisal of what we believe as to the nature of God, man, and the universe. We do not need a theology that resorts to the paradoxical, subjective, and non-categorizable, as the existentialists have done. The existentialist emphasizes the absurd. He asserts that man needs to be rescued by God. Where he discusses God in any objective way whatsoever, he does not bother to overcome any of the ambiguities of the traditionalist view. On the contrary, the existentialist makes things worse since, in his resort to paradox and his glorying in contradiction, one can never pin him down. Modern Judaism needs a theology that takes the findings of science seriously but that does not slavishly accept science as the only truth, as the naturalists do who attempt to base religious values on a scientific view of nature.

Why should we try to base the purposeful on the purposeless, the meaningful on the meaningless, and the valuable on the valueless?

The modern Jew requires a new theology so that he may worship a God he not only needs but can accept intellectually and morally.

Rabbi Solomon B. Freehof

THE PURIM PUZZLE

When Rabbi Solomon Freehof speaks, his listeners are enraptured. Wisdom, erudition, humor, eloquence and a sense of urgency combine to cast an irresistible spell. When he writes, his readers fall under the same enchantment. There have been countless rabbinical commentaries on the meaning of various Jewish holidays but few written with the compression, adroitness and pertinency of this brief essay on the meaning of the Purim holiday, which celebrates the rescue of the Jews of ancient Persia from slaughter through the evil machinations of a king's counselor.

Rabbi Freehof, spiritual leader of Rodef Shalom Temple in Pittsburgh, Pennsylvania, is the author of numerous books of biblical commentary including the *Book of Psalms,* the *Book of Job,* and a *Preface to Scripture.* He is also former president of the World Union for Progressive Judaism and the Central Conference of American Rabbis.

The runaway slaves stood before the Red Sea and heard the roar of Pharaoh's approaching chariots. In their panic they assailed Moses with outcries and threats. To which he gave the answer: "You be silent. God will fight for you."

This became the classic attitude of Jews in times of danger. Their ultimate hope for victory and rescue lay in their confidence that they and God were on the same side. The Psalm (20:8) put it: "Some trust in chariots, but we trust in the name of the Lord our God."

In the Book of Esther there was a perfect opportunity to proclaim this classic Jewish trust in God. Mordecai had pleaded with Esther to risk her own security in order to save her people. Then he wanted to say to her: If you prefer to avoid the risk, we will do without you, for help will come to us from God. He does say that (Esther 4:14), but he makes the statement in a curious circumlocution. He says: If you fail us, help will come to us from *some other place*. It is clear that the author of the book consciously sidesteps mentioning the name of God which in such circumstances would come automatically to the lips. This leads us to understand why the name of God does not occur even once in the Book of Esther. This is far from an accident. It is a conscious avoidance. The author wanted to write a completely *secular* book.

This purpose is puzzling, and it leads to a further puzzle. There can be no doubt that the Jews had become a deeply religious people, taught by prophets, psalmists and rabbis, actively participating in the public and private study of holy writings. Yet this deeply spiritualized people took enthusiastically to the secular Book of Esther and manifestly made it their favorite book in the Bible. If a book is to be judged by the creativity which it evokes, then the Book of Esther was one of the most influential books in the life of Jewry. It is in relation to the Book of Esther and the Feast of Purim which it ordained that the greatest self-expression was evoked, not from the leaders and the scholars but from the masses of the people themselves. It was at Purim that they had their masquerades, their first popular stagecraft, and their wild hilarity. There is no festival, major or minor, and no biblical story connected with a festival, which has evoked so much self-expression from the Jewish people. Why?

PENROD SCOFIELD

[45]

The frequent answer is that Purim was the opportunity for comic relief in the seriousness of Jewish life. Undoubtedly there is truth in that explanation. But it cannot be all of it. Jewish life was not devoid of joy on the Sabbath and Passover. The relief which Purim brought was more than a comic relief; it was also a *theological* relief. It was a declaration of another, a popular, explanation to the meaning of the Jewish experience.

The classic religious explanation of Jewish suffering is that the people of Israel have sinned, and that for their sin God has sent punishment to them. The very suffering, being God-sent, will purify them and lead to their redemption. This doctrine, both humble and hopeful, was taught by the prophets, and is inherent in the Book of Judges and was repeated in the older liturgy on every holiday: "It is because of our sins that we were exiled from our home."

Jews religiously believed this truth and in many ways were ennobled by it, being led to repentance and ethical purification. But they also knew in their heart that the classic doctrine does not tell the whole story. Sometimes they suffered and were innocent of wrong-doing. Sometimes their punishment came from bitter hatred; and since at times their suffering was due to evil men, not to God's intention, the deliverance must come from clever men without God's direct intervention. This human explanation of Jewish experience is represented in the Bible only in the Book of Esther. Here the Jews are endangered not because of their iniquity, but because of the evil of Haman. Here they are rescued, not by God's direct intervention, but by the lucky fact that one of their brave girls became the queen and one of their clever boys became councilor to the king of Persia.

The story represents a spiritual, or at least a psychological need of Jewry. At least one day of the year Jews wanted to say: Yes, we have been sinners and we deserve punishment but also we have been innocent and we ourselves must outwit our enemies. Purim is therefore the necessary secular footnote to the regular spiritual doctrine. It is the exception voiced by Jews to the doctrine proclaimed by Judaism. Deliverance from God is met with solemn thanksgiving. Deliverance by a clever brother and sister is expressed in dancing and hilarity. Judaism is almost never puritanical. But to the extent that it is lenten, Purim is its Mardi Gras, but a Mardi Gras with a meaning.

[46]

Rabbi Balfour Brickner

A BLUEPRINT
FOR JEWISH SURVIVAL

> Rabbi Balfour Brickner is known in key cities throughout
> the country as the host of the program "Adventures in
> Judaism," which has twice received the Ohio State Award
> from the Institute for Education by Radio-Television. His
> personality and style are refreshingly free from the pom-
> posities and heavy locutions of the rabbinical stereotype,
> both on the pulpit and at the studio microphone. In this
> article he cautions clearly that survival for the Jew is not
> likely unless there exists in the soul of this people "the
> passionate will to survive."
>
> Rabbi Brickner is director of interfaith activities for
> the Union of American Hebrew Congregations, the Cen-
> tral Conference of Amercan Rabbis, and associate direc-
> tor of the Commission on Social Action of Reform
> Judaism.

Rosh Ha-shono. Another New Year. American Jews gather by
the millions in synagogues. Chances are that the size of the
congregation will be good this year. It is easy to be "in shul" this
Rosh Ha-shono. Since Rosh Ha-shono and the Labor Day week-
end coincide, it's not even necessary to take the day off from
work to go to temple. No "conflict of interests." No conflict of
conscience to resolve this year.

But, in some congregations, particularly those in and around
New York City, attendance will be down. Some of the "faithful"
will have made a holiday out of the Holy Day, "observing" the
Day of Judgment in the mountains, at a "resort synagogue"—the
latest manifestation of Jewish vulgarity. And it is likely that in
this season of renewal, the rabbi's Rosh Ha-shono sermon will in
some way touch upon the theme of "American Jewish survival."

The subject has been on everyone's lips lately. Besides, the
survival theme is a "natural" for this time of the year when the
mood is one of introspection, of re-examination and honesty. We

[47]

try to catch a glimpse of the future of our Jewish selves in the mirrors of our past and present.

Do we have a future—or only a past? Are we spiritual parasites living on the unearned increment of past glory? Discussions see-saw from total cynicism to unrealistic optimism. Despite these naive extremes, most of us remain concerned. Questions continue to nag and annoy the opulent giant that is American Jewry. Perhaps it is time to try to bend a few of the question marks into exclamation points.

By its own elemental definition, "survival" simply means re-maining alive. All living things naturally seek their own survival. So considered, the phrase "Jewish survival" does not mean more than a quantitative continuance of a group called Jews. On these terms, of course, American Jews will survive. Since there is less and less reason to hide our identity, our quantitative presence is likely to continue.

But, will we survive *as Jews* in a sense more than nominal? This is a qualitative question based on a more probing examina-tion of the word "survival"—the continuance, by a group, of ancient uses, customs and beliefs to the present and into the future. Will there be a future for Judaism or merely a future for Jews—a future for a group whose faith and culture keep us separate and discernible from the rest of the community? Never before have there been so many Cassandra-like voices crying "No" to the possibility of Jewish survival in these terms. Much evidence can be marshalled in support of their contention:

Whether or not one accepts as valid those statistics on inter-marriage now so widely quoted, there can be little doubt that the rate of intermarriage has increased dramatically in the last decade or two. (The statistics may be questionable but the fact stands.) And hasn't intermarriage always been the litmus paper of a declining commitment to Judaism by Jews?

Many of our young people find their Jewishness and their Judaism irrelevant to their quest for identity and a meaningful life. Our college campuses are certainly not hotbeds of religious fervor.

Many of us exhibit a troublesome indifference to Jewish disciplines even though we hold nominal memberships in con-gregations and send our children to religious schools. Such activities are becoming more social than theological. For this group, Judaism "is not unpleasant, it is just unimportant."

[48]

By far the most disconcerting is the apparent reality that those we call our Jewish intellectuals seem to live on the periphery of Jewish life, critical, aloof, removed from the survivalistic stream. Their identification seems to end with the accident of their birth.

These are the arguments for despair. They are powerful. Nevertheless, Jewish survival—in the deepest sense—is possible. And there are forces operating within the American sociological pattern which leave room, not only for Judaism to remain alive but also to grow.

The word "ghettoization" does not usually evoke positive feelings. We think of the ghetto as a condition of alienation imposed, not chosen. While such "ghettoization" is commonly understood as that tendency on the part of an ethnic, cultural or religious group physically to cluster together, it can also be understood as a state of mind, a way of thinking, a pattern of behavior. It is sometimes related more to mood than to place. There are people who, though they live in "mixed" or "balanced" neighborhoods, continue to "live Jewish." Even if every community in America were to open tomorrow to any and all, regardless of income, within a short time the same "pockets of ethnic groupness" would probably develop again. People like to live with their own kind.

There are survivalistic values in these Jewish enclaves of ours. Physical huddling is not altogether negative. Isolate a Jew in some non-Jewish setting and the danger of attenuating his meaningful attachment to the Jewish group increases appreciably. The chances of a Jew being lost to *k'llal yisroel* (the Jewish people) are greater in a Jewishly barren, isolated spot than they are when he lives in a community that offers him a synagogue, a Jewish community center and other institutions and agencies of Jewish life, for these are the vehicles of Jewish survival and development. The clustered Jew of America today may not work in or for his surrounding Jewish community, but as long as he is in it, that community surely works for and even upon him.

Let this much be said for such voluntary enclaves; despite the fact that they are not in themselves forces for qualitative Jewish survival, if properly nurtured, they can be used as means to encourage patterns of Jewish living that can lead to intellectual and emotional strength. They should *not* be dismissed categorically as evil.

America is moving quickly from a society which understood and explained culturally the differences among its citizens to one which sees and explains some of those differences in religious terms. More and more, we Americans are distinguished not by what we eat or wear or the language we speak, but by what we profess. Our pluralism is religious rather than cultural. Christians ask Jews not where they came from, but what they believe. They want to know: Do Jews still see themselves as a covenant people? Do Jews consider themselves a people with a sense of religious mission? Are Jews a people whose raison d'être for continued existence is an unshakeable belief in a God who operates in and through history? Such questions indicate that our non-Jewish friends have been thinking about our religion more searchingly than we have.

One doesn't wish to be stigmatized as a "Protestant" Jew—a Jew who accepts his identity in terms of religious faith alone. The word "Jew" is rich in connotations and not all of them are pejorative. Phrases like "community," "peoplehood," "historic ties," add to our sense of mission and our understanding of ourselves. A Jew cannot be understood in credal terms alone. But what does all this mean for the average Jew? You and I must not only grapple with the two questions, "Can the Jews survive?", "Can Judaism survive?" but add a third: "Is it desirable that we survive?"

If our survival is desirable, it is because Judaism has a unique contribution to make to human existence. Judaism offers a view of man neither unrealistically hopeful nor corrosively despairing. Judaism sees man as vibrant, with an infinite potential for the evolution of his soul. Man is capable of the worst but can be better tomorrow than he is today. This bias toward optimism has always caused Judaism to set the highest standards for its own adherents and to hold up challenging criteria to all of humanity.

Jews have struggled hard to meet these standards in the spheres of family life, community morality—compassion—self-discipline and through intellectual, political, aesthetic and practical achievement. The efforts to meet such standards have not met with total failure. Such optimism has motivated Jews to bring order and inspiration to life even in the face of death, even when the Ghetto of Warsaw was about to be annihilated. In the wartime bunkers of Lodz there was theater. When Israel faced the Goliath of Arab aggression there was song. Judaism teaches men to laugh in the midst of tears.

Judaism offers man a view of the cosmos relatively uncluttered with the appendages of irrational notions. Men are challenged to probe, to inquire, to understand and thus to arrive at belief rather than accept the principles of faith through blind confidence in authority and superstition. One is drawn through understanding to come to the Jewish conclusion that there is a purpose in what happens, order in the universe, Mind at the center of all. So there comes to be perceived a sacredness in all events. We worship and pray, not to beg favors but to express emotionally our conviction that all is sanctified, that the universe is permeated by the breath of God—or what the poet William Rose Benet called, "the dust which is God." Judaism tries to translate the impersonal Mind of the universe into a personal God concerned with the world of human events. Every Jew should understand these concepts, but the individual is never threatened with rejection or expulsion if he fails to concur with the conclusions of this theology.

Judaism also stands in awe of memory, almost idolizing the principle of remembering. This faith of ours sees memory not merely as a tie that binds one generation to another or the past to the present, it uses memory as a sensitizer, as a "life-softener," as a source of rootage. In an age where so much is so brittle, so impersonal, so fleeting, so rootless, the elevation and preservation of that which makes for roots and stability is well worth struggling to preserve.

But where and how will these ideas find expression? In our urban and suburban voluntary ghettos? In our synagogues? In our religious schools as they are presently constituted?

The frontier of American Jewish survival is still the synagogue, the oldest bastion. One is reminded of the biblical phrase: "The stone which the builders have rejected has become the chief cornerstone." For so long the builders of American Jewry rejected the synagogue. Remember the Jew who loved Yiddish, or Hebrew or *kenedlach* but who had only contempt for God? His days are numbered. In his place, we find the modern who comes to the synagogue not in faith but in search, desperately hoping to find something to satisfy a deep hunger for meaning and a sense of plan and purpose. He will not long remain in the cold, sterile synagogue which has, in all honesty, been so typical of our own movement. He is no longer afraid of his emotions. Psychology has taught him that emotional expressions are a necessary and valid part of his life. He knows that which stimulates the heart need not stupefy the mind. Emotion is an energy and like all energy it needs channelled expression. Frozen rituals, a silent congregation which witnesses but does not worship, hidden choirs singing unrecognizably esoteric music, do not channel the emotions, they dam them up. Our congregations suffer from an emotional deficiency. It paralyzes the faculty of creative imagination which distinguishes religion from a moral philosophy or from some vague system of ethics. And we have let this happen precisely at a time when what we most need is a vivid imagery, figures of speech and emotional expressions by which to articulate our reasoned ideals. Unless we begin immediately to revise our worship in such a way as to give our people an opportunity to truly and traditionally express themselves, we will find that we will have lost an important vehicle for survival and with it the credo we seek to transmit.

Any blueprint for tomorrow's Judaism must contain not merely a revitalization of our present religious school structure; it must dare to dream of and to work for the creation of a radically new tool: the Jewish preparatory school.

Reality prompts the observation that American Reform Judaism cannot sufficiently intensify its Sunday schools, or week-end schools, or week-day Hebrew schools to develop in the next generation a group of men and women whose life will be so suffused with a knowledge of and a commitment to Judaism, as to enable them to withstand the onslaughts of faithless intellectualism. For this, we need to create quality institutions of education where the best and brightest of our youngsters can have their learning laced through with the insights and values which Judaism possesses and which it can indeed bring to bear on all knowledge. American Jewry can and will afford a "Jewish Exeter" or a "Jewish Andover" where the finest classical education can be fused with the finest classics of Judaism. Why shouldn't our students learn Hebrew as they learn Greek and Latin? Our parents bend heaven and earth to enroll their children in a St. Albans or a Friends School or a Milton Academy. There are as many who, seeking the Jewish survival of their progeny, would be as eager to enroll their young in a school oriented toward Judaism rather than toward some form of Protestantism.

On the college campus Judaism can be and should be taken out of the realm of the extra-curricular and placed in the classroom where it would be taught to one and all on a credit basis. A nation-wide program to subsidize Jewish scholars, artists, writers, enabling them to touch our young in the places where the young can be reached—the classroom and the laboratory—is both realistic and possible. All it takes is a will and American Jewish money.

Survival must spring from a passionate willingness to survive. Jewish survival can only come out of the conviction that Judaism still possesses indispensable values for existence in our world. American Judaism can translate this conviction into commitment. When Jews are convinced that retaining the affirmation of their Judaism will not reduce them to the state of being less authentic, less universal persons, they will move toward Judaism with far less hesitation. When they realize that Judaism makes Jews *more* authentic, *more* universal, that such a faith opens the mind rather than closes it—that it frees the soul from fear rather than encasing it in anxiety and apprehension—then American Jewry will no longer be alienated from American Judaism.

Our Judaism today is more demanding, more self-searching, more intellectually and emotionally exacting of itself than ever before in our long history. It is ready to meet the challenges of our expanding horizons. We can fashion of our faith a way and a people of whom generations to come may say with respect and gratitude, "Our predecessors did not forsake Him, nor His commandments, nor His earth, nor its humanity." We can earn that encomium by making a beginning and by beginning to make it now.

Charles Raddock

HANNAH,
THE "REBBE" OF LODOMERIA

One of the strangest stories in the colorful history of the Jewish sect called *Hasidism* is the tale of the "Virgin of Ludmir"— Hanna Rachel Werbermacher, who shocked the Orthodox Jews of eastern Europe by her aspirations to become the first woman rabbi.

Charles Raddock offers a fascinating portrait of this strange woman as a kind of footnote to his three-volume history of the Jews, *Portrait of a People,* which appeared in 1965.

Mr. Raddock is a journalist and former political editor of the Worldwide Press Syndicate.

The story of the "Virgin of Ludmir" (as Hasidic chronicles allude to her) is a case in point. Hannah-Rachel Werbermacher, a sort of Joan of Arc personality, began her controversial career by revolting against her femininity. Joan of Arc, as you recall, shocked the Catholic hierarchy of France by wearing men's clothes, and was burned at the stake when she was barely nineteen for heresy and sorcery.

But Hannah-Rachel—of Vladimir-Volynskiy, in the Ukraine—met no such end, though she shocked her contemporaries by strapping the phylacteries (*tefillin*) around her left arm and head every morning, as faithful Orthodox male Jews do. What is more, she finally became a Hasidic "rebbe," was credited with working miracles, lived to be ninety, and even gained a male following in the manner of some of the famous Hasidic "rebbes" in pre-Nazi eastern Europe.

Jewish scholars have almost unanimously ignored her and so far as I know, only one play and one novel were based on her turbulent life, though far less controversial Hasidic figures have inspired innumerable works of fiction and stage. Though Hannah-Rachel died barely sixty years ago, she is already a legend. The

[54]

task, therefore, of piecing together her life and work involved going through fragmentary Hasidic data scattered through the voluminous literature of her vanishing cult, and a week of sleuthing in Jerusalem's Hasidic quarter.

Freudians would probably ascribe Hannah-Rachel's "Hasidism" to an "Electra Complex," and trace her behavior to psychosexual disorders. Hasidim however, unfamiliar with Freudian terminology, tell a much simpler story in their dreamy *klausen* (haunts) when they discuss the lives of the Hasidic saints. This then, is *their* version.

At the turn of the nineteenth century, in "Ludmir, on the Lug river," which is now part of the Soviet Union, a Jewish shopkeeper named Monesch Werbermacher had been counseled by the local rabbi to divorce his childless wife, as indeed the Talmud suggests when a couple has been childless for at least ten years. But Monesch was deeply in love with his wife and refused to abide by talmudic injunction.

Instead, he turned to a prominent Hasidic "rebbe" the so-called "Seer of Lublin," Rabbi Yakov Yitzhak ha-Levi Horovitz, noted as a miracle worker. Indeed, after the renowned Hasidic divine prayed for the Ludmir shopkeeper, his childless spouse bore him a daughter a year later.

Though Orthodox Jews usually prefer a male child (for a male child, among other things, can take his *formal* place in the faith) Monesch took a vow upon himself to exert every effort to give his daughter Hannah-Rachel the kind of upbringing usually given a son. In short, while his daughter could never become a rabbi, there was no reason why he must deny her a full-fledged "rabbinical" education. He would indeed grant his belated child all the boons of "masculine" intellectual training.

As soon, therefore, as the little pig-tailed creature was of age (in eastern Europe, "of age" meant what we call "pre-school" age) he ignored his wife's misgivings about his plan and even the counsel of the eminent rabbi whom he had at first consulted, and placed Hannah-Rachel in the most exclusive *heder* in town where, behind a screen which separated her from her boy schoolmates, she took her sacred instruction—the only female pupil in the official Hebrew schools of Lodomeria and its environs. It was not customary in those days to give Jewish girls an advanced Hebrew education.

[55]

Hannah-Rachel did not disappoint her parents. Soon she distinguished herself as a model Talmud student and, needless to say, they were proud of her intellectual attainments. But much as they at first doted on her, they soon had reason to view her precocity with misgivings. For she began to avoid the company of other children, hardly spoke to anyone, and after school hours would shut herself away in her room, poring over her esoteric books. After a while she began to ignore her parents too, never even speaking to them unless they spoke to her first.

After months and months of such anti-social behavior, her manner had become so solemn and her conversation, such as it was, so moody, it seemed, that her father questioned the wisdom of his bold experiment in feminine talmudic training. Her mother, probably weakened from her belated childbirth and distraught over her little daughter's strange silences, which would often last for days, died. Hannah-Rachel was then only nine.

As would happen in a small, tightly-knit Jewish community, malicious neighbors began to gossip and to spread the word around that the orphan was queer. Widower Monesch appealed to the rabbi to release him from his vow. His plea granted, he removed the child from the *heder*. But that only aggravated the situation, for the child could not tear herself away from the huge talmudic tomes. She intensified her studies, withdrawing into her bedroom sometimes for days, swaying in singsong over the sacred folios as old talmudic scholars are in the habit of doing, intoning the sacred passages in a kind of ancient liturgical plainsong.

As soon as she was twelve, Monesch decided to marry her off. It was not unusual in those days for parents to arrange "matches" for daughters who had reached puberty. But when her worried father broached the subject to her one evening, Hannah-Rachel replied wryly that she had no inclination whatever to be "as other females." Thus, unable to cope with her—for he was a simple, plain-spoken man, and she an articulate "scholar"—he decided to consult the celebrated Hasidic divine Rabbi Mordecai of Chernobyl. (The "Seer of Lublin" was no longer alive.)

Reluctantly Hannah accompanied her worried father to the small farming village of Chernobyl, about fifty-five miles northwest of Kiev, which was famous in the tight world of Hasidism because of the "Chernobyler" preacher, as he was known among the plain folk of the Ukraine. In her presence, the great sage upbraided the anxious father for having subjected the impressionable child to the holy books. Whereupon Hannah herself interrupted the sage and—on talmudic grounds—proceeded to debate the distinguished scholar on the controversial question of a woman's role in the Jewish faith!

Indignant over her unheard-of effrontery, Rabbi Mordecai, though otherwise a kindly man, harshly reminded the arrogant little girl that the ancient scholars had expressly forbidden the study of the holy books to females and that no parent had the

MORTON GARCHIK

right to interfere with "God's intention." A woman's fate, he argued, was matrimony and the bearing of children.

Hannah would not hear of marriage. But the rabbi, a practical psychologist, took Monesch aside and gave him an idea. It was just after Czar Nicholas I had decreed that every Jewish boy from the age of twelve was to be taken from his home, catechized, baptized and rigidly trained for military service to Mother Russia. Everywhere in the Jewish Pale boys were snatched from their homes, and in no time the armories of Kazan, Nizhni-

Novobrod, Kiev, Smolensk, Pskov, Kherson and Vitebak—even the old barracks of Lodomeria—were swarming with newly-baptized recruits in their "marriageable" teens, Rabbi Mordecai reminded Monesch Werbermacher.

Monesch got the point. Every morning he could be found at the ancient barracks currying favor with Russian captains, sergeants and lieutenants. Laden with pipe-tobacco, vodka and choice Jewish delicacies, he finally managed to bribe an officer commanding a Jewish contingent to release one of his younger recruits Saturdays, in his custody.

Thus it came to pass that on the following Sabbath day, an officer brought a Jewish trainee to the Werbermacher household. Hannah regarded the uniformed Jewish lad calmly, and blandly reminded her father that it was her duty to instruct the boy in matters of piety, since he was undoubtedly being indoctrinated by the "baptizers." A happy Monesch observed that his problem child proceeded, with unaccustomed friendliness, to wait upon the youth and, throwing away her erstwhile reticence, grew remarkably talkative in his presence.

For several weeks boy and girl spent the Sabbath day in "talmudic conversation." Hannah seemed particularly pleased that the personable dark-haired youth, some eight years her senior, did not find it necessary, as had the Preacher of Chernobyl to question her devotion to matters of religion and intellect. She presented him with a prayer-scarf, which she had crocheted during the week. Monesch secretly wondered where his bookish daughter had suddenly acquired the feminine art of crocheting. Nor could he fail to observe how, on Friday afternoons, she would stand long before the mirror—something she had never done before, for she had always looked upon mirrors as things of vanity—leisurely weaving her auburn braids into a fashionable though modest coiffure. He also noted that the usual melancholy expression of her gray-blue eyes had vanished, and as she cheerfully busied herself tidying up the house, the jubilant parent felt profoundly grateful for the great preacher's shrewd suggestion.

Suddenly one morning, Monesch was called to the barracks to be curtly informed by the officer in charge that his young Sabbath guest had been shipped off to Omsk—and would not return until he had served the Czar for twenty-five years! Hannah stalked about the house; though she did not weep, her heartbreak was obvious. The next morning she left the house and remained away until nightfall. Monesch had no idea where she had gone, but did not dare question her.

Her disappearances became more frequent until one day, her pale face taut with determination, her tiny figure wrapped in her mother's woolen shawl, her auburn braids done up in a knot under a *Babushka,* she slunk through the muddy alleyways of Lodomeria, past the market place and the ruins of the historic church, beyond the barracks of the town. There, at the top of the hill, was the Jewish cemetery.

Hannah prayed at her mother's grave all afternoon, invoking the spirit of the woman whose belated motherhood she had hardly ever acknowledged with a gesture of filial devotion. Night came, and the girl fell asleep beside the tombstone. She did not waken till after midnight. Frightened, she began to run across the indiscernible gravetracks, stumbling over headstones and shrubbery—her dangling shawl caught on a headstone, and its sudden release threw her to the ground. She lay there in terror until the following morning when a gravedigger making the rounds discovered her quivering body.

For several days she lay in bed, in a trance. Then one morning, as Monesch in phylacteries and *tallit* stood at her bedside intoning the prayers, she called to him weakly. In a whispering voice, she confided to her father that she had just come from the Heavenly Assembly (*Yeshivah shel Maalah*) where they had conferred upon her an *oversoul* (*Neshamah Yetaereh*)! Having uttered these strange words, she slowly rose from her bed, walked to the cupboard from which she removed a phylactery-bag—the bag that contained the prayer-scarf and phylacteries she had given her erstwhile Sabbath companion—and proceeded to don the sacred male vestments! Monesch looked on in silence. . . .

Having completed the morning prayers, Hannah took out her long-neglected Talmud and once again her voice rose up in talmudic singsong. . . .

Hannah-Rachel was nineteen, Hasidim testify, when Monesch Werbermacher joined his spouse on the hill overlooking Lodomeria. The "holy virgin," as they came to call her, disposed of her parental home and shop following the traditional thirty-day period of mourning, and settled in a two-room hut near the Jewish market place. There her "rabbinical career" began.

Worshipping every morning in prayer shawl and phylacteries,

as men do, but as women are forbidden to do, constantly immersed in the sacred books, she lived alone, completely isolated from the Jewish community, though her hut stood in the very heart of it. Word soon spread concerning *"a holy virgin in Lodomeria who dwells in a little green hut and whose behavior is like unto that of a male and who performs miracles like the great Hasidic wonderworkers. . . ."*

Pious women, and then some of their menfolk, so-called Hasidim, gradually gathered around Hannah-Rachel—until the *"Grüne Stübel,"* as the hut was named, became the meeting-place of a sizable congregation, presided over by Hannah-Rachel Werbermacher. They crowded the large anteroom of her hut on the Sabbath to listen to her sermons, and after a while her fame spread beyond the banks of the Lug River, on which the town stood.

From remote areas of Volhynia, Podolia and Galicia, the lame, the halt and the blind began to set out for the "green hut," seeking benediction and divine intercession. Scholars too made their appearance, out of curiosity at first—picturesque figures supported by gnarled wooden staffs, carrying burlap knapsacks—to hold learned discourse with the "holy virgin." But only through the tiny window of her sanctum would Hannah exchange words with the pilgrims. No male was allowed into the little room which served her as sleeping quarters, chapel and study.

Before long Hasidic circles across eastern Europe buzzed with conflicting rumors about the "incredible" conduct of this Hannah of Lodomeria. Rabbis waxed indignant over the reported masculine behavior of "the virgin." Some of them agreed that the "maid" was possessed of an evil spirit and her cabalistic homilies were but the foul "utterances of Satan. . . ."

They proceeded, one by one, to assail her with endless missives. They began, to be sure, on a conciliatory note, such as: "To the holy virgin (*b'tulah*) of Lodomeria in the name of all the Disciples of the Besht and his saintly followers," but always ended with a stern warning that she cease and desist from her unorthodox acts and return forthwith to conduct befitting a Jewess.

Hannah-Rachel calmly refuted their erudite and irate arguments by citing talmudic chapter and verse in sanction of her piety. Thus defied, the rabbis threatened to excommunicate her. They called upon their faithful followers to rise against the "maid" and her "misguided illiterates." Since the movement of Hasidism, though almost a century old, was still suspect in certain learned sections of eastern Europe, the rabbis issued instructions by letter and messenger that no God-fearing Israelite "come within four ells of her and her defiled assembly, nor marry into the desecrated households of her supporters, and to wage the war of God against Satan now flourishing in the profaned community of Lodomeria in the guise of a female!"

Some of Hannah's enemies even rumored that her heresies had reached such a brazen point that she was seeking religious asylum in a Greek Orthodox convent! The Mother Superior, it was declared, had offered the "maid" protection on the pretext that the Jewish faith gave no official recognition to "holy women." The "holy war" reached such a climax one Sabbath afternoon, when the Hasidim took their Sabbath stroll, that a riot broke out in front of the green hut, and rocks were thrown into the window of the "maid's" chapel. Fortunately Hannah was not hurt but after the skirmish that followed with the "maid's" supporters, the cobblestoned alley was bespattered with blood.

Hannah's opponents finally discovered that the late Mordecai of Chernobyl had once counseled marriage for her, and a Hasidic rabbinical committee of three was formed to make the journey to Lodomeria quietly, without fanfare, to have it out with her. As a committee of three, they constituted a *beth din,* a court of law, as it were, with civil, criminal and religious jurisdiction that Hannah could not in good conscience repudiate. They had heard that she was versed in talmudic law, and therefore did not fear that she would defy their duly constituted authority. The original plan of Rabbi Mordecai Chernobyl, who had passed on when she was only sixteen, appealed to them; but where would they find a bachelor to take this rebellious female in wedlock?

Upon their arrival, they announced themselves to a long-faced scribe at the rickety table in the anteroom of the green hut. Forthwith the "maid" granted them an audience in her chapel. They were the first men ever to be admitted into her *sanctum sanctorum.*

All day long the three Hasidic rabbis remained in conference with "Rabbi" Hannah-Rachel Werbermacher, discussing the pros and cons of woman's role in Judaism. The rabbis, well aware of her adolescent precocity, were of course prepared with incontrovertible talmudic arguments, for they finally convinced her that marriage need not preclude her pious activity, though a public career she must abandon forever.

Hannah consented to marry the pallid, long-faced scribe, her senior by many years, though she herself was no youngster any more, and the three rabbis took turns performing the wedding ceremony under an open sky, as is customary among the Hasidim, and for dowry Hannah even pledged her green hut—and, at the triumphant suggestion of one of the celebrants under the *Hupah,* her prayer-shawl and phylacteries as well! These sacred vestments would now be worn only by her husband, as tradition indeed prescribed. . . .

But lo, the next morning the bride drove her husband out of the green hut and demanded a writ of divorcement! When he protested loudly, threatening to call the rabbis to his aid, she told him that she had never intended the marriage to be more than a matter of form. She had agreed to it, she said, for the sake of appearances only and had no inclination whatever to live as other women.

The rabbis could do nothing but wash their hands of the whole affair. Turning a deaf ear to the enraged husband's demands, they refused to take any further matrimonial action against the "maid." Since a woman could not by Mosaic law secure a divorce herself, but since Hannah-Rachel had none the less refused to live with her husband as man and wife, the rabbis called an extraordinary conclave and by unanimous vote excommunicated her and her followers from the Hasidic community.

Alas, Hannah was now quickly abandoned by friends and followers — a lone and brooding figure in the "grüne Stübel." Except for several kindly, devoted old crones who visited her secretly from time to time, she was ignored by everyone. Unable to endure the ostracism for long, she sold the hut and, shaking the dust of her native Ukraine from her feet, went off to the Holy Land, Palestine. . . .

In the Hundred Gates quarter (*Me'ah She'arim*) of old Jerusalem the Virgin of Lodomeria, however, soon managed again to acquire something of a congregation, and set up a modest Hasidic "court" of her own.

There are still some Jerusalem inhabitants who remember the short, gray-eyed little woman, hurrying each morning to the ancient Wailing Wall, with prayer-shawl and phylacteries bulging from a purple reticule, followed all the way by pious souls begging her benedictions. On Sabbath afternoon, one of them told me in 1951, when I first visited Israel, the "Maid of Lodomeria" would preside in her modest home over her followers, her table decked with twelve little shew-breads baked by herself, as was the custom in the "courts" of the great Hasidic rabbis of the Ukraine and Poland and among the Cabalists of old. And on the eve of the Feast of the Law (*Simhath Torah*), this old patriarch told me, he remembered how dozens of pilgrims would come from Hebron, Tiberias and Safed to pay tribute to the female rabbi and behold her leading the traditional processionals with the Scrolls (*Hakafoth*), also a ritual restricted only to males.

And on the day preceding each Blessing of the New Moon, the aging Hannah would conduct her feminine devotees to Rachel's Tomb on the road to Hebron, there to deposit the hundreds of petitions for "matriarchal intercession" accumulated during the previous month. On every anniversary of the death of the Matriarch, Jacob's favorite wife, the "maid," together with her worshipful disciples, would hold vigil for a day and a night of public prayer and reading of Psalms.

Thus, my Jerusalem informant told me, the "maid" spent the last portion of her life. He could not recall, however, whether she was ninety or ninety-one going on ninety-two when she died. The year of her death, so far as he could remember, was 1905, however.

[63]

Rabbi Jay Kaufman

A NEW JUDAISM
IN ISRAEL

This report by Rabbi Jay Kaufman deals with the efforts of non-Orthodox Judaism to gain a foothold in Israel over the protests of inflexible opposition.

He is executive vice-president of B'nai B'rith in Washington, but prior to this post he was the vice-president of the Union of American Hebrew Congregations. In that capacity he organized several pilgrimages to Israel of leading groups of reformed Jewish leaders.

In 1962 Rabbi Kaufman spent a sabbatical leave in Israel, where he fanned the flame of an incipient liberal religious movement in that country. As chairman of the Israel Committee of the World Union for Progressive Judaism he worked with the six existing Israel Progressive congregations and with the Liberal Leo Baeck School of Haifa to advance the cause.

Israel has its first Reform synagogue building — and a four-year-old Reform congregation which will worship in this cool, tree-laced edifice of Jerusalem stone.

For a long time there has been speculation as to what would occur when Reform Judaism — known abroad as Progressive or Liberal Judaism — finally came to Israel. Some prophesied violent and even bloody rioting, others a rush on the part of unaffiliated Israelis to participation in the dignified and meaningful worship of a Reform service. Neither prediction has proven true — so far.

The legal documents of the purchase by the World Union for Progressive Judaism are signed and properly filed in the Jerusalem municipality. The Israeli newspapers have carried the story so that everyone in the city is aware of the event. There have been no demonstrations of protest. The Jerusalem Reform congregation for whom the purchase was made and the new Herzeliah and Nazareth Reform congregations have been per-

[64]

mitted to worship without any interference, even though they advertise the time and place of their services regularly in the press. So, too, the purchase of the estate in the very heart of Jerusalem, has been consummated without discord. The enclave adjacent to the Bezalel Art Museum provides three buildings, one of which will be used for the synagogue and the other two eventually for educational, administrative, and youth facilities.

If there have been no demonstrations, is the congregation truly Reform? I can recall being mistaken by terminology. In 1946 I attended the Sabbath service of a Jerusalem congregation I had been told was "Liberal" and which received an annual subsidy from the World Union. I found that men and women were seated separately, the traditional Siddur and Torah service were retained in their entirety. The only innovation was a sermon in German.

Present day Israel Reform, on the other hand, is characterized by the family pew, the organ, and an original liturgy utilizing selections from several liberal prayer books, translations from the *Union Prayerbook*, spiritual poetry, and original prayers. Its theology reflects a point of view consistent with that of other World Union congregations throughout the world.

The Jerusalem congregation, after much experimentation and study, has completed its first Friday evening prayer book and it will be used by the other Israel Reform congregations as well. The service provides for a great deal of congregational participation. In fact, almost the entire service is sung to varying melodies by the congregation. There also are individual readings, sometimes of poetry, sometimes of biblical selections. The reader on the pulpit or an individual congregant rises quietly, according to plan, from his seat in the congregation, to offer the reading. This provides for a beautiful and deeply moving worship experience, one that may well have its influence on Reform congregations everywhere.

The new synagogue building in Jerusalem is not to be confused with the Hebrew Union College's new school of archeology being constructed in Jerusalem. The school has been described as a synagogue, in spite of efforts by College authorities to correct this misconception.

World-wide announcement by Rabbi Solomon Freehof, president of the World Union, of the purchase of the synagogue in Jerusalem serves to prompt attention on the prospects — and very serious problems — of the infant Reform movement in Israel. Many widely-held assumptions must be re-examined also in view of the remarkable activity stimulated by Rabbi Jerome Unger, sent to Israel several years ago by the World Union.

The prospects are promising. Rabbi Unger has been able to assist in the birth of two new congregations in Herzeliah and Nazareth — both of which held their first High Holy Day services in 1961 — and to program Sabbath worship. These are fragile shoots. They require much care, more than Rabbi Unger can provide, moving across the country as he must, as Israel's only active Reform rabbi. The two congregations need buildings and a permanent, resident rabbi. Until then their future is precarious. Their problems are analagous to those of a new suburban congregation in the United States. A congregation is born in a flush of enthusiasm, during the era of part-time rabbi and rented hall it toddles erratically. Stability is gained only when the group attains its own rabbi and structure.

The Israel congregation, moreover, will experience other difficulties. Two of the three essential needs of the American Jew filled solely by the synagogue which impel congregational membership are notably absent in Israel. The American Jew comes to the synagogue for a religious experience, for the Jewish education of his child and himself, for the opportunity to enjoy the fellowship of his coreligionists. In Israel the latter two needs are met *outside* the synagogue.

The child in Israel gets a broad and rich Jewish education in the public school system. His knowledge of Bible, Hebrew, Jewish history, and literature is more extensive than could be imparted elsewhere, even in the most effective Jewish day-school. The emotional and social needs, the sense of companionship, and the gaining of Jewish contacts so well met by the American synagogue are here superfluous.

The Israel Reform synagogue will concentrate, therefore, on providing a religious experience. This can be seen even this early in the emphasis made by the three congregations. There is a deep concern with the intent and meaning of the prayers; a wrestling with the God concept in sermons; a growing awareness of the need to deal with the problems of personal and social ethics, and to provide them with a theological mooring.

The circumstances surrounding the purchase of the synagogue should, in addition to all else, spur American Reform Jews to rout one ugly and egregious canard: that the Israeli government, as often implied and sometimes stated openly, has opposed Reform Judaism and denies freedom of worship to Reform Jews. This is an untruth — and an outrageous one.

The government agency of Israel which sold the three-building estate to the World Union for Progressive Judaism was fully aware of the purpose to which it is to be put. Other government agencies have been helpful in unraveling red tape and overcoming the obstacles Rabbi Unger faced.

The imputation that the government of Israel lends itself to discrimination against Reform Jews is not only fraudulent, it affects adversely the attitudes of some Reform Jews in the U. S. *toward* Israel. This alleged denial of religious liberty is set forth with distressing frequency by Reform Jews in many American cities as a warrant for non-cooperation and even for withholding of funds from indispensable campaigns — starting with the United Jewish Appeal and the Israel Bond drive, and running through the entire gamut of philanthropies in behalf of the Jewish state. This piece of mischievous misinformation may be refuted easily today. The .facts of the peaceful purchase of the Jerusalem synagogue, plus the freedom enjoyed by the three congregations constitute dramatic evidence.

This is not to deny the serious problem of the non-separation

A young member of a liberal Jewish congregation in Israel.

of "church and state" in Israel, a problem in whose solution Liberal Judaism in Israel is sure one day to play a critical role.

At present, only rabbis paid and licensed by the Ministry of Religions are permitted to perform weddings. What will happen when, in the future, a Reform rabbi seeks licensing in Israel? Rabbi Maurice N. Eisendrath, President of the Union of American Hebrew Congregations, posed that question to Israel's Prime Minister David Ben-Gurion at the time of the first UAHC pilgrimage to Israel. Mr. Ben-Gurion replied that he would use all his influence to see that the Reform rabbi was granted such permission. However, he felt strongly that the Reform rabbi should be a citizen of Israel and not just a visitor, and that he should be serving his own Reform congregation. On his visit to the United States in 1961, Mr. Ben-Gurion met with Rabbi Eisendrath and inquired when a permanent Reform rabbi would be in Israel serving one of the Reform congregations.

A distinction should be made between the Israeli government, which has not restrained or repressed Reform Judaism, and the Orthodox community of Israel whose opposition will continue to be relentless and ruthless.

The increased activity of Reform in Israel — as exemplified by the congregations, the Hebrew Union College school of archeology, the Liberal Leo Baeck High School in Haifa, the Reform services Rabbi Unger has been conducting in children's villages, the Bar Mitzvahs and conversions he has performed, the more frequent mention of Reform in the press — has served to bring a sharpened response from Orthodox circles.

Orthodox spokesmen have made their position clear. When faced with the alternative of having a Reform movement bring large numbers of unaffiliated Jews into the synagogue, or having these Jews remain permanently out of the synagogue, Orthodoxy unequivocally chooses the latter. They explain that as long as the Jew remains away from the synagogue, he will be conscience-ridden and may one day be won to participation in Orthodox Judaism. Once involved in the Reform synagogue, he feels religiously fulfilled, there is no pricking sense of guilt. Better non-religiosity with the hope of possible involvement, with the very real danger of total apostasy, than Reform!

Examples of Orthodox pressures are becoming evident today. Hotels have recently found themselves without available rooms when facilities are sought for a Reform service or Bar Mitzvah.

The threat of retaliation from the Orthodox *mashgiach* who supervises the *kashrut* of the kitchen is real, and could bring about financial disaster. A few families whose businesses involve a broad spectrum of the buying public have indicated that they would prefer the Reform service, but cannot affiliate because of the very probable economic boycott which would result.

Israel Orthodoxy, contrary to what we often hear, is neither dormant nor declining. It is a vital, vigorous movement, enjoying a flush of funds poured into its coffers from all over the world, and especially from the U. S.

American Jewry has much more at stake in the development of a Reform movement in Israel than may appear at first glance. Outside of North America, Liberal congregations are in an arrested or struggling position. Only in Israel are there prospects of a colorful and creative movement likely to pour new ideas and forms and zest into the stream of Reform worship and theology. If Reform fails in Israel, we stand in danger of becoming an isolated Anglo-Saxon movement, eventually rendered sterile by our own inbreeding, deprived of a cross-pollenization gleaned from spiritual expressions in other cultures.

What will happen to Reform Judaism in Israel? Will it receive the succor it requires from American Jewry during the tenuous, tender years of its incipience? Will it stir Israelis toward the creation of an indigenous form of forward-looking Judaism to meet the crying need of young Israelis, or will it fail — so that Orthodoxy or indifference will be the sole alternatives? Will a thriving Reform help render asunder the constrictive bind yoking religion and the Israel state? Will a flourishing Israel Reform fructify American Reform with fresh, compatible patterns?

The donor whose gift made possible the acquisition of the Jerusalem property, a member of the Board of an Eastern seaboard congregation, requested that his gift be an anonymous one. He said, "The knowledge that I am an active participant in the spread of Reform Judaism in Israel, in adding strength to the world movement, and in bringing to Israel Jews the sense of rich fulfilment which Reform has brought to my family, is glory enough."

Such fulfilment, for those in Israel who seek to live by a new Judaism in terms related to the twentieth century world, is more than a remote hope now.

[69]

Paul Kresh

EDITORIALS

In conventional editorials, the editor, if not the publication, takes a stand on some issue of the moment. It seems to me there are fresher ways to put over an editorial point of view than through the usual rhetoric. Why should not the devices of poetry, playwriting, fantasy, even fiction be brought into play to express an editorial viewpoint?

Two of these pieces, one in the form of a letter to the Lord from a bewildered supplicant and the other a reply from a "corresponding angel," appeared in successive issues of the publication. The third is an editorial essay on the nature of prayer.

"The preparations of the heart are man's, but the answer of the tongue is from the Lord." — *Proverbs*

Dear Lord,

Now that the excitement of the Chanukah season is out of the way, perhaps you will have more time to consider problems like mine. It all started during the holiday, as a matter of fact. Frankly, when the oil that was supposed to last for eight days burned out after one, I began to doubt You. I wrote to the manufacturers and got back a form letter containing an apology — but no refund. It was shortly after that I took my children off the bus and out of school.

The trouble is, I think, a kind of aortal cessation. Am I dead, or sick? I don't think so. Put a stethoscope to my heart and it can be heard ticking away, healthily, steadily. And that must be where the trouble lies: nothing is able to make it beat faster anymore.

We stopped watching television for a while, but the kids wound up with too much energy, and we had to turn it back on.

[70]

To tell you the truth, I don't even see the commercials now — or hear them, either. I turn the sound full up, but nothing gets through to me. I can't remember brand names. My wife thinks I just don't care.

She must be right. I try to care, but I don't. For instance, in November I took one look at the list of candidates and walked out of the booth without bothering to vote.

What can touch me? What will move me? How can I go back to believing in You? Or in me, for that matter?

Oh, they're at me all the time. Listen, You should see the junk mail I get. The pleas for funds. The call for volunteers. I can spot the stuff without opening the envelopes. Out it goes.

On my way to work every day I like to stop for a minute at the newsstand and stare at the headlines. (I think it's important to know what's going on.) I might as well tell You, the names could be numbers for all they mean to me. Mississippi, Vietnam . . . Foreign words and phrases.

I see that this morning the pickets are holding up larger signs than yesterday. Maybe they think my eyes are failing. Ah, if they'd only show me a slogan I could believe in!

Hunger Hurts. Suppose Nobody Cared?

Suppose not?

We shall not be moved.

Every morning I also pass a figure up on a high ledge, the same one each time, crouching there, poised to plunge.

"Jump!" I holler. I always do. "Jump! Jump!" Eventually he will.

Across the street some woman is being raped and beaten. I join the crowd and watch. What a weariness. Am I my sister's keeper?

All the big words they use — megaton, overkill. What's one more little murder to me?

Yesterday, as I turned the corner, a starving old lady clutched at my clothes. I brushed her off. She could rend my garments, but not my heart.

Now, I understand a super-civilization from another galaxy is trying to get in touch with me. Please tell them to leave a message. I'll try to get back to them. I would rather hear from You.

The fact is, I used to believe. I used to feel things. I even used to pray.

[71]

When I sit in Your sanctuary, which I seldom do, I experience nothing.

I sing the psalms, recite the proverbs, repeat the sonorous clichés of prayers. Nothing happens.

Let everything that hath breath praise the Lord.

And wake me up when it's over. I am inured, innoculated, inviolable. Nothing touches me. Nothing moves me. Nothing matters.

Please write and tell me how to believe in You, how to pray to You, how to praise You. Or roar at me out of a whirlwind. Tell me of Your lightning and Leviathans. Deliver the answer of Your tongue, that magnified and sanctified may be Your great Name.

Your devoted servant,

Man

Dear Man,

The Lord has asked me to underscore his regrets at the long delay in responding to your letter, which has been turned over to me for reply. The Most High feels it would be inappropriate for Him to answer you directly, since it is evident that you do not really believe in Him. How can anyone who does not believe in man possibly believe in God?

We here in heaven were reminded by your complaints of the airplane pilot who told his passengers. "I regret to inform you that we are lost — but let me reassure you that we are still traveling at 800 miles an hour." It seems to us that here is summed up the condition of your species in this age. Yet, were you to slow down for a bit, you might see signposts all about you which are there to help you to find yourself. On the other hand, you would have to open your eyes to be able to see them.

You ask if you are dead. I would say in a way you are. You have eyes and see not, ears and hear not. Even so your heart beats, although nothing, as you say, can make it beat faster; and since you are *troubled* by the fact that nothing touches you, nothing moves you, perhaps the conscience in you is still somewhat awake, and that must be a part of God alive within you.

The Lord has asked me to remind you that He created and abandoned several worlds before he fashioned yours. He would have you ponder on the methane-poisoned wastes of Jupiter and the other giant planets which He left lifeless, on the red deserts of arid Mars where only the yellow dust blows and life is lowly or non-existent, on the stifling cloudquilt of Venus, the fiery face and frosty back of uninhabitable Mercury, the deathly silence of the pocked moon that awaits your imminent arrival. And then He would like you to look around again at your earth, with its green mantle and abundant waters and myriad shapes of life, crowned and climaxed by the shaping of you to have dominion over His verdant planet. He would recommend that you open your pinched nostrils, your sightless eyes and tonedeaf ears to the scents and sights and sounds of teeming Nature — the beauty everywhere — yes, and the ugliness too. The good, and also the evil. The psalms, and also the day's newspaper. For you are afraid to live because you are afraid to suffer, and have withdrawn from pleasure in simple abject terror of pain. But how can he who is numb to suffering expect to remain sentient to joy?

Once only the Lord flooded your earth and drowned it, yet even then there was one man worth saving, and the covenant God signed with that man after the Flood contained a promise that the planet would not be destroyed a second time. But there is another end to that bargain, and you are not living up to it. As you yourself point out, you are scarcely living at all.

Choose life!

If you can not longer pray with words, try deeds. Become involved with the living world. By the faith you say you once professed, every Jew is responsible for every other Jew — and so, by extension, every man for every other man. Reach out your hand and heart to the afflicted and that hand, and that heart may learn to feel alive. Then if you try to pray with words your prayers will perhaps be invested at last with the breath of honest faith.

In brief, it is the hope of heaven that one day you will awaken, become aware of the wonders of creation, come to believe again

[73]

in man through men, and through that belief find your way once more to faith in God.

Until that time, God has asked me to express his wishes for your well-being, to assure you that a good doctrine has been given to you, and to advise that you forsake it not.

Sincerely,

A Corresponding Angel

What is Prayer?

A man might rummage the world and wonder.

Can it be seen?

At noon in the city of Milan the sunlight strikes the cathedral soaring toward the sky, making it glitter like a great hymn frozen in the shapes of the stone. Sometimes at dusk in downtown New York the skyscrapers seem to huddle together, stretching their steely necks in reverence. You have seen a woman with her eyes squeezed shut tight as her husband circled the earth in a capsule, and you knew you were watching the act of prayer.

Can it be heard?

"Santus! Sanctus Sanctus!" sings the choir in Beethoven's *Missa Solemnis,* prayer wrought in exquisite and solemn shapes, almost too beautiful to be borne by merely human ears. The cantor lifts his voice in the Kol Nidrei, on the eve of the Day of Atonement, and the sound goes up, surely to the vaults of heaven. Maimonides avowed that the very spheres of the planets give forth a perpetual music in praise of their Creator. In early spring the tongues of new leaves in a stretch of wood murmur and whisper, and what are they whispering if not their joy at the wonder and beauty of life, the largess of nature, the glory of God?

Can it be taught?

Men thought once they could teach prayer by torture, and burned and bound and beat their victims until this deity or that was acknowledged and exalted. Others suffered infinitudes of pain but kept their counsel, punishment could stop their mouths but not their souls. Prayer can be taught, but not without love.

Can it be legislated?

Countless are the laws that have sought to make prayer compulsory, but the dust covers them. So deeply have some detested the freedom of their fellow creatures that they have made laws to cover every act and thought. That the souls of men have remained inviolate is their greatest grief. Such hated the frail boats that brought men to America, seeking religious freedom. Now they hate the court that once again upholds the private and sacred nature of prayer.

Prayers that are mouthed are not prayers. Prayers recited by rote are not prayers. Prayers made compulsory by acts of the state surely are not prayers.

Prayer is a dialogue between man and God. When I am in doubt as to what it might be — or even whether it might be — I remember a look on my father's face many years ago at the start of a service for the Jewish New Year. He was dressed in a new suit, his face was shining — not with the smug, self-righteous look of the father in the poster that would sell prayer like a product — but with a special wonder. God was about to renew his contract with men, and cleanse the slate of the world for a new beginning. My father waited in his seat in the synagogue expectantly, without guilt, without guile, without hypocrisy, but with a deep intimacy that excluded all others — even myself — from that formal conversation. He was not reciting words at a signal from a school teacher. He was engaged in the actual experience of "communion with God and recognition of His presence."

What is prayer?

Whenever I recall that moment, I believe I understand.

What's Ahead in the Year 2000?
The Union of American Hebrew
Congregations' time capsule.

The
World
of Action

"What doth the Lord require of thee,
but to do justly, and to love mercy,
and to walk humbly with thy God?"

Micah VI:8

Next to reportage of the day's news, nothing is so perishable as political writing. Indeed, for a quarterly how to treat the aspect of the publication's responsibility to inform and to deal with immediate controversial issues is always a dilemma. The rapidly shifting state of the world's fortunes may render obsolete the most thoughtfully expressed and carefully documented opinion in the political realm. We have seen in our own time how quickly even the most fantastic speculation of science fiction has been dated by the rush of scientific progress. So with politics and social action. The war that is denounced in today's article may be over by the time the publication in which it appears is in the hands of its readers. A political biography is more enduring. So is that kind of reporting which projects its facts in the perspective of history.

Here are some of the pieces it was felt were not likely to "perish in a night." They still retain the quality of being relevant without being merely transient.

Flora Rheta Schreiber

WHAT'S AHEAD
IN THE YEAR 2000?

> In 1960, a questionnaire was sent out to Reform Jewry
> around the country asking them to predict what Jewish
> life would be like by the end of the present century.
> Before the microfilm of these answers was placed in a
> "time capsule" to be opened in the year 2000, the answers
> were turned over to Flora Rheta Schreiber for a sum-
> ming up of "how Jewish life and life in general may look
> when the capsule is opened."
>
> Miss Schreiber, a frequent contributor to the country's
> major magazines, author of several books, teacher and
> lecturer at the City University's new College of Police
> Science and at the New School for Social Research, con-
> structed these word pictures of things to come.

In the year 2000, when man has conquered outer space, what
changes will have occurred within inner man? And in the outer
life that he shapes for himself? What life in general, and Jewish
life in particular, at the threshold of the next century?

This is the substance of the questionnaire sent out by the
Union of American Hebrew Congregations in 1960 in connection
with the dedication of its expanded House of Living Judaism in
New York City. The questions circulated among several thousand Americans including persons prominent in politics, religion,
science, and the arts, as well as among Jewish religious leaders
and representatives of the 605 member congregations of the
UAHC. The answers were then photographed on microfilm,
placed in a time capsule, and will grace the building until
October, 2000, when it is presumed there will be someone
around to tabulate the results and measure the forecasts against
the realities. But prophecy merely as prophecy has stirred the
human imagination since the days of the Delphic oracle, Nostra-
damus, and, most importantly, the biblical prophets themselves.

[79]

And wishful forecasting has always expressed man's profoundest longing and aspirations. And, whereas the idea of a time capsule is not new, this is the first time capsule to preserve not things, but ideas—the hopes, the vision, the aspirations of man, vintage 1960, for special delivery to his equivalent in the year 2000.

Significantly, the "prophets," instead of foretelling doom by benefit of nuclear war, unanimously affirm that good old terra firma will still be here in 2000.

Perhaps New Yorkers will fly to Los Angeles in one hour; perhaps private airports will encircle the landscape as garages do today; perhaps man will grow taller, and cure himself with a pill given him by some centralized doctor. More likely, despite any Wellsian intimations of gloom to come, the consensus of respondents believes that the essence of man will remain the same.

Though men will, by then, have striven for one world with a single government representing all the majority, prediction is that "one" world will not yet exist.

In that still-divided world of 2000 the prognosticators point to the U.S.A. and the U.S.S.R. as the chief world powers, with China second in importance, Great Britain third, and Germany trailing in fourth place. The complete omission of France sharply jolts our recollections of *la gloire française.*

Peace may reign in 2000, but a two-to-one majority predicted that even by then there will *not* have been demonstrable progress in disarmament. The same numerical majority however, raised pens firmly to write that between our day and that halcyon one, no world war will have taken place. Unplagued by war, we shall, however, have faced at least one full-scale depression, our capsulized Cassandra warns us.

Racial segregation, the specter that haunts our conscience today, will, according to these crystal gazers, have passed from both the American and the African scene. So, among others, asserted Lyndon B. Johnson, the Democratic nominee for U. S. Vice-President, Eleanor Roosevelt, New York Mayor Robert Wagner, and Dr. Edwin Dahlberg, President of the National Council of Churches of Christ.

Senator John F. Kennedy, who was campaigning for the Presidency at the time, asked that some statements of his views concerning separation of church and state be included in the capsule.

The Germany of 2000, East as well as West, will have a

Democratic government, the answers foretell. In the United States, too, a major realignment of political parties will have ironed out unreal differences between present parties and will have brought a more viable union of true interests.

Medicine, taking giant steps, will have extended man's tenure on this planet of ours. Cancer, says the overwhelming majority, will have been conquered. And a smaller group, but still a majority, thinks, too, that heart disease and the common cold will have ceased to plague us. Yet optimism breaks down where schizophrenia is concerned. No, say these prophesiers, schizophrenia, still uncurable, will continue to torment mankind. (Yet the facts indicate that, at this writing, in 1960, schizophrenia, far more than cancer, heart disease, or even the common cold gives promise of responding to treatment.)

What of things Jewish? How will they have changed?

By the year 2000, say the prognosticators, a book on a Jewish theme will have won the Pulitzer prize, a Jew will have run and even been elected as Vice-President, although not as President of the United States. (Eleanor Roosevelt and The Right Reverend James A. Pike, Bishop of the Episcopal Diocese of California, differing on this subject from the majority of respondents, however, assert that a Jew will indeed become President.) Changes in Jewish journalism will be evident, too, both in the disappearance of the Yiddish press, per se, and in the emergence of an English-Jewish daily newspaper.

Jews will not have formed a United Jewish community, lament these Jeremiahs. Nor will Jewish funds in the year 2000 be raised primarily for overseas needs; rather will these funds be directed towards home use. A clear majority maintains, too, that a United Jewish Appeal, Hadassah, and the Jewish war veterans will still be going full steam ahead, but only a relatively small group sees such long term survival for the Israel Bond Drive and the Zionist Organization of America. And, says the majority, a peace treaty will govern relations between Israel and the Arabs.

Neither in the United States nor in most other countries will anti-Semitism have flared into active life. Yet, behind this optimism there is the implication that anti-Semitism will still exist and there is the darker foreboding that even in the year 2000 anti-Semitism will be most rampant in Russia and Germany.

What of the expectation for changes in the Jewish religion?

Clearly the prediction is that Reform Judaism will be the dominant faith of American Jewry. A two-to-one margin agreed that none of the branches of Judaism whether Reform, Conservative, or Orthodox, will have merged. The same margin believed that attendance at Reform Jewish schools in America will shift from once to twice a week. An equal number of respondents predicted, too, that by 2000, Jews will be practicing their religion openly in the Soviet Union. As for the Union of American Hebrew Congregations itself, while the crystal ball gazers foresee that some 1000 Reform synagogues will be members of the UAHC, only a little less than half of the replies anticipate a new name for the Union or that it will sponsor parochial schools. The most popular name predicted, incidentally, is "Union of American Reform Congregations."

A tie as to whether or not there will be women rabbis in Reform Jewish pulpits leaves the matter to unravel itself. And only time will reveal the evolution of a changing Reform position on matters of fundamental theology.

An overwhelming majority maintained that the religious revival current today would be extant, too; that the social action movements existing among various religious groups today will have increased and the intermarriage between Christians and Jews will have become much more widespread, whereas intermarriage between Catholics and Protestants will have increased but not as much.

A majority of nine-to-one believed that a Roman Catholic will have been elected President and a two-to-one margin agreed that the religion of candidates will no longer influence the American voter. The majority thought, too, that religion would not be taught in American public schools; that there would be a closer understanding among the three major religious faiths in America. A smaller group, but still a clear majority, maintained that religious influence will have brought about a betterment of moral standards in American life. But little change was anticipated in the Catholic position on birth control.

President Dwight D. Eisenhower, a textbook name to students in 2000, asked that his "Prayer of Our People," a part of his Second Inaugural Address, be included in the time capsule. In a letter to Rabbi Maurice N. Eisendrath, President of the Union of American Hebrew Congregations, President Eisenhower affirmed that this message expressed his personal views and highest hopes "for the people of our land and for our neighbors around the world." "When it is read again in the year 2000," said the President, "I hope mankind will have made progress along the lines indicated." The prayer reads: "Before all else, we seek, upon our common labor as a nation, the favor of Almighty God. And the hopes in our hearts fashion the deepest prayers of our people. . . . May we pursue the right—without self-righteousness. . . . May we know unity—without conformity. . . . May we grow in strength without pride of self. . . . May we, in our dealings with all peoples of the earth, ever speak truth and serve justice. . . . May the light of freedom, coming to all darkened lands, flame brightly—until at last the darkness is no more. . . . May the turbulence of our age yield to a true time of peace, when men and nations shall share a life that honors the dignity of each, the brotherhood of all."

And so, seeking a new dignity for man in 2000 as in 1960, how will the changes wrought affect, too, his well-being and his happiness? And, if man is the measure of all things, perhaps it is this question that is the most significant of all.

Interestingly, many, answering this question, this tell-tale forty-eighth, believe that in his emotional life man will not have changed. "Changes," said Marion B. Ross, President, Temple Beth-El, St. Petersburg, Florida, "will not affect the happiness of the average man; happiness comes from within — not from without." To this question "What is happiness?" that has badgered man through the ages, Rabbi Theodore S. Levy of Temple Israel, Waterbury, Connecticut, has a tender and touching answer: ". . . I will be 75 and my wife will be 72—our children will be in their mid 40's. With all the scientific wonders of that day we will all be in the prime of life — living and enjoying every moment of it."

Albert Vorspan

TEN WAYS OUT
FOR TIRED LIBERALS

Albert Vorspan is program director of the Union of American Hebrew Congregations and director of the Commission on Social Action of Reform Judaism.

In addition to many articles on intergroup relations and other issues of social justice, he is the author of *Giants of Justice,* published in 1960, and, with Rabbi Eugene J. Lipman, co-author of *Justice and Judaism* and *A Tale of Ten Cities.* Mr. Vorspan, who participated in a crucial civil rights demonstration in St. Augustine, Florida, wrote this scathing satire on those who would give lip service to civil rights principles but are unwilling to be personally active in the struggle.

A college student was once asked what he would like to get out of college. "Me," he replied. This story is appropriate to the mood of a rising number of white liberals—including many Jews—in their response to the unceasing demands of the racial crisis in American life. These whites are battle-weary, irritated, tense, guilty, frightened and they nurse feelings of rejection and anxiety. What they would like to get out of the civil rights struggle is . . . themselves. And they are succeeding. Would you, too, like to get out of the nerve-wracking pressure chamber of the Racial Revolution? There are escape hatches. The following are recommended as highly effective "outs," tried and tested in communities throughout the country. These "outs" are respectable, effective and popular. Indeed, they are quickly becoming the clichés of white resistance.

OUT #1: *"Why Can't Negroes Pull Themselves Up By Their Own Bootstraps The Way We Did?"*
This "out" requires skipping lightly over the obvious differences between the Jewish and Negro situations. Acknowledge

[84]

that the Negro has his troubles, but don't admit that the American Negro has been crippled by white society—a society which today demands he get out on the track and compete with white runners. Forget that Jews brought to America a rich cultural heritage, that when they faced anti-Jewish discrimination, some changed their noses and/or their names. Ignore the fact that Negroes have learned many things, but they have not yet learned how to get out of their black skins. If these elementary facts can be conveniently overlooked, or at least disparaged ("Oh, I know they've been segregated and all that, but . . ."), Out 1 should be all you need to assure a graceful exit.

OUT #2: *"I Believe In Human Rights, But Negroes Are Just Going Too Fast And Pushing Too Hard."*

Don't weaken this one by conceding that Negroes have to run as fast and as hard as they can if they are to stand still. As a matter of fact, Negroes haven't succeeded very well even in staying where they were. Are our big cities more segregated today than they were ten years ago? Are our suburbs white nooses around the necks of our black belt inner cities, and our schools getting more segregated all the time? Is it true that some 800,000 white pupils, for example, have left the New York City public school system over the past decade and that they have been replaced in large measure by Negroes and Puerto Ricans? Never mind. Never mind that desegregation in the South is moving at so glacial a pace that only 1 per cent of the Negro school children of the deep south have been integrated ten years after the Supreme Court decision; that Negro unemployment is twice that of whites; that for Negroes this is the depression of the 1930's all over again; that half of the youngsters out of work and out of school are Negro; that almost half of American Negroes are trapped in a cycle of poverty which, like wealth, is inherited from generation to generation! Some wise guy may ask you: "Negroes are pushing too fast for *whom?* Too fast for *what?*" If this happens, switch quickly to

OUT #3: *"I'm For Civil Rights, But I Will Not Go For The Breaking Of The Law And Civil Disobedience."*

This one is a trump card and should be played with strength. No sensible person can deny that some demonstrations have been ill-advised, some have undoubtedly been harmful to the civil rights cause, and there will be other unwise and impulsive adventures in the future. Don't fall into the trap of referring to the current struggles as a revolution because no revolution has ever been pretty and manicured . . . not the American Revolution, nor the French Revolution nor the birth of the State of Israel. The important thing is to denounce the demonstration and bloody riots in Harlem—a blockbuster of an example. Do not try to imagine the depths of despair from which they spring nor to understand this fact. When the Negro does not irritate our conscience through demonstrations, *we don't know he exists.* He is invisible, living on the wrong side of the tracks and the wrong side of the color line. If he refuses to be invisible, to be quiet, to accommodate himself to your desire for social peace, if he *will* be noticed, this is a definite threat to your peace of mind. Did Jews condemn violations of the Nazi Nuremberg laws? Did Jews protest the illegal immigration of Jewish refugees into Palestine? Never bring up such comparisons. If you extend the same standards to Negro demonstrators, you blow your advantage. This "out" has a good moralistic ring. It demonstrates that you are an independent fellow who calls the shots frankly as you see them. While putting you on record *for* Negro rights and *for* law and order, the beauty of it is that it also takes you right "out" of the battle.

OUT #4: *"Civil Rights, Yes, But Forced Integration, No!"*
This is a sweetheart of an "out." It touches all the bases—civil rights, freedom of conscience and a robust opposition to any semblance of coercion. It hits like a hammer, but at all costs avoid being forced to define your terms. What is "forced integration" anyway? Is prohibiting discrimination in hotels and resaturants "forced integraiton"? Is forbidding discrimination in employment "forced integration"? The force of the government *is* behind these, true, but if it is force we oppose, let's knock out compulsory education, income tax, the military draft and traffic rules. By all means, don't paint yourself into the corner and begin suggesting how non-discrimination and civil rights can be achieved *without* the force of law. You will wreck the whole "out" because it can't be done. The history of America is testimony to the futility of depending solely upon long-range education, voluntary suasion and "changing men's hearts" in the pursuit of human rights. But don't get into this. Just purse your

lips and proclaim: "Nobody is going to tell *me* who I should . . ."

OUT #5: *"They Don't Want Our Help Anymore!"*
You can get a lot of mileage out of this. Certainly you can
quote some of the wilder and more demagogic statements of
Negro extremists. You can cite examples of white men who have
been eased out of the civil rights leadership though they have
devoted their lives to the struggle for equality. In referring to
Negroes, talk about "them" in a grand sweep. Don't be specific
about Negro leaders, because Roy Wilkins, James Farmer, Martin
Luther King, Whitney Young, Bayard Rustin and every other
important Negro leader acknowledge that the Negro Revolution
cannot possibly be won by Negroes alone. They realize that
Negroes represent only 10 per cent of the population, and that
the civil rights movement must necessarily be joined to a fight for
massive social and economic measures to eliminate poverty, wipe
out slums, improve medical care and achieve full employment.
Such an undertaking—nothing less than the remaking of American society—requires a coalition of Negroes and white liberal,
labor, Jewish and other progressive forces in American life. But
these facts should in no way muffle the note of hurt pique about
what "they" are saying and doing.

OUT #6: *"After All We've Done For Them, Negroes Are
Anti-Semitic Anyway."*
This argument is, of course, only good by and to Jews because
non-Jews who are anti-Negro tend to be anti-Jewish, too, and
they might see Negro anti-Semitism as a sign of redemption.
For Jews, this argument has real appeal because Jews *have*
done a great deal for civil rights, including help in the organization and progress of the NAACP, passage of civil rights
legislation, foundation funds for Negro education, voting for
liberal candidates and many similar contributions. Play up this
side of the coin and maybe the discussion will not get around to
looking at the other side of the coin at all. That has to do with
the flight of Jews from racial problems of the city to the white
sanctuary of suburbia; the fact that the sole and inherently unhappy contact which most slum Negroes have with Jews is as
landlord, pawnshop owner, liquor store owner and loan shark;
the sullen and often ugly resistance of Jewish neighborhoods in
New York City and elsewhere to school integration plans and

other devices to achieve equality; the almost total lack of peer-to-peer contact between Jews and Negroes; the frequent exploitation of Negro maids. A 1964 study of racial attitudes in Chicago found Jews highly prejudiced against Negroes and Puerto Ricans, "more prejudiced than non-Jews were against Jews."

But, nonetheless, there *is* Negro anti-Semitism and it is probably rising. Attacks by Negroes against the Chasidim in Brooklyn have happened—and they were brutal and unprovoked, and so were the attacks against Jewish merchants in Harlem. These examples should be waved aloft like a bloody shirt, because what Jew can fail to be incensed or shaken by these developments? It is sure to evoke an historical visceral response. You might even be able, depending upon the vulnerability of your listener, to raise the spectre of an "American Mau Mau." In general, stick to emotions and fearful images, because the facts are that Negro anti-Semitism is not very high, as proved by the *Newsweek* poll, that it is largely subsumed in a general distrust of whites, and that responsible Negro leadership condemns it at every turn.

The thing to do is to play on the ingratitude of the Negro who, shockingly, looks upon the Jew as part of the white power structure and the benevolent community establishment which, North and South, has robbed him of his dignity and his manhood. If Negroes don't like us, they can fend for themselves. Whatever this attitude lacks in logic, charity and Jewish principles, it more than compensates in its susceptibility to human weakness and wounded pride. For greater results, couple with Out #5.

OUT #7: *"Rights Must Be Earned, Not Handed Out On A Silver Platter."*

This "out" lacks something in sophistication and should be used advisedly, but it does conjure up the spirit of rugged individualism and pioneer sturdiness which Americans honor so warmly in the breach. Of course, we do not withhold the right to vote from stupid and corrupt "rednecks" of Mississippi, but we do expect a Negro college professor there to "earn" his right. We do not deny access to our hotels and restaurants to pimps and addicts and adulterers and illiterates and field workers for the Cosa Nostra, but it is true that these worthies have earned their rights by having achieved whiteness which, after all, only a fraction of the world population has thus far accomplished.

A note of caution on this "out." *Don't try it on an American Negro.*

OUT #8: *"Where Were They When 6,000,000 Jews Were Being Killed By Hitler?"*

Rather nasty, but contains an element of surprise. Who knows where American Negroes were in the 30's since, until recently, they were invisible in American life?

During the war, of course, many were in the armed forces, helping to destroy Nazism, though they had to do this under rules of segregation more akin to the spirit of Nuremberg than of the United States Constitution. But the nice thing about this "out" is the implication that, if American Negroes really cared they could have stayed the hand of the Nazi murderers. Another implication is that, despite the irritations which Negroes face, this is really minor compared to what Jews have known.

In restoring to Out #8, it is necessary to gloss over the situation of the Negro in America. For, though America has never used gas ovens, we have—for 300 years—visited spiritual and psychological death upon generations of black men. Negro youngsters in the slums, we now know, are freqnently lost in the race of life before they even get to the first grade, their self-image distorted, their self-esteem destroyed, their incentive for learning blasted, their spirit shrivelled by poverty and by the narrow world of their experience. And yet most of white America acknowledges no more responsibility for that than did the good, fat burghers of Germany for what was happening in the smoking crematoria in their countryside.

OUT #9: *"It's Not A Matter of Integration At All; It's A Matter Of Education."*

This "out" should not be advanced as a hypothesis; it should be pronounced as a latter-day revelation from Sinai. Contend that strengthening the quality of Negro schools is the only goal that is important, not "moving kids around on a chessboard." But do not drop your voice lest some zealot inquire: "Isn't that separate but equal?" If that does happen, switch your argument ever so slightly so that it goes: "It's not a matter of integration at all; it's a matter of economics." Concede anything, dodge and weave, but do not grant that integration is the moral essence of the entire issue. Because, after all, everybody knows that racial integration was a popular banner when it meant kids in Little Rock, or James Meredith at the University of Mississippi or the terrible things that happened in Birmingham. But *now* when they talk integration they're talking about *your* plant, *your* block, *your* school, *your* job and *your* serenity. As everybody knows, such things are reckless, create severe tension and "simply cannot be accomplished overnight."

OUT #10: *"Integration Is A Fine Ideal, But It Just Causes A Strain For Both Colored And White Kids."*
Telling because true. There is a strain. It is a difficult ordeal for both races. But don't discuss the alternatives because they are all unpleasant, including the failure of American democracy, the alienation of the rest of mankind, the decay of our cities, the continued sense of racial superiority by white Americans, the toll of psychological damage, waste of human resources and the price of welfare subsistence for the blacks. Integration is the key to whether or not America can fulfill its own vision of equality and effectuate a multi-racial and open society. And the strain of adjustment to a better, larger society is the kind of creative tension which leads to growth in human relations and enlargement of the human spirit. Integration is the key to whether or not Americans can learn not only to accept but to *cherish* differences, thus joining a world of diversity, of dynamism, of variegated color and of teeth-rattling change. Integration is the challenge of living and working with all people. Don't try the old chestnut that Negroes don't want integration; they do. If they win it, that will be because equality is an aspect of their humanity and is not our gift to bestow or withhold. But you keep out of it. Mind your own business. "Am I my brother's keeper?" doesn't mention black brothers.

These are among the best and most viable "outs," You may find others in the heat of argument. By selecting those best fitted to your own needs, you may build yourself a sturdy case for washing your hands of the entire untidy problem. By all means, don't use them *all;* you certainly don't want to appear to be a bigot. You needn't feel guilty using these "outs" judiciously because they have become quite fashionable as the sound of the turtle is increasingly heard in the land — the snap of heads pulling into their shells.

To keep you from getting confused, avoid reading the Bible,

stay away from synagogue, don't talk to any Negroes except your maid (and these days you can't even be sure of *her*), and reserve your passions for your private world. Find peace of mind and ease of sleep . . . these are the advantages which the dead have always had over the living.

Rabbi Charles Mantinband

FROM THE DIARY
OF A MISSISSIPPI RABBI

When Charles Mantinband was spiritual leader of Temple B'nai Israel in Hattiesburg, Mississippi, he kept a diary of his experiences as chairman of the Mississippi Division of the Southern Regional Council, an interracial group.

The contents of that journal revealed dramatically the awkward and insecure position of Jews of conscience living in communities where bigotry may be directed for the moment at some mere minority but where the infection ultimately threatens the civic health of everybody.

Rabbi Mantinband is now with Congregation Emanu-El, in Longview, Texas.

MAY 3, 1962: On to Jackson, for a meeting of the Mississippi State Council—a small but select group who could exercise influence under strong leadership if they moved in concert and lived up to their name. But alas, the Catholic bishop and the Protestant lay leader, who called the session together, now deem it expedient to withdraw. The rabbi is left holding the bag. I delivered the keynote address, but with half a heart and no great hope.

MAY 5: Our congregation is in a dither. The Jackson press reports our story, full of distortion, but mentioning the names of those present. The White Citizens Council threatens it will know how to deal with these subversive traitors to the southern way of life, in due course and at the proper time. Our members have visions of bombings, smearing, and boycott. Happily, we kill the story, as inaccurate, in the local press and radio.

MAY 6: Off to Georgia in behalf of the United Jewish Appeal. This will give my *medina* a brief cooling-off period. Good thing I am not away from home on a Chatauqua assignment to some Negro institution!

[92]

MAY 8: Congregational meeting, with 100 per cent attendance, and everybody on time. Rabbi pleads guilty to the charge of taking his religion seriously and applying its principles to day-to-day living. My president thinks that my identification with liberal causes does the Jewish people no good. A friend suggests that anything that divides the congregation as small as ours is costly. Another wants to know "why must the rabbi mix with the niggers? Let us just sell to them and keep them in their place." Everybody lets off steam, and nothing is resolved. But I will not compromise.

MAY 9: Brookhaven cancels my biweekly visit. "We're through," comes the report, though it is not clear whether the little congregation is through with the rabbi or with Judaism. But I suspect they are not through with the race problem.

MAY 10: Some of my temple teachers visit the local college president, urging him to restrain "his friend, the rabbi," in inter-racial affairs. They receive scant encouragement. I hear that the Catholic monsignor visited one of our membership meetings while I was away, and pleaded with our people to stand up for the rabbi instead of standing in his way in the work that he is doing. These are good friends.

MAY 14: Notwithstanding my identification with efforts to improve race relations in Mississippi, the local Ministerium elects its sole Jewish member (me) as its president. Only in America. . . .

MAY 17: Until the congregation decides what to do about their rabbinical problem, my wife and I don't know whether we are coming or going. Lincoln University at Oxford, Pennsylvania, will confer an honorary doctorate on me next month, but as with the George Brussel Award, and sundry other honors, I deem it discreet not to share this news with the membership.

MAY 22: Another congregational meeting. Once more—100 per cent attendance. Grudgingly, they concede that my position is morally correct and consistent with the noblest teachings of Judaism. They realize, too, that they cannot interfere with my personal life, even though my activities make them apprehensive and nervous. They claim, however, that whenever their rabbi appears in public, people identify him with all Jews and, inevitably, as the spokesman of their congregation. And so, I promise to avoid bi-racial meetings "for the time being," to curtail press publicity "wherever possible." The local press is hostile and inflammatory. I still remember the front-page story in the *Hattiesburg American* years ago, with its caption: "Local Rabbi Says Race Relations Stink." The newspapers are no better than our demagogic politicians.

MAY 29: Apparently the storm is over. Now we have "other interests" to occupy our attention. Luckily, I have life tenure! I have consulted counsel to make sure of my legal and moral rights in the present dilemma, making no secret of it to the temple board. As far as one can measure, in terms of speaking engagements, committee responsibilities, and the like, there is no apparent loss in my popularity or status in the community. Anna and I make plans for the summer—Confirmation, a meeting of the Central Conference of American Rabbis, travel abroad.

SEPTEMBER 15: Students from many Northern universities are finding their way to our door to discuss Dixie mores. Brandeis University is especially well represented as are certain national magazines, which sense a big story on Mississippi in the offing. I help where I can, but ask them to keep my name out of print. The U.S. Justice Department is ready to prosecute Forest County in the matter of voter registration discrimination. Only a handful of Negroes here are allowed to vote, despite the United States Supreme Court, the Justice Department, and two Federal laws. A number of attorneys for Uncle Sam—Jewish and Christian —show up at temple services.

SEPTEMBER 17: It seems to me that the evidence against our county registrar in the case against Forrest County is overwhelming. If the case were to go to a jury, segregation would be preserved at all costs. Prospective Negro voters continue to receive instructions by volunteer leaders—college students, largely —in filling out forms and interpreting the U.S. Constitution. The racists call them "outsiders and agitators," naturally. The Columbia Broadcasting System plans a documentary, to tell the story to the whole country. I doubt it will be shown in Mississippi.

SEPTEMBER 21: The clouds gather as James Meredith prepares to matriculate at "Ole Miss." Here is the governor's golden opportunity to pose as a hero and the savior of a sacred cause. Meredith's legal advisors have learned what pitfalls to avoid. The Federal government will use armed force if necessary to carry out the court's decree. The mood of the state is ugly and defiant. I hope and pray for the best, but fear the worst.

SEPTEMBER 29: On Rosh Ha-shono Eve, forty-eight hours before the outbreak at Oxford, colleague Rabbi Perry E. Nussbaum of Jackson introduced a prayer at the beginning of his service, which was both eloquent and moving. It said in part: "All men are brothers, whatever the color of their skin. Our state is part of these United States. We cry out in dismay that Mississippi should set itself up against the nation, that statesmanship has surrendered to political opportunism. O Lord, we are small in numbers, yet we can remain great because of the legacy our

MANNY KURTZ

[95]

fathers have bequeathed to us. May we stride into the future, sustained by the truths of Torah. Give us the strength to declare that we are Americans, and will abide by our nation's laws. In the light of the Sabbath and the New Year hopes, we pray. Amen." The prayer was well received and printed in the Jackson Temple Bulletin.

SEPTEMBER 30: A Methodist brother calls to my attention an editorial in the *Methodist Advocate,* state periodical of this Protestant denomination: "Where state or national laws cancel out human rights, Christians have to make their choice. The State is not supreme. Men of good will and conscience owe their ultimate loyalty to the Giver of all law." This colleague confided in me that the periodical had come in for severe condemnation and criticism. One large church in this area had cancelled some 300 subscriptions.

OCTOBER 1: At the very hour President Kennedy addresses the nation appealing for restraint and respect for law and order, rioting breaks out on the Ole Miss campus. The sad story of loss of life, property, and morale is all too familiar. Mississippi vies with Cuba, the astronauts and the World Series in the headlines. Federal troops by the thousands pour in to protect this lone, courageous Negro. They will probably have to remain, though it is hoped in fewer numbers, as long as he remains a student. And Governor Barnett is a hero. Never was his popularity greater.

OCTOBER 2: Is it any wonder that our Jewish people tremble? After all, they are merchants for the most part, and depend for their survival upon the good will of their neighbors. The economic, political and social pressures on all sides are fearsome. One can understand their misgivings when a rabbi identifies himself publicly with a progressive or liberal cause. They could wish that the NAACP had as its chief counsel someone whose name is not Jack Greenberg. They were embarrassed when, among the Freedom Riders, there were Jewish students and not a few rabbis from other parts of the country. They remain silent and neutral. Happily, there has been a minimum of anti-Semitism in our midst, nothing resembling that caused by fulminations of a Bilbo or a Rankin in another generation. If we could keep it this way. . . .

OCTOBER 10: In my capacity as president of the Ministerial Association, I have written an editorial which appeared in our daily newspaper. It was well received. In the spirit of the Jewish High Holy Days, the message calls for soul-searching and personal inventory. It urges our citizens to seek, through penitence and prayer, the renewed and improved life. It scores those who are forever shifting responsibilities to others, who have not the humility to say "Chotosi" — "I have sinned."

OCTOBER 12, COLUMBUS DAY: Yes, "Only in America" could all these things happen. From the Delta I hear from a reliable source that Judge Earl Solomon, Municipal magistrate in Greenville, dispensed swift justice to both Negro and white hoodlums who, in the wake of the Oxford rioting, disturbed the local peace . . . that many Jewish citizens in that Delta community added their names to a list of a hundred other townspeople, in a large paid advertisement that appeared in the *Delta Democrat Times,* condemning lawlessness and urging we remain Americans, first, last, and always.

OCTOBER 15: Amazing to see how many Confederate flags fly from automobiles, and how often you hear the refrain, "The South will rise again." Letters in the press are overwhelmingly anti-Kennedy.

OCTOBER 24: A new voice in Mississippi. An upstate rabbi, altogether a Johnny-come-lately, crashes the press—the *Memphis Commercial Appeal,* no less—with his picture and all: "What America needs is more Mississippi, not less." And then goes on to denounce Communism, our state policy on Berlin and Cuba, repeating over and over again, "If Mississippi had its way." This reactionary Jewish voice curiously complicates our situation. It does not represent the thinking of the other rabbis.

OCTOBER 25: "This, too, shall pass." We have ridden out the storm. There is a temporary calm. Cuba is the news. All the local rumors and threats are forgotten. Yet how can one be optimistic? It is better to take a long-range view and prepare for a long haul, best to be on the alert lest the lunatic fringe in our midst make mischief, which it can do upon slight provocation indeed. Our hope is in young people who have an innate sense of right. Witness the editor of the daily paper on the Ole Miss campus. And this conversation recently with the president of my temple youth group:

RABBI: Do the events on the Ole Miss campus at Oxford upset you?

SUZY: "Upset" is hardly the word. It distresses me, and makes me sick. To think that civilized people should lose all sense of law and order, and give way to violence and mob behavior. It's a disgrace.

RABBI: The authorities at Jackson argue that they are within their legal rights in denying James Meredith admission to the University—in other words, that the federal government has invaded their rights as a sovereign state.

SUZY: All the courts have ruled otherwise, Rabbi. Unanimously, the judges have declared that massive resistance and interposition are unconstitutional. Much as we dislike it, if Mississippi showed no respect for the decision of the Supreme Court, what else could the President do, except to send in Federal troops? Even the mayor of Oxford has testified that this action was necessary.

RABBI: If integration came to your school, how would you feel about it? Would you attend classes?

SUZY: It would take some time to get used to the idea. After all, we've had segregation in our schools for a long time. But education is so important, that I know I'd attend classes. I'd try to be civil and behave well. I know that some day this change must come, probably before I'm finished with my schooling.

OCTOBER 26: In Chicago in mid-January there will be a National Conference on Religion and Race, sponsored by the National Catholic Welfare Conference, the National Council of Churches, and the Synagogue Council of America. The Central Conference of American Rabbis has designated me as one of its delegates. If ever there is to be peace, brotherhood, and good will in the world, I know it must spring from religious motivation, from religiously inspired action for justice. This is the centennial of the Emancipation Proclamation. How long, oh God?

Charles Angoff

LOUIS D. BRANDEIS:
A FOOTNOTE

> The field of partisan biography has always been afflicted
> with the curse of personality worship. Today it is a going
> industry devoted to hiring competent journalists and
> commissioning them to turn mortal men into idols. As
> a result, few of the biographical sketches which cross
> our path ever find their way into print.
>
> In this treatment of the late Supreme Court Justice
> Louis Brandeis, however, we get glimpses not of a god
> but of a human being.
>
> Charles Angoff is the author of a series of novels about
> American-Jewish life, including *Between Day and Dark*,
> *The Bitter Spring* and *Summer Storm*. His most famous
> biography is *H. L. Mencken: A Portrait From Memory*.
> The author is currently professor of English at Fairleigh
> Dickinson University.

The name Louis D. Brandeis was spoken often in my father's
home. He lived in the Back Bay, where the Yankees and the
rich Jews lived, while we lived in the West End of Boston, which
then was a slum. My *Alta Bobbe* (great-grandmother) referred
to him as a *landsman* (literally, one coming from the same town),
even though she never saw him face-to-face. She was very proud
of him, as only a ninety-year-old Jewish woman can be proud
of another Jew. He was to her the full proof of America as the
land of opportunity. "Think of it," she said, "a Jew talks to the
President of the United States, to Governors, a Jew, think of it!
Only in America can this happen!" My father and mother were
also very proud of him, for Brandeis spoke out in behalf of
Jewish affairs, in behalf of Zionism, spoke in temples and
synagogues. My Alte Bobbe had only one complaint against
Brandeis. He didn't have a beard. "It is not fitting," she said,
"for a great Jew not to have a beard, just as it's not fitting for a
mountain not to have trees. But I won't tell anybody." My

father's objection was that Brandeis had not gone to *cheder* (Hebrew school) and probably did not observe many of the *mitzvot* (obligatory acts) that every good Jew should observe. "Still," my father added, "he's a Jew, a good Jew; all American Jews should be the way he is. I'm not judging."

I had never seen Brandeis face-to-face either. But he was a hero of mine from the time I was not more than ten years old. I wanted very much to see him. I read somewhere or overheard someone say that Brandeis was in the habit of taking walks up and down Beacon Street in the late afternoon of every week-day and in mid-morning Sunday.

I told nobody what I had in mind. My parents had warned me against going off by myself. But that didn't worry me. There were seven of us children at home, with less than two years between us, and mother was so busy with the youngest ones that she wasn't too conscious where the rest of us were. Besides, I was the oldest, and I felt I had certain vague privileges. So one Sunday morning, right after Hebrew school, I walked over to Beacon Street and sat on a curb, facing the Boston Common. There was hardly anybody on the street, and I began to feel both lonesome and a little foolish. I stood up and started walking slowly. Then, off in the distance, I saw a tall man approaching. I waited for him. He got closer and closer to me. Now he was very close. His suit was rather messy. I was sure his suit hadn't been pressed for a long time. His shirt collar was clearly too big for him, and he hadn't had a hair-cut for weeks—his hair seemed to go in whichever way. From the pictures I had seen of him in the newspapers, I knew at once that this was Brandeis. I was thrilled as only a ten-year-old can be thrilled when face-to-face with his hero. I adored the Lincolnesque figure of Brandeis. As he passed me, I smiled at him, and he bent a bit toward me and smiled back. Then he walked on. I remained standing. Then I ran after him and walked alongside of him for a few feet . . . I smiled at him . . . he smiled back at me . . . and now he was far ahead of me.

I rushed back home and told my father and mother. "I saw Brandeis! I saw Brandeis! I really saw him! Really. I walked with him. He smiled at me."

"Good, good," said my father. "He's a fine man."

I didn't see Brandeis again till I was about fifteen. At the time there was a Ford Fall Forum in Boston, which presented free public lectures every Sunday night in a hall next to the Boston State House on top of Beacon Hill. I read on the bulletin board that Louis D. Brandeis was to talk the following Sunday on a topic having to do with the conflict between Big Business and Small Business or something of that nature. Of course, I had no interest in either Big Business or Little Business. In my house, the order of the day generally was No Business. My father was a tailor and frequently out of work. We got along somehow, but money was never plentiful. But I did want to hear Brandeis, for he was still my hero.

Mr. George W. Coleman, the chairman, introduced Mr. Brandeis in glowing terms. Mr. Brandeis got up slowly, and it took him about two minutes to walk from his seat to the lectern which was only a few feet away. He looked pretty much the same way he looked when I had last seen him, five years before, though his hair was now much grayer. He spoke softly, quietly. I was disappointed. I had heard in the meantime that he was a great lawyer, that he had battled with the Metropolitan Life Insurance Company and other insurance companies about savings bank life insurance, and had won out, also that he had had battles with various railroads entering Boston and had shown them how to make more money by reducing passenger rates and freight rates. . . . Somehow I had imagined that these battles entailed pounding on the table, shouting, stamping the floor. And here my hero was talking gently, almost as if he were in our parlor.

But slowly my disappointment changed to admiration. I noticed with what an amazing mass of information he was building up his case, with what rigorous logic he was drawing conclusions from this information, and what a mountain of persuasiveness he was slowly erecting. He was finished. He turned slowly toward his chair, and again it took him what seemed like two minutes to get to it. He sat down. The entire hall was silent. Suddenly, as if someone had pushed a button, the hall burst into a storm of applause and the applause mounted and mounted. A shudder of delight ran up and down my spine. I felt goose pimples on my arms and my face.

I rushed home and told my father. I told him how quietly Brandeis spoke, how gentle he was, and how persuasive. My father listened, then said, "Good, good, my son. I'm glad you heard Brandeis. Always remember that real wisdom, real intellectual strength, is always gentle and quiet. Don't ever forget that."

I didn't see Brandeis again till many years later, not till the first administration of President Franklin D. Roosevelt. I was in Washington. I went to the Supreme Court on a day when arguments were being presented. There on the dais sat Chief Justice Hughes and Justice McReynolds and Justice Butler and Justice Cardozo and my man, Justice Brandeis. His hair was still unruly. It was now all white. But something marvelous had come to his face. It was translucent and kindly and sharp and all-patient and all-knowing. He looked like a prophet of ancient Israel.

A man was arguing a case earnestly before the Court. Some of the justices were asking questions. Justice Brandeis asked no questions. He was merely looking intently at the man. Now and then he bent forward a bit the more clearly to hear what the man was saying. I had the feeling that the man was more concerned about the continued silence of Justice Brandeis than about the questions from the other justices.

The presentation of the argument was finished. The Court rose and began to walk out. Justice Brandeis rose slowly and walked out slowly. He was still tall, but now his shoulders were much rounder.

I walked out into the street. Again a shudder of delight went up and down my spine. And I was proud that I belonged to the same ancient people that Justice Brandeis belonged to.

[102]

As A Tale
That
Is Told

_____

"We bring our years to an end as a tale that is told"

Psalm 90

The resurgence of Jewish fiction in recent years has been so great that the editor is confronted almost with an embarrassment of riches. It is sometimes difficult to tell the subject of Jewish fiction from that of fiction in general. Jewish writers dealing with subject matter loom large on the literary scene: Saul Bellow,

[103]

Philip Roth, Bernard Malamud, Isaac Bashevis Singer, Herbert Gold. . . .their names are ubiquitous. Everywhere in print their works are being praised or getting castigated. The relation between the work of these writers and the aspirations of religion is peculiarly close. Our storytellers, with some exceptions, no longer soothe or flatter us. Their tales not only reveal what happens next but depict their subjects in the mirrors of their insights. Gone, and good riddance, are the self-consciously charming projections of the "Jewish" image designed for export to a non-Jewish world. Yet the stories and novels of these writers are more moral in their import than the manufactured works of their predecessors.

In the best of their stories, Jewish writers today are less like minnesingers and entertainers, more like the prophets of old who stood on the steps outside the palace exhorting the multitude to do better, unafraid to denounce the king himself.

Fashions in fiction are ever changing and already the contemporary Jewish hero with his sexual conquests, weltschmerz and pride in being a maladroit schlemiel is turning into as much of a tired tintype as his predecessor who worshipped Marx. You will not find either of these fellows here.

Dan Jacobson

GOLD FROM AFRICA

Dan Jacobson was born in South Africa and now lives in England. He is the author of five novels, *The Beginners, The Trap, A Dance in the Sun, The Price of Diamonds, Evidence of Love* and one book of nonfiction, *No Further West*. He is a frequent contributor to a wide range of magazines on both sides of the Atlantic. His short stories have appeared in *The New Yorker, Atlantic Monthly, Harper's Bazaar* and *Commentary*, and a collection of them, *The Zulu and the Zeyde*, published by Atlantic Monthly Press, became the basis for a successful Broadway "comedy with music" starring Menasha Skulnik. "Gold From Africa" later became the opening chapter of *The Beginners*, a panoramic story of a Jewish family. The story begins on the Cape Town docks at the turn of the century and culminates in a touching encounter at a railroad station in Bremen, where the generous instincts of the Jewish traveler overcome his practicality — the triumph of heart over mind.

In the spring of 1906, two young men said good-by to their father on Cape Town Docks. The father was a tall, handsome man, upright and slender; what was most striking about his appearance was the contrast between the whiteness of his spade-shaped beard and the darkness of the hair of his head. The contrast made his face seem strong and decisive, almost dramatically so; but there was no strength in the grey, short-sighted eyes: only a weak bewilderment and amiability.

His single leather bag had been stowed in the cabin that he was to share with eleven others during the journey to Southampton; now he and his sons, Benjamin and Meyer, stood on the deck. It was a clear, bright day; from the boat Cape Town looked like a village, compared with the huge bulk of Table Mountain which stood immediately behind the town, altogether dwarfing

PENROD SCOFIELD

it. The town was no more than a scattering of iron roofs, of church steeples, of gables, of trees; then the mountain rose, at first gradual in its slope and faintly green with grass, but soon rising sheer, precipitous, and bare, slashed here and there by great gulleys that zigzagged down its flanks. Darker and lighter shades of brown yielded to the blue of distance and height, and then, abruptly, the ascent was cut off by the wide, flat top of the mountain. Beyond the mountain there was only the clear sky, and the sun shining.

The three men made little conversation, as they leaned over the rail, looking at the confusion of Cape colored porters and white passengers below, and occasionally glancing at the stillness and emptiness of the mountain above. The brothers looked much alike, and very little like their father. They were both thick-set men, the elder more powerful in build than the younger, who was hardly more than a boy; they both had heavy features and protruding lower lips; they both wore their hair brushed directly back from their foreheads. Once when a porter slipped and stumbled, Benjamin, the older brother, laughed briefly; the father looked anxiously to see what his son was laughing at, and smiled too, though he had seen nothing. At last, Benjamin said impatiently, in Yiddish, "It's time to go. Come, Meyer. Good-by, Father."

Avrom Glickman's eyes filled immediately with tears, and he held out his arms to his son. Reluctantly, ungraciously, Benjamin yielded to his father's embrace, and broke from it as soon as he could. Then it was Meyer's turn. He too embraced his father stiffly. He said, "Tell Mama we're waiting to see her."

Nodding, holding a hand of each of his sons, Avrom said, "I'll bring Mama back with me. I'll bring her safely."

"Good, that's what we want."

Avrom was reluctant to let his sons go. "I'll tell Mama what fine boys you are. She'll see for herself when I show her the money we've saved."

Benjamin could not restrain himself. "We've saved?" he repeated ironically. Then he nodded, and smiled, and removed his hand from his father's grasp. "We must go now. It's late, the shop is waiting."

A moment later they had left him. With trembling hands Avrom felt inside his pocket for his spectacle-case; he opened it and took out the wire-rimmed spectacles and put them on. One earpiece jumped away from behind his ear, but he let it lie against his beard in his anxiety to watch his sons go down the gangway. But already he was too late. He could not see them on the gangway, nor on the quayside. Without waving or waiting they had just left him on the boat, among so many strangers, to face the risks of a three-week journey on the sea. Tears of self-pity came into Avrom's eyes, and he sniffed deeply and wiped his nostrils with the back of his hand. Then, with a gesture that was already a habit he touched the inside of his jacket, whereit was weighed down with the fifty gold sovereigns he was carrying back to Latvia—enough to bring his wife and two youngest children back with him to South Africa.

[107]

He remained at the rail, looking about him with curiosity and interest. The tears had soon dried in his eyes; on his lips now there was a faint, absent smile. A steward moved about the deck announcing through a megaphone that all visitors had to leave the ship immediately; around Avrom people were embracing, laughing, crying. A group on the quayside began singing "Auld Lang Syne"; long paper streamers were thrown from the deck onto the quay, and children rushed to pick them up. People blew kisses to one another and screamed their last messages; the boat gave a deep, prolonged hoot that made the boards of the deck quiver. Blue, red, and yellow, the streamers fluttered and broke, and the people on the quay began to recede, their hands still waving, or cupped around shouting mouths from which no sound could be heard.

As the tugs pulled the boat away, more and more of the peninsula came into view, on both sides of Table Mountain. But that edge of coastline was the first to slip below the horizon; and then even the mountain began to shrink, slowly, until all its bulk was reduced to a single brown shoulder of land, standing high out of the sea. Losing size, the mountain lost its color; it became no more than a smudge, a tiny mark on the horizon; then it was gone.

Avrom remained on deck, until it was out of sight. His sons, he knew, would be back at work. And Avrom was relieved to be on his own. He had his ticket, he had some pocket-money, he had fifty sovereigns to bring back home. There was no one on the boat who knew that the money for the ticket, his pocket-money, and the fifty sovereigns had all been saved by his sons, and none by himself, out of the miserable wages they earned, the one as a grocer's assistant, the other as a butcher's assistant, in slum-shops in the colored area of the town. There was no one on the boat who knew of all the jobs that Avrom had failed to keep, while his sons had been saving; of the horses he had bought with borrowed money and sold at a loss, of the dairy business he established in a backyard with a single cow that had died, of the surplus army blankets he had bought from a fellow who hadn't had them to sell. The reproach Avrom felt in his sons' gestures and words lay behind him, under the horizon; his wife's asperities were many weeks ahead.

A stiff breeze was blowing on deck, and Avrom roused himself. There were surely some other Jews on board with whom he could talk. Cheerfully, humming under his breath, he set out to find them.

Several weeks later Avrom sat on an empty platform on Bremen station. He had arrived safely in London for a few days with a distant cousin, and then taken the steamer to Bremen. Now he waited for his train to the East. He knew that he was on the right platform, and though he knew also that he was several hours too early for his train, he was determined not to move from the platform until it came in.

While he was sitting there, with his leather bag on the bench beside him, a train—not his, as he soon ascertained—pulled in at the platform and disgorged its passengers. They hurried away, and in a matter of minutes Avrom was left apparently alone on the platform once again. The train stood empty, its engines hissing and sending steam up to the grimy glass and iron roof far above it; then slowly it clanked away. Avrom stared at the rails, and at the grey platforms that ran parallel to one another beyond, until the black roof arched down over a row of offices and kiosks clustered around the station entrance. He had been sitting for an hour already; on an impulse he began walking down the platform, simply to stretch his legs. He carried his bag with him. The platform was a long one, he walked at a leisurely pace, and his eyesight was poor; thus, it took some time before he realized that in fact he was no longer alone on the platform. On a bench at the far end sat a mother and four children.

Almost as soon as he saw them, Avrom saw too that they were Jewish. The woman was wearing a brown wig; the boys, under their caps, wore *payess* trained to go over their ears. They were neatly dressed, in overcoats belted at the back. Something about the way they were standing around their mother arrested Avrom's attention; then he saw that they were trying to comfort her. She was in tears. Avrom hesitated, not wishing to intrude; but his curiosity would not let him creep quietly away from them.

Cautiously he approached; when he was a few paces away he cleared his throat and asked, "Is there anything a Jew can do?"

The children turned startled, clean faces towards him; then the mother looked up. She was a young woman, Avrom saw with surprise, and a good-looking one, too. Her brows were black and severe under a wide, pale forehead; her eyes looked the darker for the tears within them and on her eyelashes. Her small colorless lips were turned down, woefully.

"Can I do something to help you?" Avrom asked again. He put his bag down on the platform. "What's the matter, woman? Why are you sitting here and crying?"

The woman covered her face, and burst into tears again. Her children stared suspiciously at Avrom; the face of the youngest suddenly puckered and he, too, began to cry loudly. His brothers followed his example. The noise was pitiable and embarrassing; Avrom retreated from it a few paces down the platform. The woman's luggage was scattered about the bench; and, at last, because he could think of nothing else to do, Avrom began to gather it together. He piled it neatly in a heap, and then retreated once again.

A little later, Avrom sat together with the woman on the bench. Her story was sad and simple. She came from Latvia, and was on her way to America, to join her husband who was already there, and had sent her the money to come. On the train which had brought her to Bremen she had lost, or had had stolen from her, the handbag which contained her money, her tickets, and her travel documents. She knew no one in Bremen; she could go neither forward nor back; she could only sit on the bench, she said, and pray for help, for a miracle, her own death.

What could Avrom do? He knew no one in Bremen. He had his own train to catch. He told her to go to the police, and to ask them for the address of a rabbi. There must be someone, some organization, which would help her. But even as he offered it, his advice seemed to Avrom useless, of no help. He stood up and walked around the bench; he patted the children on their shoulders; he sat down again beside the woman. Rising within himself there was an impulse that at first he could translate only into a wish that his train would come soon, immediately, and carry him away from the woman's misery; and then only into anger. "Go!" he shouted at her harshly. "What are you sitting here and waiting for? Go!"

His harshness shocked and frightened her. She looked once more at him, stood up, and reached for her bags. Each of the children took one, she took two. Bowed, wretched, puny, the little family group began to trail away down the platform. Avrom sat on the bench; he watched them go, then he turned his head to avoid seeing them. He waited for some minutes before looking again in the direction they had gone. He could see them no longer. Avrom gave a sigh of relief and pain, a groan. He struck himself on the chest. It was there that there lay the impulse he hadn't dared to confess to himself; there lay the answer to the woman's plight.

A moment later Avrom began to run after the group. He shouted as he ran, words, oaths, prayers. Now his only fear was that he would be too late; that they had already left the platform. But he did manage to catch up with them. Without a word, he tore open his coat, he ripped at its inner lining, he took out the heavy purse with the fifty sovereigns in it, and held it out to the astonished woman.

She stared at him uncomprehendingly. "Take!" Avrom shouted, in a tone even harsher than the one in which he had told her to go. "Take, it's gold from Africa!" He thrust the purse towards her, then actually flung it at her. It struck her on the arm, and fell to the ground. He was in tears; his chest heaved and with every breath, he could feel the lightness of his coat, relieved of the weight he had carried in it for so many weeks, over so many thousands of miles. And he felt, with that lightness, an extraordinary sense of release, as though he had discharged an obligation he had been laboring under for longer than the time that had passed since he had met the woman, longer than his journey, at least as long as the years he had spent in South Africa. As though someone else had made the gift, Avrom was rewarded, while the purse still lay on the ground, by the sense he had of the world as a place where charity was available, after all, to people who were in need of it. He was rewarded even by the thought of his sons, toiling in squalor, saving their pennies, not knowing that the money they had saved for one purpose would be diverted to another. Their ignorance, their innocence, seemed profoundly touching to him; and Avrom himself remained ignorant, would always remain ignorant, of how much of revenge against them there was in what he had just done. All he was conscious of at the moment was loving-kindness, and it embraced the woman, his sons, and himself, indiscriminately.

The woman seized his hand and kissed it, moistening it with her tears. She had taken his address and sworn that her husband would pay back every one of the sovereigns; she had called him a righteous man, a protector of orphans, an angel of God. Then she left him, she to continue her journey, he to continue his.

The joy Avrom felt sustained throughout almost the remainder of his journey. He traveled on one train; then on another; in the cart of one carrier and in the cart of another. It was only when he was a few miles away from home that, without warning, his happiness and self-satisfaction deserted him. He had been so carried away by his own sense of benevolence that previously he had actually looked forward to telling the story to his wife and to his cronies in the village; now, more simply dejected than self-reproachful, he began to dread the moment of his arrival.

The reaction of Avrom's wife to the news was worse, far worse, than any he had anticipated. In the last chill hours of his journey he had tried to prepare himself against hearing her screaming, seeing her rolling on the floor and tearing her hair, perhaps even trying to attack him physically. But there was nothing; only silence. From their mother her sons had inherited their stocky figures, their full features, and protruding lower lips; but what in their expressions was vigorous and full, in her had been worn into a naked heaviness of the bone, a rigid clamping of the jaw. For four years she had been waiting to be called to join her sons, bringing with her the boy and the girl who still lived with her. Occasionally a remittance had come; more often an assurance that they were saving, that they hadn't forgotten, that the money was being put together. And at last the father had been on his way, with the money that would redeem those years, the departures before them. And now he was here, without the money, the years behind wasted, a waste of years ahead.

She did not say a word. She stared forward at the bare floor. Then she rose, to begin preparing their meal. The father stood at the door. "The woman will pay the money. Her husband will send it to us."

She did not seem to hear him. That night when he came into bed she turned her back on him. "I'm your husband," he protested. "I've come back after a long time." She paid no attention. Soon she was asleep.

Avrom lay on his back and prayed that the woman's husband would send the money soon, soon. He was ashamed of the prayer, but he uttered it fervently, silently, his lips moving in the dark.

The prayer went unanswered. It took four years before Benjamin and Meyer had saved enough money for Benjamin to make the long trip home, and to escort all the family—but for his sister, who had grown up and had become betrothed to a man in the village—to their new country.

[112]

Philip Roth

THE MISTAKEN

Ever since Philip Roth won the National Book Award
for his short story collection *Goodbye, Columbus* in 1960,
his work has been the center of critical controversy. His
merciless examination of middle-class Jewish mores, as in
his novel *Letting Go,* resulted in further national prizes
from some Jewish groups and attacks by others.

In this story about the death of a Jewish gangster the
author calls our attention to the insensitivity of death
itself, as well as of the living.

Dear Mother:

If you were watching TV tonight you know the news—Murray
Miller is dead. Who would ever have dreamed that Murray's
funeral would have a coast-to-coast audience. And what a
funeral! Simonized Cadillacs, Hamburg hats, mink stoles, and a
limousine full of flowers, the names of which Murray wouldn't
have known if he'd lived to be a million. And pallbearers with
faces pulled long enough to honor a dead pope, and beneath
those black suits, not a one of them without a bullet scar or a
knife wound or, tucked in a monogrammed billfold, a swindled
dollar. I don't want to sound bitter or envious. A man afraid of
cutting himself with a bread knife doesn't envy thieves their
lives or money. Nor do I mean to sound hard about Murray. Poor
Murray, he paid. He was sitting in his living-room, as was I just a
minute ago. His wife, his two little girls were with him, watching
TV. Then all of a sudden four men crash through hs window
and bang, bang, Murray is dead. Before the shots it must have
been a terrible moment for Murray. For which crime, he must
have thought, for which crime? And believe me, he had reason to
wonder. To even the score they would have had to kill Murray a
hundred times.

But maybe Murray didn't wonder at all. Perhaps I'm just wondering what *I* would wonder if four men came through my

[113]

PENROD SCOFIELD

window. For which crime? Who in the world couldn't think of half a dozen to satisfy a gunman . . .? But this is probably all very confusing to you. You probably don't even remember Murray Miller, the kid who was my best friend for almost a year. He would come by in the morning and we would go to school together. He was always very small, and had red kinky hair, and on his left hand he had the extra thumb. He was the one whose face I held in the snow until he almost drowned. Do you remember that day? I know you—if right this minute we were face to face, I know you would walk away, refusing to remember. I can see you turn to the stove to stir something, and you would say, "You're crazy, it's thirty years already, what good to remember yesterday's newspaper?" But I want you to remember because I want to explain. Explaining is always in order, regardless of all the years. Would Murray have made any sense if he'd cried to his assassins, "I don't have to explain to you, that union business is ancient history? It's sixteen years last January we dropped Boss Seratelli in the Passaic." Would that have convinced anyone? Not at all. In January the Passaic is cold as the Bering! Could he have pleaded, "Look, don't talk to me about the black market—I've a wife, two girls, a house, and I belong to three charitable organizations? I haven't done a crooked thing since 1945." I was ready to say, no, that would've made no sense either, but now I hear my own in the other room, and I think maybe it would have. But this is beside the point. I just want my explanation listened to for once. Don't tell me it's too late. If it straightens out our hearts, what difference if the explaining's done on Doomsday? Who knows when a blood vessel will give out in my brain, or when I'll get electrocuted turning on the TV set? Men thirty-nine years old are dying every day. Let me explain.

Surely I don't have to remind you of the house we lived in thirty years ago on Gracie Avenue. You probably know every nick on every step of those wooden stairs that led down the three flights to the street. I can see you and the bristle-brush and bucket washing from our door down to the second floor landing, right to the Shetterley's door, and *boom*, stopping! So perhaps your recollection is only of the top flight. And you remember the neighborhood? The Gracie Avenue trolley? Why waste time. What I want to write to you about is me. Now don't turn to the soup again. Relax. I have children of my own. Mothers are *supposed* to know the steps they scrub better than their chil-

[115]

dren's troubles. Please, for once, pay attention. Then if you want to stir soup, go ahead.

The night before that awful day, Dorfman, the grocer, had died. You weren't the one who told me this, by the way. Death didn't exist in our house—we turned our backs on it. The day after arguments we forgot them. The troubles, the uglinesses, all the rotten things, were hidden behind a screen, like the cat's sand box. I didn't even go to my own father's funeral because I was too little. . . . But if I'm to sit here recalling every grievance, I'll be sitting here all week. Just recounting all the things you "protected" me from would keep me up all night. Let me get back to Dorfman. He had been playing pinochle with friends, he got a pain in his chest, and he went to the bathroom for a minute. When he didn't come back, they went to see what had happened. And there he was, sitting on the bowl, his pants around his knees, dead. Murray and I heard this from the tailor, and I remember that even while I was listening I was wondering if my father had died that way. Or, as a matter of fact, if everybody did. What trouble I had with my bowels for the next week!

So Dorfman was dead. It was the only time outside of the Jewish holidays that his store was closed. And right there, despite all you had done to protect me from knowing, I knew everything about the power of death. I thought about that Closed-for-Business sign all day, and then, walking home from school, I thought about it some more, for Murray and I walked by the grocery again, just as Mrs. Dorfman was repairing the damages from the day's closing. It had snowed for a week, and the sidewalk, the trees, the rolled-up store awnings, everything was white, except for the two trolley tracks that shined all the way up Gracie. And now comes the explanation. The reason I held Murray in the snow was that he stood at the window of the grocery, staring in at Mrs. Dorfman as she threw radishes and lettuce and tomatoes into a big cardboard box. She jammed celery in on top of the tomatoes, splatted rotten eggs on top of the celery, and all the time Murray was so close he was steaming up the glass. She threw and threw and threw—I'll never forget it—and after a while it seemed she was throwing away everything in sight, spoiled or not. Right in front of our eyes, she was going crazy. I couldn't bear to see it, and I said to Murray, "C'mon Murray, c'mon." I must have said it a hundred times, but he didn't move. Suddenly, I felt angrier than I ever had in my life, and I grabbed him by the hair and said, *"C'mon!"* His eyes got red as his hair. Who you pulling? You! Yea? Yea! And I don't remember who swung first, but next thing we were rolling in the snow, me and my best friend. And I was screaming at him—"You shouldn't stare at dead people! You shouldn't!" I didn't even know what my words meant, or didn't mean, but I screamed it over and over. And then, in an instant, all my anger hardened into fear, a terrible knot of it, and I pushed his head as far as I could in the snow, and shouted at him every dirty word I knew. I don't think I've ever been so frightened in my life.

And then someone grabbed *me* by the hair and I was standing up. Murray turned over on the mushy ground and only when he looked up did I realize I'd almost drowned him. He was coughing up globs of snow as though he were a magician. Meanwhile, the hand that had grabbed my hair had found my ear and was trying to pull it off. The fingers smelled from rotten eggs. "You ought to be ashamed!" she screamed at me. From the angle my head was at, I couldn't see her face, just her long black dress swishing against her black snow-tipped shoes. She was screaming, "There isn't enough trouble? You have to make more? There isn't enough trouble in the world? God'll punish you good," she said, shaking me. "God'll punish you. God sees!" And then she let go of my ear and lifted Murray from the ground. She held up his left hand, the one with the two thumbs. *"Look,"* she said, waving the hand in my face, "a cripple, a crippled boy you hit!" And Murray, he didn't say a word, the poor cripple. Mrs. Dorfman held my arms then, and she said to Murray, "Go ahead, pay him back, pay him back good. . . ." And he did, and then when I got home, you did, which I'm sure you don't remember.

And that's all. That's it. And now what do I expect to happen? I —

He drew a long dash where he'd intended to write a word. And then his mind was empty of words, and he sat back in his chair. With the pen still in his hand, he began to read what he had written, but when he'd gotten only as far as Murray Miller's breath steaming up the grocery window, he tore the letter in half, then in half again. He dropped it into the waste-basket beside the desk and went back into the living-room.

The news was long over, and now his plump, pretty wife and his thin, pretty eight-year-old daughter watched Edward R. Murrow as he toured, room-by-room, a famous opera star's New York apartment. His son, two, was in bed. The boy and girl were not twins.

His wife looked up, and before she even asked, he said, "Just looking over some accounts." Why tell her the truth? She was a practical woman, whose sentiment was bounded on four sides by reason. She would think little of his beginning a lifetime job at nine o'clock at night. And besides, what is a man with children of his own doing explaining his childhood to his mother?

"You only missed the living-room," his daughter said, glancing up. She had her mother's round face and thin features, so far. God forbid his nose should blossom on that face. But what could he do about that? Noses, tempers, soft teeth are predestined. If, like his, her nose was supposed to bend, it would bend. Yet, deep as he was, buried in her cartilage, what help was it? Even loved ones mistook good for evil, evil for good. You told them the truth, and that hurt. You hid the truth, that hurt, too. His own mother had loved him. That made things better?

Only worse.

His window rattled, and at the sound of it he reached across and took his daughter's hand. No gunmen came crashing through. He had been a good man, or maybe just a cautious one. Either way, he was thankful for it—he hadn't been a father long enough. And yet, the longer their love continued, the greater care he'd have to bring to it. He would have to plot, scheme, allow not one mistake!

"Your fingers are all ink," the girl said, holding his right hand to the light.

She said it, and he felt, suddenly, looking at his hands, un-burdened and sad. They were only a man's hands. What could he do? Narrow as her chest was, it must guard a heartful of his mistakes already.

Isaac Bashevis Singer

GETZEL THE MONKEY

Isaac Bashevis Singer is considered not only the greatest
Yiddish writer alive but also one of the best authors writing fiction in any language. Born in Poland in 1904, he
came to the United States in 1935.

Mr. Singer's novels include *The Family Moskat, Satan
in Goray, The Magician of Lublin* and *The Slave.* He is
the author of such celebrated books of short stories as
Short Friday, Gimpel the Fool and *The Spinoza of
Market Street.* Although critics like Irving Howe have
called Singer a genius and praised him for his ability to
make us see the Jewish life of the eastern European past
through alert and twinkling eyes, the Yiddishists accuse
Singer of exploiting and distorting this material. Certainly he is a master storyteller.

"Getzel the Monkey" is the story of a mimic. Its simplicity is deceptive, for between the lines shines through
the shrewdest understanding of human nature — and of
the nature of mimicry itself.

My dear friends, we all know what a mimic is. Once we had
such a man living in our town, and he was given a fitting name.
In that day they gave nicknames to everybody but the rich
people. Still, Getzel was even richer than the one he tried to
imitate, Todrus Broder. Todrus himself lived up to his˙fancy
name. He was tall, broad-shouldered like a giant, with a black
beard as straight as a squire's and a pair of dark eyes that burned
through you when they looked at you. Now, I know what I'm
talking about. I was still a girl then, and a good-looking one, too.
When he stared at me with those fiery eyes, the marrow in my
bones trembled. If an envious man were to have a look like that,
he could, God preserve us, easily give you the evil eye. Todrus

[119]

had no cause for envy, though. He was as healthy as an ox, and he had a beautiful wife and two graceful daughters, real princesses. He lived like a nobleman. He had a carriage with a coachman, and a hansom as well. He went driving to the villages and played around with the peasant women. When he threw coins to them, they cheered. Sometimes he would go horseback riding through the town, and he sat up in the saddle as straight as a cossack.

His surname was Broder, but Todrus came from Great Poland, not from Brody. He was a great friend of all the nobles. Count Zamoysky used to come to his table on Friday nights to taste his gefilte fish. On Purim the Count sent him a gift, and what do you imagine the gift turned out to be? Two peacocks, a male and a female!

Todrus spoke Polish like a Pole and Russian like a Russian. He knew German, too, and French as well. What didn't he know? He could even play the piano. He went hunting with Zamoysky and he shot a wolf. When the Tsar visited Zamosc and the finest people went to greet him, who do you think spoke to him? Todrus Broder. No sooner were the first three words out of his mouth than the Tsar burst out laughing. They say that later the two of them played a game of chess and Todrus won. I wasn't there, but it probably happened. Later Todrus received a gold medal from Petersburg.

His father-in-law, Falk Posner, was rich, and Falk's daughter Fogel was a real beauty. She had a dowry of twenty-thousand rubles, and after her father's death she inherited his entire fortune. But don't think that Todrus married her for her money. It is said that she was travelling with her mother to the spas when suddenly Todrus entered the train. He was still a bachelor then, or perhaps a widower. He took one look at Fogel, and then he told her mother that he wanted her daughter to be his wife. Imagine, this happened some fifty years ago. . . . Everyone said that it was love at first sight for Todrus, but later it turned out that love didn't mean a thing to him. I should have as many blessed years as the nights Fogel didn't sleep because of him! They joked, saying that if you were to dress a shovel in a woman's skirts, he would chase after it. In those days, Jewish daughters didn't know about love affairs, so he had to run after Gentile girls and women.

Not far from Zamosc, Todrus had an estate where the greatest nobles came to admire his horses. But he was a terrible spend-thrift, and over the years his debts grew. He devoured his father-in-law's fortune, and that is the plain truth.

Now, Getzel the Monkey, whose name was really Getzel Bailes, decided to imitate everything about Todrus Broder. He was a rich man, and stingy to boot. His father had also been known as a miser. It was said that he had built up his fortune by starving himself. The son had a mill that poured out not flour, but gold. Getzel had an old miller who was as devoted as a dog to him. In the fall when there was a lot of grain to mill, this miller stayed awake nights. He didn't even have a room for himself; he slept with the mice in the hayloft. Getzel grew rich because of him. In those times, people were used to serving. If they didn't serve God, they served the boss.

Getzel was a money-lender, too. Half the town's houses were mortgaged to him. He had one precious little daughter, Dishke, and a wife, Risha Leah, who was as sick as she was ugly. Getzel could as soon become Todrus as I the Rabbi of Turisk. But a rumor spread through the town that Getzel was trying to become another Todrus. At the beginning, it was only the talk of the peddlers and the seamstresses, and who pays attention to such gossip? But then Getzel went to Selig the tailor, and he ordered a suit just like Todrus' with a broad fox collar and a row of tails. Later he had the shoemaker fit him with a pair of boots exactly the same as Todrus' with low uppers and shiny toes. Zamosc isn't Warsaw. Sooner or later, everyone knows what everyone else is doing. So why mimic anyone? Still, when the rumors reached Todrus' ears he merely said, "I don't care. It shows that he has a high opinion of my taste." Todrus never spoke a bad word about anyone. If he was going down Lublin Street and a girl of twelve walked by, he would lift his hat to her just as though she were a lady. Had a fool done this they would have made fun of him. But a clever person can afford to be a fool sometimes. At weddings Todrus got drunk and cracked such jokes that they thought he, not Koppel Venngrover, was the jester. When he danced a kozotsky, the floor trembled.

Well, Getzel Bailes was determined to become a second Todrus. He was small and thick as a barrel, and a stammerer to boot. To hear him try to get a word out was enough to make you faint. The town had something to mock. He bought himself a carriage, but it was a tiny carriage and the horses were two old nags.

PENROD SCOFIELD

Getzel rode from the market place to the mill and from the mill to the market place. He wanted to be gallant, and he tried to take his hat off to the druggist's wife. Before he could raise his hand, she had already disappeared. People were barely able to keep from laughing in his face, and the town rascals immediately gave him his nickname.

Getzel's wife, Risha Leah, was a shrew, but she had sense enough to see what was happening. They began to quarrel. There was no lack in Zamosc of curious people who listened at the cracks in the shutters and looked through the keyhole. Risha Leah said to him, "You can as much become Todrus as I can become a man! You are making a fool of yourself. Todrus is Todrus; you stay Getzel."

But who knows what goes on in another person's head? It seemed to be an obsession. Getzel began to pronounce his words like a person from Great Poland and to use German expressions:

mädchen, schmädchen, grädchen. He found out what Todrus ate, what he drank, and, forgive me for the expression, what drawers he wore. He began to chase women, too. And my dear friends, just as Todrus had succeeded in everything, so Getzel failed. He would crack a joke and get a box on the ear in return. Once, in the middle of a wedding celebration, he tried to seduce a woman, and her husband poured chicken soup down the front of his gabardine. Dishke cried and implored him, "Daddy, they are making fun of you!" But it is written somewhere that any fancy can become a madness.

Getzel met Todrus in the street and said, "I want to see your furniture."

"With the greatest pleasure," said Todrus, and took him into his living-room. What harm would it do Todrus, after all, if Getzel copied him?

So Getzel kept on mimicking. He tried to imitate Todrus' voice. He tried to make friends with the squires and their wives. He had studied everything in detail. Getzel had never smoked, but suddenly he came out with cigars and the cigars were bigger than he was. He also started a subscription to a newspaper in Petersburg. Todrus' daughters went to a Gentile boarding school, and Getzel wanted to send Dishke there, even though she was already too old for that. Risha Leah raised an uproar and she was barely able to prevent him from doing it. If he had been a pauper, Getzel would have been excommunicated. But he was loaded with money. For a long time, Todrus didn't pay any attention to all of this, but at last in the market place he walked over to Getzel and asked: "Do you want to see how I make water?" He used plain language, an the town had something to laugh about.

Now, listen to this. One day Risha Leah died. Of what did she die? Really, I couldn't say. Nowadays people run to the doctor; in those times a person got sick and it was soon finished. Perhaps it was Getzel's carryings-on that killed her. Anyway, she died and they buried her. Getzel didn't waste any tears over it. He sat on the stool during the seven days of mourning and cracked jokes like Todrus. His daughter Dishke was already engaged. After the thirty days of bereavement the matchmakers showered him with offers, but he wasn't in a hurry.

Two months hadn't passed when there was bedlam in the town. Todrus Broder had gone bankrupt. He had borrowed money from widows and orphans. Brides had invested their dowries with him, and he owed money to nobles. One of the squires came over and tried to shoot him. Todrus' wife wept and fainted, and the girls hid in the attic. It came out that Todrus owed Getzel a large sum of money. A mortgage, or God knows what. Getzel came to Todrus. He was carrying a cane with a silver tip and an amber handle, just like Todrus', and he pounded on the floor with it. Todrus tried to laugh off the whole business, but you could tell that he didn't feel very good about it. They wanted to auction off all his possessions, tear him to pieces. The women called him a murderer, a robber, and a swindler. The brides howled: "What did you do with our dowries?" and wailed as if it were Yom Kippur. Todrus had a dog as big as a lion, and Getzel had gotten one the image of it. He brought the dog with him, and both animals tried to devour each other. Finally Getzel whispered something to Todrus; they locked themselves in a room and stayed there for three hours. During that time the creditors almost tore the house down. When Todrus came out he was as pale as death; Getzel was perspiring. He called out to the men: "Don't make such a racket! I'll pay all the debts. I have taken over the business from Todrus." They didn't believe their own ears. Who puts a healthy head into a sickbed? But Getzel took out his purse, long and deep, just like Todrus'. However, Todrus' was empty, and this one was full of bank notes. Getzel began to pay on the spot. To some he paid off the whole debt and to others an advance, but they all knew that he was solvent. Todrus looked on silently. Fogel, his wife, came to herself and smiled. The girls came out of their hiding places. Even the dogs made peace; they began to sniff each other and wag their tails. Where had Getzel put together so much cash? As a rule, a merchant has all his money in his business. But Getzel kept on paying He had stopped stammering and he spoke now as if he really were Todrus. Todrus had a bookkeeper whom they called the secretary, and he brought out the ledgers. Meanwhile, Todrus had become his old self again. He told jokes, drank brandy, and offered a drink to Getzel. They toasted *l'chayim*.

To make a long story short, Getzel took over everything. Todrus Broder left for Lublin with his wife and daughters, and it seemed that he had moved out altogether. Even the maids went with him. But then why hadn't he taken his featherbeds with him? By law, no creditor is allowed to take these. For three months there was no word of them. Getzel had already become the boss. He went here, he went there, he rode in Todrus' carriage with Todrus' coachman. After three months Fogel came back with her daughters. It was hard to recognize her. They asked her about her husband and she answered simply, "I have no more husband." "Some misfortune, God forbid?" they asked, and she answered no, that they had been divorced.

There is a saying that the truth will come out like oil on water. And so it happened here. In the three hours that Getzel and Todrus had been locked up in the office, Todrus had transferred everything to Getzel—his house, his estate, all of his possessions, and on top of it all, his wife. Yes, Fogel married Getzel. Getzel gave her a marriage contract for ten thousand rubles and wrote up a house — it was actually Todrus' — as estate. For the daughters he put away large dowries.

The turmoil in the town was something awful. If you weren't in Zamosc then, you have no idea how excited a town can become. A book could be written about it. Not one book, ten books! Even the Gentiles don't do such things. But that was Todrus. As long as he could, he acted like a king. He gambled, he lost, and then it was all over; he disappeared. It seems he had been about to go to jail. The squires might have murdered him. And in such a situation, what won't a man do to save his life? Some people thought that Getzel had known everything in advance and that he had plotted it all. He had managed a big loan for Todrus and had lured him into his snare. No one would have thought that Getzel was so clever. But how does the saying go? If God wills, a broom will shoot.

Todrus' girls soon got married. Dishke went to live with her in-laws in Lemberg. Fogel almost never showed her face outside. Todrus's grounds had a garden with a pavilion, and she sat there all summer. In the winter she hid inside the house. Todrus Broder had vanished like a stone in the water. Some held that he was in Cracow, others that he had gone to Warsaw. Still others said that he had converted and had married a rich squiress. Who can understand such a man? If a Jew is capable of selling his wife in such a way, he is no longer a Jew. Fogel had loved him with a great love, and it was clear that she had consented to everything just to save him. In the years that followed, nobody could say a word against Todrus to her. On Rosh Hashona and Yom Kippur she stood in her pew in the women's section at the grating and she didn't utter a single word to anybody. She remained proud.

Getzel took over Todrus' language and his manners. He even became taller, or perhaps he put lifts into his boots. He became a bosom friend of the squires. It was rumored that he drank forbidden wine with them. After he had stopped stammering, he had begun to speak Polish like one of them.

Dishke never wrote a word to her father. About Todrus' daughters I heard that they didn't have a good end. One died in childbirth. Another was supposed to have hanged herself. But Getzel became Todrus and I saw it happen with my own eyes, from beginning to end. Yes, mimicking is forbidden. If you imitate a person, his fate is passed on to you. Even with a shadow one is not allowed to play tricks. In Zamosc there was a young man who used to play with his shadow. He would put his hands together so that the shadow on the wall would look like a buck with horns, eating and butting. One night the shadow jumped from the wall and gored the young man as if with real horns. He got such a butt that he had two holes in his forehead afterwards. And so it happened here.

Getzel did not need other people's money. He had enough. But suddenly he began to borrow from widows and orphans. Anywhere he could find credit, he did, and he paid high interest. He didn't have to renovate his mill, either. The flour was as white as snow. But he built a new mill and put in new mill-stones. His old and devoted miller had died, and Getzel hired a new miller who had long moustaches, a former bailiff. This one swindled him right and left. Getzel also bought an estate from a nobleman even though he already had an estate with a stable and horses. Before this he had kept to his Jewishness, but now he began to dress like a fop. He stopped coming to the synagogue except on High Holy Days. As if this wasn't enough, Getzel started a brewery and he sowed hops for beer. He didn't need any of this. Above all, it cost him a fortune. He imported machines, God knows from where, and they made such a noise at night that the neighbors couldn't sleep. Every few weeks he made a trip to Warsaw. Who can guess what really happened to him? Ten enemies don't do as much harm to a man as he does to himself. One day the news spread that Getzel was bankrupt. My dear friends, he didn't have to go bankrupt; it was all an imitation of Todrus. He had taken over the other's bad luck. People streamed from every street and broke up his window-panes. Getzel had no imitator.

No one wanted his wife; Fogel was older than Getzel by a good many years. He assured everyone that he wouldn't take anything away from them. But they beat him up. A squire came and put his pistol to Getzel's forehead in just the same way as the other had to Todrus.

To make a long story short, Getzel ran away in the middle of the night. When he left, the creditors took over and it turned out that there was more than enough for everybody. Getzel's fortune was worth God knows how much. So why had he run away? And where had he gone? Some said that the whole bankruptcy was nothing but a sham. There was supposed to have been a woman involved, but what does an old man want with a woman? It was all to be like Todrus. Had Todrus buried himself alive, Getzel would have dug his own grave. The whole thing was the work of demons. What are demons if not imitators? And what does a mirror do? This is why they cover a mirror when there is a corpse in the house. It is dangerous to see the reflection of the body.

Every piece of property Getzel had owned was taken away. The creditors didn't leave as much as a scrap of bread for Fogel. She went to live in the poor-house. When this happened I was no longer in Zamosc. But may my enemies have such an old age as they say Fogel had. She lay down on a straw mattress and she never got up again. It was said that before her death she asked to be inscribed on the tombstone not as the wife of Getzel, but as the wife of Todrus. Nobody even bothered to put up a stone. Over the years the grave became overgrown and was finally lost.

What happened to Getzel? And what happened to Todrus? No one knew. Somebody thought they might have met somewhere, but for what purpose? Todrus must have died. Dishke tried to get a part of her father's estate, but nothing was left. A man should stay what he is. The troubles of the world come from mimicking. Today they call it fashion. A charlatan in Paris invents a dress with a train in front and everybody wears it. They are all apes, the whole lot of them.

I could also tell you a story about twins, but I wouldn't dare to talk about it at night. They had no choice. They were two bodies with one soul. Both sisters died within a single day, one in Zamosc and the other in Kovle. Who knows? Perhaps one sister was real and the other was her shadow?

I am afraid of a shadow. A shadow is an emeny. When it has the chance, it takes revenge.

Meyer Levin

CHICAGO, AMERICA

> The author of the best sellers *Compulsion* and *Eva* has
> been writing with honesty and energy ever since his
> major novel *The Old Bunch* was published in 1937. His
> latest novel, *The Stronghold*, is his fifteenth and deals,
> as so much of his work does, with Jewish life. He now
> makes his home in Israel.
> There are many stories about the experience of grow-
> ing up Jewish in this country in the days when the proc-
> ess involved outright encounters with anti-Semites and
> violence but this seemed to us one of the most forthright
> and powerful of the genre.

When you saw the big fellows, the Italians, standing talking
together by the saloon, or in front of the poolroom, or going back
inside the place to a secret room in back there, they were the
Black Hand. Harry was sure of it. In the back room of the barber-
shop, too. In blood secrecy. They could murder you or rob you or
cut you up and nobody could do anything because the Black
Hand was all-powerful, even a policeman was no good against it.
If you opened your mouth your tongue would be cut out.

Paulo said so. Maybe Paulo's big brother Attilio was a Black
Hand and knew the secrets. When Paulo's father couldn't pay the
rent for the flat upstairs, Harry's father, from the back door of
their own rooms behind the print-shop, would watch the Italians
going up and down. He would mutter, but he would not bother
them. Even Harry's father was afraid of what the Black Hand
could do to you.

But something even more powerful that could do things to you
was from inside the church on Taylor Street. Even the Black
Hand was afraid of the church and the priests.

Bushwah. There was no such thing as God. Especially theirs.

But if not, then what did they do in there in the church? The
nuns with their angel faces and voices? The priests in their long
black skirts?

Aw, who's afraid of them? They're just spaghettis.

Sometimes when he was making a delivery for the shop, and he had to pass the church, Harry lingered even as he hurried. Just to catch if anything was going on there in their church.

The rope cut into his fingers; a printing package was always heavy, the paper was heavy. He was supposed to take a street-car, delivering, and only walk on the way back, but if the package was for Simon's Clothing Sale or some other customer on Halsted Street he usually saved the car-fare, lugging the package on foot. The handbills banged against his knees, and the rope cut into his fingers. He was saving. Not to buy anything, but to have five dollars. Then he would see. He would see how it felt to be rich. And after that maybe he would buy something with the money.

Once, right in front of the door of the church, Harry set down the package, to change hands. Two Italian women came out, and as the door slowly closed he saw candlelight inside, and the highest ceiling he had ever imagined, and all shining white and gold-trimmed pillars and arches.

Right near the church was a store for church things, long candles that they bought just to burn up, and crosses—that was Jesus Christ on the cross, and the painted blood was where the nails were stuck in him. And there was a handkerchief with very sad eyes.

Somehow Harry could never look at Jesus on those crosses. He got all hot and crawly and angry inside. He wanted to yell, It's a lie!

Exactly what, he didn't know. But it was a lie that the Jews did it to him.

This Friday afternoon there were four packages to deliver, and Harry couldn't carry them all at one time. His big brother Zalman was trying to finish a press job for Friday night. It was always like that at the end of the week, trying to clear everything away for *Shabos*. Because Ma always wanted to make Shabos, even if they weren't religious.

The packages were for the *shul* on Maxwell Street, some advertising for the *Pesach* holiday, and the printing had to be at the shul before the sun went down.

"Take Paulo the Italian, give him a nickel to help you," his mother said.

So they started out, the two of them with the packages. It was still daylight. Harry went up to the front of the shul, and Paulo waited on the street, not sure he could come in. Harry opened the door. Nobody inside. "You wait here," he told Paulo. "I'll go in back and see if I can find somebody." Even if his father didn't believe in all that stuff, still, he felt funny taking an Italian inside a shul.

Past the rows of benches, there was a door. And three steps down, in a passageway, he ran into the *shamos,* the sexton, a real old-style one with a long coat and a yellow beard and yellow broken teeth. The shamos started scolding him right away. "Why so late? Already yesterday it should have been here! What's the matter with your father? An *apikorus*—a scoffer—an atheist he can be, but a job is a job!" Talking, talking, the shamos came to the front of the shul with him, opened the door, where Paulo waited with the packages, and said to bring the packages inside.

Paulo was wise already that Jews kept their hats on, so he didn't give himself away as they lugged in the packages. The shamos switched on some lights. It was not a large shul; besides the benches there was only a little platform at the end, with a cabinet with an embroidered shawl over it, and a little gas-light burning in front of it.

The shamos took the packages, saying he couldn't give the money as he had already put all the money away for Shabos.

"My pa said I can't leave the job without the money, I have to bring back the money or the job," Harry declared.

The shamos spit and swore, what kind of Jews were they, not trusting a shul, but Harry said it wasn't dark yet and nobody had to come to *davven* so it wasn't yet Shabos. "He is telling me!" the shamos shrieked. "The son of an apikorus is telling me when is Shabos and when is not Shabos!" But Harry hung onto the packages, feeling ashamed because all this was in front of an Italian. Finally the shamos grumbled and went away. Harry guessed it was to get the money.

The moment he was gone, Paulo asked, "Well, where is it?"

"What?"

"What you got in your church. Where is it?" Paulo kept turning his head, as if expecting to see some kind of secret magic.

"It's in there," Harry said, indicating the embroidered shawl. "Behind there."

Paulo started toward the cabinet.

"You can't touch it! Your hand will fall off because you're a *goy.*"

Paulo looked at him, with that uncertain smile. Still, he didn't touch the shawl. "What's behind there?" he asked.

"It's a Torah. It's got the holy words written in it."

He knew holy was the bunk, but just because of the wop something inside him wanted the power to be there. And even if it was the bunk, his mother kept Shabos and kept kosher. She said it was because she was used to it, and not because she believed God would punish her if she made a mistake with the dishes.

They moved together, closer to the curtain. There was no sign of the shamos. Harry had a crazy feeling it was like peeking under a lady's skirts.

Paulo was nervy. He pulled the curtain aside and took a quick look. It was the long round things like big rolling-pins, wrapped in red velvet. That was where the Jewish secrets were. Only a rabbi could touch them.

"Inside is writing," Harry said. "You couldn't even understand. It's not even in Jewish. It's in Hebrew."

"*Gazlunim*—thieves!" From behind, the shamos came screeching at them. "Don't touch it! Bandits! Bums!" Seizing Harry by the shoulder, he slapped him hard in the face, and demanded, "To *cheder*, you go? To learn? What kind of Jewish boys are being raised? *Atheistim!* He shoved the money into Harry's hand. "*Gerout! Gerout!*"

Walking back on Taylor Street, they talked of the powers of their Gods. "If the Jewish God is so strong," Paulo said, "why do Jews always get beat up?"

"Yah?" Harry said. "What good is your wop God? Your old man don't even make enough to eat."

"A Jew can never be president," Paulo said.

"Yah? Did you ever hear of a wop being president?"

"You ain't got anything in there," Paulo said. "A church is ten times as rich, with statues all covered with gold."

"That's where they got your money," Harry said.

"A church protects you," Paulo said. "You can't do anything to a Catholic, or you get it!"

Suddenly Harry saw the connection. "They got the Black Hand," he said.

"Naw!" Paulo wouldn't give anything away. "That's different."

Harry demanded directly, "Do you believe in the church and God and all that bushwah?"

"The old lady takes us to the church," Paulo said. "Sure. Christ is God. I'm a Catholic."

"Yah. They put you in lace dresses like sissies."

"You just say that and I'll tell Pasquale you said that and they'll take a knife to you and you'll never be a man."

It was like paying off one for one when they went inside the church. Paulo had dared with the shul, so Harry had to dare with the church. Besides, going inside with Paulo was like a truce when you can go into the enemy side.

The church was very big, with the ceiling so high you could hardly see the top. The colors were red plush and gold, and there was a beautiful big statue of a lady holding a baby, and there were real hand-painted paintings, Paulo said. Then, way up in front, was their Jesus hung on a cross. He was as big as a real man, and Harry stopped short on seeing him, because he was the color of real live people, not a statue or dead.

Instead of the anger he always felt about it, and even though he knew none of it was the fault of the Jews, Harry now felt shame. Coming into their place somehow made him feel ashamed, sneaky. And everything was so rich. He couldn't look at Paulo.

Here, too, the whole place was empty. Paulo walked away down to a railing, in front, and there behind the railing was a table covered with a gold-embroidered cloth, and on the table were silver cups and things.

Then Paulo motioned to him, "Hey, c'mon." Paulo went through a little side door into a small room. Harry was scared to follow, but scared to stay alone where he was. He slipped after Paulo into the closet-room. It was almost like an office. And it was not so scarey any more. There were cabinets with glass windows and he could see all the lace dresses that the priests sometimes wore on the streets on Sunday when they had their religious parades. And there was a table with a big silver cup.

"It's okay," Paulo whispered. "This is where the kids that wait on them in the mass, the altar boys, they come here to dress up." He lifted the silver cup. "It's the blood of Christ in here," he said.

"Aw, that can't be."

"Sure. That's the sacrament."

"How can it be blood?" Harry said. "How could there be blood enough for all the churches in all the world all the time?" Paulo was silent. Looking at the goof, Harry didn't feel ashamed any more, but excited. He could prove the whole thing. He could prove the whole thing was a fake and then it would be sure proof that the Jews didn't really do anything to their Jesus. If he could prove it wasn't blood then the whole thing was a fake.

"It's dago red," he said. "It's the wine, that's all." And he could see that Paulo wasn't really sure. "You don't believe in all that bushwah?"

"When you take the sacrament," Paulo said doubtfully, "the priest says that's when it turns into the blood. Then you can pray for anything."

Suddenly a blind anger came over Harry. How could anyone be so dumb? How could they all be so dumb? He stuck his finger into the goblet.

"Watch out!" Paulo cried, in a ghostly voice. "Something'll happen to you!"

Harry pulled out his finger, wet and red. He put it to his mouth. "Vino," he said. He dipped it again and pushed it to Paulo's lips. He felt Paulo's tongue touch his finger.

The two of them in the half darkness, alone, were secret conspirators, explorers fallen into a strange jungle. "All right, you want to know if it's blood," Harry said. "Gimme your knife."

Paulo didn't think he'd have the nerve. Paulo thought of him as a scaredy sheenie.

As Paulo handed him the opened blade, Harry knew that he had it over Paulo for once for sure; he was the tougher. "What you gonna do?" Paulo asked.

Harry pressed the blade point against his finger. To himself he said, "Who's a coward?" and he was surprised that he didn't flinch or even feel the cut. The blood came, a bubble on his finger. He put the finger against Paulo's mouth. There. Taste it. That's real blood. Now you know it's bushwah, that stuff. It's bunk. "The whole thing is bunk," he declared triumphantly.

Paulo was staring at him with that dumb dago look. From that moment, Harry knew he would always be the boss between them.

And even more. He could boss the whole world. Nobody could bunk him. He had done a terrible thing and what had happened to him? Nothing.

Paulo was silent. He put back the cup.

Harry felt a little dizzy now, over his own bravery. They had been lucky, nobody had come. Maybe the priests were all eating supper.

They went out, Paulo showing him the back way, as though he

[133]

didn't feel like going through the church again. They walked around the outside of the church, and just as they got to the front, a bunch of wallios were passing. Big guys, from the last grade in school.

It was nearly dark, and Harry turned his face as though he were trying to see something, the other way. Maybe none of them knew him. At the same moment he felt a piercing throb in his cheek, as if a hot wire had been stabbed through there, a pain so sharp that he put his hand up to his jaw.

The movement must have attracted their attention. The gang of them came to a stop, and lingered by the gate. There were four or five of them, and Harry knew the big one, that was Vincenzo, the biggest guy in the school. He could break your arm by twisting it behind your back. He smoked, he was smoking now, and giving the kids that tailed after him a little pull on the butt. But maybe Vincenzo didn't know who he was? Maybe Vincenzo didn't even know he was a Jew.

Yet in the same moment, Harry knew one thing to do. He slipped the money out of his pocket; it was in a special little purse he always carried for the job money. He stuffed the purse quickly into Paulo's pocket, whispering, "Here, you keep hold of this." There was no time to switch his own private money which was still loose in the pocket.

As he and Paulo came to the gate, the gang was watching them. But they even got through the gate and were on the sidewalk. Then Vincenzo stuck out two fingers at them, like a pistol. "Who you for?" he demanded.

A wave of relief swept through Harry. Because it was only the password for the big election. "D'Angeli for Alderman!" he called out. And, "D'Angeli!" Paulo said.

Vincenzo eyed them suspiciously. "Sure. D'Angeli!" Harry repeated. "He's Italian. The hell with the Irish!" But instantly he knew he had said too much. Vincenzo grabbed him by the wrist, "You're a sheenie!" Already, Harry felt his arm twisted behind him in the terrible grip.

"I ain't!" he gasped.

"You! You bastard Jew, prove it!"

The whole gang was around him, pushing and tough. A couple more guys grabbed him, while out of them came that special laugh that was for sheenies. They played out their knives. "Don't!

[134]

don't!" he gasped. He would never be a man. They would laugh, laugh. "I'm his cousin!" he yelled, grabbing Paulo.

"Sheenie Jew bastard you lie!"

Another yelled, "He was spying in the church!"

"What were you doing in the holy church!"

Two of them grabbed Paulo, and Vincenzo turned on him. "What'd you take him inside the church for?"

"I'm his cousin! I'm his cousin!" Harry gasped.

"All right. Say something in Italian," a guy with a blade out commanded.

Another one laughed, "Say a prayer."

He babbled, "Madonna mia, Madonna mia—"

With a wild roar they were on him. A hand smacked across his mouth. He felt he was being torn to pieces. He was reaching, trying to wriggle out, and all the time Paulo was backing away, backing away. Vincenzo was yelling, "What'd you take him inside for? You let a sheenie Jew spit on our Holy Virgin Mother, what's the matter with you?"

"Aw, he didn't do anything," Paulo mumbled, almost crying.

In the twisted scramble, all of them on top of him, Harry just then tore loose, scuttling like a bug to get away, and was almost free when Vincenzo, holding Paulo with one hand, grabbed him with the other, and held him up like a rat, and spat on him and laughed.

"What'll we do with this sheenie?" Vincenzo put it to the gang.

They began pushing and kicking Harry along the street. Paulo just stood back, with his face like he was going to bust out crying. Desperately, Harry gasped, "Paulo, call my big brother!" Maybe that would scare them off, though he knew in his heart it was no use. He didn't have a big brother that would come roaring with a baseball bat. Zalman would maybe go tell a policeman, and after that—. Harry saw himself found in the alley all cut to pieces, a rat that called cops. "Paulo! Get Attilio! Get your big brother Attilio!"

"Oh, yah?" They grabbed Paulo too, and shoved him along, with his arm, too, twisted behind his back. Now the prisoners were turned off into an alley, and Harry at once knew where they were headed for. It was the shed behind the fruit store, the shed he had so often passed in dead envy, it was their secret meeting-place, and with a strange elation within his terror, he knew he would at last be inside, even if he had to die there.

[135]

They had some trick of opening it, he couldn't tell exactly, but a plank was pushed aside and someone put his hand behind. At that moment, as Harry tried to catch onto the trick, his arm was given an extra twist, and tears blinded his eyes, and he let out a yell. A foot landed in his crotch, and he fell onto the dirt inside the door, cutting his hands on stones.

There was a candle in a tin can, and he could see a skull and crossbones outlined in black, burned into the planks of the shed. Vincenzo was seated on a crate, and more of the gang kept coming in. Pasquale came in, he was in their gang too, and when he saw Harry he let out a yell, "You got him! Hey, lemme have him!"

"Naw," Vincenzo ruled. And turning to the whole crowd, "What shall we do with this sheenie, he was caught doing it in the church."

"I didn't!" Harry screeched.

"Shut up!" He got a terrible kick. All around, he could see them playing with their switch knives. Now they would do it to him. . . . That's what they had him here for. He could see it in their faces. He heard it in the way they laughed. He was trapped.

"Hey look!" Pasquale yelled. "Look at the scared sheenie! Ya ya Ikey—!"

They roared and jumped around him.

Paulo watched and grinned. He could kill Paulo.

And then way inside of him something wild, sure, was telling him there was a way to win. Even when they had you on the edge of the cliff there was a way to be smarter than the villains. And the wild something that was quivering in Harry told him that this was the moment, this was the exact time to fool them, and save himself.

"Honest fellows, honest I didn't do anything. I went to see the priest!" he blurted out. "I want to—honest, I don't believe in being a Jew, I want to be a Catholic."

For a second they stopped. Then Pasquale jumped on him. "You shut up you dirty Jew bastard I'll kill you."

"Honest! honest!" he shouted. "I wanted to ask the priest, I swear by Jesus Christ."

As the awful words came out of his mouth, he wasn't sure but maybe something would happen to him. Something still might strike him where he lay. Or they would kill him straight for using those words.

A couple of them made a move toward him, but he looked

hard at Pasquale, and he saw the big dago wasn't sure any more. The other one, Vincenzo, was standing up now like a judge.

"Ask Paulo!" Harry insisted. "Ask Paulo if I didn't ask him to take me—"

From the floor, Pasquale picked up two sticks; he crossed them and thrust them at Harry. "Kiss the cross!" he commanded. Vincenzo was pulling at a new cigarette—maybe now they would brand him with the burning cigarette? Maybe they would cut a cross on his skin, with their knives—a cross on his chest. Would he be able to hide it, at home?

The sticks were against his mouth. He kissed.

Dark, behind, Harry felt the reproachful eyes of his mother as though she stood watching. She would kill them all, but she was sore at him, too. Always, forever, this would be in her. Maybe she really believed in Moses and all that. But his father didn't believe in God, so why should he care what he did now? Still, to kiss a cross. Aw, bushwah. So what if he did? They made him.

"Say, The Jews killed Christ. The Jews are Christ killers."

That was easy, he had already done that once when they caught him in a corner of the schoolyard. "The Jews are Christ killers," Harry said.

"Say, Kill the Jews!"

Harry spat on them. In his mind he spat on them. Fangoo, the dirty wops. But he was fooling them. They would let him go. "Kill the Jews!" he repeated.

"You lousy kike punk you don't mean it." They were suddenly all over him again, punching him, their shoes in his guts. "I mean it, I mean it, kill the Jews, oh Jesus, oh Jesus!" he shrieked. Why didn't cops come? Why didn't his brother come looking for him because he hadn't got home, and find him here?

Vincenzo was standing close in front of him now. "Prove you mean it."

"I'll do anything you want." They were all closing in on him again, and he heard himself bawling. "Whataya want, lemme alone, lemme go, whataya want!" And with a great sob he pulled his own money out of his pocket. "Here! Take my money! Here!"

"Hey! The sheenie got money!" Pasquale shouted, and Harry let the change be torn from his hand, there was over a dollar, he knew, his own personal money. And at the same time, the gloating was inside him, for he had fooled them again, he had given the job money to Paulo, they would never get it.

[137]

Howling was all around him; they grabbed at his pants, tore his pockets looking for more money, then they were off of him and fighting with each other. Vincenzo was shoving amongst them, swearing and taking nickels and dimes from everybody, and then in a wild roar, nearly knocking down the walls, they were all gone, rushing out with his money.

Harry pulled his pants together. His stocking was torn, and there were scratches bleeding on his arms and face. He was sure he had a black eye. But he had got out of it. He had fooled them, and saved the real money.

Paulo came up to him. Paulo was hit too, but Harry didn't care, the dirty wop traitor. Paulo was trying to hand him the little purse, but Harry said, "Naw, you keep it till we get home." No use taking any chances.

From the doorway they looked carefully down the alley. Then they ran across and climbed a fence and got into the back yard of a house, and crossed through to their own street.

As they got to the house, Harry said. "All right, give it to me." Paulo gave him the purse. He couldn't look at Paulo and Paulo couldn't look at him. Paulo was going upstairs. Harry opened the purse and found a coin. "Here, a nickel I owe you for the job," he said.

The wop took the money.

"My God, what did they do to him!" Harry's mother shouted as he came inside the door. She seized him as if to make sure he was alive, feeling his arms, his body, then tenderly touching his bruises. "Wild beasts! Even in America! The *maloch ha-movis*—the Angel of Death—should take them, in acid they should burn! Savages they are, not people! To have to live among them—!" She turned on the old man, as if he were to blame for living here. Then she demanded, "Who did it? How did it happen? I'll tell the police! Zalman!" she shouted at her older son, "Go to the police!" At the same time she pulled Harry to the sink and started to wash him. He jerked away. "Ow! It hurts!" He felt tears coming. Somehow, now he was in the house, his last strength was gone. His lousy big brother sitting there, not even caring.

"They jumped me, some dagos by the church," he sobbed.

"A boy can't even go in the streets!" his mother cried accusingly at the old man. "*Oi! golos!* I told you he was too small to go with the packages!" And touching Harry again, "They should put them all in jail!"

[138]

His father came close, shaking his head over Harry's wounds. "By the church?" he repeated. "Paulo was with you. What did they attack you for?"

Now he could even say that all of the job money had been taken. But if he did, they wouldn't ever know how he had fooled that dirty gang, how he had got the money safe. "They took my money," Harry said. "Everything I had in my pockets."

"No!" Zalman cried. "That's robbery! It's not just kids fighting. They can be arrested!"

"A lawyer we have!" said his father.

"They paid you the money from the shul, and the gazlunim took it?" his mother asked.

"They tried to but I fooled them. I gave it to Paulo to hide. They got all my own money, they searched me." With the words, the whole thing came over him again, the knives open, the hands grabbing him, the cross at his mouth. In a burst he started to bawl. He didn't even hear the whole family marveling that he had fooled the gang of murderers and saved the money.

"You see! a head on him! a Jew learns!" his mother gloated.

"How much did they take from you, Harry?" his father asked.

At least he had a right to raise that up a little. "I had over two dollars. Two dollars and a half my own money."

"Give him!" his mother said. But his father had already reached into his pocket.

"A plague on them, a plague on every one of them, and their fathers and mothers, the wild beasts!" his mother cursed. "Who was it, Harry? Do you know their names? Can you recognize them?"

Harry said he knew them, some big guys from school. He told the whole attack now, the knives, the shack in the alley, and even the names, Pasquale and Vincenzo, the Black Hand he was sure, and he knew who some of the other kids were, one was named Joe. They were in last grade. They were almost as big as Zalman.

"Go start with the Italians. The Black Hand. They'll kill you!" Zalman said.

Harry told all, in the rush of words, except about the church, the cross. Except about yelling, Kill the Jews. That was his own part of it. Some things you did, you could never tell anybody. Now he had started a life of his own.

[139]

Hugh Nissenson

THE AMERICAN

> Hugh Nissenson's stories have appeared in *Harper's,*
> *Commentary, Esquire, Playboy* and other leading periodi-
> cals. "The American" was later included in *A Pile of*
> *Stones,* a collection of his short stories published in 1965.
> We chose this story because it deals with the wide gap
> between the experiences and aspirations of the immigrants
> to New York's lower East Side in the days before World
> War I with a compassion that manages rigorously to ex-
> clude both nostalgia and fatuous sentimentality.

Hester Street, number 225. The house where my cousin Shulim
and his parents lived has long since been torn down. A furniture
warehouse stands in its place. Yet, sometimes, even now, at the
age of sixty-five, he will go and gaze at the spot where they
rented a three room cold water flat in the winter of 1913, after
moving from the Brownsville section of Brooklyn, to try their
luck on Manhattan's Lower East Side.

"Actually, it was two rooms and a kitchen," he says. "Freezing,
with one toilet out in the hall for the whole third floor. It was a
terrible winter. A week after we moved in, the pipes froze.
Pfew!"

With his hands in his pockets, puffing on a cigar, he'll spend an
hour or so strolling up and down the block before he grabs a cab
to go home. He's a retired pattern-maker with a pension from the
I.L.G.W.U., who lives with his daughter on Madison Avenue and
85th Street. She worries about his staying out late, but once in a
while he makes an extra stop at Greene Street, where he and his
father worked in a dress factory for six dollars apiece a week.

As he describes it, they faced each other across a wide table,
sewing sleeves on Singers that dripped oil into wooden dishes
they held on their laps. The vibrating needle reverberated in the
boy's head. At night, he sometimes dreamed that his numbed
fingers slipped and were pierced to the bone.

[140]

Saturday, the Jewish Sabbath, was the only day they had off, the only time the boy seemed to be able to think. In the mornings and evenings, he and his father went to Temple Israel, on Orchard Street, to pray. The Ark, with its purple curtain and gilt lions holding a bronze tablet of the Law in their paws, filled the boy with an inexpressible joy. In spite of everything, he knew that there was a God, a merciful Lord of Creation, who had granted him and his family a chance to come to America, and begin a new life. They had fled Odessa in 1906, after a pogrom. Things were rough in the States, but they were going to get better, the boy was convinced of it. Next year, or the year after that, if all went well, he planned to enter night school and get a high school education. With an education, in America, anything was possible. He could become a clerk or a salesman, or maybe some day save up enough money to go into some kind of business for himself.

Then, one Saturday, at noon, when the morning service in the synagogue was over, and they were about to go home, his father suddenly gasped and grabbed his arm.

"What is it, Papa? What's the matter?" Shulim asked.

"Nothing. Why?"

"You're as pale as a ghost."

"It's nothing," his father repeated, sitting back down on the bench. The color was beginning to come back to his face, but the expression of stupefied horror in his moist, dark brown eyes remained the same. What—or whom had he seen? The boy looked up. Walking up the aisle to his right was a little man with a greying reddish beard.

"Who's that?" Shulim whispered.

"Where?" his father asked. Straightening up, he folded his prayer shawl and led his son out into the street. The red-bearded man was gone.

"Do you know him?" asked Shulim.

"Who?" said his father. But when they got home, and sat down to dinner, he leaned across the table and announced to his wife in a trembling voice: "Moscowitz is here."

"Moscowitz?"

"From Hamburg. The boat."

They exchanged glances over their steaming bowls of soup, but refused to say anything more. So that was it, thought Shulim, picking up his spoon. This Moscowitz was someone his parents knew from the ship that had brought them all from Hamburg to New York. Then what was all the fuss about, the boy wondered.

According to what he heard around the neighborhood the following week, Moscowitz was a respectable and charitable widower who lived alone on the next block, supported by his son, who had a job as a traveling salesman with a sweater firm uptown. As a matter og fact, it was the old man who had donated the gilt lions for the Ark, in memory of a daughter who had died in Europe on the way to the States. And sure enough, there he was, at the next Saturday's morning service, seated in the place of honor, on the front bench, next to the east wall. His beard waggled when he prayed. So his son had made good!

Sweating over his sewing machine the next day, Shulim glanced up at his father's bony, yellow face. At the age of fifty, his beard was completely grey. But Moscowitz was retired. How had his son gotten his start? Had he gone to school, or gotten the job with the sweater firm on his own—beginning as a stock boy, perhaps, and working his way up? By now he was probably driving his own car, and making seventy-five or a hundred dollars a week. Shulim tried to imagine what a job like that would be like. It would mean traveling all over the States in his own Ford, or maybe even a Maxwell, or Pierce-Arrow. He would wear starched white shirts, a clean one every day, with detachable celluloid collars and bow ties. At the fancy hotels where he stopped, the bellhops would carry his sample cases. But best of all, his father would be able to quit work. He pictured him reading the Yiddish paper in bed, with his morning glass of tea, and making a donation to the synagogue of new silver bells for the Scrolls of the Law. Bells? Handles, too, made entirely of silver, or a stained glass window, inscribed at the bottom with his name. The problem was, how to begin?

The foreman heaped another pile of cotton dresses on the table before him and he went back to work. By evening, he had it all figured out. Moscowitz's son would get him a job. If the sweater house had hired one boy from Hester Street, then why not another, willing to work just as hard, for the chance to learn the business, and prove his worth?

The boy counted the days until Saturday. The only trouble was that when his father saw Moscowitz in the synagogue, striding up the aisle with his ivory-handled cane, he averted his eyes.

[142]

"Yes, all right, I knew him," he finally admitted after dinner at home.

"His son too?" asked Shulim.

"Yes, his son too."

"What was he like?"

"It was a long time ago. He was a little boy."

"Was he smart?"

"His father thought so."

"As smart as me?"

"I suppose so. I tell you I can't remember. He was seasick the whole trip. Your mother soaked bread in coffee and tried to feed him, but he couldn't hold it down. Why do you ask?"

"They say he has a very good job."

"Do they?" said his father. A heavy smoker, except today, on the Sabbath, when it was forbidden for a pious Jew to light a fire, he sucked on a wooden match and closed his eyes.

"Do you think the old man would remember you after all these years?" Shulim asked.

"Your father's exhausted. Let him sleep," said his mother, coming in from the kitchen, and sitting down. The boy stared in silence at the plaster peeling from the ceiling above his head. With the rat holes in the woodwork stuffed with rags, the room had never been as hateful to him as it was now. It was freezing. He could see his own breath when he spoke. Old man Moscowitz lived in number 321, a building that had hot water and steam heat.

"Why doesn't Papa speak to him?" Shulim asked his mother. "Maybe his son could get me a job."

"Keep your voice down," she told him, a finger to her lips.

The weeks passed. Now, whenever he saw Moscowitz in the synagogue—as an additional honor, the old man was invariably called third for the reading of the Law—Shulim was tempted to take matters into his own hands, and introduce himself. The rumor was that his son was about to return to New York from an extended selling trip to the Midwest.

"I'll speak to him then," Shulim decided.

But a few days later, when he caught a glimpse of the salesman getting out of his car on Orchard Street, the boy discovered that he had lost his nerve. It was nine o'clock at night. He had just finished work, and he was ashamed of his oil-stained pants

WILLIAM STEINEL

and the threadbare sweater his mother had patched at the elbows with squares of red cotton snipped from a quilt. He
stepped into the doorway of a liquor store to watch. It was
Moscowitz's son, all right; there was no mistaking him. Taller
than his father, and fatter, with a ruddy face, he had the same
pale blue eyes and thinning red hair. He even carried the same
kind of cane. There was a girl with him, hanging on his arm, who
wore a feather boa, and a dark blue coat. The salesman whispered in her ear, and she laughed.

They disappeared around the corner, and Shulim inspected
the car. It was a new Maxwell, a shiny black four-seater, with a
leather covered cone clutch, and real leather seats. How fast
could it go? Unless he missed his guess, it had a 25 h.p. motor at
least, or maybe even more. The polished steel fenders reflected
the boy's pale, grinning face.

"But why can't you just say hello?" he asked his father as soon
as he got home.

"Because he wouldn't remember me."

"His father would."

"Yes, that's possible."

"Then do it for me," said the boy.

"I can't."

"But why not?"

"Because I have nothing to say to him."

"Well, to begin with, you could talk over old times. Hamburg and the boat."

"Impossible."

"Why?"

"Because that's where he left her."

"Who?"

"Moscowitz. The old man."

"No, I mean who did he leave?" asked the boy.

"His daughter."

"I don't understand."

"It's very simple. He had a daughter but he left her behind in Hamburg because she was sick and they wouldn't let her on the boat."

"How do you know?"

"I was there. Yes, I saw it all. It was the night before we sailed. I was up on the deck having a smoke, and there he was with his son and daughter. The girl was in his arms, all wrapped up in a woolen blanket, coughing, and spitting up blood. He carried her all the way from Lublin, her father says, but one look and the captain tells him that it's impossible. Against all the health regulations. She would infect the whole ship, and even if she managed to get to America alive, the authorities there would only send her back."

"Is that true?"

"It's the rule."

"What happened then?"

"They called a doctor. A little German with a blonde beard and a gold watch who took her pulse. 'Two, maybe three months at the most,' he tells them. 'That is, if she's lucky. Probably less.' 'Three months?' says Moscowitz, opening his purse. Eight or ten marks are all he has left, and what's worse, he has no German visa. If he stays in Germany for more than a week, they'll send them all back to Lublin where the girl's mother died of the same thing."

"So he left her just like that?"

"The doctor took her to a charity hospital. 'It's all right, Papa,' she says, when they're loading her on the ambulance. 'I'll wear my green dress.' "

[145]

"What'd she mean?"

"Who knows? She was not out of her mind from the fever. Moscowitz kisses her hand and cries. 'What else could I have done?' he asks me all the way across. 'Go back to Lublin? Do you know what Lublin is like for the Jews? What about my son? Look at him. A strong, healthy boy, absolutely brilliant. Doesn't a boy like that deserve half a chance?' "

The salesman stayed in New York for another week. After work, as exhausted as he was, Shulim found himself roaming the neighborhood looking for the Maxwell. What a car! The advertisements in the newspapers—'The Maxwell; perfectly simple, and simply perfect'—proved him right. It had a 25 h.p. monobloc, side valve engine, and this year, for the first time, it was going to be raced at Indianapolis.

Indianapolis! Would he ever get to see Indianapolis, Des Moines or Chicago now? He crossed Orchard and Ludlow Streets. America was waiting for him. There were vast open spaces and cities to be conquered out there, a fortune to be made by any young man who was willing to work hard, and who knew his stuff. Essex Street. He had read somewhere that in Chicago there were great hotels with marble columns in the lobby, where a traveling salesman could press a button in his room, and be served a steak dinner, on a silver plate, by a waiter dressed in a red jacket and boiled shirt. Where had he read about that? He couldn't remember. On Canal Street, an old drunk with white whiskers, and a gash on his forehead, clotted with blood, brushed up against him, and staggered by, muttering under his breath. In the gutter, a push-cart peddler was seized with a sneezing fit that left him purple in the face. A Jew, obviously. Where was he from? Were his kids going to be push-cart peddlers too? The boy headed home. It was a warmish night, just after a rain. The wet streets were jammed with Jews, Irish and Italians dragging their tired feet, grateful for a breath of fresh air. The plumbing in 225 was still clogged. As he walked up the stairs, the boy thought he heard a rat scuttling on the second landing. It was pitch dark. He leaned against the broken bannister and held his breath. The hallway stank. He was suffocating. It was already past midnight. Tomorrow morning was here. He would be up at five as usual to go to work. What for? What was going to happen to him? Had his parents brought him all that way for nothing?

Next Saturday evening, Moscowitz brought his son to synagogue for the final service of the day. Shulim watched them out of the corner of his eye. As far as he could tell, the gilt lions dedicated to the memory of his sister made no impression on the salesman at all. Perhaps he didn't know the truth. Even when his father was called up to read a portion of the Torah aloud, he looked impatient and bored. Once or twice he yawned behind his hand. When the congregation was called upon to stand, he rose with a groan. No, Shulim decided, it was inconceivable that he knew what had happened to his sister. The boy looked at the Ark which had just been closed, and the gilt lions. Old man Moscowitz resumed his seat, and smiled at his son, who shook his hand. Did the old fool really think he could bribe the Almighty with a pair of plaster lions covered with gold paint? How old was the girl when she had been deserted? Had she been older or younger than her brother? Older, probably, thought Shulim. He imagined her at fifteen or sixteen with red hair, in that green dress that revealed her developing breasts. She hadn't realized what was being done to her. But how did these things work? Had the fever broken before she had died? Supposing one night she had awakened in that strange hospital with a perfectly clear head? Would God permit such a thing? He pictured her trying to speak with the blonde doctor who had come into the room to take her pulse. It was horrible. Wasn't Moscowitz afraid? America, a hundred dollars a week, and a new Maxwell with red leather seats for his son. What good would it all do him when God had His revenge? And what about the salesman himself? Would he be punished too? He was yawning again. On Monday, he would be off on another trip.

It was getting dark. The service was almost finished. The rabbi lit the candles in front of the Ark. In the flickering light, the gilt lions seemed almost alive. Their elongated shadows leaped on the east wall. A warning, thought Shulim, as he and his father stood up to leave. The ravening mouths and curved talons were a warning to Moscowitz of the divine justice that was soon to be meted out.

"What can you expect?" says Shulim. "I was just a kid. Actually, the story has a happy ending. The old man lived to be eighty-one and the last time I heard of the son, in 1924, he was in business for himself, knitwear, and doing very well."

[147]

Burton Bernstein

THE BOSTON
DINNER PARTY

Many of Mr. Bernstein's clever and perceptive stories about Jewish life in New England have appeared in *The New Yorker*, where he is a staff writer. "The Boston Dinner Party" is an amusing yet troubling study of snobbery. It was later included in a book of Mr. Bernstein's stories called *The Grove*.

The wedding invitation, looking as if it had been dipped several times into a dish of quick-drying heavy cream, arrived in the same mail as the note. Typewritten on a plain piece of white paper, the note had a quasi-military formality about it. It was from the bride-to-be's uncle, Endicott Brand, and it announced his intention of giving a dinner party at his Beacon Hill home for Robert Kurtz and Doodie Brand the night before their February wedding. Then, at the bottom of the paper, was Robert's suddenly familiar stark, upright handwriting: "Hope you can make it! Robert."

There was no problem about making it. I'd just have to leave New York for Boston a little earlier on the Saturday in question. The problem was did I want to make it. I had pretty much lost touch with Robert since I had come to New York to work, and the few times I had run into him over the last five years, I was forced to admit to myself that I found him fairly boring—in that special well-let's-examine-all-the-possibilities way an old friend who becomes a lawyer is boring. However, he *was* an old friend, albeit a summer one, and I felt duty-bound to attend every moment of what promised to be his greatest achievement so far.

It occurred to me, while driving over the February gray Wilbur Cross Parkway towards Boston, that as long as I had known Robert Kurtz, he had never been called any name but Robert—never Bob, nor Robbie, nor Bert—just Robert. I spent a long stretch of the remainder of that drive trying to figure out why.

Boston was going under in a sleet storm when I arrived. Snow had fallen earlier and the wet sleet hammering down on top of it like globs of gruel turned the downtown area into a raging sea of porridge. The driving was dangerous and by the time I reached Dave Eisen's apartment house, where I was staying for the week-end, we were already late for the party. Dave Eisen was the third member of the summer triumvirate from the Grove. Dave, like Robert, had elected to stay in Boston after college but, unlike Robert, he had gone to work for his father. Robert was currently employed in his future father-in-law's ancient Boston law firm.

I left my bag at Dave's and together we dashed back to my car. We crept with the almost blind traffic towards Beacon Hill, leaving a symmetrical wake of slush when we could get moving. To make matters worse, many streets leading to Beacon Hill had become one-way since I was last in Boston and I was becoming very confused.

"When is Robert going to become mayor or governor or something and straighten out this damn city?" I asked Dave, once he had pointed out the latest secret formula for driving up the Hill on a slippery evening.

Dave lit a cigarette nervously. He never quite trusted machines, especially when the elements were working against them. "It won't be long after tomorrow," he said through rapid inhalations. "All that's left for him to do now is trap the Irish vote, and he's working on that with the maid he just hired. She's still got the dew of County Cork behind her ears."

With the motor and tires whining wildly, we ground slowly and unsurely up the Hill, traveling sidewards most of the way. "You know," I said, tensely peering out the windshield, "I can believe it, knowing Robert. This wedding business and Doodie and all that perfectly fits the famous Kurtz timetable, doesn't it?"

"Ah, you remember," Dave said. We were almost at the summit of the Hill, so neither of us dared say anything more until we were positive we would make it. Dave involuntarily pushed against the dashboard, as if to help the car along by some human effort. Finally, we arrived at the top and I slipped the car up to what I thought was the curb and considered it parked.

"The Brand house is just over there," Dave said, pointing down a side street. He was breathing more easily now, walking through the heavy slush. "Everything's always worked out just so for that guy," he went on, "ever since he let us in on the schedule of his life back in the Grove. He planned out every step and by God it worked. I'll tell you something: I'm jealous of Robert. Not so much of him, really, but of how he gets whatever he goes after, Exeter, Harvard, the Law School, the Law Review, the Judge Advocate commission in the Army, the proper Boston law firm, and now the perfect girl—Miss Governor's Wife of 1980. My God, it's right out of Marquand at his worst! Things like that aren't supposed to work out so smoothly for nice little boys from the Grove, but for him they do. I've never seen anything like it!"

"You're sounding bitter, Dave," I said teasingly.

Dave slipped slightly in the slush, but regained his balance with a graceless maneuver. "Yeah," he said, when he recovered, "you laugh because you live in New York and don't give a damn, but you should see it up close, like I do. And it's not just sour grapes, either."

We stood before the awesome front door of the Brand house. It was the sort of place I had spent my youth viewing in passing, without ever thinking or caring too much about what was going on inside—at least no more than I would care about what went on inside Martian dwellings. But rapping the brass knocker, I suddenly felt like a child being dared to play a trick-or-treat prank on the local police chief's abode. Dave was ill-at-ease himself in his dark, loose-hung way, as he stamped the sticky snow off his shoes. "Have you ever figured out why nobody—not even us—ever called Robert anything but Robert?" I asked him. Dave bunched together his heavy black eyebrows, flecked with drops of sleet. "Yes," he said. "He never let us."

A white-aproned maid opened the door to reveal a *Holiday* magazine two-page, four-color spread of gracious living in Boston. Even the room's occupants seemed to have struck assigned poses for a non-existent portrait camera. The flawless tableau shattered when Robert rushed over to greet us, as we emerged from the hallway. "Hey," he almost shouted. "Great to see you guys. You made it. *Great!* Come on in and meet everybody." I noted quickly that Robert was much the same as ever: absurdly tall, with that developed Harvardian slouch, those smooth, unclassifiable features, and that constant nonchalant aggressiveness. Just his haircut was a little less boyishly short.

With a controlled gush, Doodie Brand appeared at Robert's side. She was a pert, pretty, sandy blonde girl, whose face, since the first time I had met her years ago, had taken on a curiously mischievous cast, as though she were about to announce to all present that if they cared to observe their shoes, they would find that they had all been given hotfoots. She happily accepted our heartiest congratulations and wishes for the future. "Now Robert and I will have to get you boys hooked next," she said coyly. "I've got two redheaded prospects here tonight—you know, the Armstrong twins. Anyway, come meet the family."

The family included Norman and Mary Brand, Doodie's parents, Chad Brand, her brother and Robert's best man and Harvard classmate, and Endicott Brand, her uncle and our host. Above the roaring fireplace was a commanding portrait of a dour, white-haired lady, obviously the late Mrs. Endicott Brand. A perusal of Norman Brand, while he laboriously pumped my hand, told me he was quite drunk.

"You boys would be Robert's summer friends, right?" Mr. Brand said thickly. He had a kind of sly teddy bear look, which set him apart from his older, more distinguished brother and law partner, Endicott. "I've met Robert's winter friends, but I believe this is the first time I've met his summer ones. My own son, Chad, is one of Robert's winter friends, aren't you, Chad?" He put a fatherly arm around his son. "Chad wants to go to Washington and work for some government agency, instead of staying in his father's law firm like a good boy—like Robert here. Robert's a good boy, don't you fellows think so?"

Robert saved us the embarrassment of answering by throwing back his head and laughing a bit too forcefully. The others joined in with less spirited laughter. "Yes," Mr. Brand went on, not choosing to hear the reactions, "Robert instinctually knows where his bread is buttered, isn't that right, boys?"

Endicott Brand took hold of my arm and Dave's. "I think we'd better get Robert's friends a drink, or they'll never catch up to you, Norman," he said quietly. "We always forget to keep Norman away from the bar on special occasions like weddings. He's fine unless there's a special occasion."

"That's not true, 'Cott," Mr. Brand said pleasantly. "I've been known to get exceedingly drunk on the most ordinary occasions."

"Oh, Dad," Doodie whined with mock irritation. "Behave yourself. How often does your only daughter get married?"

"You have a point there, Doodie, my girl," Mr. Brand mumbled. His wife good-naturedly tugged his arm to lead him off, but as he turned to follow her he collided with a plump, old-young man, who had the puffy, rosy cheeks and wide eyes of an aging seraph. "What have we here?" Mr. Brand said, loosing himself from his wife's grasp. "Oh, have you gentlemen met the Right Reverend Hocking?" Dave and I shook hands with the Reverend. "Reverend Hocking is going to marry Doodie and Robert tomorrow," Mr. Brand continued, smiling emptily at the clergyman. "It's all part of the Great Boston Compromise. You see, the Reverend is with the Unitarian church—or is it the Universalist one? I always get them mixed up."

Reverend Hocking threw back his head and laughed, almost in imitation of Robert. "You should know, sir, you hired me," he said, with a childlike joviality.

"So I did, so I did," Mr. Brand drawled. "I'm used to Episcopalian weddings, you must understand. However, you brush up on your invocations for tomorrow, Reverend. I want everything to go off tickety-boo." Mr. Brand had a lot of trouble pronouncing the last word.

Reverend Hocking performed his laugh again, with a little less verve, though. "Don't worry about a thing, sir," he said, patting Mr. Brand's shoulder as if he were dusting it. The others had slipped away during the conversation, and Mr. Brand was at last persuaded to follow his wife, leaving the clergyman alone with Dave and me. Fortunately, our host reappeared with a maid holding a tray of martinis. "Well," he said, once we had our drinks in hand, "to the bride and groom!" We drank to the bride and groom, who had merged into a circle of guests across the room. While our host kept the three of us in conversation about the weather in Boston, I managed to scan the room quickly. Not far away were Robert's parents, sitting stiffly on a large settee and chatting with anyone who dropped by to pay his respects. A very thin, birdlike woman, who seemed vaguely familiar, sat between them, nervously examining the faces around her. She clutched a martini glass uncomfortably, bringing it close to her lips from time to time, but never quite daring to place it between them. She noticed my glances towards her and turned away, like an edgy robin. Then, all at once, she smiled fully at me, displaying very pink gums. I excused myself and headed for the settee.

"Oh, look who's here, dear," Mrs. Kurtz said to her husband as I approached them. They both seemed glazed with pride. "Isn't it wonderful?" Mrs. Kurtz asked, grasping my hand in both of hers. "Milton and I love Doodie and her family so. They're just the most wonderful dignified people, aren't they?"

"You don't see homes like this in the Grove—or even *Newton*— eh, boy?" Mr. Kurtz said confidentially. He raised his elbow as if to nudge me in the ribs, but he suddenly thought better of it. "These people really know how to spend their money. I was telling my wife that these old Yankees—"

Mrs. Kurtz cut him off, as I remembered she always did, by merely straightening her posture and looking away. "Have you met Robert's Aunt Ruth—Mrs. Greenspan?" she asked.

I shook hands with the frail, nervous woman sitting between them. "I think I met you once in the Grove, when I visited," she said in an unsure voice.

"Aunt Ruth is from New York," Mrs. Kurtz offered still erect and holding her drink just above her lap. "She's one of Robert's favorite aunts, so she came all the way up to Boston for the wedding, just like you did."

"Whereabouts in New York do you live?" I asked Robert's aunt.

"Before my brother—Ruth's husband—passed away," Mrs. Kurtz said before her sister-in-law could answer, "Ruth lived on Central Park West."

"Now I got a little flat off the Grand Concourse," Aunt Ruth finally got out. "It's very comfy for me all alone, with the children grown up."

"Well, boy," Mr. Kurtz interjected, "what do you think of our Robert? Practically just out of law school and already he's making a regular name for himself." I told Mr. and Mrs. Kurtz that both Doodie and Robert were lucky to have each other, and all the parents should be very proud.

Robert called his parents over to a circle of people nearby. I was about to edge out of the way myself, when Aunt Ruth gestured quickly with her arthritic hand for me to bend over towards her. "You're a very good friend of Robert's, aren't you?" she whispered in my ear. I could think of little else to do but nod. "So what do you think?" she continued. "Is he going to be happy with this girl and all his fancy in-laws?" While I was pondering what to say, she went on. "Well, I don't mind telling you, I'm not so happy about all this. There are so many nice girls around, what does he have to get mixed up with these people for? A brilliant lawyer like him doesn't need anybody."

[153]

Out of the corner of my eye, I saw Dave looking at me with a pained expression. He was still conversationally trapped with the Reverend Hocking. "Don't worry," I said to Aunt Ruth, patting her bony shoulder, "everything's going to be fine. Excuse me, I have to join some friends."

Actually, Robert, hopping from group to group, performed the rescue operation for Dave. "Take your drinks in to dinner," he was telling the Reverend and Dave as I pulled up. "You may need them; the Brands love to make speeches at dinner."

Robert herded us into the dining room, a plush Georgian affair dominated by a fastidiously set table. We squinted at our place cards and I found myself between the two red-headed maids of honor, the Armstrong twins, and across from Aunt Ruth. Once we were seated, Endicott Brand, with the bride- and groom-to-be on either side of him, nodded to Reverend Hocking, who, neatly picking up his cue, bowed his head and waited for complete silence. "Lord, we thank Thee for what we are about to enjoy," he said angelically. I noticed that Aunt Ruth's lips were moving almost imperceptibly when she raised her head a few seconds after the others. She looked across at me questioningly.

"That was very nice, Reverend," Norman Brand said, shifting unsteadily in his seat. "Very nice indeed. No frills, no redundancies. Performed with dispatch. Good job!"

"Thank you," said the Reverend, forcing a smile.

Doodie leaned over towards her father. "Daddie, now you behave yourself," she warned, leveling her finger at him.

"Yes, dear, eat your soup," Mrs. Brand added. "It'll do you good."

The talk blurred into a dozen conversations. The redhead on my left, Mary Jo Armstrong, seemed contentedly assigned to talk to Dave, who was on her left, so I allowed myself to be attached to her twin, Mary Lou. For a girl of twenty-one or so, she possessed what appeared to be an extraordinary amount of baby fat, which gave her the rounded, immaculate quality of a Breck Shampoo advertisement. She kept things rolling by launching infinitely enthusiastic monologues. Her sister apparently took the same tack, and between the two of them, I felt as if I were attending a junior prom planning committee meeting.

". . . So the whole thing just kills me anyway," Mary Lou was saying, bobbing her curly head almost in perfect time to her speech meter, "because if it wasn't for Robert getting so mixed up between me and Mary Jo—everybody does, actually—he probably never would've met Doodie in the first place, or at least not so soon, anyway, and we all wouldn't even be here tonight. I guess you don't know the whole story, though, do you?"

"No," I answered, "I don't think I do." Although the food was beautifully prepared and served, it had a kind of institutional taste to it. The wine was very good, however, but it was making my mind wander.

"Well, anyway," Mary Lou continued, neatly placing her knife and fork in an inverted "V" on her practically full plate of pot roast, and turning intimately towards me, "it was this way. It was a scream, really. You *do* want to hear about it, don't you?"

"Yes," I said brightly. "By all means."

"Well, anyway," she went on, "Robert and Chad were very close friends at Eliot House, but Chad never got around to formally introducing Robert to Doodie because she was going steady with George Wilkinson, who is older and some kind of distant relation on Doodie's mother's side. Anyhow, everyone figured that, naturally, some day Doodie and George would be married, so everyone just kind of accepted it when Doodie never went out much with anybody else except George from the time she first started in at Radcliffe. I must say they really were made for each other, but that was before Robert. Well, you'll never get Chad to admit it, but he wrangled an invitation for Robert to the Harvey's Christmas party by pulling all kinds of strings, and then Chad asked me if I'd like to go with Robert. Of course, I had plenty of invitations—both Mary Jo and I did—but I said sure because I thought it would be fun, since Robert was a new face and so forth. So then Chad brought Robert over to the house to pick up Mary Jo and me, and they find Doodie there, because George was coming over to pick her up. Well, then Robert starts this whole routine about which one of us is which—just like everybody does when they meet us because we're so identical and all—only Robert was miles funnier about it than anybody else. He's so naturally witty anyway, don't you think? So we all went off to the Harvey's together and for the whole evening Robert hardly knew I *existed*. I mean he kept making Doodie laugh by telling her she'd have to stay close by him so she could help tell Mary Jo and me apart. It was just kind of love at first sight for him and Doodie from that very first moment on. Poor George never had a chance after that, the way Robert rushed Doodie with flowers and beautiful love letters and poems and everything. Doodie wanted to break up with George right away, only the Brands said she ought to wait. I guess they weren't too happy about Robert at first because of, you know, everything. But they were secretly engaged anyway, even when they were in college. George left college and went in the Marines to Korea or some place, so that helped the situation. Mary Jo and I were the only ones who knew about it because we and Doodie were always such close friends. . . ."

There are times when I feel I am living in a movie and this was one of them. Perhaps, it is from seeing too many movies, or perhaps, from not seeing enough of them, but ever so often I find my mind wandering according to standard cinematic techniques. For instance, while Mary Lou was talking, my eyes were focused on some dinner roll crumbs slightly to the right of my plate. The crisp, angular crumbs began to mesmerize me, so that it was almost painful to take my eyes off them. Then, Mary Lou's voice slowly faded and the crumbs dissolved, with all the predictability of a Warner Brothers flashback, into a sunny lake, Lake Massasoit. My mind's camera took in, with a glorious panorama shot, the marshy cove of the Grove, Pond Avenue with its cluster of bungalows, the community raft, the family rowboats—all just as they were on any given summer afternoon. Then, there was a reverse shot of the Massasoit Lodge directly across the lake. The Lodge was a richly rustic summer resort, where old Boston families came to swim, fish, play golf, and sail. The people of the Grove considered the Lodge a never-never land that was forever barred to them, so they chose to avoid talking about it and, after a while, even caring about it.

Medium close-up of the Lodge's sandy beach (the only one on the lake). Robert, David, and myself, all about sixteen years old, were heading towards that beach in my outboard motorboat. Robert was sitting on the prow, squinting ahead and looking for all his worth like a young man inherently bound to the sea. Dave was huddled on the middle seat, grimacing and trying to avoid the spray and exhaust fumes. I was busily steering from the stern.

"All right," shouted Robert above the motor, in his best Captain Bligh tone, "now push the stop button a few times, but don't stall it out till I say so."

"Hey, look, Robert," I shouted back, "let's do it some other time. They'll kick us right the hell off." He pretended that he didn't hear me. Not wanting to act cowardly, I pushed the stop button as he ordered. The motor accommodated by skipping and even backfiring before it roared to life again. Robert peered unabashedly at the beach full of people lounging on blankets and under umbrellas, and they began to stare back at us. Then he flicked his hand at me several times. That was the signal, and I obediently made the motor stall out completely. We coasted smoothly in towards the beach. Before the bow touched the sand, a lifeguard scampered down from his white tower and waved at us.

"Hey," he said, as Robert leapt expertly from the prow onto the sand, "this is a private beach. You have to be a guest of the Lodge."

Standing every bit as tall as the lifeguard, Robert looked him right in the eye. "Say, our motor just conked out," he said easily. "We drifted in here so we could change the plugs. Nice place you got here."

The lifeguard was worried. "Yeah," he said, "well, get your boat off to the side there and fix it where the guests aren't swimming. And don't spill any gas on the water or the manager will have my head. You guys aren't from that place across the lake, are you?" Dave was beginning to pale under his tan.

"Hell no," Robert laughed and stuck out his right hand. "My name is Robert Forsythe, from Boston. My friends and I use this lake once in a while when we're not in Maine. Mind if I take a swim?"

The lifeguard examined us from behind the protective shield of his sunglasses. "Yeah, I guess it's O.K.," he said slowly. "Only make sure you don't bother the guests any." Robert grinned at Dave and me and ambled down the beach discreetly behind the lifeguard.

Dave and I climbed out of the boat and pushed it towards the less populated end of the beach, where we convincingly tinkered with the motor. "What's the crazy sonafabitch doing now?" I asked Dave, who had a better sightline to watch Robert in action on the beach.

Dave gently struck the engine block a few times with a wrench and, turning his head slightly, said, "He just sat down next to a real piece—one of those Miss Kimberley's School-type girls—and he's giving her some kind of line, I guess. Now, some guy is coming over and talking to him and pointing over here. . . . Now the guy is walking away and Robert and the girl are laughing and going into the lake."

"No kidding," I whispered incredulously. "Is he really doing it? I'll say one thing for him—he's got nerve." We tinkered for another ten minutes or so and then I told Dave to stay with the boat while I walked up the beach to get Robert. He was sitting amiably on a blanket next to a tall, delicately tanned blonde girl, whose breasts were just beginning to fill out her latex bathing suit. As I approached them, I felt strangely underdressed, although I was wearing bathing trunks and a T-shirt, just as Robert was. Digging at the sand with my right foot, I told Robert the motor was fixed and we ought to be starting back. "You guys go on ahead," he said casually and grinning infectiously. "I'll walk back or something. Don't worry about me." He didn't introduce me to the girl.

". . . So then they came back from Rockport, all officially engaged and everything, and their parents got together for a kind of conclave and they all made plans for the wedding. Robert and Doodie got the idea of Reverend Hocking doing the ceremony, so everybody was finally satisfied there. Isn't it all just like some kind of wonderful romantic story from the Middle Ages?" Mary Lou's question made the bread crumbs and the dinner party reappear in brilliant focus again. I looked directly at her for what seemed the first time in several hours. "Yes," I said, "It sure is."

The servants began to clear the dinner plates away. After an exchange of smiles, Mary Lou concluded that I was an unrewarding dinner partner and gave her full attention to Chad, who was on her right. While lighting a cigarette, I glanced at Aunt Ruth and discovered she was gazing straight at me. I flashed her an are-you-having-a-good-time? expression, and she turned away quickly, as if I had caught her in some devilish act. One of the maids came around behind her and attempted to take her plate, but Aunt Ruth surprised the maid by handing it to her. Mrs. Kurtz observed the episode and immediately said something to Aunt Ruth through her tightly stretched lips, which made the older woman appear jittery and unhappy.

The strangely piercing sound of a half-filled water glass being struck several times by Endicott Brand's teaspoon abruptly halted the conversations around the table. The host rose to his feet, his weight resting on his finger tips which remained on the table, and he heavily cleared his throat. "Ladies and gentlemen," he began slowly, "we often say in the Brand family that you have to work for your dinner. Well, tonight it can hardly be called work, really. To my mind, it's true pleasure, for we are here to celebrate a wedding tomorrow of two young people who are very close to all of us. If anyone knows a greater pleasure than that, I wish he'd let me know about it. My niece Doodie and Robert have chosen each other as partners for life, and basking in their radiance of this happy situation, I propose a toast to their continuing joy, good work, and success." He raised his wine glass and the rest of us arose with a bumbling of chairs and toasted the couple. Doodie and Robert looked at each other imploringly and clinked glasses, which caused everyone to laugh in a patronizing manner. There was a second or two of indecision, while those standing wondered whether to reseat themselves or not. Norman Brand made up our minds by starting to speak.

" 'Cott has expressed our feelings quite eloquently," he said, his speech still a little thick, "but there is one thing I am supposed to add as the honorable and esteemed father of the bride: I have not lost a daughter but I've gained a son. Well, all I can say is I must have gained quite a son if he could turn Doodie's head. A lot of young men have been trying to do that for years now, and, as far as I know, Robert has been the only successful one. It will be interesting getting to know our new son better, and I would like to go on record right now as saying, 'Welcome to the family, Robert.' "

Mr. Brand slumped down into his seat, as the ensuing applause reached its loudest point. He seemed to have spent more energy on his speech than he wanted to. Beaming alarmingly, Robert leaned across the table and shook hands with him, which lengthened the clapping for another few seconds. Again, there was a slightly embarrassed moment, while the guests searched each other's faces to see who would make the next toast. Someone suggested that Mr. and Mrs. Kurtz should speak, but Mrs. Kurtz refused for both of them, claiming they weren't good talkers. Aunt Ruth's face had become so tense that her chin had all but disappeared. I thought she looked sick. Finally, Reverend Hocking tinkled his glass and smiled benignly at his audience.

"As the representative here of the Divine Power," he said, in a more authoritative voice than he had used all evening, "and as the person who will bind Robert and Doodie in holy matrimony tomorrow, I feel I should offer my blessing at this time. These two—whom I am proud to call my friends—came to me and asked me to marry them. Nothing, as Mr. Brand so well put it, could give anyone more pleasure. In this particular case, it is indeed a deep honor I shall never forget, serving two individuals of varied backgrounds under one God's Ordinance. I wish you both the very ultimate of health and happiness."

Through the applause that followed, Robert arose and attempted to begin a speech of thanks. However, before he could gain everyone's attention, Aunt Ruth was shakily on her feet, clutching a slip of paper as if it were a governmental proclamation. "*Robele,*" she began, her voice cracking. "*Robele,* just a minute, please, darling. Let me say something, please, to the people before you talk." Mrs. Kurtz furiously tried to whisper to her, but Aunt Ruth didn't seem to notice. The room became

PENROD SCOFIELD

eerily quiet, as if everyone had just been informed that a bomb was hurtling towards the house and would arrive in exactly ten seconds.

Aunt Ruth coughed and, summoning her second wind, said, "Ladies and gentlemen. There is an ancient prayer of our people, which it is appropriate to say when two people get married. You will excuse me, but I want to say it now—for my nephew Robert's wedding: *Y'vorecho Adonoi. . . .*"

She pronounced the Hebrew words exultantly, like a political prisoner addressing his firing squad. Suddenly, I found myself imitating the open-mouthed expression on Robert's face; I realized what I was doing and looked at Dave. The corners of his mouth were slightly upturned in a controlled smile. Several guests, including Mrs. Brand, solemnly bowed their heads, while Mr. Brand mechanically played with a teaspoon on the table-cloth. Mr. Kurtz discovered that his tie needed constant straight-ening, and his wife seemed about to cry out in rage. "And now I will translate the prayer for everybody," Aunt Ruth went on doggedly, when she had finished reciting the Hebrew. "May the Lord bless thee and keep thee; May He cause His countenance to shine upon thee; and be gracious unto thee; May He lift up His face unto thee and grant thee peace."

Aunt Ruth slowly sat down. She seemed enormously relieved and managed a twitching smile at Robert and Doodie. Those whose heads were bowed tremulously lifted them. Dave reached around behind Mary Jo and tucked a wad of paper in my coat pocket. I surreptitiously extricated it and, cupping it in my hand, glanced down. "Mistah Kurtz—he dead," the pencil scrawl read.

Norman Brand put aside his teaspoon and turned towards Aunt Ruth, cocking his head slightly. "Do we drink to that or what?" he asked her.

Aunt Ruth grinned in a way that changed her features drastically. "Certainly you may, Mr. Brand, if you want to," she answered. Mr. Brand slumped back in his chair and didn't drink.

Our host was the next person to break the silence. "Mrs. Green-span," he said, "I want to thank you for that lovely prayer."

"You're welcome," Aunt Ruth mumbled, without looking at him.

"Well now," Endicott Brand went on briskly, readjusting him-self in his chair, "I think we've earned our dinner. Shall we take our coffee in the living-room?"

Herbert Gold

NICHOLAS IN EXILE

Herbert Gold is the author of *The Man Who Was Not With It, Therefore Be Bold, The Optimist* and *Salt* as well as of short stories and essays that have appeared in leading magazines and anthologies.

"Nicholas in Exile" was picked for this collection because of its ingenious revelation of how a hatred pronounced dead comes back to life to chill the air in a seemingly serene tropical setting.

With our first meeting on the terrace of the Hotel Oloffson at its station on a tropical hillside rising from Port-au-Prince, Nicholas greeted me as a long-lost, long-mourned, spiritual brother. "A white man — man of culture," he quickly explained in his rapid, slightly stilted, peculiarly idiomatic English: "a man who knows the score in literature, music, and art. These Haitian monkeys, it's not a matter of their color, there are some smart ones — they just don't have enough of Western civilization behind them. Naturally there are always the smart ones."

I was too flattered to argue the point. Infected by the traveler's loneliness and passivity before an offer of pleasure or distraction, I allowed Nicholas to take me over with his energetic thrust of sudden intimacy. I had no friends in this steaming Caribbean corner of oblivion. Nicholas DeManheim, manager of the hotel, obviously knew everybody, and everything that was going on. He was short, stocky, jolly, with a shock of sun-bleached hair falling over merry blue eyes; he was French — "well, not entirely, *mais quand même j'ai fait mes études à Paris!*" — he seemed French anyway, and he had the rare gift of instantaneous rapport. I knew nothing at all about him, but accepted his petition to be my brother. I sighed with relief. I was ready to let him help me settle into my year at the Université d'Haiti. Charm may have been a commodity he sold, but he really had it to sell.

He also gave me a rate at the hotel. He found me an elegant room, away from the noises of rum and fun, drink and quarrel, with a painting of a cockfight on one wall. The room had a little flowered porch of its own, propped up against the hillside on stilts, and a view of the algae-encrusted swimming pool just below, half-hidden by banana and mango trees; and further on, blue hills and mountains, blue bay, the smoky city spread out along the curve of sea. The original buildings of the hotel had been the residence of a president of Haiti who had grievously insulted his people and had consequently been torn limb from limb by a mob. It is said that parts of his body were eaten by his enemies. His son was still alive, in his eighties, elegant in a white suit and carrying a white cocomacaque, the traditional Haitian aristocrat's walking stick. The Son strolled about mostly at dawn, breathing the unbreathed air, he explained; he wore green catskin shoes to preserve his virility. Emaciated and haughty, in a white suit and a celluloid collar, he occasionally crossed over from his own little house nearby to visit the scene of his father's martyrdom. His rage had been converted to amiable smiles. He was determined to be virile forever.

Nicholas told me stories about Haiti. He entertained and informed me with the natural cynicism of the European flung inconsiderately upon this alien heap of coral and mountain, amid an alien people, neither African nor French, crippled by poverty, stubborn, undependable. They always answered "yes," no matter what he asked them. It was the traditional yielding resistance of the slave. "Is this the way to the Magloire house?" "Yes." "Will you do this job?" "Yes." No matter which way it really was, no matter what the servant's real intentions about the job, Nicholas suffered much trouble in the kitchen with the waiters and cooks, and with the maids, and with the porters and shoeshine boys and everybody. It was a pleasure, he declared to talk things over with me. And sweaty but relaxed, he hustled me into his blue 4-CV Renault to carry me up the mountain to the little house in Petionville where he lived with his wife and child. "I have amended the Mosaic law," he said. "Honor Thy Wife and Son!"

While Nicholas was almost French, a former student in France, *"Français de coeur,"* as he said, his wife was really French. She had orange hair and freckled skin and pale green eyes, washed paler by the sun, not the storybook Frenchwoman at first glance; but she spoke with the hard *r* of the Parisienne and there was no doubt about the affiliation of her cynical, gay, reserved spirit. Their child, little more than a year old, was being given a tough and loving inauguration. He already knew how to swim, paddling for dear life in their tiny pool, while his mother waded alongside, keeping her hand cautiously beneath the straining, protuberant baby belly. Later we ate a tropical salad by the pool of their rented house. Nicholas smiled and smiled and nodded modestly over the earnest compliments I offered him on his family. Occasionally his face would cloud and become distracted, as for example, when the barefooted servant forgot to serve us some necessary item of the menu in its proper order.

"*De la crème fraîche! De la crème fraîche, espèce de putain!*"

The country girl, who spoke Creole, not French, was confused by her master's anger. Since she ate mostly rice and beans and, on special occasions, pork, mangoes, and bananas, and little else, the variety and complexity of a foreigner's meal was still beyond her easy unravelling. Nicholas paid her about six dollars a month while she was learning. Later she might earn eight dollars a month. But not until she learned to bring the fresh cream along with the fruit salad.

"I don't take cream on fruit," I said.

"Neither do I," he said, "but that animal has to learn. They are nothing more than animals. Do you know this was a rich country when the French were still here? And now look at it." He raised his chin and I looked at that instead. "They call this freedom. They are enslaved to themselves — apes, monkeys, animals — nothing better."

"Well, they're trying to move forward. They're building . . ."

But I achieved only a feeble level of praise for Haitian progress. And indeed, the country is the most depressed in the Western Hemisphere. It was difficult to argue abstractly about national freedom in the midst of misery and a military dictatorship. The French should not have left in 1804, Nicholas said. Toussaint L'Ouverture, the slave leader, is thought to be a great man, but what is his legacy in the Haiti of today? Misery, torture, corruption, and cynicism. The barefoot servants being cursed by mulatto and black masters instead of French ones. Dulled abandon, incomprehension, and failure. "You don't like it? But look at it!"

But then, to ease my liberal malaise, Nicholas handed me his wriggling son to hold in my lap. He cooed at the child with the adoration of a man given a first son after crossing the middle of the journey of his life. We admired it together. Nicholas' wife, Aurore, smiled and laughed and said little. Watchful of the world, sometimes chattering, she remained aloof from the eager warmth which Nicholas chose to radiate in my direction. Mme. DeManheim's moated sufficiency unto herself would be charming and reassuring to a man who was very certain of himself. At that time I responded more easily to Nicholas' short-cuts to friendship — flattery, urging, intense listening, joking.

Nicholas and I disagreed about some matters. He had contempt for the Haitians on a racial basis: "Fresh out of the jungle, my friend. What else can you expect of them?" I resisted this line and he seldom pushed it any further. But he smiled and winked in my direction when a servant made a mistake, before he began his *engueullade,* the good hard-mouthing he believed that they needed. When he lost his temper in a rage at a servant, his wife just took their son in her arms and held him until the gust was past. Then, subsiding, Nicholas apologized to Madame and me for his shouting and the meal continued.

Nicholas enjoyed one frequent Haitian companion. Roussan Garou was six feet four inches tall, almost blue in color, emaciated by cirrhosis of the liver, furious-eyed and very intelligent — a poet. He had the lofty look of those tribesmen who can stand motionless, like cranes, with one leg folded against the other at the knee. He was a Haitian racist who hated whites, hated mulattoes, except during the rare days when he was sober. Then he would sit with Nicholas and me on the terrace of the Hotel Oloffson, drinking American canned fruit juice and describing how France must provide the third force of mediation between the Soviet Union and the United States. This task could only be accomplished with the aid of its sister republic, Haiti. And of course, first it would be necessary to wash Port-au-Prince in the blood of the exploiters, whoever they might be. He grinned and lifted his glass to toast me in Dole pineapple juice.

"Of course," he assured me, "a citizen of the republic of letters like yourself has no other nationality . . ."

Nicholas beamed.

"And like our friend Nicholas, too, a European gentleman on these distant shores . . ."

Nicholas threw his arms across our shoulders in a rush of

PENROD SCOFIELD

happy feeling. He had brought the three of us together. What a pleasure! He ordered another can of chilled juice. He cursed out the waiter, who had brought the can on a plate instead of pouring the juice into a pitcher. When Nicholas put his arm around Roussan's shoulder and clutched it, the poet gazed at me from the yellowish whites of his eyes with a measuring, challenging stare. He did not return the ebullient European gesture. He was a poet, not a *Quartier Latin* student.

The three of us went on sipping Dole pineapple juice and discussing world politics at a table on the terrace of the Hotel Oloffson perched on its little slope up from the steaming port city. Down the hill a bit, the National Palace glittered in the sunlight, its cellars filled with the President's personal stock of munitions. The world and politics provided subjects for reverie in Port-au-Prince, that retracted corner of the universe. In order to share words, one must talk.

When Roussan went off, stepping precariously in his continual illness, Nicholas waved goodbye and even blew a kiss from the tip of his fingertips. The stalk of a poet revolved slowly as if the flying kiss had hit him on the neck. Gravely he saluted, turned, walked on, stopped, and bowed to the ancient Son in his green

[166]

catskin shoes, taking an unusual late afternoon stroll, risking his virility in the breathed air of the Port-au-Prince afternoon.

Nicholas said, as Roussan disappeared down the winding road, "Decent chap. Drunkard like any Haitian with a brain in his head. Of course, his poetry is just addled brains. The cerebral matter must be like scrambled eggs — eggs scrambled, what? in Rhum Barbancourt.'

"He talks rationally enough now."

"He's sick, that's why. Can't stand up under thinking, got to drink. It's the emotions that break down, not just the brain. Come on up the hill, let's have dinner at home. My boy recognizes you — refresh the little chappie. At this age they have short memories, you know?"

And he urged me into the little blue 4-CV. I was homesick and susceptible to the flattery of his attention, the baby smiles of his son, the undemanding gaiety of his orange-haired wife. We clattered up the two-lane mountain highway, dodging in and out of traffic, and I studied fatalism with my eyes shut. On the steep side of the highway, in the ravine, there were the wrecks of automobiles, sinking among refuse, grasses, and wind-fall rocks in the dry trickle of mountain water.

Along the road, Haitian peasant women, balancing on their heads their loads of produce for the market, walked downhill in a steady procession, talking softly or silent, following each other in a ceaseless line. Others, with empty baskets on their heads, made the long climb back up the mountain on skinny legs with a scale of dust covering them. Occasionally they would scramble into the ravine to bathe in the stream. They carried away whatever was useful in the destroyed automobiles, but there was not very much they could use.

"Animals," Nicholas said if one stepped in the roadway. He gave me the traditional upper-class Haitian advice for an auto-mobile accident involving a peasant: *Make sure he is dead.* Back up if necessary. If the pedestrian is injured, you must pay hospital expenses; if killed, seventy dollars for the funeral. "The doctors are thieves. The hospitals are rackets. The whole family lives on what you give them for medicine. *Back up,*" he said grinning.

Then, as if this reminded him, he reported a bit of gossip about Roussan Garou. Roussan had been in charge of supplying foreign women to the previous president of the Republic of

[167]

Haiti. He had gone on shopping trips to Cuba and Jamaica, with diplomatic accreditation. "Now of course," said Nicholas, "he is confined to poetry, since the new regime has made other arrangements. Naturally he favors reform — immediate turnover."

The charm of my new friend may be hard to find in this cold chronicle. But malice about others does not immediately put us off; we think ourselves immune when we see the sparkling eyes of the friend. His malice may even flatter us with a sense of our own superiority to it while the malicious one's tender fantasy is busy pleasing us. You have to imagine the melancholy of a traveler, his hopes for a gregarious tropical evening after the blistering day, and the power of smiles, winks, and random assumptions of complicity to force a friendship into life. And there was more than malice to Nicholas. He loved music, he had written a novel, he spoke languages, he knew the score. He reacted vivaciously. He was in touch. I could mark off his judgments as whimsical quirks. It was plain hard to make severe judgment of a man who so obviously wanted to be liked.

We sat in the cool of the evening and discussed student days in Paris. His nostalgia for the Left Bank was contagious. Sometimes, deep in rum, we sang a scatological song, "*Le Quartier Latin*," traditional among the medical students of Paris; we talked about Bergson and the school of Bergson, the Dôme and the Select, and the special quality of French girls. "A French girl who doesn't love him." Nicholas said, "is better to a man than a woman of any other nationality who might happen to adore him. Yes? Yes? You agree?"

I had no quarrel with this observation. We had found several grounds for friendship. I pitied him: Did his wife love him or was she merely good to him?

Then one evening it happened that we were exploring together the bars of the Boulevard Harry-Truman, the one spacious avenue of the city, designed for elegance upon the leveled debris of a waterfront slum. It had been built for the Exposition by President Estimé; there were palm trees and cafés and medieval ruins which dated back to 1949. With plaster construction and a high percentage of the expenditure going for peculiar Caribbean extra profits, it took only a few years to produce crumbling walls and picturesque ramparts worthy of ancient Rome, or at least of Cinecitta. Thick-leaved plants followed in the path of smaller weeds; soon whole trees were pushing through the cracks of the luxurious halls and galleries. Among the desolation of the wide boulevard, the broken pipes and breached foundations, several bars — Whiskey à Gogo, the Casino Italien, and a few others — kept afloat with their bit of neon, their tourists, and the nightly crop of celebrating Haitian men with their patient women.

We drank in the Whiskey à Gogo. At about midnight Nicholas suddenly bethought himself of his wife and son. This reminded him of things beautiful, things eternal. The piano! he decided. He had been a child prodigy of the Seventh *Arondissement* Right now, at this very moment, we would go home for a concert. He would play for me, for me alone, and for his wife and child, too. In the cool of the Haitian night, in the heat of the bar, it seemed like a fine idea. We emerged from the Whiskey à Gogo and made our way, sideways and distracted, down the walk past the Casino. Nicholas wore the look, both happy and worried, of a man without a job who has suddenly, unexpectedly, found a bottle of rum in a paper bag. He believed his luck, but doubted it. He staggered a little.

The evening made me ridiculous, too. I was not used to the jolt of rum-soda, the drink of choice in Port-au-Prince. I was taken by a pointless whimsicality as we passed the brutal little pack of black Buicks and Cadillacs which surrounded the Casino, the usual sign that the President of the Republic, plus cronies, bodyguards, and ladyfriends, was busy relaxing from the cares of state inside. Sleepy policemen leaned with their submachine guns against the black fenders, fighting off their yawns. They blinked at us in the dark and wondered when the President would relieve them from their travail. Overhead, tropical sky with blinking stars; at eye level, ruins, palm trees, bodyguards with black weapons, the Boulevard Harry-Truman. We were encircled in the dark as we uncertainly strolled past the police cars.

A silly joke possessed me. One of the black police cars had its door swung open. I took Nicholas by the shoulder and shoved him toward it, saying like a cop, "Get in there!"

He stiffened. He turned cold as ice, and sober, with his lank hair fallen over his forehead and his icy eyes blazing. He pulled away from me, hissing, *"Don't you touch me."*

It was as if we were different beings in another time and place. The language and style were of another period.

The evening was abruptly over. The violence of his revulsion, the violence of his reaction against me, set us both out of gear. We had nothing to say to each other. We parted within a few minutes.

Something peculiar and incomplete kept nagging at me all the next day. My friend's fear and rage reminded me of something.

At last I went to an American police officer who had been assigned to the Port-au-Prince police to help them develop a department of scientific investigation — fingerprints, chemical analysis, and so on. I asked him to find out what he could about the history of Nicholas DeMannheim. "For a pal, why not?" he said.

That evening he drove up to the Hotel Oloffson. On his way to my room he passed the cheery time of day with Nicholas, who was getting ready to speed up the mountain in his little blue 4-CV toward his red-haired wife and his son. The policeman found me and said, "It's easy. Nicholas is under a sentence of death in France." Many international criminals can make a comfortable home in Haiti if they keep up their payments to the proper officials. Haitian politicians are less demanding than most. "But it's only politics," the policeman assured me. "Nicholas was a student in Paris during the Occupation. He was only a student. There was a resistance movement. They say he was a Gestapo informer."

I'm not sure I thanked my friend the policeman. A man responsible for torture and death at the hands of the Nazis should have been indentifiable by some manifest sign. That he could have a pretty wife, a baby son upon whom he doted, an interest in music and art, a taste for conversation, a boyish charm — in theory, yes. We all know this. But the fact of a living Nicholas, grinning and ingratiating, now filled me with horror. There was also a horror of myself for not recognizing him. It made me fear again. I was unsafe. The world was filled with hidden enemies. I did not speak with him in the days that followed.

And yet Nicholas was not my enemy, not any longer, not in this altered world.

Nicholas himself understood that some pause must come to our friendship. He could not have known what I had found out about him, but the evening had ended in a way which, with his discretion alerted, forced a beat of respite. Our friendship had been too sudden; now he would draw back.

But at last one night he again came to my room in the hotel, knocked, and waited till I opened the door to him. He brought with him a bottle of rum, two glasses, ice, and little bottles of soda. He sat down at my table and served us both. His face was red and congested with the effort he was making. It had all been worked out in his imagination, and worked out to such automatic utterance that his suavity vanished, his control disappeared, his timing was off. He pronounced the conclusion of an imaginary discussion he had been having with me. He knew my lines and wanted to give me the cue as rapidly as possible. "I cannot bear living in this place any longer," he said. "I must leave. I can write, translate, work at many jobs. I need your help. Help me get into New York. In New York I can work at a job fit for a man of my background." He talked on rapidly, disjointedly, never saying "America" or "The United States." "I know New York well, though I have never been there. Aurore must not stay here any longer. She insists. You can recommend me. An affidavit. I need a little help. You have been . . . I have helped you. My son must have a chance to be raised among civilized people — not these savages, these apes. It's for him, too — you like my son, don't you? In New York you have friends. Do it."

I was foundering in the rush of his feeling, his hope and desire sent my way. Whether I was fond of his child, whether I gave a new weight to his contempt for Haitians, even whether or not I could do anything for him at the embassy if he had been condemned by a French court — all this was irrelevant. *Merely political,* the American policeman had said. I held to my simple idea. No reproach would be adequate; there was nothing else I could say: "No, Nicholas. No. I won't do it."

He stood up and an empty bottle of soda somersaulted to the floor. It bounced without breaking. He looked at me with eyes which were suddenly very thoughtful and considerate of me. His mouth was still moving slightly, as if, with the sound turned off, he was continuing a lecture about how much he needed to go live in New York. His tongue was working on the inside of his lips and the muscles of his cheeks. At last he spoke aloud. He spoke wearily, pitifully, not wanting to; he spoke because it was expected of him; he uttered the word as if asking in still another way a favor of me. He said : *"Jew,"* and waited for me to hit him.

[171]

Jo Sinclair

THE MEDAL

Jo Sinclair is the author of *Wasteland* the 1946 Harper prize novel, *Sing At My Wake* and other books. Miss Sinclair's stories and articles have been published in *Saturday Evening Post, Esquire, Harper's* and other periodicals.

In this story of the effect of a Jewish hero's death on his young son, she takes her characters to the very edge where sentiment teeters on the brink of bathos without ever letting her tale deteriorate into a tearjerker. The result is a moving study of the springs of grief.

Cleveland was almost as hot as Washington had been, and Mildred felt stifled as she paid the taxi driver. Josh had taken the suitcase; he was on the front porch now, digging in a pocket for his key.

When the taxi pulled away, Mildred walked very slowly. She could not bear the idea of going in; the house was so much Phil's. The screen door closed behind Josh without a sound, and she found that unbearable, too. A boy should let a door slam automatically, she thought almost querulously. How long after death do we have to tiptoe?

She came into the living room, made herself snap up the window shades at once, welcoming the noise. She heard her son's soft steps at the back of the house, and shrank from the thought of the evening stretching ahead.

Where would she continue to get the casual talk? Again, she would have to mask her grieving loneliness, avert her eyes from so many things—a photograph, the piano Phil had loved to play, his big chair.

In the dining room, Mildred rolled up the shades quickly, then went through to the kitchen. The roses on the table were full blown—velvet red, yellow, named Mirandy and Eclipse. Phil had known all his roses by name, as he had planted them or cut them for the house. And she had called their names silently two days ago, as if cutting the two roses for him, just before it was time to leave for the airport.

She permitted herself to relax for an instant, let the sorrow roll over her completely. A woman could not, most of the time. She could not groan, or cry like a lost female animal left alone. The child turned her from bereft wife and hungering lover into the pretense of strong, calm mother. The child was unknowing but rigid censor. Even in her own bedroom, late at night, a woman must not mourn her dead beloved with anything but choked weeping. A boy lay sleeping in the next room, too young to be awakened by such frightening sounds of yearning.

Mildred added water to the vase, mechanically straightened the tablecloth. She thought wearily that she should be proud of Josh, instead of resenting his implacable presence. He had not cried once. It was she who had gone to pieces inside when the telegram had come. Josh had seemed to turn into an expressionless boy, somehow taller, unbelievably quiet.

And that queer look of detachment had stayed with him, through even the flight to Washington—his first plane ride. The quiet boy had walked with her into the White House, a walk which had made her own legs tremble. Mildred remembered the President's kind eyes as he shook hands with her son. "How old are you, Joshua?" he had asked. "Twelve, sir," her son had answered, and the President had said: "I'll bet everyone calls you Josh." The boy: "Yes, sir, they do." The President, very, very gently: "I know how proud you are of your father." And that courteous, stony-quiet voice: "Yes, sir. Thank you." The blue ribbon had gone about Josh's neck. When the President stepped back, the medal had looked too large for the slender, thin-faced boy.

Mildred went back to the living-room, to telephone Phil's mother. Dialing, she heard the soft steps in the bedroom. The tiptoe steps of mourning; somehow, Josh kept repeating Phil's death, over and over.

"Hello, Mother," she said into the telephone. "We just got home, dear. Are you feeling any better?"

Amelia Goldmark's deep voice answered with eagerness. They were very fond of each other, the candid old woman and the younger one whose own mother and father were dead.

"It was a fine trip," Mildred said. "He's a little tired, but I do think he enjoyed the plane. And we had time to see a little of Washington."

Carefully, she answered the impatient questions. Her mother-in-law was in her late seventies, and their family doctor had forbidden the trip to Washington. As Mildred described the presentation, her eyes were on the photograph of Phil, which stood on the table near the piano. He was not in uniform, and she was glad. It was Phil in the picture, the man of home and garden and advertising agency, the tall and boyish husband who studied at the kitchen table and looked up at midnight to say: "That's it for tonight, Mil. How about that corned beef sandwich?"

"I'm anxious to see the medal," Phil's mother said.

"It's beautiful," Mildred told her. "So simple. We'll tell you all about it tomorrow. Are you sure you feel up to temple?"

As the deep, old voice told of a phone call from the Atlanta cousins, Josh came into the room. He had changed into denims and a short-sleeved shirt. A feeling half resentment and half anguish swept through Mildred as she saw him take from his pocket the case that held the medal, put it down on the table. A little more awe, please, she thought achingly. Not every father wins his son the highest honor his country can give.

Josh went out to the front porch and sat on the top step, his shoulders hunched. The picture lit up for her again of the way he had stood in the Rose Garden of the White House—so quiet, poised, like a little stranger she had never seen before.

All through the presentation, Mildred had remembered with a kind of agony Phil's garden, the look of his bare arms and thick, black hair in sunlight as he pruned his roses. The words of the citation had come to her in jerks, a phrase fading, the next one too stark: "Captain Philip David Goldmark . . . veteran of World War II . . . killed . . . his valiant leadership and courageous fighting . . . far beyond the call of duty. . . ."

Amelia Goldmark said reluctantly: "Well, I had better let you rest. Tell Joshua his dog's been good as gold. I suppose you're coming for him later? Those two hate so to be separated."

"I'm not sure, Mother. If Josh isn't too tired."

"Well, we'll be together tomorrow, anyway." The deep laugh had a quaver in it. "Frankly, Bozo's wonderful company. I'd like another day of him."

[174]

Mildred went to wash her face and change into a house dress. She unpacked quickly, put on lipstick. Then, still moving briskly, she went out to the porch, leaned against the rail near the hunched figure.

"Darling," she said, "Grandma says Bozo's been a perfect gent of a visitor. Want to drive over and bring him home?"

"Why don't we get him tomorrow, or something?" Josh said.

It was so unlike him that Mildred's stomach lurched. The street was very quiet, deserted looking. Somewhere a screen door slammed, but no one came out into the hot stillness.

"Fine," she said. "I think we'd better have a little supper now. Going to set the table for me?"

Without a word, Josh followed her in. "Just spoons," she said, fighting to retain the casual tone. "We'll have cornflakes and sliced peaches. Plenty of cold milk."

It was a summer dish he loved, but he made no comment. As they sat, Mildred kept her eyes from the vase of roses, began to speak with simulated interest of the fall semester, which would begin in three weeks. She taught mathematics at a junior high school halfway across the city, and on her way each morning she dropped Josh in front of Moreland School. Phil never needed the car because the rapid transit to his downtown office was within walking distance of their suburban home. Had been within walking distance, she amended that thought carefully.

"Are you looking forward to working with the public address system at school?" she asked, making herself smile.

"I guess so," Josh said, not looking up. He was eating listlessly.

"Miss Buchanan told me it's perfect preparation for the speech and drama classes you want later on," she said doggedly, and talked on and on to the silent boy.

Yes, later on, she thought grimly, unable to keep the flooding memory under control. Later on, Phil was to have finished law. One more year of evening classes, of books and briefs spread over the kitchen table. And he had planned to go on making a living at the agency during the long haul of establishing himself as a lawyer. His old joke! "Commercials, PR, legal advice, horticulture lessons? See Goldmark."

When the interminable meal was over, Mildred said brightly, "Run along, darling—there aren't enough dishes for two. Why don't you see if your friends are out in the street? It doesn't seem as hot now."

[175]

Josh disappeared at once. The tears came as she washed the few dishes and put a fresh cloth on the table. If only she could be alone for one day—just Mildred, mourning Phil, and no child near enough to stop her wild screams of grief.

She lit a cigarette and sat near the windows, looking out at Phil's lovely yard until she felt under control again. But her feet shuffled with exhaustion when she went to the living-room.

It was cool there, dim with the approaching dusk. With a start, she saw that Josh had not gone out. He was sitting in Phil's chair. Quickly, she snapped on the table lamp, then went to the standing lamp behind the piano. The light made the wood shine.

"Feel like practicing?" she said cheerfully.

"Mom, no," Josh said, his voice ragged.

"Would you like me to play something?" she went on with an effort. She had to get normal life back into this house!

"No, thank you," Josh said, and he sounded almost frantic.

His resemblance to his father hurt too much. The face long and thin, the same texture of hair; he had Phil's and Amelia Goldmark's mouth, curved and strongly traced. At the old woman's dinner table, every Sunday, Mildred had never failed to feel a tenderness, a delight sharp as a little ache, at the sight of those three faces marked so indelibly by generation. It had overjoyed her to be close to the three high-strung creatures, so aware of their needs and of her own capacity to minister to them. She had never doubted that capacity for a moment, until today.

Street noises drifted into the room. The live sounds warmed her a little. There was such a spell of death in the house. Phil would have hated it.

Deliberately, she said, "Darling, please don't forget the medal tomorrow. For Grandma to see. Better take it to your dresser now, so you remember it in the morning when we leave for temple."

Protest stiffened his entire body. They had not talked about the medal once, in Washington or on the trip back. They had not talked about Phil, for that matter, Mildred thought quite suddenly.

"Mom, I can't," Josh mumbled.

"Can't what?" Mildred asked, beginning to feel frightened.

"I'm not going to temple," he burst out. "I don't want to. Ever."

She felt sick, a little dizzy, but she said in the calm voice she had created for him: "And afterward, we'll spend the day with Grandma, as usual. She's looking forward to hearing about our

[176]

trip. She wants to see the medal, hold it for a while. But, of course, you'll take it home again—it belongs to you."

"I don't want the medal," Josh cried. "I want Dad."

His outcry made a slash of pain in Mildred's head. She wanted Phil, too. Wildly, rawly; no substitute would do. But, instinctively, she started toward Josh, to comfort him. To her bewilderment, he jumped up quickly, as if he wanted to run away from her. She stopped at once, looked at him helplessly.

The quiet pose was gone. He looked lost, anguished, as if the telegram had just come.

"Why did he have to die?" Josh demanded.

The bitterness in his voice made Mildred's heart spiral downward. She felt the sudden bleakness of failure: all along, through the happy years of his growing, Phil and she had been so sure that they were preparing a child for life, carefully interpreting the inexplicable in his world along with the facts.

She managed to say, "It isn't for us to answer. That meaning is God's. We both know that."

Josh shook his head. Stunned, she saw his refusal of all the years of unquestioning faith. This was the boy who had listened as raptly to Bible stories as to fairy tales; then, old enough, plunged into Sunday school and Hebrew classes. Only a few weeks ago, he had been studying wholeheartedly for his Bar Mitzvah.

"Josh," she said, her throat dry, "please talk to me."

"Well, don't tell me God," he blurted. "Like the rabbi did. What *reason* is there, Mom? You can't tell me. I know you can't."

He walked away so quickly that he lurched, but he stopped at the screen door and stared out. For the first time since he had been born, Mildred felt her son as a fear instead of an exciting, joyous challenge.

"He was in the big war," Josh said coldly, his back still to her. "That was plenty. Plenty."

Yearning for some kind of right answer, Mildred managed a few lame words: "Some men feel duty strongly. Not—just a one-time thing."

He whirled around, said with a strange, harsh anger, "It wasn't duty! Nobody can kid me. Not the rabbi—not God. Why are you? Don't, Mom! He already did his duty. More than a lot of guys. So why did he die? All I want is a reason. A *reason*."

"Josh, don't—please," she begged.

"They—they give you a medal, and—. What's such a far-away war got to do with Dad? Or the U.N.? Nobody else on our street volunteered. Nobody in temple. Just Dad. For what?"

His eyes were not a boy's, and Mildred felt the unreal terror of trying to grope toward a strange child.

"I just want a reason," this stranger said to her insistently. "Why'd he go? Why'd he get—killed?"

At that last word, which came out slurred with pain, Mildred cried out unthinkingly, from her heart: "Oh, my dearest, I miss him just as much as you do. I love him just as much."

Josh winced. The anger, so false, turned into the honest thing at last—the grief he had been hiding all along. He went slowly back to the couch, sat heavily. As she saw the sprawling body, the hands loose and pitfully awkward, Mildred's world righted itself for the first time since Phil's death.

The shocking knowledge was in her, suddenly, that she had gone away from her son in the weeks since that death. In her own bereavement, she had left him alone. The boy's composure had been a relief to her, not an anxiety.

And there was a deeper shock underlying this one. Josh's questioning of his God, his temple, the lovely pattern of religion his short life had contained with such certainty, brought her the sickening realization of her own uncomforted spirit. In permitting her unabated pain so long, her continuing hunger for Phil's arms and body, hadn't she also questioned a life-long belief?

Mildred came close to Josh, but made no attempt to touch him. He would not want to be held now, babied; that was one of the few things she knew for sure at this moment. Looking down at her son, she saw his father's eyes in a beginning face—his grandmother's eyes. The beautiful, deathless procession of generations wound through her heart; how had she forgotten the faith and hope mankind made of its children by giving them, by forever replenishing its family and its world?

And she thought, with hurt for Josh: A child's inheritance. Did I really think it was a medal? That honor and pride were all he needed, to hold in his hands for riches—father to son?

A feeling of shame came with the awareness of how she had put away Phil's words for herself. She had considered them her own, precious and private possessions left to a woman by her man. And she must have thought, without verbalizing it: Besides, Josh is a child. What could a husband's words mean to him? A lover's words? He doesn't need them. I do.

The shame was something she was not used to, and she had to brace herself to go on with the somber facts: She had seized the words and hidden them for her own comfort, though they belonged as much to Josh. A child needed all of the inheritance. Not just a medal. Not just prayers, either; for look how the old patterns of ritual, of preparation to live as a man under God, could turn meaningless when the heart was unprepared. This boy needed every bit of his inheritance. There must be such a thing as armoring yourself with the broad rituals of mankind—that make the human being, as well as the Jew.

Very suddenly, Mildred could think of Phil's smile without pain, without the loneliness and yearning which had sickened her memories.

"You want a reason, Josh," she said. "Why he went. Knowing he might not come back. He did know that."

Her son stared up at her, his eyes narrowed against the pushing tears.

Mildred nodded, said softly: "Sometimes a reason is just there. Inside a man. What he thinks and feels—believes—like part of his body."

Phil had sat in this room before leaving, and had talked to her. And now, as quietly as Phil had spoken, she talked to their son.

"Your father loved every part of life," she said. "Worked at it, wanted it every minute. There was no room in him for dying."

The word, dying, no longer hurt, and Mildred knew that she had stopped the senseless fighting of Phil's death. She had to walk for an instant, the thankfulness a feeling of almost explosive physical relief.

When she turned, leaning back against the piano, she was able to go on: "Your father used to laugh a lot. Remember? And there was something he'd say often—when he felt particularly good. When a favorite rose opened early. When we had potato pancakes for Sunday supper. Simple things. He'd say: 'For a Jew-boy in this world, this year, I'm mighty happy. Mighty satisfied.' And he'd laugh—but it wasn't ever a joke. If he were the type, it would have been a solemn laugh."

Josh's eyes began to absorb her words, and Mildred's memories lost the last vestige of sickness.

"A reason? Oh, Josh," she said tenderly. "Well, let me try to tell you. Before he left for the big one, that first war in his life—my life—he sat in this room and talked. You hadn't been born, but—oh, we used to talk about you a lot."

[179]

She smiled. "Your father had you named long time before you were born. Well, that night, he said to me: 'You know, I'm crazy about this country, this street, this house. Sometimes, Mil, I think about my grandfather and grandmother—who happened to come here from Germany. Who happened to get to a place called Atlanta, Georgia, first off. Young Jews. Just a little money— enough to buy needles and thread, a few other things for a peddler's kit. No Nazis then, eh? Just the little pogroms, the usual European Jew-hate. Small potatoes—but not to Goldmark the immigrant. So—a young Jew peddled on the roads of Georgia. He had kids. He brought his family up to Ohio for better bread-and-butter. And, Mil, I think of our kid. How maybe our Josh'll go to the same school you and I met at. And Mother—think Josh'll love Ann Arbor as much as Mother did? As much as we did? I do.' "

Mildred stopped for a second. Then she took a deeper breath, smiled again at the boy listening so intently.

"That's the way he talked that night," she said. "Just a kind of —wondering. I remember he said: 'I think of our pretty house, Mil. And the way I decided I'm going to be a lawyer some day. When it's possible. Because of a word like Nazi in the world. Far away from my house, my city, my darlings. Far as God—near as God. And how that's O.K. with my world—Phil Goldmark wanting to be a lawyer all of a sudden. Remembering his grandfather's choice—doing a repeat, because that word "choice" is just as good to a grandson, and to *his* son. I tell you, Mil, I'm crazy about this country.' "

Josh's face twisted. "Oh, Mom," he muttered.

"You want a reason," Mildred said. "To hold in your hands instead of a medal? The reason was always the same for Phil Goldmark. The second time he went to a war, we sat here together again. In this room. Now you were in the world, too. We felt you up in your bed, sleeping. The house was full of you, and we talked. Of so many things—people. You, us. A world of countries. The way even Grandma had been born in this country— down in Atlanta—so far from a word like Nazi, that the world was hearing again. Names like Eichmann, Khrushchev, Nasser, places like Havana, Moscow, Tel Aviv, Peiping. And yet things, names and countries, the world—they're never far any more. Far and near as God. That was your father's way of saying it. A word like Nazi. So far from his son, his wife, his mother—even *her*

[180]

mother and father. A word like 'choice.' He loved that word."
Mildred added, very softly, "He said to me: 'In case it ever
comes up, Mil, this Jew-boy is still crazy about this country. This
city, this street. The way "choice" hollers in this street. The way
this street, this house, is going to go on hollering "choice" loud
enough—always.' And he laughed. You know—that laugh of his?"

Josh jumped up and ran toward her. She met him with her own
hungry embrace. He was crying. Mildred held him tightly, let
him cry, her lips against his hair.

When finally he looked up at her, she saw that Phil actually
had given him his reason. Josh's eyes were quite still.

"I kind of forgot about Dad," he said. "Isn't that funny? Just—
forgot. The way he talked, the way he was. You know, laughing
that way? But no joke—ever. How he meant it, all the way in his
eyes, even laughing. Even—dying, I guess he'd mean it all the
way. Like what he told you, and—and you just told me. I just
kind of forgot."

"I almost did, too," Mildred said in a low voice, and kissed
him.

She watched him drag out his handkerchief and mop up. After
a while, she said shyly, "Feel like taking a look at the yard
before bedtime?"

Josh nodded, took her hand in the old, casual way.

They walked through the house, out the back door. In the
yard, a light fragrance seemed to hem them in like delicate
boundary lines. When first the house had been bought, Phil had
said with a pleased laugh: "Well, I'm going to have a smelly
garden, Mil. Always wanted one."

Now, as Mildred and her son walked in the darkness of the
yard, they knew the phlox as they passed it, and the scented
yellow lilies, the roses Phil had selected so carefully for their
perfume. They stopped at the back property line, where the
lilacs—long past blossom time—made a tall, thick hedge of green.
They could see the kitchen windows shining with soft light. The
night noises of their neighbors came into the yard, muffled, comfortable.

"Isn't it beautiful here?" Mildred said. "Let's plant a tree this
fall. Back here, where there's plenty of room for it to grow."

Josh was silent for a moment. Then he said jerkily, "Yeah, let's.
Right here, Mom. This city, this street. This—house."

[181]

Jack Ansell

THE ONLY ONE
IN TOWN

> Jack Ansell, a resident of the South for many years, is
> author of *His Brother, The Bear.* "The Only One In
> Town" deals with the effect of the racial issue on a
> Jewish storekeeper who tries to preserve his integrity in
> a small southern town. Mr. Ansell is with ABC-TV in
> New York.

The town of Twosboro is easy to miss, if you are driving more
than thirty miles an hour along Highway 25. There is a small oak
arrow on the left side of the road, and just below it the words,
Twosboro 2 Miles. But there has been so much rain in the
north-central areas of Louisiana lately that the w, the s, the b,
and the r have faded sadly, and are just now barely distinguish-
able. A speeding eye sees only T o o o, which has been mistaken
for everything from a new kind of traffic sign to an advertisement
for Toololoo's liver remedy, which is very popular in this part of
the world. They have been so busy in Twosboro lately that no
one has had time to repaint the wooden arrow.

Until last week there were one thousand seven hundred thirty-
nine residents in Twosboro. Marcus and Lillian Greenbaum were
the only Jews. They owned and operated one of the two clothing and dry goods stores on Lacey Street, the seven-block business
section of Twosboro, as had Marcus' father, Abram Greenbaum,
before him. The firm of A. Greenbaum and Son was sixty-seven
years old last week. Marcus was forty-six on Monday.

It started on Tuesday, just before noon. Marcus and his wife.
Lillian, were stacking levis on the open counter to the right of
the store's new all-glass door when Daniel Culp, the manager
of the only supermarket in Twosboro, lumbered in. Daniel Culp
always lumbers in, just as he always lumbers out. Daniel is a tall,
rangy, candle-limbed man with a pallid face at once so round
and so sad that it seems forever to be begging a return to the

[182]

right body. Daniel never says hello or good-bye. He stares at you from baby's eyes until you feel guilty of some small neglect, then with an innocence so artless it turns you to marble, he says laconically what he has come to say. He said what he came to say on Tuesday.

"Marcus. We was some of us noticin' only a hour so ago how you was the only man in Twosboro not to been signed up by the White Citizens Council." He paused with a hint of forbearance. "We think you better do that little thing, Marcus."

Marcus Greenbaum, whose hair was thinning, ran his thick stubby fingers through the random strands along his forehead. "I told Chet Tulley when he came around last week I wasn't interested in joining anything, Daniel," he said. His wife, Lillian, looked down at the levis. Her eyes were anxious slits.

Daniel Culp's soft, high voice never changed its level. His voice is popular in Twosboro at the semi-annual Baptist revivals. "I tell you somethin', Marcus. Man's sure got a privilege of changin' his mind one week to the next. This week ain't last week. I ain't Chet Tulley, neither."

Marcus, who is a full head-and-a-half shorter, and considerably broader, looked slowly up. "You don't need me, Daniel. One member more or less doesn't make or break the Citizens Council."

"We need you, Marcus. Know what I mean? We need you. We got to have you, Marcus. Okay I send Chet back around?"

Marcus' lips were pale and pursed. "No need to, Daniel," he said.

Daniel leaned imperceptibly forward but he appeared to Marcus like a man toppling from stilts. "You got a love on for niggers, Marcus?" His brown infant's eyes were black.

Lillian Greenbaum's head jerked up like a frightened fowl's. The veins were heavy in Marcus' neck. "There's no need for that kind of talk between us, is there, Daniel?" It sounded less a question than a soliloquy. Marcus, who had never found a particular joy in talking, often sounded as though he were talking to himself.

Daniel Culp smiled. "Nobody means to be rude or nothin', Marcus, and we've knowed each other most all our lives I reckon, but it ain't hard in a town size of Twosboro for a Jew and a nigger to wind up in the same stall. I don't like bein' outspoken like that, Marcus, an' I'm only sayin' it for your own good. You an' your good folks been fine citizens since Twosboro come into

[183]

bein' awmost, but this thing's big, Marcus, it's got everybody all worked up in nearbouts ever town around here. There's durn near as many niggers as there are whites in Pachatoula Parish, Marcus, and we got to be organized a hundred per cent proper. Why, them coons could get theirselves organized faster'n jack-rabbits the way this NAACP thing's goin'. No matter what else you may of got wind of, all the Council's set out to do is see none of them radical notions starts stirrin' 'em up. An' maybe if any one of them black boogers starts yappin' 'bout his rights, sort of show him what his rightful place is. Leastways in Twosboro. Reckon you better sign up, Marcus. I'll tell ole Chet to drop back by. Nice to seen you, Lillian."

When Daniel Culp had lumbered out, candle-limber and candle-sallow, Lillian Greenbaum turned a plaintive face, and her voice was shrill. "You lost your head, Marcus? Have you gone and lost your senses, Marcus? It's not enough to be the only Jewish people in this town? You have to be God yet, too?"

Marcus seemed not to hear her. He didn't answer. A curious smile started to mingle with the return of color to his lips. He always smiled like that when he was hurt, or lonely. He began arranging the levis in small neat stacks again, studying his edged precision with a heavy, slow respect. He knew how it irritated Lillian, this terrible detachment he assumed now with such cruel deliberateness. But he couldn't do otherwise. There was no talking to Lillian any more. He only ended up in some inarticulate corner, desperately stuttering the pathetic explanations for what he had yet to explain to himself.

His thick plodding fingers paralleled his thoughts. For the hundredth time since Chet Tulley had come by the store last week he asked himself what he was doing. He found no answer, not even the thinnest solace of pride. He was too small a man, he knew, to experience pride which somehow wasn't wanted or shared. He was alone, and he wasn't certain why.

It was strange. He was not a very smart man, and certainly not a brave man, and scarcely a man stirred to the bowels by the plights of whole races and creeds. If anything, he was a dismal, diffident man. These things he knew, or thought he knew. He was too simple a man to understand the maze of social consciousness, much less rear up to defend it. But when Chet Tulley had held out the small white card, itself so oddly anonymous, he had said no without pause or inflection. And all because of some confused chemistry in which he—who in Twosboro so often forgot he was a Jew—had suddenly, near shatteringly, remembered that he was. It was nothing he could turn into a convincing word, not even to Lillian. He recalled with a painful flush how he had said to her after Chet Tulley left the store, "I think maybe for the first time in my life I'm near to knowing what it is to be a Jew," only to have her glower back as she might to a child or a fool. He had stayed to himself for hours after that, thinking about himself, and about Twosboro, and about being a Jew. He had known so few Jewish families in his life, outside his own and Lillian's. They went to nearby Mannerville or to Lillian's home in Vicksburg for the High Holy Days, but the rest of the year they were Jews in name—in Twosboro. He had lived his life in Twosboro, speaking the Twosboro tongue, thinking the Twosboro thought. And now for the first time in that life he was apart from the only people, the only home, he had ever really known. And no one to understand it, least of all himself.

Here again, as always, his mind reached its stale dead end. His hands reached by rote for another stack of levis.

Lillian was raging on, as she had since last week. "What's a name on a piece of paper, Marcus? Nothing. Absolutely nothing. Lord! These people are our friends here, Marcus, they're the people we play gin with and watch television with. They're our customers, Marcus. Are you forgetting that, too? They're our *customers*. Do we play gin rummy with the *shvartsahs*? Are we living up north somewhere? This is the south, Marcus, it's Twosboro, we live right down here in Twosboro. . . ."

Marcus heard her, and pretended he didn't; and he felt neither guilty nor noble; and he knew, almost dumbly, that the fear in her voice was not false.

On Wednesday, Chet Tulley—the only sober barber in Twosboro and an unkempt, faltering man—came by again, and held out the white card with calloused fingers and guarded eyes. Marcus said, as gently as he was able, "I'm sorry, Chet, but I just won't do it." Lillian's eyes moved heavenward, and for a moment glazed stunningly mad.

Daniel Culp returned on Thursday, bringing with him the president of the Pachatoula Bank and Trust, Adam Sanders, who is a quiet and prosperous man, and whose family in the early days of Twosboro had made it possible for Abram Greenbaum to settle there. Daniel Culp said little, while the benign banker—

noted in Twosboro for licking the wounds which others have made—assured both Marcus and Lillian that they were two of the most highly respected people in the whole of Pachatoula Parish, as were Abram and Sarah Greenbaum before them, God rest their beloved souls, and that the only thing the good citizens of Twosboro were asking was that some nominal allegiance be given where allegiance was so assuredly due. Marcus, almost mesmerized by the deep honeyed drawl, thought for an instant he was actually agreeing to everything the ingratiating little man was saying, but when Daniel Culp said sharply, "We give you ever chance there is to give, Marcus. Don't blame us none whatever gits set loose now." He realized that a voice he could not rightly call his own had again managed the unqualified no.

That afternoon three Negro customers, to whom they had been selling for years and even used for odd jobs around the house, came into the store, and Lillian turned away from them with accusing abruptness, while Marcus waited on them with the dull familiarity of a lifetime, and tried—dispassionately—to bring them into some kind of balance with himself, and with Daniel Culp, and with Lillian, and with Twosboro. And couldn't. They were colored and he was white. They were Negroes and he was . . . a Jew. He felt suddenly as implausibly ancient as he felt curiously unborn. He wished for a single exquisite second he might feel that what he was doing he was doing out of great love, or great compassion, or great wisdom or reason or truth. It seemed so simple to feel simple humanity. It seemed so barren to have to think, again and again, I cannot put my name to this injustice because I am a Jew. It seemed so foolish and so foreign in Twosboro. He wondered—as he watched the undaunted colored people laugh themselves like children out of the new glass door—what his father might have done in his place. But his image of his father was as dim as his own tired question. He was tired to his soul.

On Friday morning he and Lillian walked the ten short blocks from their house to the store, and it was almost as if he had expected to find exactly what he found. A. Greenbaum and Son was a jarring cavity in the center of Lacey Street. The glass window and door had been totally shattered, and there was nothing inside but overturned counters and racks, and random pieces of soiled material and torn clothing which looked foolishly like castoffs at the end of a masquerade. Marcus gazed upon the scene as hollowly as it upon him; and although he was faintly aware of the deep gurgling noise in Lillian's throat, which sounded peculiarly as though she were drowning, he could not lift an arm to comfort her nor find the voice for anger.

They left Twosboro that night, saying little to themselves or each other. They drove to Mannerville, some fifty miles to the north, where he had a cousin, and only once during the still dark drive did a word pass between them. That was when Lillian, her head pressed against the plastic seat cover of the car, said between closed teeth, "Not even one of your precious *shvartsahs* to tell us good-bye." But the words were merely a natural lining to the emptiness that clothed him. There was no one and nothing to fight. It was as if something had been ordered, something ordained, and he but its helpless purveyor.

Somebody remarked in Twosboro yesterday that since everybody in town is now solidly behind the Council it wouldn't hurt them any to get the sign on Highway 25 repainted. There are one thousand seven hundred and thirty-seven residents now of course, although Daniel Culp's wife, Mary Alice, is expecting another next month. There are six hundred and sixty-three Negroes and one thousand seventy-four whites. There are no Jews in Twosboro.

Richard M. Elman

TIMMY

Mr. Elman is a frequent contributor to *The Nation, Paris Review, Saturday Review* and other leading publications. He is the author of the novel *A Coat for the Tsar*.

At a time when relations between Jews and Negroes make a hot potato for political discussion, Mr. Elman's story of a Jewish widow and her friendship with a Negro maid is particularly pertinent — a frank and disturbing look at a curious but utterly believable symbiosis.

Mrs. Golden's children rarely visited her. She didn't mind, although she told them that she did. Edgar, her husband, was like the children; he was always busy with one thing or another, and that Mrs. Golden didn't care for any of his activities wasn't necessarily his fault. Edgar was a fine provider, an energetic, active sort of man who had gotten quite far rather early in life and thought he should still be going somewhere. The only trouble was his wife hadn't cared to make the trip with him. She had liked it much better in her comfortable home. Bitterly, once, Mrs. Golden had accused Edgar of inspiring the children's neglect for her, but even as she spoke she saw this wasn't so. She knew her husband would have liked the kids to spend more time with their mother if only to relieve him of some of the burden.

Not that you could honestly call Lilly Golden a ball-and-chain; she was far too meek, long-suffering, devoted, and was considered by most strangers to be a good wife. Although she and her husband rarely saw each other (except at breakfast), or spent time with each other (except on those combination business-trip vacations which Edgar liked to take), they knew deeply that their marriage was inextricable in the same way that some dreams make one aware that one is dreaming. If Lilly happened to be awake at night when Edgar would come home from one of his trade banquets or dinner meetings, she would register the proper notes of protest and solicitude at being awakened while always making sure to ask him questions about his day. Drowsy, bored, yet somehow strengthened by her husband's return, Lilly would lie back and listen to Edgar thump about in the darkness while he undressed, proud that she had sustained the loneliness once again. Shuddering when the covers were rolled back, or when Edgar brushed against her with a gross caress, she had schooled herself never to move away. Pretending sleep, she would wait until he had dozed off, and then she would get up, would walk out into the parlor, and stare blankly at the evening paper for an hour or so.

During the day Lilly found that being alone was an exhausting chore. Then she tried hard to be "self-sufficient" in response to Edgar's constant declarations that he was not going to live forever, but as she was not a club woman and did not like to window shop in Manhattan or to go to museums or matinees, the hours dragged. Her three sons, their wives, and the grandchildren might have kept her company, but the daughters-in-law frightened Lilly; the sons were now businessmen themselves; and she knew enough not to want to interfere in the raising of their children. Consequently, her main companion had to be Timmy.

Timmy was about the same age as her mistress and she had been with the Goldens as a day worker ever since the children were infants. The two women got along well. Boisterously, each entertained the other without ever being mean or condescending; with Timmy in the house, Lilly did not need to feel so shut in. From 9 A.M. to 5 P.M. on Mondays, Wednesdays, and Fridays, the two women carried on a running kaffee klatsch and pajama party. At times they giggled together like schoolgirls; at other times Timmy called her mistress "ma'am" and "honey" and never Lilly, but that was merely a convention; they talked to one another like old friends.

Timmy was a tall, heavy-set colored woman who had once been slim and pretty. She had a brazen stare and the skin along her arms and shoulders had a smooth, deep brown luster. Only her high cheekbones and her long delicate eyelashes gave an indication of her former voluptuousness. Otherwise, in her tattered stocking-cap with her sleeves rolled up above her crinkled elbows, she gave off a perfume of starch and bleaching fluid and affected a plodding, goonish sloppiness in comparison with which Lilly Golden looked withered, skimpy, almost un-formed—a frail, not quite blonde woman with narrow hips and shoulders, whose large blue, staring eyes seemed so much brighter than her habitually drab printed bathrobes. Placed alongside Timmy, Lilly could not help but look meager indeed.

Yet she would spend hours in the kitchen with the colored woman, gossiping, or smoking cigarettes, or just watching those big soft shoulders and strong arms plod through the ironing. "How's your sister these days?" Lilly might ask. ". . . You know the one I mean . . . the one who needs insulin . . . don't you remember? I gave you the money. . . ."

"Oh that one," Timmy would say with a good-natured smile, "that one that has the diabetes," signifying that she had been caught in an earlier lie or an exaggeration. Hurriedly then, as she creaked back and forth against the ironing board, Timmy would find a way to change the subject, or she would begin a long dissertation on the family's squalid condition in far-away Pine Ridge, Georgia. She would squeal, "That reminds me," and then would throw Lilly completely off the scent by quickly nar-rating one harrowing New York adventure, followed by a second one, in the process of which the names of dozens of exotic gin mills, movie theaters, barbecues, and hotels might be summoned up as evidence. Tying her bathrobe tightly about her waist, Lilly would sit cross-legged on the kitchen stool, a shrewd inquisitor. She could always tell when Timmy was lying, but she never cared to catch her up and make her stammer; she preferred to hide her secret glee behind the terry-cloth lapels of her robe.

Because Timmy had never married, to Lilly's knowledge, the first question every Monday would invariably be: "How was your week-end? How did the boys treat you?"

Then Timmy's thick, tinted lips would break into a rare frown. "Missus Goldenhoney," she would say, wiping a hand along her bandana, "sometimes I think them men creatures oughtn't to be allowed to carry on the way they do."

What followed then would be a salty discourse concocted half of Bessie Smith and half of Mary Worth. Timmy's escapades with the men of Harlem or Bedford-Stuyvesant had not ceased at the menopause. They always seemed to begin with her stepping out with one man, losing track of him, then running into a second, an even older friend. But, despite the inept plotting, the years had

taught Timmy to color such improbable yarns to Lilly's satisfaction with numerous strand-like asides and great quantities of
a dark rhetoric of the streets that permitted her to invent infinite
epithets with which to allude to the act of love, or to such actions
as dancing, boozing, or even singing in a church choir. All these
experiences breathed life when Timmy told them, and the result was that Mrs. Golden might frown, or sigh, or make little
clucking noises of disapproval with her tongue, but she would
find herself muttering "Ah yes," and "Go ahead," and "Then what
happened?"

Even over lunch, the colored maid's lusty monologue might
continue. If Timmy was too busy with her housework, Mrs.
Golden would prepare the sandwiches and brew tea. Then they
would sit down opposite each other. Later, if it was a nice day,
Mrs. Golden might get dressed to do her shopping. Otherwise,
she would order by telephone and they would spend the afternoon in more talk, with Lilly following Timmy about the house
to issue the kinds of instructions which after twenty years were
no longer necessary.

Usually, then, the two women would talk in a confidential way
about the Golden family. In the master bedroom, Mrs. G would
pitch in with the moving and lifting of heavy objects as she related what a busy man her husband was; one at a time, through
her sons' deserted lairs, she would discuss what eventually should
be done with the various pieces of sporting equipment, books,
records, and souvenirs that still lay around on the tops of night
tables and bureaus, catching dust; or she would show the maid
the newest snapshots of her grandchildren, or tell her dry, unin-
teresting stories of their latest antics. In the face of all this,
Timmy played her role convincingly; she was polite without
ceasing for a minute to attend to her chores. She made no secret
of the fact that she didn't like any of the other Goldens. "Them,"
she called the children, and Lilly no longer winced when she
heard the word. She was much too pleased that she could have
this intimacy with Timmy and she never felt that she was permitting the girl liberties. When Edgar asked if she had paid "the
schwartsa," she did not rebuke him, for she knew the name was
important to him for his image of himself, but she almost never
used such a word herself, and if she did she crossed her fingers.
The fact was that when her maid had left the house Lilly Golden
thought only about her next visit.

[191]

That is why, when Edgar died suddenly in his sleep of a heart attack, Timmy was the first person she wanted to come and be with her.

The children lined up solidly against that idea. On the morning of the funeral, when the maid was out of earshot in the kitchen, they argued that Lilly could afford a real companion, a college girl or another widowed lady like herself, not just a colored maid. They also suggested that Mrs. Golden sell the house and move into an apartment nearer the city. When Lilly raised her voice in protest, her eldest son puffed out his cheeks just like Edgar, and declared: "Mother, please. We know you're still upset."

It rained for the funeral, and the cold, dreary affair went off according to a precise timetable. There were the usual number of staged and unstaged outbursts; there was even a moment of genuine pathos for Lilly when the coffin was lowered into the grave and she found that she could not release the pocket of dirt that had been thrust into her hands. Afterwards, she and the children returned to the old house for a cold luncheon prepared by Timmy, but Lilly retired as soon thereafter as possible, and when, early the next morning, the children returned for a visit along with two of Edgar's brothers, the assistant rabbi, and the family lawyer, Lilly greeted them by announcing her plans with dry eyes:

She would keep the big house and ask Timmy to sleep in. She did not want to go away on a trip; she did not think it would be fair to live in White Plains with her eldest son; she did not want her sister in Minneapolis to come and stay with her a while. "We never got along when Edgar was alive. Why should we now?" Lilly asked. "Besides," she added, "Flora has no sense of humor and Timmy does." She preferred Timmy, or to be left alone, if need be, for she wanted time to think. Patiently, Lilly explained that just so long as she had someone to do the heavy cleaning and cook for her occasional guests, she would be happy, but her second son, Robert, exclaimed: "Honestly, Mamma, it sounds so impractical."

Lilly didn't deny that it was. "That's the way I want it . . . and I can afford it," she simply said.

"Besides," she smiled vaguely again, as if her colorless smile and her colorless voice were conspiring together, "I won't be lonely. There's TV and the telephone and a great big world outside."

"But Mother. . . ."

Lily held up her hand to demand silence. "If all else fails, I'll have my memories," she said.

This sentiment took everybody by surprise. The three sons thought: "She means memories of us." The daughters-in-law smiled guiltily together. "Jesus," went the astonished lawyer, and even Edgar's brothers mused: "Memories of him. The old girl liked him after all. God help her."

Then, because none of the sons had wanted Lilly to move in with them in the first place, one by one they relented and it was agreed that she was to do as she pleased, as long as the situation was manageable, if she would release some of the money from the estate to compensate the younger Goldens for the valuable property on which the house stood.

Wearily, Lilly agreed. It was small blackmail for her freedom, she thought, as she signed all the necessary papers, kissed her children, and made them promise to visit her often with the little ones. Then the lawyer had to go and Edgar's brothers sat around coughing, whispering, and glancing at condolence cards, before they, too, departed.

On the very next morning, Timmy came to work late as usual, but Mrs. Golden didn't make her intentions known to the girl on that day or the next, for she was still too busy receiving visitors, and when the last of these had departed, she preferred to remain alone in her room. It was not that Lilly felt timid. On the contrary, she felt sure that Timmy would be more comfortable in that large suite of rooms in her attic than in some Harlem tenement, and she had promised herself not to impose any restrictions on the maid. If she didn't make the invitation right away, it was because she wanted to endure her isolation for just a little while longer; for the moment, it gave her a kind of joy.

Ever since that morning when she had opened her eyes to find Edgar dead alongside her, Lilly had hardly a moment to make her peace with that part of her life that began and ended with Edgar. To be finally alone was like waking from a bad dream to be assured by somebody you wanted to trust that the dream had been a fact and now the real dream was to start; and when she looked down into Edgar's rude, cold eyes for the last time, Lilly wondered if it weren't all hallucination. How else had she ever been tamed by such a man? Death had twisted Edgar's lips and blanched his cheeks, turning his expression sullen and pathetic. How then had he managed to frighten her so in their former life together? When she was alone she pondered this question as she meandered about the big house in her peignoir, going from room to room, throwing out letters, magazines, and papers without discrimination, save for the fact that she touched everything that had once been Edgar's with a faintly pleasurable sense of dread.

For nearly two weeks she lived that way. Timmy was given a vacation with pay; for a few days the phone was lifted off its cradle; and she told her family not to worry and not to try and see her for a while. Getting up when she pleased and going to sleep when she pleased, Lilly Golden drew the shades about her, threw away the stacks of black-edged cards without acknowledging them or the wreaths and flowers from her late husband's Gentile friends, and lived for the most part on coffee and on the baskets of fruits and sweets that kept arriving. She wandered through the house, her eyes glancing from the television set to the sliver of daylight beneath the drawn shades, or to the ancient sepia photos of her husband and the babies that were on the mantel, and while she made preparations for her new mode of life, she was not stirred to thoughts of Timmy. But on the Monday of the third week after Edgar's death, the maid returned.

It was a warm, springish day in late March when Lilly woke up quite late in the morning from a dream about New Orleans, where she had spent her honeymoon, to find that the shades had been raised and that the sun was streaming across her face brightly. At first, she was alarmed by all the sunshine and the ringing stillness to the air, until she detected Timmy's familiar whistle coming from downstairs in the kitchen. Then she looked up and noticed that the television was still lit from the night before with tiny incandescent specks, although it made no noise now save for a low, steady, shushing sound. Lilly jumped out of bed. She rushed to the machine and flicked the switch. Slipping into her robe, she hurried out of the room and down the hall to wash her face and comb her hair in the bathroom. Presently, she was hurrying again toward the stairway when she stopped herself short, cinched the belt on her robe once more, and began to walk downstairs slowly into the kitchen.

[194]

The first thing she saw was Timmy's broad bent back. "Good morning," she called to the girl, who had already set up her ironing board and was going over the last of Edgar's shirts. Between puffs of steam, Timmy lifted her head gracefully, "I got your juice ready," she announced, without yet looking around.

Lilly's glance went to the counter near the sink, where Timmy had placed a setting for breakfast. There was light toast in the salver and the percolator stood on the stove, warmed by a smudge of blue flame. On the ironing board, alongside Timmy's elbow, a cold cup of coffee stood.

"Why, that's very sweet of you," Lilly said, trying still to get the girl to turn around. She went toward the counter.

"Maybe you should give the juice a stirring," Timmy suggested.

"Yes, I will . . . of course," murmured Lilly, glancing sideways as she walked past and noticing Timmy's bright green pinafore and the new pink bandana that held her straight hair in place against her head. At the counter she spun around and met the girl full face. She had expected a smile but was greeted with a stare and a slow look of irony around the corners of the mouth. "You look well," Lilly said.

Timmy nodded: "Uh huh."

"Very well indeed," Lilly added. As she downed her juice with a quick toss of the head, she heard the iron sizzle against the shirt front. Then Mrs. Golden walked to the stove and poured herself some coffee. Lighting a cigarette, she sat down on the kitchen stool, simultaneously kicking her bright gingham slippers off her feet and curling her white toes around the chrome stool support, to watch Timmy glide over the shirt front and to sip her coffee.

"Well?" she asked.

And again: "Well?"

But the maid was reluctant to start a conversation, so Lilly finally had to add: "Well, how was your vacation?"

Timmy pretended to frown. "Trouble," she mumbled, "nothing but trouble, expense, and aggravation."

Lilly's heart began to pound. Then, aloud, she heard Timmy add: "Didn't even get to Pine Ridge. Didn't get nowhere. Stayed home most of the time with Bill and watched teevee. Well, you know," she explained rather archly, as if an explanation was in order, ". . . Bill . . . he's my new fella . . . he don't like to go nowheres. . . ."

"Oh?"

Timmy's body heaved. She dipped the ends of her fingers under the dripping sink and sprinkled the area around the blue ESG monogram on Mr. Golden's shirt. Tiny currents of steam shot out when she placed the hot iron over the monogram. "God damn Bill," she mumbled grouchily.

"Men are like that sometimes," Lilly said, trying to console her.

"Oh, but I didn't mean," Timmy started to say, before succumbing to a giggle. Then she smirked: "You said it, sister. You're lucky to be done with all that. Maybe Jewish men are different. . . ."

"No." Lilly shook her head. Then she decided to be bold. "I didn't know you had a new man," she said. "Tell me about him. What's his full name? What is he like? What does he do?"

The smile faded from Timmy's lips. "Name's Bill," she replied, folding Edgar's shirt and reaching down into her wicker basket for another damp white bundle. "Bill don't do nothing much," she added with a grunt.

"Oh, Timmy. I'm sorry," said Lilly again. The expression had been formed without her choosing it. She had expected more from Timmy—a story, a ribald explanation of Bill's do-nothing attitude—but that was no reason for her to be sorry, and when the maid remained silent as she wrung out the shirt between her pudgy, dark pink hands, she wished she could recall the phrase. "He don't do nothing . . . that one," she heard Timmy say, almost belligerently, bending low over the plane of the board now so that her ample bosoms were pendant behind the pinafore, and when she saw her reach for the hot iron again, Lilly suddenly blurted: "Timmy. . . ."

The maid looked up.

". . . I don't know whether it's necessary for you to do Mr. Golden's shirts with such care now," Lilly said.

Timmy's smooth forehead was dense with perspiration and her hand was clutching the iron. "No, ma'am?" she asked, incredulously.

"No," Lilly announced, gaining courage. "As a matter of fact, there's a lot of Mr. Golden's stuff lying around that we ought to organize and throw away. I tried to do some things when you were gone, but I didn't know where to begin or what to do with certain items. There's all his suits, for instance. Some are like new. My husband was quite a dandy, you know. Maybe your Bill can use them?"

"*No, ma'am. Not Bill,*" the maid spoke loudly and sternly. She stared hard at Lilly as if delivering a prepared lecture. "Bill wouldn't like no hand-me-downs. . . ."

Lilly's throat went dry: "I see. . . ."

Turning away, she tried to close her eyes, to shut the incident from her thoughts, to dissociate herself from this second blunder. She realized she might have offended her old friend by offering a dead man's clothes to her new lover. Negroes, she knew, were apt to be superstitious. But she had meant no offense. She swore she hadn't. She had only thought that Bill might want to make use of such nice clothes. Walking barefoot to the stove to pour herself a second cup of coffee, Lilly could feel Timmy's eyes upon the back of her neck, and she was aware of a strong, cheap perfume. "Ma'am?" she heard. Spinning around so that she spilt some of the coffee into the saucer, Lilly saw the maid staring down at the wilted monogram on the damp white shirt.

She whispered: "Yes?"

"Ma'am," Timmy's lips moved again.

"Yes," she replied.

"Maybe you don't understand what I meant. . . ."

"Oh, never mind," Lilly interruped.

"But Mrs. Goldenhoney. . . ."

"Timmy, I think I understand and I certainly didn't mean to offend your Bill; however, I do think we ought to try and dispose of these things come what may."

She waited patiently for the colored woman to agree with her, but when not another word was said, Lilly lit a fresh cigarette from the still-smouldering butt end and began to speak again in a hoarse, croaking voice. "Timmy," she asked then, "along these lines . . . what would you say . . . how would you like a full time job?"

Timmy gave no sign that she had understood. She brushed the sweat off her forehead and again started to lift the iron.

"*Didn't you hear what I asked you?*" Lilly's throat began to hurt. "Do you understand what I mean?"

The maid breathed heavily. "I heard you and I understan' and I was thinkin' about it. . . ."

"Well . . . what do you think?"

"Well now, Mrs. Goldenhoney, I think that's darn nice of you, but, ma'am," she smiled, "you see, I don' know's if Bill would like that idea. . . ."

"But he can sleep in with you. What is there not to like about it?"

"Oh . . . you know," the maid turned shy.

Lilly could no longer contain her curiosity. More than ever before, she felt that she did not know and that Timmy was not trying to understand what she had offered her. "Do you always do what this Bill likes you to do?" she asked sharply. Then: "Why him and not the others?"

Timmy mimicked shock. Her mouth fell open. "Because Bill . . . he ain't like any of the others," she said, and when Lilly didn't let on that she had understood, Timmy added: "I mean he's different . . . treats me good. Them others . . . they don't give a good goddamn for old Timmy . . . all except Bill. . . . He's serious with me. Now do you understan'?"

She paused to see if her message had been understood before adding, with another curious heave of her shoulders: "Matter of fact . . . Bill, he say he don' want me to work here at all no more. He say I could do much better in a factory. But I keeps telling him about you and how you needed me now that the Mister is passed away and he say okay . . . okay, maybe you should stay on a while, Timmy, until she is straightened out with the estate and can move in with her folks. . . ."

The maid's voice trailed off as she saw Mrs. Golden clap her hands over her burning ears. Then it rose again for a moment, but Lilly clearly was no longer listening. The dullest of headaches was coming on her and she had already begun to reply in an uncanny echo of a voice: "That's very understanding of Bill. Thank you, Timmy. Bill is very understanding and you are being too kind . . . but . . . I hadn't planned to move in with my *folks* ever. . . ."

Timmy interrupted: "Mrs. Golden, you oughtn't to talk that way. . . ."

"*Why not?*" Lilly cried. "*Don't you understand that I don't like them any better than you do?*"

The maid did not answer. She merely shook her head as a further warning to Lilly before turning away to resume her ironing. And Lilly, wanting to beg her now to stop, became strident: "*Why are you treating me like this?* You're lying again, aren't you? You. . . ."

[198]

But in the middle of that last sentence, a sudden surge of humiliation went through her. The extent of her own impudence became unbearable as she perceived that Timmy would never have considered such an arrangement even if there had been no Bill. Then Lilly felt terribly meager and embarrassed in the presence of the stout, complacent colored woman. She pushed aside her stool and walked to the doorway. But spite got the better of her once again. Turning, she announced: "I am going upstairs to dress. Then I am going shopping. When you get a chance I want you to clean out Mr. Golden's closet. Keep anything you think Bill will like. I'm sure he can't be *that* particular."

"Uh huh."

That special grunting sound of the maid's pierced Lilly's being, draining the spite from her so that—for a moment—she stared at the stolid figure bent low over the ironing board with a quiet tenderness, but when she tried to imagine Timmy once more as she had in her fantasies, her eyes filled with tears and she had to flee upstairs.

Twenty minutes later a hot bath had revived her sufficiently to allow her to dress and stand fully clothed for the street on the top landing. As she went down the stairs, Lilly heard Timmy vacuuming and humming to herself in the living room. She said nothing to the maid as she rushed out onto the front steps, but when she returned from the supermarket and the bank an hour and a half later, still wide-eyed from the unaccustomed glare of day, Timmy had fled. The old house was deserted once more. The shutters banged; the floors rang with her footsteps; and there was not even a note left behind, although Timmy had not taken any of her uniforms and had carefully placed Edgar's shirts on the bed above her pillow.

That evening Mrs. Golden could not sleep. As she lay in the darkness of her room with her eyes open she imagined as if in a dream that Timmy had been caught in a tenement fire and was dying of burns. Rushing to the hospital by taxi, she knew that she would offer to forgive the maid, but when she was ushered into the dingy, tiled hospital room she saw Edgar's naked white body lying on the bed.

She cried out.

Early the next morning a man called on the telephone.

Timmy was taking a job in a factory, he said. She was not going to do housework any more. Whatever was still owed, Mrs.

[199]

Golden could send care of Bill Dawson at Post Office Box E 120, Bronx 11, N.Y.

"Did you write that number down?" the man asked.

Sprawled across her bed, Lilly Golden swallowed painfully as she assured the man that she had copied the address.

"Timmy says it comes to twenty-nine dollars and seventy-five cents for three days plus carfare and for you to send a money order, not a check," the man said then.

"All right," went Lilly, before realizing that she had something more to say, a message to give. She added: "I hope Timmy will be happy and that she will forgive me for what I said. I was sorry that she had to leave so abruptly."

But when she heard the dial tone break in she knew that Timmy's boy friend had already hung up.

Barry Spacks

THE THREE
LITTLE KITTENS

Barry Spacks is professor of English at the Massachusetts
Institute of Technology, and author of many short stories
which have appeared in distinguished literary quarterlies.
In this fable, Mr. Spacks skates on the thin ice of
dialect and the kind of humor no longer too fashionable,
without once being offensive or heavy-handed.

It happened in December. Cold? I'm afraid to blow my nose it
might chip off, that's how cold. It's so cold I'm wearing three pairs
of pants, and going down the street to open the store I see my
breath come from my mouth in a puff like a white balloon, so I
look like a character from a comic strip who's got nothing to say.
All right—cold. I'm walking to the store and what do I see? Three
kittens. I see three kittens, without mittens. Now it just so
happens that in my store I sell mittens, all kinds. In fact, mittens
is a specialty with me, so naturally I'm interested that these three
kittens shouldn't have between them a single pair of mittens on
such a day. I think to myself, maybe it's a problem of size, they
couldn't get fitted? In the store I knew I had plenty of mittens
small enough for a flea, much less a kitten—so maybe I could be
of service? Also, as I come along, the kittens begin to cry. Well,
what do you think, I got a heart like a stone? Naturally, I go
over to inquire the trouble. I say, "What's with all the crying,
kittens? Could anything happen it's so bad it couldn't be worse?
Please, stop crying, tell me, what is it?"

The head kitten sniffs and says, "We lost our mittens, so we
shall have no pie."

"What?"

"You heard me, Pop."

"Well, that's nothing," I said. "Nothing. Stop crying already—
think of the kittens starving in Europe. And as far as you lost

your mittens, so big deal. You come along with me to the store, you buy yourself each another pair of mittens, and it's not such a tragedy already."

Well, that was the right thing to say. All of a sudden no more crying, and I'm walking down the street with three kittens beside me. How do I feel? I feel *wonderful!* Believe me, a good deed warms the heart on a cold day. No, no, I'm perfectly happy with these kittens, you understand—already they looked to me a little shifty, with not such nice manners—but I said to myself, Charlie, I said, how many would stop on a day like this to worry about kittens? and the answer I got was: precious few. It gave me a little pick-up, you know?

Anyway, we come to the store. I open up, I go to the back, and sure enough I find a carton of super-small-size mittens, left from a hundred years already.

"Kittens," I said, "take a look. Here's a fine piece of merchandise, and I'm making a special price. Take three pair it costs you a buck each"—you got to understand that I myself paid already approximately 87 cents a pair for these mittens—"A buck each," I said, "bear them away and use them in health."

"So who has money?" said the smallest kitten, and like that they're crying again, "waaa, waaa, we lost our mittens, we don't get no pie," and so forth. I tell you, it was terrible.

"Don't *cry*," I said. "Please. Stop crying, all right?" One thing I can't stand, a kitten should cry.

"Listen," I sai*d*, "*take* the mittens. Here," I told them, "take, take. Only don't cry."

Well, naturally they stopped crying, and again I felt very pleased with myself. This is not a way to run a mitten business, but what can you do, send them out in the street barehanded? They scrambled all over each other to get at the box.

"You don't have something in leather, maybe?" the middle-

[202]

sized kitten asked. These were wool, but very nice, believe me. Top quality.

"Look," I said, "for the price you're paying, be satisfied."

"Sure, Pop," said the largest kitten. "Thanks."

"Thanks," said the middle kitten, and the smallest one too, and they're gone, each with a pair.

Okay. I'm feeling good. I settle down with the paper to wait for a customer—it's not too much to ask?—but nothing happens. Gradually it gets warmer, the steam is coming up. My blood begins to circulate a little. My bones are thawing. In fact, in the chair behind the counter slowly I'm dozing off to sleep, when the little bell from the door tinkles, and it's the kittens. Crying.

"Weh's mir," I groaned, *"now* what's the trouble?"

"Waaa," cried the kittens, "waaa, waaa, waaa. Again we lost our mittens."

"Impossible!"

"No, it's true," said the head kitten.

"And listen, no *mittens*—" said the middle kitten.

"—no pie," said the little kitten.

"Besides which we're freezing our paws off," the head one put in.

"Look," I said, "what do you think this is, the Be Kind to Animals? This is a store, not a charity institution!"

But they're crying even more.

"What do you want from me?" I said, "Didn't I already give you some mittens?"

Louder. And louder.

"Weh," I said, "all right, take, take. But be more *careful* this time."

"Sure, Pop," said the head kitten, and that's another three pair gone with the wind.

And not a word of thanks.

And who's back, exactly five minutes later? You got it.

"Now wait just a second," I said.

"Waaa, waaa," they start, "the three little kittens, they lost their mittens . . ."

"Dummkopfs! You can't hold on to a pair of mittens for five minutes?"

"That's the long and the short of it," says the head kitten.

"Okay," I said, "I'm sorry. But no more. You got to learn the hard way."

So the middle kitten says, "Listen, what do you expect? We're only kittens. If we had any brains we'd be running a store already like you."

And they start to cry worse than ever. "Okay," I shout, "okay. Take. Take. Only stop crying. And be *careful*."

Another three pair. At this rate I'll be out of merchandise before a customer comes in the store. But all right, I think, it's charity, it's deductible. And when the bell tinkles next time, I don't even look up from my newspaper. "Again?" I ask. "Uh huh," they reply.

Well, it keeps up all morning long, kittens and mittens, mittens and kittens, the whole morning. Finally there comes a time to stop: from almost a gross I got left three measly pair.

"No more," I told them. "No more!"

"We'll cry," said the smallest kitten.

"So cry," I said. "Who cares?"

"But we won't get no pie," said the head kitten. "Be reasonable, Pop."

"Out," I hollered, steeling my heart, "out of the store!"

And how did I feel then? I felt *terrible*. I couldn't help thinking about those kittens, freezing in the cold. Crying. Not getting no pie. All right, I told myself, they're careless, they're ungrateful, but what can you expect from a bunch of kittens? I said to myself, Charlie, you got no heart? I said, what, considerations of business expediency should dry up the milk of human kindness?

Never! I cried, and I snatched up the last three pairs of mittens and ran out in the cold to find them. A crazy, mishugina thing to do? A soft-headed, sentimental gesture?

You're darned right!

[204]

Because I came around the corner, freezing already—in my rush I didn't even put on my own mittens—and there they were. With a folding table. And a little cash register. And a crowd of kittens I've never seen before. Customers. And a sign:

SPECIAL!
KITTEN MITTENS
3 Prs. $1.59.

And another sign:

PIE!
15¢ a cut.

I couldn't even speak.

"Now don't fly off the handle, Pop," said the head kitten. "We *found* them again, that's all."

"We found our mittens, we found our mittens," the other two sang, gazing at me anxiously.

"See, it just so happened we found them all again," said the smallest kitten.

"So we thought, you know,—" said the middle kitten.

"Like, after all, Pop, business is business," said the head kitten.

"No hard feelings?" they all said at once.

Now what would *you* have done? Honestly? Step in there and knock those kittens this way and that? Reach in and empty the till? Jump up and down on the pie?

I gazed at the kittens. They gazed at me.

"Please," I said, "here," setting the last three pair before them, "take." And I turned back toward my store. "Hey, wait! Hey, Pop, hold on a minute!" They came after, but I out-distanced them. Life is hard, but on occasion it offers certain pleasures; I locked the door, and listened to them out there weeping away. Weeping in contrition. Choking with sobs of shame. Or was it that? I didn't dare go look to find out. Was it the sound of sobs I heard, or the sound of three little mouths, stuffing themselves with pie?

Arthur Kober

AN OLE PERSIN YOU DON'T KEEP MOVIN' AROUN' LIKE IF SHE'S A PIECE LUGGITCH

> Arthur Kober, the author of *Having a Wonderful Time* and humorous stories about Bella Gross and her family, is working on his memoirs. The device of the telephone monologue to reveal character is one of his favorite approaches but here what appears on the surface just another lampoon of a middle-class Jewish housewife turns out as a touching inquiry into the plight of the unwanted old.

Hello, Henny? . . . Hi, Henny. This is Ruthie. Listen, Henny, when we got home las' night I foun' a messitch you called me up but it was awmost happest twelve, nearly one, by that time, and I figgered, my goodness, she's prolly asleep by now, Henny is, what'sa sense wakin' you up? . . . Ha? . . . You wanted we should come over your house? . . . When? . . . Las' night? Oh, we couldn't of las' night on account Arnie, he made this here previous engagemint, which is where we went las' night.

Listen, Henny, you remember a couple months ago I mentioned you these people we met, Mr. and Mrs. Rabin? . . . Oh, certainey you remember on account I tole you they this couple who owned this big house right next the one we rented in Long Beach all doong the month Augus'. Jack Rabin, he owns a chainna discount stores—you know, refrigerators, TV sets, 'lectrical appliances and such, and his wife, Gladys, she useta be in show business, a dancer, a singer or somethin'. Anyways, their whole house, no matter where you look, she's got pitchas hangin' from the time she was in show business. This musta been a good fifteen-twenny years ago, maybe more, when a persin could put their hanns arounna waist, she was so thin. Today, like Arnie says, "You gotta get a buncha kids to play ringga-rounna-rosie, and then I betcha, their fingers won't even be touchin' yet." . . .

No, Henny, I don't mean she's heavy set. I mean she's plain fat! But she's got a simply movvelous disposition, that I mus' say.

Any case, Jack and Arnie, all doong the month Augus', if there's one thing they did, it was playin' gin rummy, but evvey single night, regella like clockwork. It was a habit, a drug—know what I mean? . . . That's right. Any case, no matter what, right after dinner they simply hadda sit down, the two men, and have their game gin rummy while Gladys and me, we'd sit aroun' and we'd schmoos, or we'd watch a little television, else we'd drive to the Lido movie house and we'd take in a pitcha show, you know, a double featcha.

Finey I hadda say to Arnie, "Fa heaven's sake, Arnie, what kine vacation is this when evvey single night you either go over to the Rabins to gamble, else Jack comes over here to gamble?" "Honey," Arnie says to me, "a vacation is a time when a persin should relax, a time when he should take it nice and easy. And believe me, honey," he says to me, "I'm takin' Jack's dough very nice and easy." "Well, I don't think that's the lease bit nice," I says to him. "Look, honey," Arnie says, "any time he wantsa quit, let him quit. Nobody's twistin' his arm he should be my pigeon." . . .

Waddeya mean, can Rabin afford it? Listen, Henny, you should see that gorgeous house in Long Beach—it's regella mansion! And his garden, Henny, a show-place with all kines flowers. Why, it takes two men alone to keep that garden up. Besides, they got their own cook, she's got a maid, Gladys, and when they drive to the city, they got a chauffered car to take them there. And you know somethin' else? The couple times we went out to dinner—you know, a restront?—Jack never, not even once, let Arnie put his hanns in his pockit. "Listen, boy," he says to Arnie, "you two are strickly my guess', see, so let's not have any argamints who picks up the check. Me, that's who!" I dunno, Henny. Somehow I din feel we should be so much obligated, but Arnie, he says to me, "Look, honey, it gives him pleasure to shell out money. So why go and spoil his fun?"

Anyways, before we left Long Beach the Rabins insistid we should give them our phone number in the city on account Jack wants we should come to his house fa dinner so's he could have a chance to win his money back. . . . Course not, Henny. He was oney kiddin'. But we got on very nice and lovely with the Rabins and they din want we should break up the friennship. Besides,

Gladys promised she's gonna take me over to Brooklyn, to Loman's, a place where they sell markt-down dresses, the exact same garmints you see in the Fifth Avenue store winders, oney you save fordy, maybe fifty per cent. She knows a girl, a sales-lady, she says, who tips her off any time they got a special sale. . . . No, no, Henny, not yet. Lemme go first and see what's what, and then after I fine out, I can let you know.

Oh, about las' night, Henny. Well, two weeks ago we get a phone call. Lo and behold, it's the Rabins. They been very busy settlin' their New Yawk apartmint, and now they are very anshiss we should come over fa dinner, which is the date we had las' night. Well, Henny, when we got to their apartmint house on Central Park West, I couldn't believe my eyes. Honesly, Henny, a regella palace! In the first place, you take the lobby alone—it's so big, like Arnie says, "Next time the firm holds a convention, I'm gonna recommend we hire this here lobby." And in the second place, their apartmint looks right over the reserwoir in Central Park, so it's like havin' your own privitt lake right in front your home. And you know somethin', Henny? That furnitcha in the livin' room, they musta spent a young fortchin decoratin' the place. It's all done in black and white—you know, zebra style, with black and white tiles on the floor and such. Arnie says to me on the way home the place reminded him of the El Morocco —you know, the classy night club. So I says to him, "Arnie," I says, "how come you know from the El Morocco? Since when you been there?" "What'sa matter," he says to me, "you never seen pitchas of the place in the Daily Mirr'?" . . . That's right, Henny. They got booths-like, with zebra stripes in the back.

Well, Henny, all I can say is I wish on all my good frienns they should live like the way the Rabins live. In the first place, they got a maid who takes your things when you come in the apartmint. Then they got another maid, she passes aroun' the horr doves while the first maid is gettin' you the drinks. Then, later, when you sit down to the meal, the two maids, they wait on you, so natchelly they mus' have a cook who does the cookin'. "My goodness, Arnie," I say to Arnie when we get home, "how you s'pose a persin can afford all that help plus such an expensive apartmint?" "My guess is the black market," he says to me. "Don't forget, honey," Arnie says, "all that equipmint Jack's sellin' in his discount houses, all that stuff was mighty scarce doong the las' war, so lotsa people came along and they shelled out heavy cash, and under the counter so the govvimint don't know about it." "Fa heaven's sake, Arnie," I says to him, "how can you say such a tareble thing?" "Listen," he says to me, "you ast me a questchin and I give you an answer. That's how." You know that Arnie, Henny. Fa evvey "why?" he's got a "because."

Oh, lemme tell you about the dinner. In the first place, the meal began with burnt grapefruit. . . . May I drop dead on this very spot if I'm kiddin'! It's a very simple recipe Gladys gimme. You take a grapefruit, cut it in half. You put sugar on the top, then you heat it till the sugar turns brown, then you're ready to serve. . . . Duckling with slices orintches on it. . . . That's right. Then the meal wound up with a simply delicious chawklit soufflé. Like Arnie says to me on the way home, "Honey," he says, "I betcha if a persin went to a high-class restront and ordered a meal fa four people like we got tonight, you know hommuch that would set him back? Plenty," he says, "believe!"

Well, after we finished eatin' we went to the playroom where they got a fancy bar with all kines comical sayin's on the wall, and right away Jack gets out some big branny glasses—snifters, you call them, and he purs in half full branny. "Go easy on that stuff, Jack," Arnie says to him. "You wanna get me drunk so soon?" "Why not?" Jack says to him. "Listen, that's li'ble to be oney way I can win all my money back. Stop wastin' time, boy," he says to Arnie, "and start shufflin' the cards awready." Gladys don't want them to gamble right away. She says it's not polite. It's O.K. in Long Beach where it's not so formal, but here in the city, she says, it's more polite to sit aroun' a few minutes and talk with the guess'. "Look, Glad," Jack says. . . . Yeah, that's his special nickname he calls her by—Glad. "Look, Glad," he says, "I got a guess' who likes to gamble. You got a guess', she likes to schmoos. So s'posin' you schmoos with your guess' while I gamble with mine. O.K.?"

So the fellas start to sit down at the card table—a regella table, I mean, with a green felt top and it's got slots on the side fa poker chips and all. So jus' when they're dealin' the cards, in comes one of the maids. What'sa matter? There's a phone call fa Jack. His sister Freda's on the phone, she's very anshis to talk to him, somethin' importint come up. Well, Henny, you woulda thought the world's gonna cave in, the way Jack started to carry on. "That goddamn Freda," he starts in to holler. "Evvey time a persin sits down to have a few minutes pleasure, she's gotta come along with some hard-luck cockamamie story whereby I awways wine up shellin' out heavy sugar." . . . Look, Henny, I'm oney repeatin' you what he said.

So anyways, he disappears and we sit there, the three of us— me, Gladys, and Arnie, and nobody is sayin' a word. Finey, jus' to break the ice, I remind Gladys about how she promised she's gonna take me to this here dress house in Brooklyn, and she says her frienn—you know, this here certain saleslady, she din call her up yet, but when she does, she's gonna lemme know first thing. Well, Henny, ten minutes go by, twenny minutes go by, no Jack. By this time Arnie is sittin' at the card table, he's playin' a little solitaire while Gladys is takin' me arounna playroom and she's showin' me auddigraphed pitchas the celebrities she's got on the wall—you know, Jackie Leonard, Buddy Hackett, Gene Baylos. Very comical what they wrote. Very.

Alluva sudden, Henny, lo and behold, in comes Jack from the other room and is he burnt up? He is simply sizzelin'! What'sa matter? It's his sister Freda again! "What's she want this time?" Gladys asts him. "Same ole story," he yells. "I simply gotta do somethin' about Mama on account she's drivin' Freda nuts." . . . O.K., Henny. If you'll kiney hole your horses, I'll tell awready.

It turns out they got a mother, she's awmost eighdy years ole *kennehoreh,* and she's livin' with the sister's family, this Freda, but it so happens the mother is not so normal, see. . . . Yeah, that's right. Listen, after all, a mother, she's eighdy years ole, you gotta 'preciate she's still alive without you worryin' she's not so right in the head. Oh, no, not this here Freda! It seems the mother's greatiss pleasure is to stann at the stove and cook. It's like a passion with her. So she cooks and she cooks, and it drives Freda crazy. In the first place, the mother won't let her use the stove, and in the second place, she can't stan' her mother's cookin'. Gives her heartburn all that fried stuff—at lease, so she says.

Another thing—accordin' to Jack, she says the mother don't like to dress up in the house. She likes to go roun' in her bathrobe with her hair hangin' down. She says she feels more comfitable that way, poor thing. But it drives Freda crazy seein' her mother slop arounna house. Besides, Jack's got a niece, Beverly. . . . Nah, she's awmost twenny years ole, a regella young lady, and Beverly claims she's too embarrassed to have frienns comin' over on account the granma in her bathrobe lookin' like the wratha God.

Beverly claims she's got no privacy when she wantsa go out on a date, on account once the granma gets into the bathroom, it takes her years to finey come out.

Freda says—accordin' to Jack, I mean, that all the mother talks about is Jack this, Jack that, what a wonnerful son he is, hommuch he helps out the family, and how tareble her life is with Freda. "If you're such a wonnerful son like Mama thinks you are," Freda tells him, "s'pposin' she goes and lives with you fa a change. You got two-three bathrooms, you got a big apartmint," she says, "so's Mama can walk arounna place any way she likes."

"Hoddeya like that?" Jack starts in yellin' to us. "I send my goddamn sister a check each and evvey month to pay the rent. When she wantsa new dress, or else my niece needs a piece fur or somethin', who goes and pays fa it? Me, that's who!" he hollers. "And lease one Sunday a month, when I'm not usin' the car, I send the driver over to Freda's place, he should take Mama and the family fa a ride in the country. But all that's not good enough

[211]

fa my lousy sister. Oh, no! Now she wants Mama should go and live with us!"

"Waddeya think we should do?" Gladys goes and she asts him. "Do nothin', that's what we should do!" he yells. "Fa cryin' out loud," he says, "I got big business men comin' here time and time again. I feed them, I entertain them, which is how I do mos' my business. A fine thing," he says, "if Mama comes bargin' aroun' in her bathrobe and starts talkin' to them in her farn accent. That's gonna look good, that's gonna help me in my business. A fat chance!" "Did you tell Freda that?" Gladys asts him. "Natchelly I tole her that. I tole her plenty, believe me." "So what'd she say," Gladys asts him. "She says Mama lived her own life and now it's time Beverly should live her life. She says if it keeps up this way, Beverly's gonna wine up without she's got no boy frienns, and all on account Mama." Oh, and that's not all. Listen to this, Henny.

She says to Jack—now get this, Freda says if Jack don't want the mother to move in with him, why not put her in some home fa ole people whereby she meets folks her own age to talk to, where she can dress how she likes without no young people bein' aroun' to pester and fuss, and where she and Jack could come and visit her a couple times a week? "Hoddeya like that crazy sister?" Jack starts screamin' again. "No feelin's, no consideration, but whatsoever! Why, Mama would have a conniption fit if I went ahead on a deal like that. Here she is," he says, "an ole lady, awmost eighdy years ole, God bless her, and my dopey sister wants we should send her away from her own flesh 'n' blood, she should go live with a bunch strangers who don't know her from Adam! Boy, was I mad!" And believe me, Henny, he certainey looked mad. And who can blame him? After all, like I says to Arnie on the way home, "An ole persin you don't keep movin' aroun' like if she's a piece luggitch." Know what I mean?

Ha? . . . Natchelly he refused. What he said, he said if she's so worried about Beverly and the boy frienns, it's about time the girl moved out to her own place, and he's even willin' to pay part the rent. At first Freda don't think it right, her oney child should move outa the apartmint and away from the family. "Boy, did I wanna blow my top?" Jack says to us. "Finey I hadda say to her, 'Look, Freda, Beverly is no kid. She's a grownup lady. Pretty soon she's gonna get married and have her own home with her own husbint and family. So what's the diffrince if she has her place now or in a couple years? After all,' I says to her, 'wadde you complainin' about bein' I'm gonna chip in mos' the rent?' "

Well, like Arnie says to me on the way home, "Honey, here is a guy with all that dough, a show-place in Long Beach and a gorgeous apartmint in town with at least three in help, and you'd think a fella like that'd be sittin' on top the world. No, sir," he says. "Believe me, honey," he says, "I'm glad I'm not in his boots, no matter hommuch he's got stashed way in his bank account."

I dunno, Henny. Me, I keep thinkin' about that poor ole mother, how nobody wants her. I tell you, ole age is a tareble thing. Tareble. You know, I keep wonderin' what's gonna happen when Jack's sister, Freda, gets to be aroun' eighdy and she's livin' with her daughter Beverly, and what her granndaughter's gonna say about havin' her hangin' aroun'. Believe me, she's gonna be sorry she behaved to her mother that way. And if she calls up Jack and she starts in complainin', I betcha he's gonna tell her, "Good fa you, you goddamn fool. After the way you treated Mama, you're certainey gettin' what you deserve. I hope it's a good lesson to you."

Ha? . . . Natchelly he refused. What he said, he said if shes the fellas. Poor Jack was so upset the whole thing, he simply got no appetite. We jus' sat aroun' discussin' the whole thing till it came nearly twelve o'clock, then we went home. Anyways, we made a date fa next Wednesday, and the boys are gonna have their game while Gladys and me, we're gonna take in a pitcha show. Listen, Henny, if you got nothin' to do Wednesday night, s'posin' you come along. Besides, I want you should meet Gladys Rabin. Maybe she'll take the two of us along when she fines out if they got a sale over there in Brooklyn. O.K.? . . . Awright, Henny, you lemme know. Look, Henny, I gotta hang up now. Good-by.

*   *   *

Mr. Kober was so fearful that his sketch might be misunderstood that he sent along this interesting letter which was published with it:

Dear Editor:
Thank you very much for accepting my story, "An Old Persin."
My work invariably produces some kind of strong

[213]

reaction from my coreligionists. When my play, *Having Wonderful Time,* was produced, there were quite a few letters from outraged Jews about my depiction of certain summer campers. My series about Bella Gross in *The New Yorker* also provoked the letter-writers. There was another series in that magazine, about a Hollywood agent named Benny Greenspan and this, like my other stories, stirred readers into comment.

One of my critics was a naval officer who was greatly exercised about my work. His letter, more intelligent and articulate than the others, took me to task for showing Jewish people in what he thought was an unpleasant light. (This was during the war and the writer felt I was encouraging anti-Semitism.) The indignant officer was Herman Wouk who, oddly enough, received the same kind of criticism he leveled at me when his book, *Marjorie Morningstar,* was published.

I write about what I see and what I hear, and, in the case of Bella Gross, about a family I love. It is not my purpose to disparage or ridicule my people. Benny Greenspan certainly is not an admirable type. The fact that he is Jewish is incidental to the fact that he uses devious methods to achieve his ends. Perhaps by calling attention to him and, through humor, revealing his shady methods. I may make him mend his ways. (A vain hope, I know.) Ignoring him and pretending he doesn't exist and/or not writing about the loud, the harsh, the cheap, the vulgar, the crude, the hustler, and the money-grubber who, unfortunately, happen to be Jewish, seems to me a silly proscription. . . .

Sincerely,
Arthur Kober

Arthur Sainer

THE DREAMING VILLAGE

Arthur Sainer is a drama critic for *The Village Voice*, a novelist and playwright. One of his plays has the intriguing title, *Charlie Chestnut Rides the I.R.T.* He is currently working on a novel, *The Adventures of Sam Needleman.*

"The Dreaming Village" is a perfect illustration of the ability of fiction to deal with a moral problem without preaching, without knocking the reader over the head with the blow of its message. All of the sociological tracts and magazine articles in the world about the plight of our senior citizens could not conceivably affect our readers' conscience as disturbingly as this story of displacement and loneliness that somehow manages never to be disspiriting or depressing.

They are tearing down the house in which my Morris died, Mrs. Peters thought to herself. She sat in the overstuffed living room, her rheumatic legs stiff, her fingers unconsciously kneading her knuckles. In this room, the old lady thought, I lost my husband seventeen years ago.

The house she referred to was a tenement in the East Nineties. Decay had long ago laid its hand softly on the structure, and yet, enfeebled as it was, the building refused to die, or even to recognize its doom. Old people clung to it and moved about its living quarters, clutching worn bannisters, conversing in the halls in broken English, puttering about stoves and lighting lamps as if time were a friend. Old Mrs. Peters herself moved with the others, creeping up the landing with her groceries, setting the table with the good linen, refusing to understand the nature of the disintegration, that a blow from any virile source could send the total structure, with its tenants, toppling from illusion to reality.

When the city condemned the tenement it ordered the occu-

PENROD SCOFIELD

pants gone by the second week in October. A steel wrecking ball would then quickly dispatch any lingering illusions. It was now the first week in October.

The city also produced new living quarters for Mrs. Peters, a clean, airy, one-and-a-half room dwelling in the Rego Park sections of Queens. The rent was considerably higher but Mrs. Peters' children undertook to see that she was not burdened financially. It was a respectable building, mailboxes were not broken and the walls were whole. Mrs. Peters had seen it and she hated it.

She hated it with such passion that all complaints previously leveled at the tenement, concerning drafts, roaches, and leaks, gave way now to a perpetual song of love.

"My husband Morris and I have lived in the house since 1913," she told the butcher one morning.

The butcher, a grizzled fellow with eyebrows like mustaches, pumped his head vigorously. His shop would soon close. He could appreciate what was ailing Mrs. Peters.

"They think a person can move just like that," Mrs. Peters told the grocer. "Since 1913, you know?"

The anemic grocer nodded. He knew.

"Just like that," Mrs. Peters said to the furry vegetable man.

"Fresh celery?" he interposed.

One night during the first week in October Mrs. Peters sat and reflected about the old days. The past, for many, is realer than the present, and Mrs. Peters called to life her husband Morris in the year 1913. Morris, a young man, had his thumbs in his pockets and they were walking through the apartment, appraising the rooms as they went. Morris gawked and nodded constantly.

"See, Morris, it's got southern exposure. That's very good, you know it?"

"Sure I know it," he lied gently.

Morris grinned, unhooked his thumbs, and lifted his hands expansively. "Lets take the flat," he proclaimed.

"Even when it's so far uptown? Maybe it's too far you should have to travel to the shop?"

"Listen to the woman. It's got southern exposure, ain't it?"

It was a clean building and there was a toilet in the apartment. That was the clincher. They gazed at the toilet in delight.

"By the way," Morris found himself casually informing friends, "about this new flat we got. Did I mention the southern exposure and toilet?"

But now he was dead. Mrs. Peters felt a twinge in her legs as she sat. It was still summer outside but she could feel in her legs the stirrings of autumn and somewhere deep down the silences of winter.

It became quite cold two mornings later and it was then that the tenants discovered two men standing before the building. The men wore topcoats over well-pressed business suits and hats shadowed their well-shaven cheeks. The men were standing, legs apart, eyeing the buliding and conversing easily. The tenants watched from bedroom windows, from the butcher shop, and from the hallway. The tenants held their breath, waiting for the men to move on, but the men did not move on. They stood and stood, conversing before that ancient structure, the wind nudging their coattails. In his shop the butcher found himself unconsciously hoisting his cleaver and Mrs. Peters found herself growing light-headed. One of the men smoked a cigarette and pointed at the structure. The other nodded, his hands jangling in his pockets. At the end of twenty minutes one of the men laughed in what seemed to the tenants brittle fashion and then both got into a blue automobile and drove off. The tenants converged on the street, voicing indignation and apprehension. They were careful not to step where the men had been standing.

By the beginning of the second week in October the weather had gotten warmer and then colder again. It simply could not make up its mind. Mrs. Peters found she was having palpitations and, on a quite chilly afternoon, bundled up and besought the family doctor. He was reassuring in a nasal way, prescribed a new medicine, advised her on a physician in Rego Park, and wished her the best. Mrs. Peters bundled her way out into the windy afternoon in time to hear the school-children squealing and watch their briefcases swinging in the crisp air. Their feet clattered on the pavement and Mrs. Peters grit her teeth without realizing it.

About that time Mrs. Peters began to have the uneasy feeling that she was involved in a betrayal. It was as if she could hear the scurrying, see herself packing, watch her neighbors fussing with trunks and barrels. It seemed that they were all whispering, trying to keep the building from knowing its fate.

But how does one communicate anything to a building? Even so, it in no way lessened her guilt. Granted, the building could not think, speak or feel, the horror awaiting it at the final moment was in no sense mitigated. Mrs. Peters found her fingers moving along the walls, found herself listening to the floorboards creaking. But what was she listening for? And what action could an old lady conceivably take? Still, she knew full well that a child had been conceived beneath its roof, a family brought up, and a husband lost forever. It was all here, in the walls, in the air. And for this gift she would soon flee the premises, leaving the house to the mercy of the steel ball.

She began thinking she would sneak out when the time came, she would put on her coat and let it believe she was only off to the grocer's to purchase grapefruit or lemons or a box of prunes. But, it was incredible nonsense—she found she was shaking her dead and that her lined face was grimacing. Buildings can know nothing, you are becoming like a child again. It's time to take the chicken out of the icebox.

One evening Mrs. Peters had a visit from her son-in-law. Milty was a plump fellow in his early forties, his frame was stuffed like a bird set for impalement, but he was active, always sitting on the ball of his rump, ready to spring.

"How's it going, Mom? Sorry to leave the old dump?"

"A little."

"I got it all arranged with the movers. They'll be in early Thursday morning. You be ready."

"I will."

"You'll like it in Rego Park once you get used to it. They got fresh air out there, Mom—and fancy stores. It takes getting used to."

"I suppose so."

"Hah hah. I gotta go, Mom. Let's have a kiss. Don't be a sourpuss."

She had put off packing for days and when at last she could not put it off any longer she understood why she had postponed it. For she began turning up articles she had not seen in years and in her hands they trembled. But decisions had to be made, even as she found them, there was not enough time to ponder, they either had to be packed and taken to Rego Park or tossed into the junk heap. And the really painful ones were a frightful problem. She wept over them and in the end packed everything. Never mind that there wasn't room, she would make room. She would fling out the new refrigerator, if need be, or she might even go without a television set, even that. It was not possible to part with the source of one's pain.

On the final morning, before she had time to consider, the movers were at the door. Then the dressers were gone, the kitchen furniture, the dishes, the photographs, the clothes, the brooms. Too fast, too fast. She wanted to speak but there was nothing to say and no one to say it to. And too easy, too easy. Am I feeling nothing? she thought. My head is going round, they have put a postage stamp on me. It's too fast, can't you understand? They had come while she was still having her cereal and when they left she discovered the spoon and the half-eaten bowl waiting for her on the sink.

Then Milty was honking for her from the car. She hurried into her coat, clattered erratically down the old stairs, her overladen pocketbook thumping against her side, and then turned to look at the house as she reached the street. But the honking confused her and she hurried into the car and huddled into the seat beside

[219]

her son-in-law. As the car pulled away she noticed several neighbors, standing almost like apparitions, before the house. She
tried to wave, to call—but too late. Were they to be carted off
as well? What were they taking with them and where were they
taking it to?

Milty drove rapidly, at one point he streaked through a red
light, he was constantly passing other cars, nervously bumping
his horn, restless in his seat. Mrs. Peters found the trip exciting.
After all, she was going to a new home, it was a brand new start.
But the wide swing over the Triboro Bridge depressed her and
when they skimmed down Grand Central Parkway and then onto
the local streets of Queens, streets busy with a sense of their
own purpose, gloom spread about her like a cape.

Late that day she stood in her new one-and-one-half room
apartment with all her old things about her. The apartment
smelt freshly painted and it smelt of new wood. At one moment
she was elated, the next moment she felt wretched. When it got
dark she forgot to turn on the lights. She sat in the old armchair
and wept bitterly. Then she made soup. The next day she
walked down Queens Boulevard, looking suspiciously at all the
shops and carefully scrutinizing the people. When she entered
the supermarket, she made her way slowly along all the rows,
appraising the canned goods, squinting at the carrots, her eyes
even coming to rest once or twice on employees in white coats.
She made a few purchases and found the transaction disturbing,
again it seemed she was indulging herself, enacting another
betrayal.

In the house she sorted out her groceries, put some in the
refrigerator and others in the cupboard. She could not get the
hang of it; it seemed she must be storing someone else's food in
someone else's house. As she was putting away the canned
peaches she had a vision of the two men with their topcoats
swaying in the breeze. She was furious, she wanted to scream, to
fling something. The peaches shook in her hand.

Often in the following days she thought of the steel ball. If
she could only know that the house was still standing. After all,
was it easy to knock down such a house? But there was no one to
ask. She thought idly of taking the train back, but subway trips
nowadays made her nervous. And besides, which way was Manhattan? They had disoriented her. Most of the time she sat in
the house and looked out the window. Her only activities were

preparing meals, shopping, and dusting. On the second Sunday the children and grandchildren came to visit. She prepared dinner and everyone made a great deal of noise and there was even a fight between the daughters-in-law. Later all the women helped with the dishes while the men smoked cigars with vigor and cursed and talked business. For a little while Mrs. Peters was happy.

It was dark by the time they left and she was tired. She sat by the window for a while, watching the lights of the speeding cars, hearing the sound of their oily engines. It seemed to her, for a brief moment, that she could hear a kind of cracking and crumbling going on in the distance.

That night Mrs. Peters had a dream. She dreamt that her husband Morris rang the bell of her new apartment and stood there grinning. He was a young man, he was the man of 1913. He held out his hand while her heart pounded and said, "I've come to take you back to the old apartment." She was overjoyed and quickly took his hand but when he wanted to hurry down the steps she had to remind him that she was an old woman and that they had better take the elevator. He said it didn't matter and then they were in the old apartment but somehow it did not quite look like the old apartment, it resembled the apartment she had lived in as a girl, before her marriage. But Morris was grinning and asked her if she wanted to dance.

"But Morris," she reminded him, "you don't dance."

But they danced and as they danced she could feel her legs growing lighter and then youth stealing upon her age. And then she saw the grocer and the butcher watching through the window, just as if God had raised them up from the ground. They smiled, encouraging her.

A Time
to
Laugh

"A time to weep, and a time to laugh:
a time to mourn, and a time to dance"

Ecclesiastes III:4

Of all the weapons in his arsenal of survival, none has served the Jew better than the power to laugh. Laughter sometimes lends immediate perspective, even to otherwise intolerable experiences. It punctures the fright of appearances and heals the sad heart. Sometimes it even reduces our severest enemies to absurdity.

American Judaism does not print jokes, although it has carried an occasional cartoon. We have preferred our shafts of humor to wing like barbed darts to some worthy target. (Much that passes for humor in our popular entertainment today is simply insult, naked of the garments of grace and wit.)

"Our sincerest laughter with some pain is fraught," Shelley said. And, indeed, under most varieties of Jewish humor sounds a pedal note of sadness.

The most civilized form of humor is the ability to laugh at one's self, a trait always conspicuously lacking in the humor of barbarians. Several of the pieces in this section indulge in self-mockery, but never in self-flagellation. There is nothing so sobering as the sight of blood, especially if it is our own!

We have leaned to the kind of humorous writing that hurts a little but never enough to spoil the heart's merriment. Here are some examples . . .

RUDOLPH J. CARRASCO

Albert Vorspan

A JEW
IN THE WHITE HOUSE

Only Albert Vorspan, director of program of the Union of American Hebrew Congregations, could have brought off with a clear conscience the kind of political ragging implicit in the text of "A Jew In The White House." The piece attracted much attention, appearing as it did shortly after the election of the late President Kennedy.

The election of our first Roman Catholic President has affected me strangely. Last night I had a dream—that a Jew became President of the United States. I awakened at dawn to find that the millennium had not yet arrived and that the White House was still a Protestant-Catholic bastion. But the dream lingers on. . . .

It all began at the political convention in 1984 (honest) which was held in the Cow Palace in San Francisco. The front-runners had faded out, and even the most obvious dark-horses had fallen by the wayside in the marathon balloting when the name of Jacob Meyer, the popular Mayor of Minneapolis, emerged out of nowhere: A Jew! Dare we nominate a Jew? Can a Jew be elected? The whispered questions swept through the tense assembly. The fortieth ballot began. Suddenly, Jacob Meyer received an urgent note, asking for an immediate private meeting with the leaders of the American Jewish Human Relations Council.

Leaving his seat, Meyer met the Jewish group in a secluded room in the basement. (It turned out later that three other Jewish organizations were waiting in three other rooms with three different views to express, but he didn't know.) The head of the organization, a distinguished, white-faced banker from Memphis placed his hand on Meyer's shoulder and said: "Jacob, we know how tempting it must be for you to go for this nomination. It is a great honor. But, Jacob, we urge you not to do it. You will open the floodgates of hatred. Remember what happened

[225]

to Smith and Kennedy? Well, what they would do to you would make those campaigns look like communion breakfasts. Heaven knows what they would do to you—and to us. Please, Jake, think carefully before you do this thing." Mr. Meyer promised to think about it, and he did, right up to the moment when Governor Arm of Pennsylvania swung his delegation to Jacob Meyer, thus assuring Meyer's nomination for the Presidency of the United States.

The morning after his historic nomination, the nominee was surprised to receive a telegram from the same Jewish organization, hailing his nomination as a "triumph of the American dream that neither religion nor race is a barrier to public office." The telegram also asked him to endorse the organization's statement that there is no such thing as a "Jewish vote" and that Americans vote solely on the basis of what is best for America. Summoning his assistant, Meyer said: "Brady, send them a telegram and tell them I endorse their sentiments completely and they are rendering a fine service to the American people. Then get Herb, Pete, and Pat on the telephone and tell them to go to work on the Jewish voters in New York, California and Illinois. I need 80 per cent in those states or I'm a dead duck."

There was, as predicted, a good deal of nastiness in the campaign which brought Meyer to the Presidency. One hundred leaders issued a manifesto, raising the "religious issue" in the election. Could a member of the Jewish faith be objective with respect to Israel? Could he dine in the Kremlin or even the United Nations or would he have to bow out of important negotiations because shrimp is served? Could he enforce the Humane Slaughter Act, without discriminating in favor of cows and poultry and against pigs and lobsters? Could he tack a m'zuzo at the entrance to the White House? Could he light the Christmas tree in the White House?

Meyer took to television and said: "My Jewish faith will have nothing, I repeat nothing, to do with my Presidency of the United States. Any conflicts between my Jewishness and my Americanism, I assure you would be resolved in favor of my oath and responsibility to all the people." This eliminated the religious issue except in one segment of the American public: Jews.

The English-Jewish press boiled over with editorials on how Meyer "has leaned over so far backward he has fallen on his

[226]

behind" and "Is Meyer a Self-Hater?" One excitable communal leader told a startled reporter that he regarded Jacob Meyer as an outstanding "anti-Semite." The reporter gulped momentarily and said: "But, Meyer is Jewish!" "Aha," shot back the leader, "That's the worst kind."

And so, Jacob Meyer became the first Jewish President of the United States.

Although Meyer ran a scrupulously ethical administration, it was not long before there was rumbling about the President's "kitchen cabinet." (One wag said a Jewish President should have "two kitchen cabinets," one for milk and one for meat.) As it happened, the one "kitchen cabinet" consisted of the President's Aunt Sophie who moved into the White House from Chicago the day of the Inauguration and fired the cook; cousin Charlie, who had never been able to hold down a job anywhere and now became the President's Appointments Secretary; and, of course, "Bubbe" Meyer, the President's extraordinary eighty-eight-year-old grandmother (quickly named "Bobby" by the Hearst press which slyly suggested she had taken over the White House like a cross between Rasputin and Sherman Adams); the President's bewildered wife, Sally (about whom the Yiddish press asked: what kind of name is that for a Jewish girl?) his fifteen-year-old son, Hiram, and twenty-five-year-old daughter, Deborah, both of whom had to be lifted bodily from their beds every Saturday morning to be marched to the synagogue with the family for the waiting photographers.

President Meyer's administration served at a time of great tension. The cabinet frequently met around the clock. Dedicated and patriotic men, they did not mind the heavy burden of their tasks. What wrecked them, in the end, was the incessant delicatessen sandwiches, flown in daily from the Stage Delicatessen in New York City. As Secretary of Agriculture Baldwin afterwards said: "I did not mind that our meetings always started an hour late, or that we had to go along with Grandma Meyer's silly plan to have a poster in every house saying EAT, EAT. What I could not take was another hot pastrami sandwich. My mind and spirit are still with you, Mr. President. But my stomach is shot."

Prior to his jet-propulsion into politics, Jacob Meyer had been a partner in a flourishing drug store in Minneapolis. His partners had been a Roman Catholic named Aloysius Kelly and a

Methodist named Frank Holman. When he became President, Meyer found that Catholic organizations, seeking to reach the White House on a host of public matters, invoked the aid of Kelly. Protestant groups made a conduit of Holman. Only Jewish groups had no contacts; so they, of course, were reduced to giving awards to Kelly *and* Holman. There was, of course, only one Jew in the Cabinet. As Meyer confided to a friend, "If you wanted more Jews, you should have picked another Roman Catholic President."

President Meyer introduced unprecedented reforms into the Government. A new and revolutionary committee structure was set up: every American was assigned to a sub-committee. The President pushed through a constitutional amendment, creating a Vice-President in charge of Fund-Raising. While it was somewhat strange at first, the people soon got used to card-calling whenever the budget had to be balanced. Indeed, voluntary contributions soon displaced the income tax. Techniques which had proved themselves in the United Jewish Appeal and the Israel Bond Drive soon began to work for the United States except that the N.A.M. refused to turn over its mailing list to the Government. No one batted an eye when the President of U.S. Steel called the President of General Motors and said: "Give or else." Every trade and profession was organized for "crisis" giving; 100 bankers gave $200,000 each year on condition they would not have to go to fund-faising dinners, banquets, "Big gifts" luncheons; and every taxpayer received a heartbreaking pamphlet annually, with pictures of starving children, dramatizing what would happen to America if contributions slackened.

The wives of the members of Congress were organized by Sally, Sophie, and Grandma into a United States Congressional Sisterhood and a nationwide bazaar brought in more money than all excise taxes put together. Washington has never been livelier. Supreme Court sessions were all followed by a collation and entertainment. An *Afikomen* Hunt was co-featured with Easter egg-rolling on the White House lawn, and the summer White House was installed at the Fontainebleau in Miami Beach (until a visiting Foreign Minister got lost in the new wing, causing an international scandal). Presiding at a White House reception, beaming at the ancient Senators whirling through the hora, passing out cigars, checking the stakes of the pinochle game in the East Room, keeping his guests' glasses filled with seltzer water—Jacob Meyer was a beloved president.

Education was the theme of Meyer's administration. Not only was a college education available to every youngster; it was compulsory. Adult education swept the country like the hula hoop.

"Other presidents like to throw out the first ball at the baseball game," the President told James Reston. "I would rather throw out the first question in the classroom."

A Government TV network brought learning to every housewife. Teachers proudly admitted their professions. A football stadium at one university was turned into an open-air museum. Colleges began giving scholarships to skinny, brainy boys whom the prettiest co-eds now clearly preferred. It was a new America —exhausting but exhilarating.

But, as it must to every Administration, a crisis came to the Meyer Administration. It did not arise, as one might expect, in the tense international situation; hot tea and sponge cake did much to drown the cold war and Meyer shrewdly gave the Russians extra-territorial rights to Disneyland. The crisis was— you should pardon the expression—domestic. What happened was that Grandma threatened to leave the White House, and the report, badly distorted, sent tremors through the nation's press. Drew Pearson, in predicting things to come, headlined: "QUEEN BEE OF WHITE HOUSE THREATENS BREAK WITH PRESIDENT OVER FOOD POLICY, SAYS PRESIDENT TOO THIN, HE'LL GET CONSUMPTION."

The Hearst Press saw a more sinister meaning in the controversy: "BOBBY MEYER IN WHITE HOUSE REVOLT; MIGHT DEFECT; CABINET MAY GO WITH HER."

The true story is this: It was a Monday evening, March 17, 7:00 P.M. The entire Meyer clan had gathered for dinner. The President said the *motze* blessing, and everybody began eating— except Grandma, who sat, stone-faced and silent, staring straight ahead. "What's the matter, Bubbe?" asked the President's wife. "What should be the matter?" replied Grandma. She didn't touch a morsel. The President, expert in domestic politics, felt the same sinking sensation that he experienced when he was about to talk to the Senator from Mississippi about civil rights. A storm was brewing. Dinner over, the President signalled everybody else out of the room and settled down to find out what Grandma had on her mind.

"Okay, Bubbe, I know you," he began. "Something's eating you. Now what is it?"

"What should be eating me?" she asked. "There's nothing eating me." Pause. "I'm leaving."

"Leaving the White House? Why, for heaven's sake? You're not happy here?"

She frowned darkly. "Okay, if you must know, I'm not happy."

The President, in spite of himself, found himself thinking in political terms. "Look, Bubbe, you can't leave. You're a key personality in the Government. You get more mail than I do. The old people love you. You have a daily column in the Yiddish press. You've become a new-type Eleanor Roosevelt. If you leave me, the press will kill me with their wild speculations. Please!" He stared at her, saw the familiar stubborn set of the chin. "Why? So tell me why?"

"In the *first* place," she said in the sing-song fashion which suggested a long and telling list was coming, "I don't like the House. What do you need such a big house? It's a *shonda*, a man with a small family should live like an Arab king! You ask me, we should move into a nice, small house—a ranch house, maybe, with a picture window. And not *shtom* in the middle of the city. In the suburbs, across the river in Virginia maybe. I'll tell you the truth, Ed Murrow, he should rest in peace, once wanted me on Person-to-Person, I was ashamed he should come here. What Jewish family stays in the city?"

"Mama!" he cried out. "I'm the *President*. This is the White House. I've got to stay here."

"What *got* to? Kennedy lived in Georgetown and Palm Beach and Eisenhower he could live on a farm in Pennsylvania and play golf, why can't you live in a nice Jewish neighborhood in Arlington and play gin and send back the servants—who needs them? Sally can clean the house."

"That's ridiculous, Bubbe! You're a smart woman, why don't you——"

"And you, Jake, you should pardon me, *you* are a *shlemiel*. A 25-karat shlemiel. All day and all night you work your fingers to the bone. Did you get a single raise? *And the drugstore. So who is minding the drugstore, they're probably running it into the ground!*"

"Bubbe, you're talking crazy."

"*I'm* crazy, eh? *And you?* Smart, smart, smart. And did you marry off your Debbie, already twenty-five years old and you should be ashamed, she's an old maid? You have—who knows?— a million people working for you but one nice Jewish boy, his father should own a nice business, you couldn't find?"

"Please, please," said Jake, trying to dam up the flood. "You must realize . . ."

"And I'll tell you also, I don't like the people you have visiting here."

"People? Now what are you saying?"

"That Roosian, whatsisname, you said I should be nice to him. A *cossack*, he should boil in oil. And the Latin with the dirty beard, I thought he was a *Lubavitcher rebbe*, turns out he's a *mishuganer* farmer sleeps in his bed with his clothes on. Who needs it? Bad enough you have Cousin Charlie snoring like you are testing your rockets in the South Room. Better I should go back to Minneapolis where a *mensh* is a *mensh*."

In the end, of course, Grandma Meyer didn't leave but it took three emergency sessions of the Cabinet to negotiate with her before she would settle back to the routine of White House life. A portable television, to watch Jack Paar, helped soften her anger and, of course, a White House Annex was installed over the Golden Age Club in Arlington, Virginia. Finally, she succumbed and told Jacob: "Okay, for the time being I'll stay. But I'm warning you. You be a good boy, because the next time I go, I go. You shouldn't take me for granite."

Jacob Meyer served two hectic terms with genuine distinction. Except for the controversiality of his grandmother, there was little criticism directed at him or his policies. Most everybody was afraid to express criticism for fear of being accused of anti-Semitism. And since every citizen served on a sub-committee, the U.S. was not merely a pure democracy, it was, like Israel, a nation of Presidents. Meyer's Administration broke the crust of old traditions and old prejudices. He left office on such a churning tide of democratic sentiment that he was able, miraculously, to pick his successor and to have him elected against incredible odds: the first Negro ever to serve as President of the United States.

Dore Schary

WHO'S THE RABBI?

> Author, playwright, director, producer, Academy Award
> winner, Mr. Schary wrote and produced with the Theatre
> Guild *Sunrise at Campobello,* directed and co-produced
> *A Majority of One* and is probably rehearsing a new play
> somewhere right now.
>   Mr. Schary is also deeply involved in Jewish life and is
> currently chairman of the Anti-Defamation League of
> B'nai B'rith.
>   This story of an attempt at introducing the ideas of
> Reform Judaism in Newark, New Jersey, during the early
> days of this century later appeared in the book *For Spe-
> cial Occasions.*

My father, Herman Hugo Schary, was born in Kurland in 1873.
He came to America the long way and the hard way, across
Siberia, into China, to Japan, and then to San Francisco. He
arrived in Brooklyn in 1893.

My mother, Belle Drachler, was born in Byalistok in 1875. Her
parents, Shaina and Baruch Drachler, fled the pogroms in 1891
and had also settled in Brooklyn.

Belle Drachler met Herman Hugo Schary in 1894 and they
were married in 1895. At the time of their betrothal my father
was gainfully employed decorating public buildings with flags
on significant holidays and my mother worked in a shirt-waist
factory. Pooling these curious resources they opened a delicatessen store. That enterprise failed. Then the Scharys and the
Drachlers moved to the burgeoning Jewish community of Newark, New Jersey.

Pa went back to decorating but his career in this field was
terminated when he fell off the Newark Courthouse while drap-
ing it in black at the time of President McKinley's death. My
parents then opened another delicatessen store and restaurant
which also failed. Then came poor but busy years of selling

greeting cards, real estate, and millinery. During this time they raised a family of two girls and two boys, the youngest of whom was born in 1905. That was me.

Mother was an exceptional cook and as a means of keeping the family afloat she made kreplach, gefilte fish, borscht, chalo, and other delicacies for less gifted neighbors. In 1913, Mother was asked to cater the wedding supper for the marriage of Susan Lasser to Peter Stone. The affair was so successful other requests poured in and in 1914 my folks bought an old house on fashionable High Street and opened the first Schary Manor, a kosher catering establishment. For the next twelve years Schary Manor was the home away from home for thousands of celebrants of weddings, Bar Mitzvahs, anniversaries, birthdays, charity banquets, and other *simchas.*

During the years we got to know almost the entire membership of the Newark Jewish Community and some of our best friends were—rabbis.

When arrangements were being made for weddings at Schary Manor we always asked, "Who's the rabbi?" The answer to the question was of some help to us because, after our years of experience, we could by the answer determine the kind of ceremony it was to be. Each rabbi had his own form of service and his own distinctive style. They also had individual ideas about the length of the ceremony. Rabbi Brodsky's rituals ran the long-

HAL JUST

est; Rabbi Hoffman of the Oheb Shalom was runner-up; and then came Rabbi Julius Silberfeld of B'nai Abraham, followed by Rabbi Solomon Foster of B'nai Jeshurun, a Reform congregation.

We knew all the habits and ways of the most popular rabbis, so the arrival of young Lewis Browne, an obscure, recently ordained member of the rabbinate in town, meant we would have to go through an orientation program until we could anticipate his demands.

There were not only differences between all the rabbis, but also an unspoken rivalry which reflected the rivalry between the congregations which, in turn, reflected the differences in the layers of Jewish life in Newark.

Rabbi Brodsky, who had been with the Anshe Russia Temple since its formation, was the chief Orthodox rabbi and undoubtedly the dean of the Newark rabbinate. He was a handsome picture of the traditional Eastern European rabbi. He was a Russian. He was tall and dignified and his long wispy white beard hung in splendid display almost to his waist. He represented with firmness and authority the active Orthodox Russian-Jewish community of the city and most of the weddings or Bar Mitzvah or *bris milo* (circumcision) ceremonies celebrated by Russian Jews were presided over by Reb Brodsky.

His wedding services were lengthy and ritualistic. A good part of them were in Yiddish, most in Hebrew, and a small part were in English. He always conluded with the words, "Now kiss your bride and be happy." My *zaida*, Mother's father, disliked this rather roguish conclusion because he believed it was too commonplace for a great rabbi like Brodsky.

Members of synagogues never hesitate to criticize their rabbis. They point out that if Abraham had the privilege of debating a point with God as reported in the Book of Genesis, then they certainly had the right to point out to a rabbi anything that displeased them. Zaida, therefore, had discussed his lack of enthusiasm for Reb Brodsky's conclusive light-hearted suggestion, "Now kiss your bride and be happy."

Reb Brodsky had listened, because he had respect for Zaida's opinions. He had stroked his beard, sipped his tea, nodded his head, and then ignored Zaida's criticism.

Israel Lipkin, a famous Lithuanian novelist, once wrote, "A rabbi whom they don't want to drive out of town isn't a rabbi, and a rabbi whom they actually drive out isn't a man."

[234]

So Brodsky had critics, as did and do all members of the clergy. He would sort out the criticisms and come to his own determination. But he remained a man and stayed in the pulpit of Anshe Russia till the end of his long and active life. And he ended all his wedding ceremonies the same way. After a while Zaida stopped talking about it, but would shake his head dolefully whenever he heard the final words.

Rabbi Hoffman of the Oheb Shalom was another towering figure of a rabbi. He was tall and heavier than Rabbi Brodsky. He had a black spade beard and a deep mellifluous voice that rolled out the ancient Hebrew prayers with awesome authority. His congregation was largely German-Jewish and they had a rather snobbish attitude toward the Russian-Jews. This was an Old World antipathy brought over and maintained in the New World. The congregants of Oheb Shalom were generally richer and did give generously to all charity campaigns. They observed the holidays in the traditional ways, but there was a difference. A service in Oheb Shalom might have all the same words, but the sound of devotion was never as loud or as passionate as the sound in the Anshe Russia.

Rabbi Hoffman's ceremonies exuded dignity and a tone of solemnity probably brought to bear because of the rabbi's appearance, which was ministerial rather than patriarchal. My father once said, "You feel you could tell a good joke to Brodsky, but you would never try and tell one to Hoffman."

There were critics, too, of Rabbi Hoffman but most of his congregation weren't too open concerning their judgments. They were afraid outsiders would repeat their opinions and that it might rebound badly to their rabbi, to whom they were devoted as the Anshe Russians were to their Rabbi Brodsky.

Rabbi Silberfeld, a comparative newcomer at the time, was a younger man than Brodsky and Hoffman and he was a different and newer type of leader. He wore no beard—only a moustache which he assumed made him look older. He had a gay and merry look in his eye. His congregation, B'nai Abraham, was an amalgam of Russian-Jews on the way out of complete Orthodoxy into Conservatism and German-Jews who were resisting the drive into Reform Judaism but didn't want the Orthodoxy of Anshe Russian since it was so typically Russian and rather Old World.

All of these congregants found a new home and a new rabbi

in B'nai Abraham and the congregation prospered. Rabbi Silberfeld had a gift with wedding ceremonies; where Brodsky's were long and sometimes incomprehensible to the less learned Jews, and where Hoffman's were a bit pedantic and solemn, Silberfeld brought peace and warmth and comprehensibility along with the necessary degree of religiosity. So he thrived and soon earned the title, "The Marrying Rabbi."

In a short time he was out-running Brodsky and Hoffman. And his congregation was outstripping the others in acquiring new members. Silberfeld brought energy to his duties, along with a faster tempo more attuned to the times and his backers.

But he also had his critics, among them Zaida, who couldn't understand a rabbi who didn't wear a beard. In addition Zaida believed Silberfeld was making religion too easy. "It's not easy to be a Jew," argued Zaida. "It's hard. And if you make it too easy, you won't be a good Jew."

Our family shifted membership to B'nai Abraham but Zaida didn't. He stayed with the Anshe Russia and while he professed to believe that Mother preferred the new temple because the women sat with the men in the more modern fashion, I think he actually believed that Ma and Pa were becoming lazy in their religious devotions. He said it didn't make any difference where I went to *schul*. He had long renounced the chance of my becoming a *talmeed*—a scholar.

Rabbi Foster was the master of the block of the B'nai Jeshurun congregation which represented the drift of the Jewish brethren in Newark to Reform Judaism. Even those of us in the family who didn't know nearly enough about our faith had misgivings about going into a temple and uncovering the head. The services in the B'nai Jeshurun used much more English and were consequently more intelligible, but they did lack the sound of piety to which we had become accustomed. Zaida wouldn't even discuss the B'nai Jeshurun. As far as he was concerned, he rendered harsh judgment that it might as well be a church.

His feelings were again a reflection of the swirling tides of disagreement that were eddying about the Newark Jewish religious life. The Reform movement was new and strange and was greeted with suspicion. Since the congregation at first was not as large, the number of weddings over which Rabbi Foster presided was smaller. When he did appear at Schary Manor, we discovered that his ceremonies were crisp and intelligent. His sermons were more intellectual than the other rabbis' and while he was learned in Hebrew, the song of his prayers didn't compare to any of the other three. Finally, his ceremonies were the shortest by at least five minutes.

But these four rabbis were by now familiar to us. There were others who came to Schary Manor, but Brodsky, Hoffman, Silberfeld, and Foster were the names we heard most often in answer to the question, "Who's the rabbi?"

Then suddenly Lewis Brown came to town. He was young, quite handsome, and his dress was unique. He wore long pointed collars and wide flowing ties. His coats were cut in the manner we believed to be "English style." He had a small clipped moustache and spoke in a cultured accent that some people said was "Harvard" and others said was "English." He charmed each lady he met as he lifted her hand to his lips. He charmed the men, too, since it was obvious he was learned without being professorial. And he had a fund of funny stories that were "mannish" without being vulgar. He hit the town like a fresh spring rain. The Jewish prophets in Newark spoke and ordained he was going to be the most popular rabbi in town. Lewis Browne's congregation was a new one called "The Free Synagogue." This name had, to Mother, a clinical sound and while she liked Rabbi Browne she couldn't understand why the congregation hadn't picked a Hebrew identification.

The members of the congregation were Reform Jews who had reformed even further than the members of the B'nai Jeshurun. They were mostly German-Jews and boasted a high number of politically liberal members. They did not yet have a building of their own and had been conducting services in various halls which they had rented for their Friday night services.

When they retained Rabbi Browne as their spiritual master, they came to Schary Manor to request the use of our largest banquet room as a regular site for their services until their building drive was completed, which would then enable them to construct their own rather elaborately planned temple.

Since we were a kosher establishment and never catered on Friday night, the banquet hall was always available and Father thought that it was a profitable arrangement which, at the same time, served a good and respectable purpose.

Zaida hated the idea. He maintained that the Free Synagogue was more of a discussion group than a temple and he looked at the proceedings as sacrilegious. Mother acted as arbiter, but she was hardly objective since she and my sisters, Lillian and Frances, all fell for Rabbi Browne's enormous charm and intelligence.

So the arrangement was made. To me, Lewis Browne was an extraordinary figure. Before I met him, he had heard from Mother that I had dreams about being a writer. He spoke to me on a level of understanding that was new because he was a writer and he told me it was a lonely business but one that could not be denied. He said that writing, too, was a religion. I was so impressed I started wearing long collars and wide ties like Rabbi Browne, but Lil said I looked ridiculous in them, and since I did, I stopped wearing them. It was one of my early frustrations.

Zaida regretted Mother's decision but didn't fight it. He would always have an early dinner and leave the house to walk to the Anshe Russia Temple before the sun set. After services there were always discussions and debates at the schul so Zaida knew he would be back long after the members of the Free Synagogue had gone. They, he knew, would arrive after dinner, to begin their observances at eight and be out of the hall by 9:45.

So the Free Synagogue took over, but lasted in Schary Manor only a few short weeks. What broke up the harmony of the congregation was Rabbi Browne's second lecture, which dealt with the life of Jesus.

Even the most sophisticated of the congregants weren't ready for that. As Rabbi Browne started his surprise sermon (which turned out to be a monumental one), there was a murmur of hushed reaction. Then a few of the congregation got up and walked out politely but hurriedly. The next departure was neither polite nor hurried. A man got up and interrupted the services by saying, "This is not the place for such a discussion. It's a disgrace in a temple. Either you stop or I resign as vice-president."

Lewis Browne didn't stop and "The Free Synagogue" lost a vice-president who took with him his wife and daughter and son-in-law.

Lil and I, who were witnesses to the debacle, had mixed reactions. I was sorry that Browne was getting into hot water, but I agreed that he had put himself there. Lil was trying to be open-minded, but she was worried about what Zaida would have to say.

Rabbi Browne, recognizing that he was on a sticky wicket, tried to turn the tide by talking of understanding. He said that fear was ignorance—that he was talking about a famous and important Jew as a man—not as the Messiah. But as he talked, it became clear that his support was dwindling. He came to an abrupt end and the service was concluded.

One or two people congratulated him, but the rest filed out, puzzled, until they reached the front hall. Then, feeling free to express their doubts, the arguments began and they were loud and passionate.

The ex-vice-president, who had waited outside of Schary Manor, picked up where he had left off and two more sober-minded gentlemen had to restrain him from hitting one of Rabbi Browne's supporters.

Rabbi Browne was quite understandably shaken by the experience and Mother offered him a cup of tea which he declined. He left, saying he would see us next Friday night. Mother asked him to have dinner with us that evening and he accepted.

Mother, after he left, told us that it would be advisable not to tell Zaida about the subject of the sermon and we all agreed that it was a discreet suggestion.

Pa came home from his Friday night pinochle game at Uncle Mike's and when we told him, he thought it was a great joke. While he liked Lewis Browne, he had said, "He talks like a rabbi but looks like a floor-walker. He won't be around by next Rosh Hashono."

When Zaida arrived, we all greeted him extravagantly to prevent him from suspecting anything. I watched for him and opened the door for him, because on the Sabbath he never carried a key nor would he even press the electric doorbell. The Sabbath was a day of rest and to Zaida everything rested, including kilowatt power. Normally, I would tease Zaida and keep him waiting for an extra few minutes outside the door. He'd wait patiently and when I would let him in he'd merely say *"chochem* —wise guy."

But tonight I had the door open when he got to the steps and I called out, "Good Shabos." However, the Anshe Russia was not an island, and in the mysterious fashion of town gossip that flies quicker than light, the word had already reached Zaida as he strolled home. He had met some friends who had been at Oheb Shalom, who had met some friends who had been at B'nai

Abraham, who had met some friends who had been at The Free Synagogue and the Jewish community was lighting up with the startling news of Rabbi Browne's sermon on the life of Jesus delivered in a synagogue.

Zaida's first angry comment was, *"Ich hub dir gesucht*—I told you so." He felt that Schary Manor had been disgraced and that he had been dishonored. Perhaps, he said, it was time for him to go to the Home for the Aged. This was as desperate a statement as the modern one, "I think I'll kill myself."

But hot tea and jam and sponge cake calmed him somewhat and he went to bed, reluctantly agreeing that, for the time being, he would not move out. But never, no never, would he ever even look at Rabbi Browne.

This presented a quick problem to Mother, who remembered her invitation to Rabbi Browne for dinner the next Friday night.

The problem was solved the next day by Lewis Browne himself, who knew Zaida, and called Mother and said that he thought it would be an embarrassment for him to come. Mother agreed.

The Free Synagogue's convocation on the following Friday night indicated a sharp drop in members. Though some new curious souls dropped by to take in Browne's next bombshell, the total figure was less. There was no bombshell. Perhaps with a touch of polite irony, Browne spoke on the Book of Job.

The following Friday the number in attendance was less. In a few short weeks The Free Synagogue as it was constituted disappeared and Lewis Browne departed from Newark leaving a rather mixed but imperishable memory in the minds of many Newarkers.

The other rabbis went back to their normal labors and from then on when we asked "Who's the rabbi?" we would hear all the other names, but never again did we hear the name, Lewis Browne.

Not till he wrote his first bestseller, *How Odd of God.* Then everybody heard his name.

Rabbi Leonard Winograd

I'M GETTING GRAY
IN THE TEMPLES

In this hilarious essay drawn from his own experiences in the field, Rabbi Winograd, spiritual leader of Beth Zion Temple in Johnstown, Pennsylvania, tells a harrowing, although good-humored, tale of how to grow old in the service of your congregants.

RUDOLPH J. CARRASCO

It all began on that sunny June day when my five-year-old son, Emil, ran down the steps of the Rockdale Avenue Temple shouting, "Daddy, Daddy, if you are a rabbi where is your beard?" I had just received rabbinical ordination, and regardless of what any of my classmates may have thought was going to be accomplished when Dr. Nelson Glueck laid his hands on me, my first-born son apparently expected me to grow a beard.

Since then I have served several congregations and have ever sought to find humor during the grim hours by remembering

[241]

that ancient exhortation: "Don't take the world too seriously because you cannot possibly get out of it alive."

Simultaneous with my arrival at my first congregation came a request for an insurance medcial examination. It has always amazed me how insurance men will cajole, tease and seduce you into filling out an application for a policy and then treat you as if you had insulted or offended them intentionally when your medical history becomes apparent. In this case the problem was my weight. I begun my rabbinical career by finding out that rabbis are not patients, as such, when they enter the doctor's office. After I had peeled to my pelt, the doctor decided to ask me a few questions. When you take out the coach's daughter you must say something to her in "Football." He felt he had to say something to me in "Religion." "Rabbi, you know one time I strated to read the Bible and I found that there were more loose women and there was more licentiousness and more sexual immorality there than in any other book I have ever read." I answered, "I have always said that there is something in the Bible for everyone."

That afternoon I made my first hospital visit after my ordination. It was indeed a memorable occasion. In the lobby of the hospital there was a directory which gave many fascinating details about each patient, such as age, address, and religion. On a small card I listed the names and room numbers of Jewish patients. My first stop was at the door of an elderly woman who had three problems. Her first problem was that she was in agony. She was in agony because she had fallen down a flight of stairs and hurt her back and her ribs. There was no position in which she could sit or lie whereby she might find relief from this torture for even a moment. My heart bled for her and I wondered if there was something that could be done to relieve her suffering. This brings us to her second problem. There was indeed something which could be done to relieve her suffering. All she needed was a corset which her daughter, who lived several blocks away, was supposed to bring to her. She had been waiting all day for this medically prescribed corset. So you see, her second problem was that her daughter was, for some reason or other, unable to bring this corset to the hospital. Her third problem was that she spoke very little English and she was trying to communicate with me. Unfortunately, Yiddish was not one of the languages taught in the public schools of the small Pennsylvania town where I had been educated, and it took a great deal of time for her to communicate her needs to me. BUT, it didn't take very long for me to move into action once I had assessed the situation. I went to the nearest telephone booth, looked up the number of this suffering woman's daughter, found my dime and called her. "Hello, this is Rabbi Winograd. I am visiting your mother at the hospital and she is in a great deal of pain. She tells me that this pain could be relieved if she could have her corset. Now if there is something which prevents you from bringing this corset to the hospital, I would be most happy to go to your house and bring it to your mother." The answer gave me one of my first *gray hairs in the temple*. "That is very kind of you Rabbi, but I feel that you should know that I do not plan to join your congregation."

My first year of "graying in the temple" rolled over me with the subtlety of a cobalt bomb and I found that springtime had come to Massachusetts. I received the usual phone call informing me that a certain Mrs. Cohen (I use the name Cohen because in this congregation there was no one by that name) had been in an automobile accident and was now home recuperating. A temple serves three human needs—religious, educational, and social. I had never met Mrs. Cohen because she had never been to the temple. She had never been to the temple for religious services. She had never been to the temple for religious school activities. She had never been to the temple for social functions. A perfect score! I called her to ask if I could go over for a visit. She told me that she would be glad to see me. I knocked on her front door and introduced myself. She was pleased to meet me. Seated in the living room, face to face, we discussed her injury. I asked her how long she had lived in our community. Answering this question she went on to inform me what city she had come from.

Smiling from ear to ear I asked her if she knew Rabbi Kochba. Her response was at least candid. "Yes, now that's the kind of rabbi we ought to have for our congregation." Unable to restrain my laughter I asked, "Well now, what does Rabbi Kochba do for the good people of his congregation that you would want me to do for our congregation?" Well, perhaps you think you have seen some pretty red faces in your time, but you should have seen the color of this one as she realized what she had said, and answered, "Well, he really stands up to those people. He tells them that a rabbi should live in a certain kind of house and they will just have to go out and find the money and build it for him." This was even better. So I responded with my smile reserved for new true friends and said, "I'll do that, will you back me up?" She answered "Well, of course the two situations have nothing in common."

She was, of course, right. The meaning of the whole thing is that no two situations are identical and that is why we need rabbis instead of tape recorders and encyclopedias. One of the important functions of the rabbi is the greeting of new residents to the community. Judaism has been spared the denominationalism which divides other religions. Since there are three movements in Judaism, it is naturally assumed that every little movement has a meaning all its own. Technically and definitively these movements are known as Reform, Conservative, and Orthodox. But then the Reform are also known as Liberal or Progressive, and the Orthodox are also known as Traditional. Of course the Conservatives do not have this kind of splintering since they are the center group, although come to think of it there are a great many Conservatives who are really Reconstructionists. Of course, a lot of Orthodox would object to being called Traditional, inasmuch as they would insist that this is not a matter of degree. One is either Orthodox or he is not. The members of this group sometimes prefer to call themselves Torah-true Jews. Although it is best to divide them into the Hasidim and the Mithnagdim. Generally speaking, as you can see, Judaism has not been plagued by the denominationalism which divides other major religions. By the way, it should be mentioned that many of the Hasidim are the Lubavitchers who have certain elements of the Mithnagdim combined with Hasidism. Then of course, there is an important branch of Orthodoxy called the S'fardim, but most Hasidim would say that the S'fardim are really Conservatives. But for this I would have to ask a friend who is Rabbi of the Sephardic Reform Temple of Curaçao because he is much closer to the situation. Now, when the residents come to the community they ask you questions like this, "Rabbi, is your congregation Orthodox or Reserved?" I answer "Neither." Then there was a man who wanted to know if my congregation was Hebrew or Reform. I answered, "Both."

Now, when I am not getting "gray in the temple" I am getting gray with people from the temple. Like the wonderful Bostonian man who sat in my home and looking me straight in the eye as we discussed my very interesting history, asked, "Rabbi, whatever possessed you to go into the 'robinhood'?" (Bostonian pronunciation of rabbinhood.) Now, when you think about it, it is a kind of logical sequence. A bunch of sisters in a sisterhood. A bunch of brothers in a brotherhood. How could he ever dream that a bunch of rabbis is not a rabbinhood, since he probably did not know that a bunch of children is a youth group? We will not discuss motherhood at this time.

They tell the story about the little girl who came home from religious school and reported that she had learned part of the Ten Commandments, whereupon she began to recite "I am the Lord by God, who brought you out of the land of Egypt." Now I do not know whether or not this actually happened, but with children we have the most fun trying to interpret Judaism. For example, at each seat in the pews of our temple, one can find a copy of the Bible in English. Each Sabbath as I prepare to read the scriptural lesson from the Torah scroll, I announce "today's reading of Scripture can be found in your pew Bibles on page six, chapter x verse y." You can imagine how delighted I was to learn that little children in our temple were under the impression that a pew was a kind of Bible.

Since an essential part of a rabbi's life centers around the thirst for education, one is constantly experimenting with methods of making instruction more efficient. We have a particular problem with the teaching of the Hebrew language, because of the Sam Levenson syndrome. I am sure you have all heard of the Sam Levenson syndrome. This is a combination of the Hebrew language and a boy with a football helmet who cannot go to Hebrew school because of a mother who is concerned with "When will he get his sunshine?" Therefore, it is quite a yoke to bear, as we seek to combine in our child football helmets, sunshine, and the Hebrew language. Naturally, a rabbi with growing children has a tremendous advantage. He can experiment on his own kids and thus save children of the temple from faulty methods. Since I had three children at the time of my ordination (a record which I would not advise anyone to try to break), I could see the unlimited possibilities of using Hebrew in the home. We decided that with baby Michael, (his Yiddish name is Mayerka, and you should hear his older brother, Harry, sing "Oh, Mayerka, Oh Mayerka, God shed his grace on thee") we would speak only Hebrew so that it would be his first language. Anxiously we waited as the months rolled by. Some day Michael is going to speak! What will be his first word? Will it be *Abba* (father) or *Imma* (Mother)? Then came the moment of decision. I had been out late at a meeting because "Why should this night be any different from any other night?" I returned home to the usual dark house with everyone alseep. Walking past baby Michael's room I was astonished as he sat up in bed and shouted "Hi-there!"

His Hebrew progress has continued at about the same level to this day. He is now five years of age and is interested in all phases of human activity. We encourage this. We seek to include him in all conversations. A month or so ago when the word "urine" was used by an adult in his presence, I asked Michael, "Do you know what urine is?" the answer—"Of course, Daddy, urine is how you say 'tinkle' in Hebrew."

Rabbis' children, as you see, have difficulty in breaking their accustomed thought-patterns in new situations. In this case, the new situation was the appearance of a foreign-sounding word in the English language. Then there was the episode of the conference in Philadelphia, when I took my children to a cafeteria for breakfast. They requested cereal as they usually do in the morning and were served with it something they had never seen or tasted before. Finally my oldest boy asked me, "Daddy, what is this stuff they put on the cereal here?" I told him that this is called cream and that it is something that we never have in our house. I was about to explain that we do not have it in our house because we are all fat enough without it. However, before I could get this explanation out, number one son again asked, "Why don't we ever have it at home?" Quick as could be my number two son gave him the answer. "Because it isn't kosher."

But if you think that it is only children who have difficulty in breaking their accustomed pattern of thought in new situations, consider a dear friend of mine, a Presbyterian minister, who won an immortal place in my heart's treasure house. During one phase of my dieting he remarked, "I know you are doing pretty well with that diet now, but we'll see how well you get along when Lent is over."

Ruth Gruber Michaels

EVERYBODY TALKS

Mrs. Michaels is a lecturer and author of *Israel Today, Land of Many Nations, Israel Without Tears,* and *Destination Palestine.* She has contributed articles to *Look, Life, Reader's Digest* and other popular publications.

The essay "Everybody Talks" is a hair-raising report on her experiences as a lecturer before Jewish audiences.

Everybody talks. And nearly everybody gives talks. There is a new kind of hunger in America—a hunger to make speeches, a hunger to hear speeches. Catholics speak; Baptists speak. Jews also speak, and listen.

Just as Judaism is a way of life, so Jewish meetings have become an American-Jewish way of life. At almost any house in almost any community, someone is lecturing in a synagogue, a Jewish community center, a Hebrew school, a club, a hotel, a rumpus room or a living room.

At this moment, from Seattle to Miami Beach, at the drop of a gavel, a small invasion army of speakers, properly fortified by kosher roast beef or bagels and lox, fulsomely introduced, will stand up behind white tablecloths, and begin speaking on everything from A (anti-Semitism) to Z (Zionism). There are fund-raising meetings, luncheons, brunches, breakfasts, dinners, teas and even coffees.

Lecturing in itself is not new. People have been singing for their supper ever since the first caveman told his friends a good fish story. Lecturing got on its feet as organized business just after the Civil War when Ann Eliza Young, one of Brigham Young's twenty-seven wives, sued her husband for divorce and then earned $20,000 a year talking about it.

In every Jewish community, the year is staked out in meetings. Like gold miners jealously nailing their names on wooden sticks along streams they dream are flowing with gold, each organiza-

[247]

tion races to capture a day on the calendar most likely to have the best turn-out and least likely to conflict with weddings, Bar Mitzvahs, golden anniversaries and, if possible, births and deaths. Each day is agonizingly appraised, like D-Day. The rites of spring are ushered in by the United Jewish Appeal, Chanukah means that the Bonds for Israel campaign is over.

In between the two giant fund-raising organizations that tower over Jewish communal life like the East and West learning to coexist, all the other organizations—the synagogue congregations, the Sisterhoods, Hadassah, Pioneer Women, Mizrachi, ZOA, ORT, B'nai B'rith, Verband, AJC (Committee as well as Congress), the Friendly Sisters of Maspeth and thousands more —hold educational meetings, fashion shows, donor luncheons, Mitzvah luncheons, study groups, forums, card parties, bazaars, award dinners, conferences and conventions.

Of America's five and a half million Jews, there is scarcely a man or child alive who has not been to a Jewish meeting. Archeologists of the future, digging among the ruins of American civilization 1964, may ponder such artifacts as a crumbling wall hung with nothing but plaques.

Along with holding meetings goes the crucial problem of getting bigger and bigger audiences to turn up for meetings. The great gimmick of our day is "The Guest of Honor."

The guest of honor is someone in the community beloved enough to bring out a host of friends, or rich and powerful enough to bring out even his competitors. (At fund-raising meetings, the guest of honor is almost always given his plaque after the money is in, lest all his friends walk out as soon as he is honored.)

Jewish meetings have a group identity; whether the city is New York, Chicago, Dallas or Peoria, the people look comfortable together. Whether the meeting is made up essentially of upper middle class, middle middle class or lower middle class, the people seem to know each other's backgrounds, foibles, culture, mores and tribal beliefs. The only real stranger is often the itinerant speaker, who, before he even opens his mouth, is ready to drop from too much well-meant hospitality.

Sometimes you discover that you have been pre-sold to the community as a combination of Demosthenes, Shakespeare and Jacqueline Kennedy. In Winnipeg, Canada, the advance publicity in the local press described me as "one of the eleven best-dressed women in New York." Since no list had ever gone beyond ten, the publicity man was sure that whoever makes up those lists would not sue him. The results were spectacular. The afternoon of the meeting itself, one of the leading citizens called the chairman for tickets. The chairman said, "I'm sorry, but you'll have to sit on the chandelier." The leading citizen said, "I don't care where we sit. My wife says we have to go. She can sit on the chandelier."

Most chairmen today have learned that brevity is the soul of good chairmanship. But every now and then you meet one who gets micromania. Once having heard the golden sound of his own voice through a public address system, he becomes hypnotized with eloquence. Speakers are just as guilty. There is a whole generation of Phudnick speakers—*Nudnicks* with Ph.D.'s.

In New York City, where chairmen and speakers are practically chained to a speedometer on their tongues, and every item on the agenda is clocked like the countdown on a moon launch, a mimeographed introduction taking exactly thirty-six seconds was sent to the chairman of a number of fund-raising meetings I was to address. Two quick paragraphs polished off my life and times, and then one chairman paused to say, "I have barely scratched the surface" and introduced me.

The ghost of Freud lurks and often smirks on the fringes of even the most somber meetings. There was the chairman who once asked the audience to rise: "Let us have a moment of silence for those who have gone on to the Great Behind."

The birth of Israel gave Jewish meetings the greatest shot in the arm since Moses called the Jews together in the desert. Jewish philanthropy, which had always been unique in its generosity, suddenly sky-rocketed. The UJA raised its sights from a few thousand dollars a year to over 100 million dollars a year. All Israel-minded organizations followed suit.

A whole pattern of Jewish fund-raising evolved, which has become the envy of non-Jewish groups—from parlor meetings and advanced gifts meetings to the big dinner itself, with the chairman, the speaker, the card-callers, the announcements of contributions, a kind of Jewish open-confessional, and finally the guest of honor.

To a speaker, each audience has a character of its own. Every audience has its own seismograph. They know when they're being talked down to; they know when a speaker is hostile or bored or distracted or exhausted. And they know when a speaker cares deeply about them and about his subject.

Each speaker too has his own integrity. He is the sum total of his life's experiences. He cannot imitate. He can only project his own image. This is his validity as a speaker.

The validity of a speech is that it gives an audience something new—perhaps a new thought, perhaps some new information, new understanding. Perhaps even a sense of purpose, of commitment, of ennoblement. Perhaps even a desire not just to listen, but to act.

Invariably someone asks you, "Don't you ever get nervous?"

Of course you get nervous. Every speech is a new challenge, and even when you have reached the exalted state where your knees no longer knock, your stomach no longer flips, the pulses in your throat no longer tick like an old alarm clock, you still feel a heightened sense of tension, a total concentration as though every blood cell in your body were focused on this one thing— this speech to be made. It is as though blinkers protect you. Nothing can distract you. You are ready to soar.

But distractions are always present. In the middle of a speech, I heard a man shout angrily, "It's enough already. Shut up."

The audience gasped. What do you do? Do you stop? Do you pretend you haven't heard? Do you run the risk of breaking whatever mood you have managed to create?

I went right on talking. When the evening was over, a red-faced man came up to me apologetically. "I had too much to drink when they served cocktails," he said. "I fell asleep while you were talking and had a nightmare. I thought my wife was yelling at me. So I told her to shut up. The worst thing is I don't even belong here. I was brought along as a guest."

Men and women lecturers have different worries. Men have to worry not to pace the platform like caged animals, not to twiddle their thumbs or keep looking at their watches or wiping their foreheads. Women worry about their clothes, their posture —not to pitch their voice too high, not to hug the microphone, not to hunch themselves on the lectern, not to wear dangling earrings or charm bracelets which distract the audience, not to wear loud dresses which fatigue the eye or necklines which capture it.

A highly dramatic woman speaker was suddenly dropped

[250]

when reports came back across the country that her dresses plunged too low and her speeches followed the plunge.

A lecturer is forever aware that he and the audience are partners. They spark each other. They both create. They create the magic together. A speaker is nothing without an audience. With it, he comes alive. He talks out of the guts of living, out of suffering and joy, out of the truth of self-knowledge.

Audiences too have their frustrations. They may come all primed to see some glamorous movie star or to hear the "hottest" Man of the Year, only to find a pinch-hitter. The movie star has flown to London to make a movie, and the Man of the Year has just been called to the White House to advise the President on the state of the union.

Having done a fair share of pinch-hitting, I am always amazed at the good nature of a long-suffering audience. When the beloved Veep, Vice-President Alben Barkley married, he cancelled all his speaking engagements for a while. In Flint, Michigan, sitting on the dais with the senators and all the officials who had come to pay homage to the Veep, I stood up apologetically. "I have pinch-hit for a lot of people," I said, "but this is the first time I have had to pinch-hit for the Great Lover."

The chairman ended the meeting gallantly. "We were sorry to miss the Great Lover, but we are happy to have had our own Great Love."

Even if it wasn't true, his gallantry helped the audience over the hurdle of their disappointment.

One spring when the Supreme Court session was unexpectedly prolonged, I was asked to pinch-hit for Supreme Court Justice William O. Douglas, whom I had known in Washington and had admired as a rare human being. A battery of judges sat on the dais. Some 250 lawyers, trained to be critical, sat in the audience. Suddenly I heard myself saying, "Mr. Chairman, Honorable—er —Honorable—how *do* you address judges?"

The judge next to me on the dais counselled loud enough for everyone to hear. "It depends on what side of the bench you're on."

The laughter and good humor broke the tension.

But the toughest assignment came the day I was to pinch-hit for the late Rabbi Abba Hillel Silver.

In the morning there was an urgent phone call. "You've got to do this. It's a terrible emergency. We have been promising Rabbi Silver to Dallas for five years. This year he finally accepted. Dallas was overjoyed. But now he has pneumonia. You've got to go. Only nobody must know that *you* are Abba Hillel Silver."

I protested that I could never be Rabbi Silver.

"The chairman says he'll take you—or cancel the meeting. Hundreds of thousands of dollars are at stake for Israel."

When the plane landed in Dallas, I pulled a hat over my eyes and tried to slink down the ramp looking as un-Rabbi Silver-like as possible. TV cameras were shooting; newspapermen stood waiting. I turned around to see what movie star was behind me. Nobody was behind me. The terrible realization came that they were shooting me.

"But I thought I was coming incognito," I muttered to the field man.

"Don't worry. They're not showing this on TV until 6:30 tonight; by that time nobody will be home. They'll be at our meeting."

We drove to the hotel; I changed for dinner, met nobody except the chairman. In the ballroom nobody was introduced to me; nobody talked.

When what looked like half the City of Dallas had finished eating its fruit cup, the chairman stood up. "Ladies and Gentlemen," he said in the voice of a mourner on Lincoln's death train. "I have sad news. Rabbi Abba Hillel Silver has pneumonia."

The sighs could have been heard from Dallas to New York. If they hadn't eaten their fruit cup, the entire audience would have left. For months I rarely ate a fruit cup without saying a little prayer that Rabbi Silver would not catch pneumonia.

There is a special quality about a Jewish audience and a Jewish meeting. It is the presence of the Jewish psyche. It is the quality of soul. It is the quality of gratitude toward America: "America was good to me. I want to repay it." It is the old man nodding his head, saying, "If my father hadn't run away from the army in Russia, I'd be ashes in a gas chamber. . . . There but for the Grace of God. . . ." It is the young college graduate who says to you, "Israel helped me find my identity."

Every meeting is an affirmation. An affirmation of responsibility. An affirmation of Judaism in America. An affirmation of life.

[252]

Rabbi Erwin L. Herman

BAR MITZVAH
A LA CARTE

> Rabbi Erwin L. Herman, director of regional activities of
> the Union of American Hebrew Congregations, wrote "Bar
> Mitzvah a la Carte" on the basis of firsthand experience,
> having just managed to survive the Bar Mitzvah of his
> own son. His indignation over the gross take-over of what
> was once a spiritual event in the life of a Jewish boy
> entering manhood is lifted out of the ordinary by his
> deceptively good-natured approach to a touchy subject.

"... *lift up His Countenance toward thee and grant thee peace.*"
The blessing completed, the rabbi rested his hands for a moment
more on the well-combed hair of the Bar Mitzvah. Then, grasping the arm of his young religious inductee and calling a "Good-
Shabos" greeting to the congregation, he walked briskly down
the centre aisle.

His walk was more than a sign that the service had ended. It
was a bridge—a swinging, swaying, suspended bridge—between
prayer and the party, between the holy and the profane. The
Bar Mitzvah celebration had begun when he reached the sanctuary door.

What followed will, for many, be unbelievable. For others, it
will be shameful. But for the rest, it will be the faithful reporting
of their own experiences or, possibly, a projection of their personal plans. What followed was not one situation, but many. . . .

Episode A: Immediately following the religious service, the
entire congregation was treated to a traditional Kiddush with a
most untraditional wine—champagne, fine French champagne.
Within the hour, the oh-so-recent worshipers were converted
into a giggling, foul-story-telling mob, hiccuping its way through
a *simcha.* And to add to the fun, the Bar Mitzvah and his play-
mates found their own joy in draining the glasses of their preoccupied parents. (Being grown-up can really be fun!)

[253]

RUDOLPH J. CARRASCO

Episode B: Immediately following the religious service, the friends and family adjourned to the social hall. Its face had been lifted—lifted up to the very rafters. For there, next to the ceiling, was suspended a large cage. And in that cage were two hundred of the brightest plumaged, loudly screeching parakeets ever assembled under one temple roof. Inspired by what moments ago had been a spiritual symphony, the guests were now deafened by a chirping cacophony, arranged by the caterer who beamed from the kitchen door. But the noise was the least of it! Thirty minutes after the meal began, served with deliberate and meticulous care befitting a lavish expenditure of funds, the toastmaster, coached by the caterer, called for attention, pointed an ominous finger to the aviary above and, ignoring the obvious yet unspoken prayers of the assembled adults and encouraged by the shrieking delight of the thirteen-year-olds, shouted the magic words that opened the doors of Chaos. The trap was sprung—and from the mouth of that suspended cage was disgorged a frenetic rainbow of color, a spectrum of nervous movement, a screeching, whistling, babbling battalion of birds, each bent upon the onerous task of reaching support below without being crushed by wildly churning wings or eviscerated by thrusting beaks. Not all of them made it quite as planned. Some landed in the hair of astounded guests and clawed their way to the firmness of scalp. Some struck the table and some the food. Some stayed and would not budge. Others sat for a moment, left a token of their presence, and flew off to torment elsewhere. In a word, when the birds came out, confusion came in. It is unnecessary to describe the hysterics of the women, the heroics of the men, the joy of the kids . . . or the humiliation of the rabbi.

Episode C: Immediately following the religious service, the friends and family adjourned to the social hall. But it was no longer the hall they once knew. Through the magic of imagination (and money), the caterer had converted the place into—a circus, of course. Not just a plain, everyday, small-town circus, but an authentic three-ringer with sawdust and poles and balloons and the promise of "anything can happen here." It did. No sooner had the guests reached dessert, when the music of the band overarched the conversation, the clowns appeared, the dogs performed, and . . . the elephant was led in. A live, flesh, blood, and tusk elephant. And on that elephant, there was a howdah, a contraption that looks like a theater box caught in a high wind. At a gesture of his driver, the beast bowed obediently before his captive audience. It was said that a mocking smile formed on his hairy lips, but this cannot be proved since the viewer beat a hasty retreat from the room.

Episodes D, E, F, etc. . . . what good does it do to add to the account? Is it necessary to describe the chopped liver or the sculptured ice or the butter-baked Bible? Or the child who ran by, waving a five hundred dollar check, shouting: "Look, Mom, another one!"?

Why have we permitted this lovely ceremony and its celebration to become a ritualistic prostitute, used and abused without love by society-starved parents and commercial hucksters? Why have we permitted the religious vows of the child to find hollow echo in the drunken vowels of the adult? Why are the congregational leaders without voice? Why are the teachers stupefied and struck dumb? Why *are* the rabbis quiet?

There is a conspiracy of silence. It is broken only by the occasional cluck-cluck of a critic . . . or the painful cry of a debt-ridden parent . . . or the anguished *whisper* of a rabbinical group. The caterer has found his new place, in the saddle of the synagogue. While he may have been stunned at the outset by the centrality of his role, he now bears his responsibilities with aplomb and just the necessary touch of arrogance. Why not? We have made it possible. No sooner is the Bar Mitzvah Sabbath date selected, then we rush headlong—to the caterer. The Haftoro portion can wait! The meetings with rabbi and teacher can wait! The caterer cannot—will not wait.

Who, then, is this imperious and artistic soul who commands our attention and demands nothing but a franchise? He is, above all else, a master of psychology who understands every nuance of our social needs and our every ache for acceptance. He is a real estate tactician who metes out the rooms of the synagogue with wondrous skill when the traffic gets heavy. He is an authority on party novelties, possessing more titillating gimmicks than a joke store and more gleaming baubles than Woolworth's. He is an interior decorator whose head seems to dance with ideas that are frighteningly imaginative and so much fun: a luau Bar Mtzvah, a baseball Bar Mitzvah, a vaudeville Bar Mitzvah. He is, in effect, an architect of our social structure who has learned to blend the secular with the sectarian, giving prominence to the former, for he reads us well.

This is the shepherd who leads us with uncomplaining conformity down the road of social acceptance. We have been good sheep—and like good sheep, we have been clipped. Enough! It is time to state without equivocation that we have had it, and to admit that we have been had, in the process. Either the Bar Mitzvah in its totality—including the party *and* the presents— regains its proper perspective as a full and satisfying *religious* experience or it gets discarded into history's wastebasket as obsolete and obscene.

If the Bar Mitzvah is to teach, let it do so, properly and in its entirety. But a child *cannot* be taught the meaning of Godliness with lessons that are crass and vulgar, the meaning of charitableness by the unconscionable spending of money, or the meaning of prayer when the benediction of his worship service serves merely as the invocation to the festivities.

If the Bar Mitzvah is to serve as a warm and formal welcome into the Jewish religious community, then let that community be worthy of the child. The act of becoming Bar Mitzvah can be a becoming act when we, who have sold it for a mess of pottage, will redeem it as our birthright once again.

Sara Kasdan

IF YOU WANT
TO SPEAK FRENCH

> Sara Kasdan, the author of *Love and Kisses* and *So It Was Just a Simple Wedding*, cannot put pen to paper without tapping the springs of laughter.
> "If You Want to Speak French" offers helpful hints not only on the study of foreign languages but on the maintenance of squatter's rights in distant democracies.

If you want to speak French go to France. If you want to speak Spanish go to Spain. If you want to speak Hebrew stay home and study unless you are already expert at it or you intend to spend at least three months in Israel studying at an *Oolpahn*, an intensive Hebrew language school where you will live in a dormitory and hear and speak only Hebrew.

But if you've studied Hebrew at home to the point where you can impress your more ignorant friends with your fluency and you feel that you will wow the Israelis with your knowledge or at least get credit for trying, just forget it. Israelis can detect an American accent from the word "ba-vaka-sha" or "please" which will probably be the first word of any sentence you try. If you say, "Please to tell me where stands the autobus to the sea shore," ninety per cent of the Israelis will reply in perfect English. If your accent happens to be as good as a Sabra's (a native Israeli), you are out of luck. The reply will be in rapid-fire Hebrew which you will not understand. If your informant elaborates on his verbal directions by pointing, you are fortunate. He will never know that you are just a tourist. If he does not point, you will smile sweetly, say rapidly, "todah rabah" (many thanks) and walk proudly to the wrong bus.

There comes a time in the life of the American tourist in Israel when he or she (meaning me) decides there is no percentage in using her hard-learned Hebrew. There comes a time when it pays to be ignorant. One of these times was on a bus trip returning to Tel-Aviv from Eilat, the southern tip of the Negev desert. It started out to be a trip on a sight-seeing bus. When we left early in the morning the temperature was 105 degrees in the shade and there was no shade. After about an hour of travel, when we were half-way up a mountain, even the bus became over-heated. I had felt none too secure about the road in the first place. I could never understand how the Israelis had glued that narrow serpentine strip of pavement to a mountain of loose dirt and rock. I suspected a secret material, perhaps American chewing gum, and felt that at any moment the road would become unstuck and slide down several thousand feet of mountainside.

The bus driver tried every means of getting the bus started. He even made a sacrificial offering of our iced drinking water to the radiator god, but to no avail. We waited on the mountainside until the regular Eilat—Tel-Aviv bus came along on its one daily run. The more aggressive of the group got seats on the bus. The rest of us had to stand in the aisle for a wild sixty-mile-per-hour drive down the mountain.

Among the seated passengers were two Israeli women, one of whom had been aggressive and offensive in two languages from the moment the tour started. She had wilfully delayed our return trip by a half-hour when the other passengers were anxious to get an early start and we were fairly or unfairly blaming her for the over-heated bus motor.

When after another hour of traveling we stopped at a roadside stand for bottles of soda water and whatever we could get to take the place of the lunch which we would miss, I managed to be among the first served. I dashed back to the bus, seltzer water and cookies in hand, and deliberately sat down in the seat temporarily relinquished by the bilingual offender, but left in the charge of her monolingual friend. "Madam," said the woman to me in Hebrew, "this seat is taken." I made like I knew from nothing. I smiled at her sweetly and offered her a cookie.

I kept the seat. The meek may inherit the earth, but they do not inherit bus seats.

Nat Hentoff

YIDDISH SURVIVALS
IN THE NEW COMEDY

To the addict of the modern periodical it must sometimes
seem as if Nat Hentoff is not an individual but a whole
corporation. His byline appears in *The Reporter, Harper's,
Esquire, The New Yorker, The Village Voice* and almost
any reputable weekly, monthly or quarterly you can name.
His favorite theme is social justice. In this piece, however,
Mr. Hentoff takes a holiday from his war against reaction
to examine the current state of Jewish humor and its roots
in the Jewish past.

When I was a boy in the 1930's, a recurrent source of neighborhood pride was the high percentage of reigning comedians who
were Jews—Jack Benny, Joe Penner, Milton Berle, Eddie Cantor,
George Burns, among them. The non-members who were too
pungently skillful to be excluded received honorary admission
certificates. It was said of Fred Allen, W. C. Fields, and Bob
Hope that somehow, perhaps through propinquity, they had
acquired the ingredients of a *"Yiddishe Kop."*

Assimilationism having accelerated since then, there is now
less overt compartmentalization-by-cultural-background. Nonetheless, it cannot have escaped even the most nominal Jew that
a similarly high percentage of the "new" comedians—the social
and political satirists—are Jewish by birth if not by conscious
practice. The compatriots include Mort Sahl, Elaine May and
Mike Nichols, Shelly Berman, and Lenny Bruce.

Except for Lenny Bruce, the others are not nearly so bold and
penetrating dissectors of our pretensions and routinized con-
victions as they have been billed, but the purpose of this essay
is not so much to analyze their philosophies, or lack of them, as
to speculate on what aspects of Yiddish humor continue to be
part of their techniques and their general way of looking at
society.

[259]

So far as it can be defined, Yiddish humor has usually been mordant, often self-critical and, in essence, has been a view of society from underneath, from the position of a partial or a total outsider. Like Negro wit, it is distinctively minority humor; and significantly, a currently popular joke among civil libertarians involved in the struggle for equal rights has Jewish antecedents. A white "cracker" about to be electrocuted for so wanton a killing of a Freedom Rider that even a southern court sentenced him to die suddenly, asks to be admitted into membership in the N.A.A.C.P. His request is granted by astonished members of the local unit. As he is strapped into the chair, the "cracker" says with satisfaction, approving his own impending death, "Well, at least I got another of those black-loving Jews."

The predecessor and mirror image of that story which I first heard concerned a venerable, pious Jew who demanded on his death bed that he be baptized a Catholic. With his last strength, he explained his action to his startled and aggrieved children. "Better," he whispered, "that a *goy* should die than a Jew."

No bitterness this explicit can be found in the work of the "new" comedians, but there are signs of similar in-group irony and solidarity as when Shelley Berman tells of his father's conviction that "all laborers are Gentiles. Even a Jew who is a laborer is a Gentile." More subtle and more reflective of the sometimes radical change in the attitude toward the Jew of certain sections of society, was an improvisatory scene by Nichols and May in which Miss May played a rootless, northern version of a Tennessee Williams heroine. "Do you know," she pleaded, "what it is like to be a *shickse* in America? All your life you think there *is* such a thing as a Gentile, but you do not believe it." Mr. Nichols tried to calm the distraught soul: "I hope I have not hurt you, pretty Gentile lady."

There are no actual Yiddishisms or Yiddish motifs in the work of Mort Sahl; but his vinegary, mocking style and the particular cadences of his speech as he skewers social and political pieties are in the direct line of such Yiddish monologists as Michael Rosenberg and Menasha Skulnik. The tempo has been increased but the punctuations are similar, as is the wry, half-questioning conclusion of each story. One expects Sahl to hunch his shoulders and turn his palms up in the traditional Yiddish gesture of ultimate incomprehension of *others'* absurdities.

Shelly Berman is even more clearly related in inflection to the

RUDOLPH J. CARRASCO

Yiddish comics of the past. His subject matter is more wide-ranging and is superficially more sophisticated (although he spends as much time on the telephone as George Jessel. ever did). Lenny Bruce accurately termed Berman "the goyishe Sam Levenson"; and Berman, though a more skilful actor, is indeed a spiritual, more cosmopolitan heir of Levenson.

Oddly, the most daring and, to some, the most outrageously unprecedented of all the new comedians is the one who uses the Yiddish words in his act as well as those sweeping gestures that used to be endemic to the Yiddish stage. Lenny Bruce evoked more different overtones from the judicious placement of one off-color word than any Yiddish comedian in history. Other Jewish terms were fused in his act with Negro and jazz argot into an anthology of advanced in-group language that crossed the boundary line of several minority groups in our culture.

What most firmly linked Bruce, however, to that Jewish tradition which predates Jews in show business, was his fierce sense of moral outrage. As Irving Howe and Eliezer Greenberg point out in their introduction to *A Treasury of Yiddish Stories*:

[261]

"Unlike American humor, Jewish humor is overwhelmingly social: its great themes are precisely those events which make the Jewish experience so tragic." Among those dominant themes is the difficulty and yet the necessity of sustaining a system of spiritual values in the face of constant materialistic temptation and equally constant obtuseness on the part of the vast majority who live mainly for instant gratification.

This moral preoccupation was pervasive in Bruce's work from his devastating account of the Sunday in a church when Christ and Moses return to earth ("O God," shouts the preacher, "look at the front door! Here come the lepers! Don't TOUCH anything! Is the poor box locked?") to Bruce's frequent self-interrogations in public as to whether he deserved high income. "I'm a hustler. As long as they give, I'll take. But I know that someday we'll have to answer for this, and I'm saving money for that day." Bruce then created the apocalyptic tribunal. Among those brought forward to justify themselves was Sammy Davis, Jr. Bruce imitated Davis telling the judges he earns between $20,000 and $30,000 a week. "But what do you do to earn so much?" the judges asked. Bruce launched into a tartly accurate impression of Davis' act. The judge was indignant: "Take away his Jewish Star and his stocking cap! And that religious statue of Elizabeth Taylor! Thirty years in Biloxi!"

In Bruce, the residue of Judaism was more his implacable morality than the high percentage of Jewish slang he used. In Berman, it is a somewhat sophisticated abstraction of the performing style of the Yiddish-American monologists. In Nichols and May and Mort Sahl, the heritage is expressed both in mannerisms and in the sardonic stance of the outsider.

In all of these Jewish-born satirists, there are sufficient remnants of the Yiddish comedic approach to indicate again that however assimilated and non-sectarian those of us become who were raised in a Yiddish environment, parts of the past cannot be rubbed off. As for our children, their idea of humor is apt to undergo a further dilution of the Yiddish style, although they will retain some of that flavor through absorbing the partially Yiddish-nurtured skepticism of Bruce, Sahl, Nichols and May, and if they're lucky, of their parents.

Albert Vorspan and Paul Kresh

A GLOSSARY
FOR JEWISH MEETINGS

> In twenty years of professional association with Jewish
> life I estimate that I may have spent practically a third
> of my waking life at meetings. Mr. Vorspan, another
> victim of that dismal label "professional Jew," claims he
> can match or surpass me. At any rate, both of us decided
> to sit down one day and supply what seemed to us a
> badly-needed guide for the interpretation of what is said
> when members of our faith gather in solemn conclave.

There are those who claim that Jewish meetings constitute a
method of capital punishment, with boredom as the supreme
penalty. This is a dire canard. Most Jewish meetings have an
explosive element which makes uninterrupted sleep—let alone
departure from this life—impracticable. The fact is, those who
do find themselves drifting off at these gatherings are, we have
long suspected, simply victims of a language difficulty. The most
meaningful exchanges are passing them right by. We are not
referring only to the salty quality of the notes that are forwarded
from hand to hand until they reach the lucky recipient whose
wry smile says worlds to the onlooker with the proper key to
their meaning; there is also the content of the deliberations
themselves.

All Jewish meetings (well, anyway, some of them) have a
purposefulness that must strike the newcomer to their midst as
exceptional. It is possible that an unprepared participant might
be able to extract the gist of, say a meeting on temple deficits,
welfare fund disbursements, or organizational programming,
without a real understanding of the special vocabulary in use.
Like a concert-goer, however, who doesn't know the score, he is
missing much. We have sent our lexicographers into the field in
the hope of filling in this distressing gap. We are now in a
position to supply you with a basic list of terms useful to the

understanding of Jewish meetings of every variety. They may even come in handy at non-sectarian meetings.

We object to the manner in which this motion has been railroaded through.
    (We had it arranged for my side to put in our motion first.)

I am sure that Mr. Berg has excellent authority to back his conclusion.
    (He doesn't know what he's talking about.)

I don't question the sincerity of Mr. Stein's statement.
    (I question the sincerity of Mr. Stein's statement.)

Mr. Glasser is a most devoted and tireless member of our board.
    (Mr. Glasser is a *nudnik*.)

I don't think we should waste time going over the minutes of our last meeting.
    (Miss Klotznick never typed them.)

Would you restate the motion?
    (They're not going to put anything over on me.)

I had some remarks prepared for me by the staff, but I feel so close to this group I would rather just speak from my heart.
    (I will now make the remarks prepared for me.)

My worthy colleague . . .
    (My worst enemy should have such a colleague.)

I don't think we can take responsibility for the behavior of every individual Jew.
(A Jewish *gonif* is on the front pages.)

I think the entire Jewish community can take pride in the achievements of this great American.
(Arthur Goldberg has been named Ambassador to the U.N.)

It lacks *tam*.
(It's for *goyim*.)

I think we must bear in mind the public relations implications of such a move.
(The *goyim* won't like it.)

Are there any further nominations?
(It's all settled.)

I'm just talking off the top of my head.
(I don't know what I'm talking about.)

I don't recall the earlier comment, but I do believe . . .
(I just woke up.)

Let's set up a pilot project.
(Let's kill it for a year.)

I missed part of the meeting, but what I heard was most stimulating.
(After I made my own comment, I fell asleep.)

Let's adopt the idea in principle and have the exact language worked out later.
(Let's kill this crazy idea and go home already.)

Let's get down to *tachlis*.
(1. Let's change the subject. 2. Let's avoid a decision at all costs.)

Why don't we leave these details to be worked out by the staff.
(It's not important anyway.)

The statement is wonderfully strong, but I think the committee should go over it.
(It's too strong.)

Would the waiters please clear the hall.
(Here comes the pitch.)

[265]

The previous speaker has already said much of what I had in mind, but it bears repeating.

(He stole the only idea I had.)

Allow me these few moments . . .

(Consider the evening shot.)

I will confine myself to a few brief remarks.

(We'll be lucky to get home for the Late, Late Show.)

Can we keep this off the record?

(The reporter is here for the *National Jewish Post*.)

Will you withhold your applause until I have introduced all the people on the dais?

(Everybody's on the dais.)

I have just returned from Israel.

(Who hasn't?)

Jewish life is at the crossroads.

(There's a new emergency—on top of the usual crises and catastrophes.)

The resolutions committee meets in Parlor C.

(The resolutions committee meets in Parlor E—in the other wing of the hotel.)

Point of order!

(Let me talk!)

I came here from a sickbed.

(I'm lowering my pledge.)

I'm glad to see the youth here, because they are the leaders of tomorrow.

(Who let all those kids in?)

A token of our appreciation for his many years of unstinting and dedicated devotion to civic and Jewish causes . . .

(Another plaque.)

We have just sent a telegram to the State Department.

(We ran out of stationery.)

I, therefore, propose we refer this interesting idea to a committee for further study.

(Let's kill this silly idea and go home already.)

Speaking for myself, I'm very glad you brought that question up.

(I was afraid some joker would bring that up.)

Everybody who knows me knows that I strongly believe Jews should stand up and be counted.

(Except in this case.)

We all admire Mr. Fergasson as a distinguished Jewish communal, civic, and philanthropic leader.

(He's a big giver.)

We thank Herb for his most detailed and thorough report. He has certainly given us food for thought.

(Let's eat already.)

Mind you, I have no objection to the principle of this project, but I simply think we should carefully examine all the implications of it.

(I'm against it.)

Our committee has proceeded slowly and cautiously.

(We haven't had a meeting yet.)

I wonder if we could return to this point a little later.

(Let's bury it.)

I'd like Mr. Berg to hear this.

(Berg, stop talking already and listen!)

This is such an important suggestion and the hour is so late, why can't we put this over to another meeting when our minds are fresh?

(Let's kill this dopey idea and go home already.)

I must say you have asked a very searching and challenging question.

(I wish I knew the answer.)

Nobody feels more strongly than I do that Jews must be in the forefront of social justice.

(Let's stay out of it.)

Our decision to pool our efforts with those of all the other synagogues in the community in developing a joint community-wide program reflects our deep commitment to *Klal Yisroel,* to the peoplehood of Israel.

(This way we can split the costs.)

[267]

Rabbi Eugene Borowitz

CREATIVE WORSHIP
IN THE COMPUTER AGE

> Rabbi Borowitz is professor of education and lecturer on
> Jewish religious thought at the Hebrew Union College-
> Jewish Institute of Religion in New York City, rabbinical
> training ground of the Reform rabbinate. His articles have
> appeared in *The American Jewish Yearbook, The Founda-
> tions of American Education, Commentary, The Recon-
> structionist* and other journals.
>   His poker-faced speculation as to what might happen
> if modern technology ever takes over the temple sounds a
> timely warning to those who would put their trust in
> machines, however brilliant.

Many years have passed since creative worship was introduced
to Reform Jewish Youth at the first National Federation of
Temple Youth National Leadership Institutes. Much good has
come from the notion that services should be designed by the
worshippers themselves, based on their present needs and utilizing all relevant materials, not just the prayerbook. By this
direct appeal to their concerns, stated in their language, appealing to their taste, our young people have learned to feel at
home in prayer, to articulate their deepest longings and their
highest hopes to God. And they have experienced the broad
variety of forms: music and dance, choral speech and pantomime,
in which worship may find adequate expression.

Yet with the passage of the years some problems have arisen.
As the Methodists, Baptists, and even the Quakers have discovered in their practice of free and unregimented liturgy,
spontaneity is difficult to combine with regularity. The persons
charged with creating the service find they are using the same
themes over and over again. Their knowledge of the resources of
prayers and music is finite and they soon run out of fresh
material. Even their sensitivity to the needs of their fellows

begins to dull and they cannot meet their congregants' desire to pray on any but the most obvious level. Often then, the efforts at creative worship end up a tasteless mixture of the customary and the new, with neither the lovers of the tradition nor those who want a more personally oriented service happy with the result.

The problem is largely one of human limits in time, energy, knowledge and inspiration. Why not, however, utilize modern technology to expand the range of creative capacity to the fullest and thus make this modern style of worship more fully effective? No committee, regardless of its scholarly or artistic membership, could be as effective in identifying the inner needs of worshippers and creating a service responsive to them as a properly programmed computer.

The inability of most leadership to diagnose the congregations' living needs week after week has obviously been a limiting factor in previous creative services. The computer can render great aid here. On the simplest level, congregants could be given a check list of varied moods and emotions, which, according to a specific code, could be phoned in to the computer before each service. Less superficial would be a series of Rorschach-like designs which would allow the worshipper to project his depth desires. The extraordinary speed of the computer would make it possible to keep this information quite current and prevent the creation of services expressive of needs which might

MARTIN SILVERMAN

[269]

have already passed. Brief experimentation could easily indicate how close to the beginning of services the worshipper could still make his concerns manifest. This process has the advantage that, having personally participated in creating the service, the congregant is more likely to attend. For its part, the computer would do what no rabbi ever could—accept every suggestion, whenever it might come, regardless of its content, gratefully and patiently, even several simultaneously.

At the last moment possible the computer would, by mathematical computation, determine the exact proportion of needs to be manifest at that service. This would be analyzed in terms of all the possible patterns of worship which have previously been programmed for the computer by a panel of experts in Judaism, other religions and the arts. These various structures are now quickly considered to see which would be most appropriate to the mood of the congregation. The possibility of too much repetition can easily be guarded against through the machine's memory device which will retain a record of the previous weeks' patterns.

A fitting form for the service having been determined, the computer would draw forth appropriate materials with which to give it substance. Again, a vast range of religious literature and music has been stored in its circuits. In a liberal movement this would obviously include suitable selections from the greatest of mankind's writing, regardless of their author's own race or creed. Here too, the proper proportion of Jewish to non-Jewish materials could easily be fixed or even varied from week to week within a given mathematical range.

One other factor might also be taken into account: the congregation's response to the previous services. A truly sophisticated installation would include provision for feedback after each service, indicating to what extent the service designed had actually met the needs of the congregation. These responses could be included as part of the computer's guidance in creating future services. Over a period of time the computer would not be working out of the expert's theory alone but out of its own real experience with this congregation.

Some practical problems are worthy of consideration. The computer should be attached to a high-speed printing device which would make it possible for each congregant to have a nice-looking copy of the service on his arrival. By determining mathematically how many people actually come in ratio to the number of calls received, at a given time of the year, in relation to the weather, the machine could produce an efficient number of copies.

Since the cost of computers is beyond the reach of most congregations, they might well be located on a regional basis, serving the various communities via the telephone installations so common to big businesses today. Perhaps the Union might undertake this valuable service. However, some provision should be made for an occasional hook-up between the computers to exchange information, lest regional differences eventually come to disrupt the unity of Reform Judaism.

Preaching too, might benefit from the use of the computer. Surely the sermon should speak to the living needs of congregants. The computer might well guide the preacher in his choice of text or approach. Since time is a critical factor in meeting needs, it would be better if the energetic preacher could stock the computer with a variety of sermons. (He too could benefit from the computer's memory and analysis of previous congregational reactions in preparing these more effectively.) In this case, the computer, while selecting materials for this service, could also choose the sermon most appropriate to it. And the electronic brain could be relied upon to keep the manuscript, if not the delivery, down to a length adjusted to the congregation's attention span.

Many exciting possibilities open up once the computer is brought into the planning process. More will undoubtedly be revealed once it is actually in use. Serendipity has proved to be one of the major factors in the attractiveness and utility of these electronic brains. Of course the costs involved in even a pilot project are very substantial. But surely in a dynamic and progressive movement such as ours there must be some individuals or foundations who would underwrite what may well prove to be a decisive break-through in twentieth century religious practice. The electronic age is here. Will not someone step forward to enable us to meet it with courage?

MANNY KURTZ

God in Bernstein's
"Kaddish" Symphony

The
Living
Arts

"Give unto them a garland for ashes"

Isaiah LXI:3

Until his untimely death in 1965, David Boroff contributed a column for each quarter in which he tried to place the season's books, plays and motion pictures in a thoughtful framework of relative rather than absolute evaluation. David Boroff could be trenchant when he chose. He was always honest. But, above all, he was fair, which is probably why our readers came to love his writing and to trust his judgment.

Today, Leslie Fiedler is doing this column and lending little comfort to the complacment.

Our music critic is Alan Rich of the *New York Herald Tribune*.

The plastic arts are discussed in each issue by Alfred Werner, who not only possesses a pair of penetratingly clear eyes but is passionately interested in the relation between art and the faith of Judaism.

A play, a film or a painting wins our consideration if it is concerned with the Jewish religion or with Jewish life, whether the author is a Jew, a Christian, a Moslem or an atheist. At the same time, we are concerned with stimulating the creation of new works of art as expressions of Judaism both within the sanctuary and in the general community.

The essays in this section were selected because they seemed to be of more than passing interest since the works being reviewed are regarded not in isolation but as examples for the expression of general principles and standards.

Rabbi Ely E. Pilchik

GOD IN BERNSTEIN'S "KADDISH" SYMPHONY

When Leonard Bernstein's "Kaddish" Symphony was introduced by the composer at Philharmonic Hall in Lincoln Center in the spring of 1964, a number of critics attacked the text of the piece as insulting and inappropriate.

In this essay, the spiritual leader of Temple B'nai Jeshurun in Newark, New Jersey, defends the composer's approach on the basis of a tradition which he says reaches back to the days of Abraham. Rabbi Pilchik is the author of *From The Beginning — A New Look At The Bible*, and *Hillel — A Book Against The Sword*. He is also the librettist of an oratorio based on the Book of Job.

We long to understand God. That longing assures our survival. "Seek Me and live," said the Prophet.

Our understanding of our God of justice and mercy has been clouded. Jewish theology has become Jewish theodicy. All of us, quietly or articulately, wonder—how could the God of Abraham, Isaac, and Jacob, the God of our Covenant let it happen? Is He still there? Does He still care?

Leonard Bernstein, who heard and amplified His "still small voice" in the "Jeremiah Symphony" returned to Him in the "Kaddish" Symphony. The "Jeremiah" is built on biblical text, the book of Lamentations. The "Kaddish" Symphony, founded on our magnificent mourner's prayer, incorporates Bernstein's own poetic words.

The world premiere of the "Kaddish" Symphony was presented in Israel. The Israelis understood it, felt it, and hailed it. When Bernstein conducted it here, at Philharmonic Hall, it evoked bruising reviews. The critics panned the music and took offense at Bernstein's running text. Schonberg of the *New York Times*, Kolodin of the *Saturday Review*, and Sargeant of the *New Yorker* joined in choral outcry: "Blasphemy!"

[275]

In *American Judaism,* Alan Rich called the text "offensive." He also disparaged the work in the *Herald Tribune.*

Winthrop Sargeant (*New Yorker,* April 18, 1964) suspected that Bernstein's spoken text "may cause a good many devout Jews to shake their heads in dismay . . . at the adjuration, criticism, and emotional denunciation" of God. Mr. Sargeant and his colleagues may be right about *untutored* "devout Jews." Those Jews who have examined each link in the chain of Jewish tradition will, like the Israeli audience, nod their heads with heart-rending appreciation. The giants in our faith firmly confronted God and vocally challenged Him.

The Jewish I-Thou dialogue with God, ranging from the biblical era to our own, may be the key to a Jewish theology for our generation. Leonard Bernstein deserves our deep gratitude for driving us back to reread the small print covering the "free and easy terms" of our contract with God.

Abraham, who first signed that eternal contract, in his plea for Sodom and Gomorrah (Genesis 18) asks: "Shall not the Judge of all the earth do justly?"

Jacob engages in a physical struggle with God (Genesis 31) and emerges the limping "Israel." The Hebrew word "Yisroel" means "One who wrestles with God." It identified that people whose prayer is the "Kaddish."

Moses, our supreme Prophet, the only one "whom the Lord knew face to face," demanded of God (Exodus 32): "Turn from Thy fierce wrath and repent of this evil against Thy people."

Jeremiah, in desperation, explodes (Chapter 20): "O Lord, Thou hast deceived me and I was deceived—For the word of the Lord has become for me a reproach and a derision all day long."

The Psalms also fairly bristle with emotional complaints against God.

What is the entire Book of Job? An Himalayan indictment of God for His enormous injustice.

Our talmudic and kabbalistic literature is punctuated with vivid parentheticals of what Martin Buber calls the "unvarnished intimacy" between the Jew and God. Go back and read the martyrdom of Rabbi Akiba (Talmud Berakot 61 b). Go back and read the account of Hadrian's slaughter of the Ten Sages ("Asarah Haruge Malkut" in volume VI of Jellinek's Beth ha-Midrash). God's "chastisements of love" constitute the cream of talmudic jest.

When we dig into medieval Jewish history we find a long bloody catalogue of catastrophes. Every auto-da-fé, every butchery, every pogrom carries its threnody in its train. Dirge and denunciation compose the cadence.

We move on to the eighteenth century. Hasidism flourishes in Russia. We meet Rabbi Levi Yitzchak of Berdichev. Martin Buber, who studied his every word and measured the Berdichever's every breath tells us: "He confronted God only as the passionate intercessor for Israel, but took Him to account, made demands on Him, and even ventured to hurl threats."

Here is a free translation of Rabbi Levi Yitzchak's Yiddish "bawling-out" of God:

Good morning Lord of the Universe
I, Levi Yitzchak, son of Sarah of Berdichev
Call you to a law-suit
On behalf of Your people Israel.
Why are you so against Your people Israel?
Why do you oppress Your people Israel?
No matter what, it is: "Command the Children of Israel."
No matter what, it is: "Say to the Children of Israel."
No matter what, it is: "Speak of the Children of Israel."
Beloved Father! How many other peoples live in the world?
Babylonians, Persians, Edomites.
The Germans—what do they say:
"Our King is a King."
The English—what do they say:
"Our Sovereign is a Sovereign!"
And I, Levi Yitzchak, son of Sarah, of Berdichev say:
"Yithgadal v'Yithkadash Shme Rabba."
Hallowed and Magnified be the Great Name.
And I, Levi Yitzchak, son of Sarah, of Berdichev say:
"I shall not move from here
Until there be an end to all this.
All this must stop!
Yithgadal v'Yithkadash Shme Rabba."

Of these deeply rooted historic fibers did Leonard Bernstein weave the spoken text of his "Kaddish" Symphony. Of these and more. Of the holocaust in our own lifetime and the poetic reverberations in the new Republic of Israel. Of Jacob Kohen's *Ha'z'aka Ha'shlishit*—"The Third Cry"—epitomizing the long martyrdom of the "chosen people" and their bitter complaint against the Chooser. Of Nathan Alterman's "From All Peoples":

When our children cried in the shadow of the gallows
We never heard the world's anger;
For Thou didst choose us from among all peoples
Thou didst love us and favor us.
For Thou didst choose us from all peoples,
Norwegians, Czechs, and Britons;
And when our children marched to the gallows
Jewish children, wise Jewish children,
They know that their blood is not counted in the bloodshed—
They only call back to their mothers:
"Mother don't look!"

The tragic protest rhymes on and on. Enough. It is too hard to bear. Let the critics of Bernstein's spoken words read the full texts. Then they will know that from Abraham to Alterman, spanning thirty-seven hundred years of Jewish history and literature, the authors and sayers of "Kaddish" did not hesitate to "speak up" to God. They abjured Him. They criticized Him. They emotionally denounced Him. And with every heartbeat they extolled and hallowed His name.

The man Job, says the Talmud, was never born and never lived. Perhaps not the individual. But Job epitomizes the Jew—the Jew living through history. And Job's excruciating confession of faith, "Though He slay me, yet will I trust Him," is the Jew's undaunted affirmation. This is precisely what the "Kaddish" means. Leonard Bernstein understood this. His critics, untutored and unfeeling, failed to grasp it. Bernstein struck the seldom-heard chord of God's immanence and man's intimacy with the Divine. A note from David's harp floated inaudibly across thirty centuries and touched Bernstein's heart. He heard it. He captured it in flight. He reproduced it with brilliant orchestral and verbal enlargement. He created of that ancient faint note a glorious symphonic hymn to the Father of Peace. One fine day we and Bernstein's critics will come around to listen to it, to understand it, and to say: "Amen."

[278]

Karl Shapiro

THE JEWISH WRITER
IN AMERICA

Karl Shapiro is professor of English at the University of Nebraska. For many years he was editor of the highly respected *Prairie Schooner* and before that of *Poetry* magazine. He is one of the country's foremost poets and critics. He won the Pulitzer Prize for poetry in 1944.

This essay on the role of the Jewish writer in a country that gives him the freedom to develop his "Jewish conscience" later appeared in the book *In Defense of Ignorance.*

In the course of collecting my essays and delivering them as public lectures I made the awful discovery that I must define my Jewishness. What has being a Jew got to do with literary criticism? Quite a bit, evidently. The mere act of defending oneself against the shallow Jew-baiting of Pound or the profound racism of Eliot constitutes a "position." And insofar as I have a position, it is bound to be something of a "Jewish positior.."

One of the chief strategic triumphs of the New Classicism has been its ability to quash the opposition, whether literary, sociological, or religious. Eliot carefully flattered the conservative mind in government, in philosophy, and in religion. Pound flattered the sense of culture aristocracy and the political authoritarianism which goes hand in hand with the religion of culture. The anti-Americanism of both writers is of that variety which connects commercialism with "mass taste" and with "free-thinking." What Eliot calls the free-thinking Jew, Pound calls the international Jewish banker. Indeed, it is the medieval image of the Jew as Shylock and Christ-killer which the Classicists perpetuate in the twentieth century. And, miraculous to report, the intellectual Jewish writers do not resist this image but tend to accept it guiltily! I refer particularly to the Jewish editors of cultural journals who purvey a kind of Marxist-Freudian anti-Semitism (in the belief that a Jewish identity is an historical anachronism) and I refer to the many Jewish professors of literature who are "new critics" and who thereby deprive themselves of any humanitarian standard of judgment. A book of verse I published called *Poems of a Jew* was most bitterly assailed by Jewish new critics, while the non-intellectual Jewish press tended to accept the poems as an awkward but serious expression of modern Jewishness.

The intellectual faction among Jewish professors, critics, and editors has been led quietly by the nose into the Pound-Eliot preserve. They were content to accept the Culture religion which in Eliot's criticism apparently subsumed any actual religion. They were content to accept Eliot's second-hand ideas of "pluralistic culture" which apparently subsumed mere nationalisms. Thus, it was precisely the "free-thinkers" whom Eliot despised who became his staunchest defenders. And those intellectuals who were not captivated by Eliot's version of the Tradition were taken in by his esthetic of the "objectivity" of the work of art. Even a critic as political in his thinking as F. O. Matthiessen convinced himself that it was somehow indecent to expose Eliot's beliefs to view. So holy was Eliot's reputation as poet, thinker, and man that criticism of his work became the chief taboo in twentieth century literature. William Carlos Williams alone dared attack the master. And for a Jew to raise his voice against Pound, Eliot, or T. E. Hulme was considered an act of savagery by the New Criticism and the New Pedagogy. It is extraordinary how much the defense of Pound has been placed on a hypocritical "Christian" footing. With what relief the intellectuals seized on the trashy and meretricious canto about humility to prove old Ezra's purity of heart! Pound on the throne of humility evidently cancels out Pound as the Great Dictator.

As a twentieth century American writer I grew up to respect the British literary tradition above all others and to share in the famous American "guilt" about our own American heritage. As a Jew I was misled by Jewish intellectuals, ex-Marxists and Freudians, to minimize and even accept the fashionable anti-Americanism and anti-Semitism of the Moderns. In all probability, I would never have been led to examine the ideas of these Moderns had I not been driven to do so—by participating in the Pound affair over the Bollingen Prize, and by having to teach modern poetry. Whatever Jewish consciousness I possess today I can trace to the writings of the American Classicists who made it their business to equate "American" and "Jew" as twin evils. This consciousness of myself as American Jew narrowed my writing for many years, erecting a private ghetto in my mind.

There is no Jewish writer per se in America. But the American writer, generally speaking, does not mention his ancestry, even if he happens to know what it is. The American writer tends to cut himself off from his past and even to deride it. There are exceptions, of course—the Henry Jameses and the Eliots—but most American writers favor the approach of Mark Twain: that dukes, kings, and ancestors are flotsam and jetsam one would do better to steer clear of. A poet from an old New England family wrote me when he saw my book, *Poems of a Jew,* and said, "You go back so much farther than I do!" He said this almost with a kind of envy, I thought. Then he added cryptically, "You write like an Arab," one of the strangest compliments I have ever had. At least, I think it was a compliment.

It is only in the last generation or two that an American Jew could write Jewishly and still be thought of as an American. Many years ago, when I was beginning to write for publication, I wrote an American poet whom I knew to be Jewish and asked him what obstacles one had to overcome to publish poems under a Jewish name. His reply was so ambiguous that I decided his own name wasn't very Jewish after all. I was not imagining things: many years later a non-Jewish poet said to me, "When I first saw your poems I thought you had an impossible name for a poet." This remark did not indicate anti-Semitism or anything of the sort, but it suggests the persistence of the British tradition in American letters until a very late date. Nowadays, the Jewish writer in America meets with no obstacle *qua* Jew in publication or in other forms of recognition, but this happy circumstance only brings us closer to the question: what *is* an American Jewish writer?

To me the answer is—an American Jewish writer is a Jew who is an American who is a writer. Everybody knows what an American is; everyone knows what a writer is; but very few people seem to know what a Jew is, including Jews, and including American Jewish writers.

[281]

I once participated in a symposium called "The Jewish Writer and the English Literary Tradition." It was published in one of the cultural journals. The question for the symposium was this: "As a Jew and a writer in the Anglo-American literary tradition, how do you confront the presence in that tradition of the mythical . . . figure of the Jew as found in the (anti-Semitic) writings of Chaucer, Marlowe, Shakespeare, Scott, T. S. Eliot, Evelyn Waugh, Thomas Wolfe, Henry Adams, etc. In what way do you find this a problem to you, etc?"

Reading between the lines, I took the question to mean: Do you think the Jew will be able to break into high literary society? That is, we were given a sociological question, one in which any element of a Jewish *mystique* was distinctly absent. And the replies also struck me as sociological, or, as we say more often, rationalistic. The replies ran along these lines:

a) The Jew defends a pluralistic culture; therefore he is attacked as "international." (The term "pluralistic" has been popularized by T. S. Eliot, whom most of the symposium felt it necessary to bow to in passing.)

b) Anti-Semitism is pathological, a disease like the black plague, and just as medieval. Get a well-doctored society and it will disappear.

c) Jews are also secretly anti-Semitic, parochial, and self-pitying. Let the Jewish writer be *more* cosmopolitan.

d) Writers like Eliot really love the Jews, but you must learn how to take insults.

e) Is anti-Semitism really real? Stephen Spender answered this way: If a Jew didn't know he was a Jew he wouldn't think he was a Jew.

The summation of the other approaches was by Philip Rahv, an honest and ruthless logician. What we must do, said Rahv, is to "conduct a struggle against the new religiosity, along with those non-Jewish intellectuals who refuse to abandon the progressive and secular outlook. This . . . religiosity tends to divide rather than unite humanity; it is historically vacuous and metaphysically permeated with nostalgia. . . ."

The best statement made in this list of responses was by Harold Rosenberg, who put his finger on the weakness of the question itself. Rosenberg noted that to move from a personification like Shylock to the sociological cliché is a serious mistake.

For instance, some German critic sees *The Merchant of Venice* with the repulsive Shylock and writes a review that says in effect: Down with the Jews. Thus Shylock becomes the Jew-with-the-knife and an instrument for political propaganda. As a result the Jew tends to blame Shakespeare for anti-Semitism.

To me the symposium was meaningless because it took for granted that religion is obsolescent, and racism the product of religion. The writers who took part in it seemed to be saying that religion is evil but Culture is good (whatever Culture is). Let's save Culture and get rid of religion.

My own answer was this, we are Jews by popular consent of the Jewish-Christian community and not by choice or ambition. We accept our Jewishness because to reject it would be a betrayal not of our electors but of ourselves. In the same way I felt when I was conscripted that to avoid military duty would have been a betrayal of my identity as an American. If this is negative Americanism then I can also call myself a negative Jew. But my election to America and to Israel gives me my total identity, the kind of identity which has never been permitted to survive in all of Europe's history.

The most curious aspect of this affair is that the Jews who are recognized writers of one kind or another shrink back from Judaism but defend, however half-heartedly, their right to be Jews. I read somewhere that a Christian writer asked a Jew what it was to be a Jew. The Jew answered, "We are a religion." This is a beautiful answer and a true one, but perhaps not true enough. We are even more than a religion.

Our symposium people seemed to interpret the expression, "American Jewish writer," to mean one who infused into the American idiom something of the Jewish idiom or of Jewish psychology. To me this is trivial; and in any case the American idiom is a vast complex of such idioms, all of which are tending toward the making of a great national (American) literature. A brilliant novel like Saul Bellow's *The Adventures of Augie March* is saturated with Jewish witticisms and sentiments; the very language seems almost a transliteration of—what? I can't read Yiddish but I recognize the idiom. And the American reader need not know of the presence of this element in Bellow's writing, for by now it is as much American as it is Jewish. What is really Jewish in Bellow lies much deeper: it is the poetry of the Jew that makes his hero what he is, in Chicago, in Mexico, wherever Augie happens to be. Bellow has translated Singer's story, *Gimpel the Fool,* from Yiddish. It is one of the most side-splitting and yet painful tales I have ever read, but it might have been written in New York instead of Poland, or wherever it came from. This is Jewishness far beyond culture, social problems, history, and the rest. It is even beyond religion, as far as I can see.

Sociological Judaism seems to me completely pointless, and the preservation of national memory for its own sake, mere narcism. The business of the Jewish writer is not to complain about society but to rise above such complaints. Nearly all social protest literature is superficial anyhow; the greater realities of difference lie below the bickerings of ideologists. I would say there are two kinds of Jewish American literature, the kind recommended by our symposium—a psychologically Judaistic literature — and the real kind, which I would recommend: a God-centered literature. That is a poor way of putting it but I will try to explain what I mean.

A merely Judaistic literature is only a kind of "regional" literature, even though this "region" takes in most of the world and all of history. In such literature the Jew may be good or bad, Shylock or the Wandering Jew or Leopold Bloom, but he is simply a man of memory, an anachronism. He is not the Jew who "lives life" as Martin Buber puts it. He is the Jew of the past, the Jew of the Wailing Wall. I once read a new *Oxford Book of Irish Verse* and was struck by the centuries-old struggle of the Irish poets to regain their Irishness, to throw off the cosmopolitanism of the world-writer, and to renew that particular consciousness which is not a "cultural heritage" but an identity. In the case of the Irish I can sense only dimly what that identity is. But in the case of the Jew I know what it is. The Jewish writer everywhere in the modern world has the problem of regaining the Jewish consciousness which, in our case, is God-consciousness. I am not talking about religion; religion is only a by-product of this consciousness. For the Jewish writer who wants to turn his back on this consciousness we can only give him our blessing and let him go. But for the consciously Jewish writer in America or anywhere else we must recognize his obligation to establish this consciousness centrally in his work, the right, so to speak, of the existence of God. If this encourages religious progress, that may be to the good; but I am not talking about religion.

Jewish creative intelligence has been driven into by-paths for centuries. We are just beginning to return to the era of Jewish philosophy, but our abstract thinking generally still belongs to the Middle Ages. We produce an Einstein who, from the religious or even political viewpoint, is a baby. We produce a Freud who foists upon the world a surrogate religion while striving mightily to destroy both Christianity and Judaism in one breath. The fantastic intellectual powers of the Jews of our time go into everything under the sun except Jewish consciousness, or to use a really lofty word, holiness.

The Jews have written one of the greatest holy books. And that book is the beginning and the end of our literature. Jewish literature is not great. Jewish philosophy is not great. Jewish scholarship—perhaps. Our contributions to science, government, law, and the humane knowledges, even the arts of music and, in our lifetime, painting, have been advanced by Jews. But the great arts of the written word have not been advanced by the people of the book. Not to any significant degree.

Our friends of the symposium on the Jewish writer in the United States were more interesting in setting up fresh literary symbols than they were in understanding a religion or in seeking the *mystique* back of it. Consequently, I think of them as literary social climbers and not poets.

As far as one can tell these things, there are only two countries in the world where the Jewish writer is free to create his own consciousness: Israel and the United States. Everywhere else the Jew seems to live on the past. Even Proust's recreation of consciousness is a kind of Jewish nostalgia. In Europe it is either nostalgia or nightmare: Proust or Kafka. The European Jew was always a visitor and knew it. But in America everybody is a visitor. In this land of permanent visitors the Jew is in a rare position to "live the life" of a full Jewish consciousness. The Jews live a fantastic historical paradox: we are the spiritual aborigines of the modern world, and we are the ethical and sometimes intellectual conscience of the modern world. History has hated us so deeply because every Jew is regarded as a living witness of the Christian and Muslim revelations—which he is. The Jew's assumption of holiness and his rather laissez-faire attitude toward religion make him a natural target in almost any historical situation. Only in America (as the expression goes) can the Jew be a natural Jew. There are fewer religious tensions in America than any place in history—the national tendency to vulgarize religion and to experiment with new sects has allowed the American Jew to relax—to emerge from the historical consciousness to a contemporary Jewish consciousness.

I was speaking of the creative man and by that I mean not only the poet or novelist, painter or composer, but the mystic and saint. Our rational modern upbringing prevents us from even thinking of God. In our time we say or think that God is for women and children. We go to houses of worship possibly, but only because it is too troublesome not to. Now the true writer and mystic does not ransack the storehouse of religion for literary plunder; rather he adds to the spiritual storehouse. He does not take; he gives. He may never even go near a synagogue or church, and in many cases in the past he has been forbidden to enter the official house of prayer. Poets and mystics are always having the door slammed in their faces; especially the church door.

This full Jewish consciousness which is today possible in America as in Israel is a way of life, so to speak. And it does not necessarily involve ritual or anything of the sort, though it may in some cases. It does not involve piety and may in fact involve the exact opposite. I am paraphrasing the modern Jewish philosopher, Martin Buber—I hope I am not corrupting what he means. He says, "The true hallowing of man is the hallowing of the human in him. . . . In life, as Chasidism understands and proclaims it, there is no essential distinction between sacred and profane spaces, between sacred and profane times, between sacred and profane actions, between sacred and profane conversations." I am not sure how many Jews accept this kind of belief, but I suppose very few. All the same, in my ignorance of my own religion, it seems to me the very core of Jewish consciousness. It is anti-ascetic and joyous—the Chasidim dance wildly with the Torah. "Man," says Buber, "cannot approach the divine by reaching beyond the human; but he can approach Him through becoming human."

It matters very little whether the American Jewish poet or novelist writes *about* the American Jew (the good artist is seldom that self-conscious anyway); it even matters little whether he lives as a Jew in the conventional sense of "living as"; what does matter is that he accept the consequences of Jewishness. He cannot escape them in any event, and I do not think he should *suffer* these consequences but revel in them.

The Jewish writer is presented with a kind of freedom which is almost inconceivable. The Jewish plus American combination only doubles this freedom.

Modern literature attempts to perpetuate the Jew as imaged in Christian theology and story. But this Jew is as dead as the Negro of the minstrel show. Both images come from the age of slavery. The Jew today is free in his mythological homeland Israel and free in America, the mythological homeland of freedom. Creatively he has begun to flourish as never before, nor can the medievalism of the New Classicists prevent this flowering, as much as they fear it. Freedom in any form is anathema to modern Classicism. Even "free verse" is not really free, says the poor fettered Eliot. And the "free-thinking Jew" is, of course, a grave danger to whatever is the opposite of freedom.

David Boroff

IS THERE
A JEWISH RENAISSANCE?

The late David Boroff was our first critic of the living arts.
Mr. Boroff added the burden of this task to his deadlines
for *The New York Times, Harper's, Commentary, Mid-
stream, Saturday Review* and the *New York Post* and to
his teaching schedule as professor of English at New York
University.

Mr. Boroff's sudden death at the age of forty-eight on
May 15, 1965, not only deprived *American Judaism* of a
brilliant critic but was a loss to the academic world, to
journalism and to American letters. His first column in
American Judaism took up the question, "Is There a
Jewish Renaissance?" Although the matters under consideration were of momentary interest, Mr. Boroff's remarks
on the fashionableness of the "Jewish thing" remain valid
and timely.

An observant high-fashion model told me recently that there is a
"Jewish thing," as she put it, among top echelon photographers.
Some of them have taken to tacking up Hebrew eyecharts on
the walls of their well-appointed studios. (What curious symbolism this has eludes me at the moment.) Certainly, there is a new
Jewish awareness, a stir of Jewish activity in the arts. Can we call
it a renaissance? Are we in the midst of a kind of Elizabethan
splendor and vitality without even knowing it? It may well be.

Let's look at books first. Some critics have been proclaiming,
with great éclat, the new era of the Jewish best seller. In the
past, only the Jew as rogue or hustler, as in *What Makes Sammy
Run,* could make the big leagues. Today what someone has
called "the house-broken Jew" inhabits the clean, well-lighted
places of best-sellerdom. Marjorie Morningstar, as the All-Ameri-
can virgin, started the trend. *Exodus* is also in the popular
American grain. It can be described as a Middle-Eastern Western. There are the same wide-screen heroics, the same black and

[288]

white portrayal of characters. Harry Golden is, indeed, a kind of schmalz-barrel philosopher — an old Yankee tradition.

But let's not oversimplify. There are still survivals of older images of Jewish self-hatred and self-conscious ethnic quaintness. Jerome Weidman's *Enemy Camp* is an example of the first. Leo Rosten's Hyman Kaplan book is emblematic of the second.

I think the truth about Jewish bestsellers runs something like this. As American life becomes more homogenized — with Jew and gentile drawing closer together — non-Jewish readers feel a tug of curiosity about their Jewish neighbors. They are, after all, the same — all bound up in a common suburbanized humanity. But there is also a difference — and it is this margin of differentiation that attracts the gentile reader. In what does it consist? Largely, I think, in the persistence of an elemental quality in Jewish life. Jews have managed to retain, to a remarkable degree, a fluent, even explosive emotionality, which is essentially foreign to the Anglo-Saxon temperament. (Italian-Americans have this quality too, but they haven't yet found their voice in American literature.)

But there is more. The Jew haunts the gentile imagination. Because there are mythic elements in the gentile's view of the Jew — he sees him either as demon or saint, malefactor or victim never as mere Man — he is perennially bemused by him.

Of course, we should not overlook the fact that Jewish readers make up a big proportion of the reading population and, almost unaided, can hoist a book to the best-seller list. Once ensconced there, a book will command a large audience of gentiles.

But best-sellerdom has its special perils. There is a cult of personality about successful writers. Readers of *Exodus,* with a display of shrewdness, acknowledge that the love story is absurd, the characters stereotypes. They read the novel, they insist, for its history, which packs a wallop. But Uris is not a historian! And Herman Wouk is hardly a theologian. Yet the public gets its Israeli history from Uris and its Judaism from Wouk's *This Is My God.* It is little wonder that professional historians and theologians have, in turn, assailed these books.

On Broadway, the Jew is also well-represented. But has a fresh portrait emerged? The evidence would suggest not. *A Majority of One,* a good-humored and charming play, is hardly a new phenomenon. It is a cross between *Rise of the Goldbergs* and *Abie's Irish Rose* — with a dash of orientalism. Curiously enough, *The Tenth Man* by Paddy Chayefsky is also an old-fashioned play, despite its Freudian trappings. Many who saw it were not persuaded by its burden of religious mysticism, but they found the deeply-steeped Jewishness engaging. It is the older characters in the play who charm us in their unreconstructed Jewishness. Yet, as Kenneth Tynan pointed out in *The New Yorker*, it was a portrait of the Jewish people, "as limited in its way as the image of Uncle Tom. These were stage Jews, whose naiveté, congenital stoicism, and inverted sentence structure displayed the same kind of folksiness that one finds, and abhors, in stage Irishmen." Anyway, how representative is a store-front synagogue in Mineola? Chayefsky ought to take a look around Nassau County.

Those who saw *Raisin in the Sun* expressed their pleasure in a play which movingly portrays the everyday crises of a Negro family. It imaginatively seized on the drama of the commonplace. The striking thing is that Jewish dramatists have not yet done for familiar Jewish life what Larraine Hansbury has done for the Negro in Chicago. Is the drama of Jewish life so lost to our Jewish writers, or muffled by habit, that they have to dip back into the past or into dusty corners? We are still waiting for Jewish-American literature that will have warmth without sentimentality, affirmation without preachment.

The same retreat from contemporary Jewish-American reality can be seen in the movies. *Ben Hur,* evidently was a tasteful spectacle (a term which, in the past, was a contradiction). It provided a sympathetic portrayal of Jews under the Roman yoke. Another big Jewish movie was *Exodus,* filmed in Israel. One wonders how Israelis feel seeing the stirring chapters of their recent history being reenacted at a time when the land is still scarred and the events still reverberate.

Jewish artists have long had an instinct for the mass audience. Reasons are not hard to find. Barred from heavy industries, Jews have had to deploy their talents at the outer borders of our economy — at what is new and fluid and accessible. It is no accident that so many of the early Hollywood pioneers were graduates of the Garment Center, where adroit timing, sensitivity, and a flair for charting the tricky currents and shoals of taste are necessary for survival. These qualities have long been in the Jewish tool kit. Merely to manage in a hostile world, the Jew has had to read its omens and portents correctly. Thus the

paradox: the Jew, once the stranger within the gates, helps interpret America to Americans and shapes images by which Americans define themselves.

But we might do better to climb down — or is it up? — from
best-sellerdom and the fripperies of Hollywood and look at the
higher reaches of American culture. Perhaps the biggest news is
that a Jewish writer, Delmore Schwartz, has won the Bollingen
Prize for poetry. This is the same award that Ezra Pound won
some years ago to the dismay of thousands repelled by his
crass anti-Semitism. I like to think that this new distinction is a
sign of the maturity of the Jewish-American literary artist. We
have produced our share of journalists and literary entertainers
(for that is what most best-selling novelists are). But the
emergence of a generation of gifted Jewish novelists and poets is
cause for jubilation. Most of them are around forty and just
beginning to hit the top of their form. Such writers as Saul
Bellow, Bernard Malamud, Harvey Swados, and Herbert Gold are
an important part of the literary landscape. Nor are they reluctant to deal with Jewish subject matter.

It is significant that the literary supplement of the *London
Times*, in a special issue devoted to "The American Imagination,"
took note of the break-through of American-Jewish letters. It is,
the article observed, the sheer energy and daring of Jewish
writers that makes them "a decisive force in American letters."
The gifted Jewish writer has moved into the middle of the
American stage rather than back to the Jewish world, but he has
retained the "preoccupations with sentiment, suffering and
righteousness, with morality." In other words, the Jewish writer
has been acculturated — not assimilated — and is uniquely in
position to exploit to the fullest his American and Jewish heritage.

How much, one wonders, does Israel influence the Jewish-
American cultural scene?

An area to watch, however, is the world of dance. There have
always been many Jews in dance. Many of the leading chore-
ographers are Jewish. Jerome Robbins and Michael Kidd come
quickly to mind. And in the field of modern dance, there are
Sophie Maslow, Anna Sokolow, and many others.

It is through dance that the exhilaration of a young country
can best be communicated, for dance is inherently a young person's medium. There may well be an Israeli influence on Ameri-

can dance conveyed in the following ways: There are, first, local groups concentrating on Jewish and Israeli dance themes, e.g., Fred Berk's Hebraica Dancers and the Aviv Group. Secondly, modern dancers in America may appropriate Israeli themes and techniques. Certainly, the appearance in New York City of the Imbal Dancers attracted large audiences, including many dancers who are quite zealous about keeping up with new dance ideas and idioms.

Modern dance seems to be in the doldrums, and one way to attain new vitality is through an infusion of another culture's high spirits. This, Israeli dance has in abundance. If the trouble with modern dance is an excess of introversion, then Israeli dance, with its sunny gaiety and buoyancy, is just what the doctor ordered. It may yet be that the next decade will witness some fruitful cultural interchange.

Leslie Fiedler

SOME JEWISH
POP ART HEROES

> Leslie Fiedler, *enfant terrible* of American letters, took
> over the late David Boroff's column in *American Judaism*
> on drama, books and films in the winter of 1965. Although
> his opening fuselage was circumspect, even conservative,
> to those acquainted with Mr. Fiedler's sizzling style, he
> soon showed that his high-spirited approach could not be
> dampened by the mere fact that his prose was appearing
> in a religious publication.
>
> In "Some Jewish Pop Art Heroes" he takes a scathing
> look at "vulgarity as style" in some recent books on Jewish
> subjects.
>
> Mr. Fiedler is professor of English at State University
> of New York in Buffalo, and author of five books of
> criticism, three novels and a collection of short stories.

It was in 1913 that little Mary Phagan was killed, a thirteen-year-
old factory girl, her attempted rape fumbled but her head
successfully bashed in and though it seems painfully clear now
that her assailant was a Negro, her boss, a young Jew called Leo
Frank, was convicted in court of her murder and lynched for it
shortly thereafter. That was 1915, the war already begun which
was to cut us off forever from that time of relative innocence;
and Americans were going in large numbers to see *The Birth of
a Nation,* greatest of all American moving pictures and storehouse of all the most vicious anti-Negro stereotypes. But just
those Georgia rednecks, who should have contented themselves
with an orgy of hating niggers and cheering the Ku Klux Klan
under the auspices of D. W. Griffiths, were letting the shiftless
and violent Negro whose testimony doomed Frank slip through
their fingers in order to indulge stereotypes more deeply buried
in the depths of their psyches than any fantasies about Black
sexuality. Harry Golden tells us that only a couple of decades
ago, back-country performers were still singing the ballad he

prints as an appendix to his best-selling book on the Frank Case, *A Little Girl is Dead,* a ballad which justifies the lynching as sacred revenge against the Jews.

> Leo Frank he met her
> With a brutish heart and grin;
> He says to little Mary,
> "You'll never see home again."
> Judge Roan he passed the sentence;
> He passed it very well;
> The Christian doers of heaven
> Sent Leo Frank to hell . . .

But why, Harry Golden is worrying all these years later, did the crowd malice of the Deep South, egged on by the rhetoric of Tom Watson, a splendid Populist leader gone sour and turned into nigger-baiter *par excellence,* why did it prefer the Jew to the Negro, given a clear choice? True enough, Frank behaved oddly in his first encounters with the police, appeared guilty of something (though God knows what), evasive, shifty; and by all accounts he seems to have been a singularly unappealing young man. Besides, he was clearly identified as a "capitalist," doubly a capitalist, since to the *lumpen* socialist mind of the American Populist capitalist equals Jew, and the two together add up to demi-devil. And in certain regards, the record seems to bear them out; for Frank did hire child labor, did work it disgracefully long hours at pitifully low wages; and if he did not (as popular fancy imagined) exploit his girls sexually, he walked in on their privacy with utter contempt for their dignity. Like most factory managers of his time, he was — metaphorically at least — screwing little girls like Mary Phagan; and in the undermind of the uneducated the line between metaphor and fact is blurred.

Besides, the kind of Georgians who lynched Frank were the inheritors of a folk tradition in which the Jew had been defined through centuries of song and story as the child-murderer. That tradition had been strong enough to influence great poets like Chaucer and Shakespeare and to create a score of ballads still sung in the rural South, so why should it not have moved the jurors, even before Frank's own lawyer had made the mistake of raising the issue of his Jewishness, and erupted finally in the fury of the lynch mob?

In European folk art, the Jew is a villain of a special kind, and before World War I the mind of back-country America was still folk and European; but in America Pop Art (which he plays a decisive role in creating) the Jew is a hero, like Golden himself: successful pop artist and pop idol — to the gentiles, of course, as well as the Jews — at the same time. No wonder Norman Mailer, fighting the hard fight of the serious writer, who bucks rather than embodies the stereotypes of the mass audience, wrote plaintively once: "If/Harry Golden/is the Gentile's Jew/can I be-/come the Golden/Goy?" This shift of the Jew from archetypal "Baddie" to mythological "Goodie," and its connection with the shift from folk culture to mass culture is immensely important yet almost totally ignored by literary critics like Irving Malin, in *Jews and Americans,* who is committed to defining the nature of the Jewish experience in the United States.

Yet Malin does not mention Harry Golden, for instance, much less other Jewish Pop Art Heroes like Lenny Bruce, Sammy Davis, Jr., Jack Ruby or Superman. Trying to fit Philip Roth and six other writers (Bellow, Malamud, Karl Shapiro, etc.) into his own seven categories (Exile, Time, Irony, Parable, etc.), he does not find an occasion for treating the difficult and essential subject I have been trying to define. Perhaps this is because "vulgarity" is not one of his rubrics, and it is the vivid and perdurable vulgarity of the Jews (so embarrassing to our official apologists) which lies at the heart of Pop Culture. No Jew on his own would have invented — thank God — the notion of a gentleman, but some Jews invented Miami Beach, some the commercial Musical Comedy, and two, Jerome Siegel and Joe Shuster, the Comic Book — or at least, the first Great Comic Book Hero of them all, Superman.

We live now at a point where the generation (they must be somewhere between twenty-five and thirty-five) that grew up on the classic Comic Book is memorializing it; making a smash success out of the revived Bat Man on TV (pop art wryly remembered is Camp, a kind of genteel tribute to vulgarity); and, I hope, buying in vast quantities the annotated anthology of the genre, *The Great Comic Book Heroes,* recently put together by Jules Feiffer, himself a veteran vulgarian.

Jules Feiffer loves the comic books a little better than he understands them, missing, I think, the essential point that they are a special kind of "junk" in the history of sub-art: *urban junk*

— their imagined world simply the city, and their heroes city boys or losers in the very world that makes and peddles the comics. (Superman is in "real life" an unsuccessful reporter.) But the dreamers in the city are, almost inevitably, Jews — and it is their fantasies by which a generation or two lived, their fantasies by which they discovered they could make it in this Gentile world: beginning in school, let's say, by drawing the pictures, erotic or heroic, which their inept neighbors needed to see before they were quite sure what they were dreaming.

Not only Will Eisner's seedy *The Spirit* was Jewish, as Feiffer sees; but all of those more WASPish looking Super-fellows, though on another level. They are Jewish versions of the goy, idealized portraits of the gentile boy who beats up the Jewish one (no wonder so many of their fictional victims had long noses and puttered about laboratories) — quite like, on their level, Bellow's Henderson or Mailer's Sergious O'Shaughnessy. Did we love them or hate them, those dumb sluggers in their lodge regalia? The answer is there in the record, as Feiffer sees quite clearly when dealing with their female opposite numbers, who remind us of that other perfect bully out of the nightmares of our childhood: Mama. "... Wonder Woman ... was every Jewish boy's unfantiasied picture of the world as it really was. You mean men were not wicked and weak? ... You mean women didn't have to be *stronger* than men to survive in this world? Not in *my* house?"

Once he has projected his oppressor as his secret self, however, the Jewish writer, on a pop level or any other, is likely to get in trouble; end like Norman Mailer — or Lenny Bruce — forgetting that he is only Jerome Siegel imagining he is Clark Kent dreaming that he can reveal himself as Superman, and coming to believe that there is only himself, i.e., Super-Jew. Lenny Bruce's autobiography, *How to Talk Dirty and Influence People*, does not take us to the point where he had fallen out of a hotel window, after having capered madly about the room and lifted an imaginary cape, screaming, "I'm Super-Jew." But it does take us through some of his earlier disguises as an Oriental mystic, Roman Catholic priest, transvestite sailor, still uncertain of his destiny as victim, persecuted truth-teller, gross and grotesque prophet — his passion called obscenity, and his madness drug addition. There was a streak of self-dramatizing sentimentality in Lenny Bruce that tempted him to see himself as Jesus Christ;

[296]

but there was a saving vulgarity which impelled him to realize that he was rather a Comic Book Hero who cannot fly. That vulgarity I'm sure he was pleased to think of as Jewish; for he was (with scarcely any Jewish education or even background, certainly none of the kind generally called "positive") much concerned with sorting out the world into what he thought of as its primary categories: "Evaporated milk is goyish even if the Jews invented it. Chocolate is Jewish and fudge is goyish. Spam is goyish and rye bread is Jewish. Negroes are all Jews. Italians are all Jews. Irishmen who have rejected their religion are Jews. Mouths are very Jewish. And bosoms. Baton-twirling is very goyish." In his sense at least, it is still hard to be a Jew; and perhaps the chief value of his book (along with the thousand laughs it provides) is to remind us of this fact.

No one would suspect it, on the other hand, reading Sammy Davis, Jr.'s autobiography; for though, like Lenny Bruce, he is an entertainer who has turned himself into a Pop Art Hero, he is one who has made it — in part, he would have us believe, by identifying with the Good Medicine of Judaism. Walking from a difficult and successful operation, he finds "a clear outline of the Star of David" impressed on his palm from a religious medallion he was clutching; he wears a mezuzah, given him by Eddie Cantor, around his neck and charms everyone; he gains the respect of Sam Goldwyn by refusing to work on Yom Kippur; he wins a beautiful *shiksa* for his wife, who then converts to Judaism and their wedding is a B. O. smash! Yet all through it of course, he is a Negro. Under such circumstances, who wouldn't be a Jew!

His book *Yes I an,* though professionally written in that insipid ghost style which robs truth of conviction and fact of reality, is not without interest. For somehow the picture of a vain, driven, essent lly unlovable man, at odds with his own Negro community (and what disheartening glimpses we have of their columnists, reporters and millionaires) and himself, emerges, a gifted entertainer who betrays almost everything and everybody but is blessed with success; and who — in this age of strange conversions — imagines that to begin to become "all right," one must become a Jew. I saw, for my sins, the production of *Golden Boy,* an utterly incredible revision of Odets' soupy play about Jews updated to get the box office that only Negro drama gets these days; and in the midst of it all Sammy Davis, trying to live the part he acted, a Negro turned Jew being the John Garfield of the sixties. And remembering, of course, Marilyn Monroe and Elizabeth Taylor, I found myself slipping away into a daydream in which Frank Sinatra (second only unto Jehovah in Sammy Davis' pantheon) would end up playing Frankie Alpine in the movie made of Bernard Malamud's *The Assistant*, and insisting upon being really circumcized in the last scene where that character becomes a Jew. And then there would be no goyim left at all in the world of pop culture, not a single one. . . .

But walking down the street afterwards, I saw the lines queued up before *Thunderball* and realized that James Bond at least was left, the last of the WASP heroes, as goyish as fudge or twirler girls: something for us to imagine ourselves when we grew weary of the mythic burden of our Jewishness. My relief did not last long, however; for just as there is (in the local drugstore, supermarket, airport newsstand) a Fanny Hillman of our own these days for every one of *their* Fanny Hills, I discovered there is also an Israel Bond, OY-OY-7, the sort-of hero of *Loxfinger*, which surely must rank with the worst books ever written. I will not let chauvinism drive me to calling it un-equivocally *the* worst; but if you have wondered where all the weary semitic jokes went since Hitler scared them out of the goyim they are here (along with Hitler himself), in such a context of Borsht Belt good humor that one must take them as innocently proffered. Next to Sol Weinstein, author of *Loxfinger*, Henny Youngman seems like Oscar Wilde; and it takes a con-siderable effort to remember the immemorial principle that, despite everything, a Jew has a right to make a living.

Vulgarity passes over into grossness not by excess but by cold-blooded commercial manipulation. What could be more vulgar, for instance, yet still pathetic at least, perhaps even tragic, than Jack Ruby who wanted, like any kid reading *Superman*, to be a hero, too; and even got the chance to do it on television. John Kaplan and Jon R. Waltz have written their study of the case, *The Trial of Jack Ruby*, to analyze courtroom strategies, not the vagaries of mass culture; but it is the latter that impressed and disheartened me as I made my way through their book: NBC offering to pick up the tab if Ruby would hire the real-life original of TV's *Sam Benedict;* Judge Brown's public denial of the manuscript about the case by which he hoped to make his fortune; Ruby's lawyers bootlegging pictures of him to sell to *Life* etc., etc.

In his own deepest consciousness, however, Ruby wanted to sell nothing, only to show the world (on television if possible) that "Jews do have guts," that under his own improbable guise Super-Jew really lived and would avenge the president that had been kind to his people. Once convicted and, he felt, vilified, however, it was quite other fantasies that possessed Ruby's poor paranoid head: fantasies that "all the Jews in America were being slaughtered," "twenty-five million innocent people," and that even his brother Sam was being "tortured, horribly mutilated, castrated and burned in the street outside the jail" — that the Jew had, in fact, become Leo Frank again because he had failed to be Superman.

But Ruby is, of course, wrong. No crowds are gathering for his lynching or his brother's; and if any ballads are being made now, they concern not his guilt but his plight, are sung not by rednecks from the hills but urban folk singers, Jews like Bobby Dylan, the inventors of "folk-rock," who surely celebrate him something like this:

> I didn't raise my chubby, sweet,
>   brown-eyed balding boy
> To go out and overdo the doin's
>   of some goy.
> He murdered a man on TV
> They say he has shot another.
> Won't you give some thought to
>   poor Jack Ruby's mother.

Alan Rich

WHAT IS JEWISH MUSIC?

> Alan Rich, whose sharp-honed style and unerring taste
> are hallmarks of his columns as music critic for the *New
> York Herald Tribune*, joined *American Judaism's* roster of
> critics in the fall of 1964.
> His essay on "What Is Jewish Music?" challenges the
> idea that composers who write out of religious motivation
> are exempt from the standards applied to secular com-
> positions.
> Mr. Rich is the author of *Careers and Opportunities in
> Music*. His articles have appeared in leading publications,
> including *Musical Quarterly, Musical America, Saturday
> Review, The American Record Guide* and *High Fidelity*.

Music is an international language, the poets tell us, and we'd
better believe it. They reckon at times, however, without
taking into account the sentimental possessiveness of certain
national and religious groups who demand a music of their own,
something which can express a private heritage and express a
private personality.

Americans around the turn of the century were obsessed with
the need for a great American repertory. Composers who received most of their training in the European tradition nevertheless returned to their own country to turn out their Indian
Suites and their ragtime symphonies and operas, usually with
a self-consciousness that vitiated their real talents. Poor George
Gershwin was bent, if not actually broken, on the rack of Great-
American-Composer worship.

Something of the same sort is happening today in Jewish
circles, particularly in Israel. There has to be a Jewish music,
we are told, before the new nation can really hold up its head
in the brotherhood of states.

Basically, there is no danger in this attitude. Certainly today's

Jewish composer has a strong native heritage to draw upon, and most of it is absolutely virgin. With few ancestors before the twentieth century — and these of primarily historical importance — today's Jewish composer is really on his own, and the sky's the limit.

A Czech, Spanish or Finnish composer of nationalistic bent today must cope with the ghosts of his musical ancestors; even an American must face the living ghosts of Copland and Harris. The Jewish composer can make his own beginning.

And indeed, the beginnings are impressive. The musical world has, for the first time in its history, a large and illustrious core of Jewish composers. Some — Copland, Schuman, Milhaud for the most part, and the Israeli Josef Tal — are not very interested in proclaiming their heritage in their scores. Others, however, are, and with results that are often exceptionally interesting.

Here, however, is where sentimentality can often rear its ugly and dangerous head. Blind acceptance of the fact of a Jewish musical repertory of serious dimensions does no service either to the composer or to the art he serves. The symphonies of Dvorak, the cowboy ballets of Copland or the nationalistic tone-poems of Sibelius are not masterpieces merely because they honor the heritage of a nation; they are viable because the composers dealt with their materials with intelligence and sophistication.

This can also happen in Jewish music. It already has, in fact. Ernest Bloch can readily be thought of as the founder of a Jewish symphonic style, and his best Jewish works — *Schelomo, Baal Shem,* the *Avodath Hakodesh* — succeed because he had the power to assimilate the materials of a native language and then to create strong and beautiful music out of his own mind. His success, from the beginning, was in the international concert halls, not merely before audiences of proud and unquestioning seekers after a particular Jewish truth.

This must be the aim, if there is ever to be an important repertory of Jewish music. The standards that must be applied cannot stem from provincial pride or sentimentality. If they do, nobody benefits, least of all the composer.

There is an old cliché in the arts: write out of your own background and experience, and the world will find you out and pay you honor. This is all very well, although I have heard the line in a lot of very bad movies. But the distinction that should be borne in mind is the same one that distinguishes a Stieglitz photograph from an amateur snapshot, or a Sunday painting from a Rembrandt. Sooner or later the responsibility of the artistic language must be faced — the use of materials in such a way that there is some distillation of raw experience into a higher essence.

This language is no respecter of boundary lines or ethnic backgrounds. Its vitality has to do with ageless principles of musical expression: not so much the materials themselves, but the way they are ordered so as to stimulate the interest, imagination and memory.

We are now faced with proof that native Jewish materials — chants, folksongs and merely the scales and harmonies out of which they are constructed — can serve the composer in a variety of exciting ways. This is fine, and there should be a tingle of pride in store for all of us in hearing these elements played by symphony orchestras and sung by big-time stars. Our pride will really be well-placed, however, when the music that results from all this can stand on its own, not merely as Jewish music, but as music.

Alfred Werner

JEWISH CONTRIBUTIONS
TO AMERICAN ART

Alfred Werner is entirely his own man — so much so that
he was recently permitted to publish a vitriolic attack on
the art exhibition sponsored by the Union of American
Hebrew Congregations in the pages of its own official
publication. Dr. Werner brings to his judgments a for-
midable background of many decades. He is the senior
editor of *Art Voices,* art critic, historian, lecturer, contributing editor of *Arts Magazine* and U. S. correspondent
of *Pantheon International Magazine of Art.* His recent
books include *Modigliani the Sculptor* and *Jules Pascin.*
In "Jewish Contributions to American Art," Mr. Werner
points out how generous American Jews have been in
contributing to the wealth of American museums and art
institutions.

Recently, a staff member of one of New York's great museums
complained bitterly to me about the losses suffered by the U.S.A.
through the many donations of art to Israel. The complaint was,
in particular, about the transfer of Billy Rose's sculpture collection to Jerusalem. In rejoinder, I gently pointed out that Israel, a
small and young nation, was still poorly endowed with works of
art, whereas most American museums own many more objects
than they can possibly display. Far from being unpatriotic,
American Jews have always contributed to the wealth of public
institutions in the U.S.A., either directly, or indirectly through
monetary gifts. Not long ago the Guggenheim Museum in New
York — itself the creation of a son of a Jewish immigrant from
Switzerland — received priceless nineteenth and twentieth century paintings and sculptures from the retired dealer Justin K.
Thannhauser, who had come to the United States from Munich
as a refugee from Nazism.

One merchant prince who helped greatly to make the New

York Metropolitan Museum of Art the finest collection in the Western Hemisphere was Benjamin Altman, who had begun as a helper in his father's dry-goods store. Altman assembled a dazzling collection which included fourteen Rembrandts, portraits by Velásquez, Dürer and Holbein, beautiful Persian rugs, Renaissance sculpture and many precious Chinese vases. He bequeathed his entire collection, with funds for its care and maintenance, to the Metropolitan Museum. Michael-Friedsam was a distant relative of Altman, and after the latter's death succeeded him as president of the B. Altman department store. Part of his exquisite art collection went to the Metropolitan Museum and another part to the Brooklyn Museum. The third Jewish collector to aid the Metropolitan Museum was Jules Semon Bache, who, from a humble cashier in a private banking firm, eventually became the founder and head of the Wall Street firm, Bache & Company.

Large-scale collecting was not confined to New York City. Jules E. Mastbaum of Philadelphia, who controlled a chain of movie theaters, became fascinated with the art of August Rodin, and acquired 98 Rodins, originals and good copies. He yearned to have them placed in a special museum, but died before the proper building was created on the Benjamin Franklin Parkway. His indefatigable widow saw the fulfillment of his dream. Thanks to this couple, Philadelphia can boast of the largest Rodin collection outside Paris. Baltimore's art museum owes its fame to the generosity of three collectors. One of them was the Lithuanian-born merchant Jacob Epstein who donated works by Hals, Rembrandt, Rubens, Titian and Tintoretto. In the building is also a portrait bust made by the famous sculptor of the same name, Jacob Epstein, who was not related to his sitter.

The other two were the sisters Claribel and Etta Cone. They were among the nine children of a Bavarian immigrant whose fortune was based on the wholesale grocery business in Baltimore. Claribel was an outstanding physician and a professor of pathology at the Women's Medical College. The two spinsters, shortly after 1900, went to Paris, where they were captivated by the work of Henri Matisse, at that time far from recognition. In the course of more than twenty years they acquired what is now the finest Matisse collection in the U.S.A. After the death of Claribel, in 1929, it was administered by Etta, and when she died, two decades later, it went to the Baltimore Museum of Art.

Unlike these six, the pioneer photographer, Alfred Stieglitz, was never rich. But as a courageous dealer, who exhibited expressionist and cubist art when nobody wanted it, he acquired paintings by such outstanding Americans as John Marin, Arthur G. Dove, Charles Demuth, Marsden Hartley, Abraham Walkowitz, Max Weber, and Charles Sheeler. Since there were no children of his union with Georgia O'Keeffe, herself an excellent painter, their collection will, after her death, go to museums.

Mildred Constantine

A HOUSE FOR OUR GOD

Mildred Constantine is associate curator of graphic design
of The Museum of Modern Art in New York. She has
directed many of the museum's exhibitions on architecture
and design and written and edited numerous museum
publications. Her deep interest in Judaism as it relates to
the arts was manifested when she volunteered to assemble
an exhibition of modern painting on the theme "Art: An
Environment for Faith" at the San Francisco Art Museum
in conjunction with the Union of American Hebrew Congregations' 48th General Assembly held in that city in
1965.

In this essay Miss Constantine suggests how the
modern synagogue can give inspiring form through architecture to religious and human needs.

*It is not necessary to go into the Holy of Holies in order to find
God. You can find Him in every place.**

"All architecture," according to Mies van der Rohe, the great
architectural innovator of our times, "must stem from the sustaining and driving forces of civilization." These forces, created
by the traditions of the past and by the complicated expressions
and flux of the present, influence every aspect of civilization.
There cannot be an involvement of art, literature, or religion
without an involvement with life. There cannot be architecture,
born out of function and purpose, expressive of the basic substance, without an involvement with life.

Religion is a piece of the changing fabric of civilization. It too
is structured of the past, the present, and the future. It is many
faceted: its past is subject to many disputatious interpretations
and its present is complicated by allegiances which have modi-

*Paul Tillich, *Architectural Forum*, Dec. 1955.

[306]

Oheb Shalom, Baltimore, Maryland.
The Architects Collaborative and Leavitt & Sons,
Norfolk, Virginia, architects, 1960.

Kneses Tifereth Israel Synagogue, Port Chester, New York.
Philip Johnson, architect, 1956.

fied and expanded the external aspects of belief and the essence of the divine spirit.

One of the major developments of our contemporary civilization has been the new temples of worship. What do we demand in such structures—a monument to the spiritual, a manifestation of the material, a home for tradition, or a transcending expression of timelessness? Can the physical, psychological, spiritual, and social factors be combined with such specifics as air, light, heat, and shelter to produce a building that represents the dynamics of architecture and religion? Can the realistic needs and requirements of a congregation be met in a devotional space in which the immanence of the divine spirit exists?

Many of our Jewish theologians and writers have indicated that there is no one or preferred form for the synagogue. The Jews have always tended to build their houses of worship in conformity with the architecture of their environment.

The Lord, requesting that Moses ask his people to make Him a sanctuary, made known his wishes as to materials, size and scale (the cubit is used as the measure—the distance between the elbow and knuckles) as well as decorative elements for the ark, the mercy seat, the table, candlesticks; for the tabernacle, the curtains (twined linen, and blue and purple and scarlet), the altar, the chambers, the holy garments, and so forth (Exodus 26).

When Solomon built the first Temple for the Lord, he embodied human acts, human thoughts, and human expressions in relation to the spirit of God. Solomon was instructed as to the length, breadth, and height of the house, the porch before the temple of the house, house windows of narrow lights were specified. The house was built of stone, made ready before it was brought to the site so that there was neither hammer nor axe nor any tool of iron heard in the house while it was being built. The house was covered with beams and boards of cedar. No stone was seen, even the floors were covered with fir. It took seven years to build and the cedar trees, fir-trees, gold, were furnished by Hiram, King of Tyre (First Book of Kings).

In our time, we have a choice. We can preserve an attachment to the past, we can adapt the characteristics and look of tradition, or we can reflect our age—change, action, movement, and create new expressions which the moral and creative resources of man can express.

[308]

Just as there is controversy in the "fitness" of aspects of Jewish belief—the conservative, the orthodox, the reformed—so there is controversy in the tangible expressions of these aspects. There are those who prefer the traditional forms without the distractions of visual elements felt to inhibit religious expression. Their belief is that the emotional aspects of worship inhibit true religious experience. They point to the Second Commandment as the source for this belief. But scholars have argued that this commandment does not really imply stricture on decoration but only on the representation of human form. The source of light, too, has been open to many discussions. On the one hand, an exclusion of the world is felt to be essential in a house of worship to encourage immersion; others have asked for houses of worship open to the world, to nature, and to the sky. It is true that intensely religious experience needs no aids, yet music, painted walls, carved wood, and other embellishments have been used throughout the ages to aid the worshipper to commune with God.

In our age of conformity, buildings of all kinds have had a tendency to look alike. However, a place of worship is not like the neon-laden theatre. Given the human equipment, the all-encompassing and progressive technology of our times, and the vast choice of materials, the architects of our time can produce a diversity of forms with which to express the current diverse spiritual needs.

It has become popular to mix "the good, the true, and the beautiful" in religious buildings at the expense of genuine spiritual and architectural expression. The temples then are addressed to the congregations and their need or demand for ostentatious display. Architects must possess a force of character, integrity, and creative instinct, to fuse the sternly practical and the inspirationally beautiful, compatible with the logic of religious demands.

As early as 1945, Eric Mendelsohn's first synagogue was also his first actual commission in the United States and one of the first contemporary religious buildings in this country. His solution for accommodating larger congregations for the High Holy Days and other social functions by means of disappearing walls and folding doors is now fairly standard procedure in modern synagogue architecture. The St. Louis Temple *B'nai Amoona* unites temple, assembly wing, and school, all tightly arranged around an enclosed garden. The temple is under a parabola which projects far beyond the front windows, thus shielding them from a western exposure. This produces a most startling and effective interior. The ark detail in scale, material, and simplicity is commanding of attention.

Philip Johnson and Walter Gropius offer two handsome examples of successful religious architecture. Johnson's classical concern for beginning, middle, and end in the organization of space is clearly reflected in his great synagogue *Kneses Tifereth Israel* in Port Chester, New York. This monumental white building is orchestrated like a symphony. It sits gleaming and quietly compelling among the trees—its whiteness heralding the approach. Out from under the sky, one enters, through large dark doors, a small low elliptical vestibule, passing through it into a bright large rectilinear hall. This classic sequence of light to dark to light spaces ends in a crescendo not a little aided by the clearly contrasting colors used on walls, on seats, on floors. This seemingly formal purity is unabashedly emotional—its physical scale meant to elevate man to a spiritual response and enjoyment.

While Johnson's building relies on its interior spaces to create spiritual elation, the *Temple Oheb Shalom* in Baltimore evokes a spiritual reaction by the emphasis of its exterior. Gropius and the other members of The Architects Collaborative together with Leavitt & Sons have successfully merged symbolic imagery with architectural expression. The four arches on the facade, suggesting the Tablets of the Laws, create a vaulted roof line. The upward sweep of the arch and the rhythmic movement of the repeated pattern creates an immediate religious character. In the interior, there is careful control of illumination. Sunlight does not enter the building directly and wall fenestration is minimal. Colorful vertical stained glass windows can only be seen on the retreat from the sanctuary above the entrance. Predominant tones of blue in the seat coverings, carpeting, and walls help to convey the remote and quiet air.

An amalgamation of art and architecture can be seen in the *Congregation B'nai Israel* in Milburn, New Jersey, whose facade of cypress paneling is enlivened by the Burning Bush sculpture of Herbert Ferber. Frank Lloyd Wright's *Beth Sholom Synagogue* in Elkins Park, Pennsylvania, expresses his creative

[310]

B'nai Amoona Synagogue and Community Center, St. Louis, Missouri. Eric Mendelsohn, architect, 1946-50.

Ark detail of
B'nai Amoona Temple
and Community Center.

originality in the evocative shape of his building—a pyramidal shape, "a traveling Mt. Sinai in glass, a mountain of light."*

The exigencies of army life produced the anonymous chapel which provided one house of worship for all denominations. This wartime device, like so many others, soon found its way into peacetime use. The *MIT Chapel*, the three chapels at *Brandeis University*, and the *Air Corps Academy Chapels* are typical of modern religious thought and experience. However similar their intent, their elements express entirely different attitudes which reflect on the ambiance in which they exist.

The *Kresge Chapel* by Eero Saarinen at Massachusetts Institute of Technology offers complete separation from the world. The one building serves Catholic, Protestant, and Jewish faiths. The main focus of this circular building is on the altar which is lighted from above by a honeycomb grille. The gilt metal reredos screen by Harry Bertoia is like a stage backdrop. Somehow it seems that the religion, as well as the building, being neutralized and distilled, has a general effect of remoteness and the structure's monumentality becomes forbidding and cold.

In contrast to this one chapel for three denominations, the three chapels of the *Interfaith Center* at Brandeis University provide separate religious facilities. They are grouped around a central pool. Each of the buildings is of block faced with brick on the facade and the interior. Each of the chapels has a different altar and ark. In the Catholic, the emphasis is on the altar; the Protestant offers altar and pulpit equal emphasis, whereas in the Jewish Chapel the emphasis is on the Art of Moses.

The synagogues illustrated range in time from 1945 to the present and are presented as contemporary architectural expressions in tune with new religious and human requirements. The heavy, low, traditional domes have given way to joyous, adventurous, and frankly proud buildings. The expansion of our spiritual needs is being given meaningful form.

Architectural Forum, June 1959

In
Other
Lands

A few have raised the exercise of travel writing to a high art but, for the most part, the travelogue is more likely to glaze the eye than to make the heart beat faster. Secretly, I think we hate to read about or even to look at pictures of places where we have not been. Put an atlas in the hands of most of us and we will turn immediately to the maps of locales we know. Yet if, as William Lloyd Garrison said, "My country is the world and my countrymen mankind," we must struggle against our innate provincialism and awaken our curiosity about far-off lands. As with other writing there is no sure formula for this. The travel writer must have the magical ability to evoke foreign places and customs so vividly that the trip becomes irresistible to the imagination. But Jewish life is so rich in color and variety, so endlessly fascinating in the variation of its customs and conditions, that we have frequently been hard put to choose between essays from one issue to the next.

The pieces included here seem to us to contain an extra dimension of understanding besides the ability to evoke the color and quality of distant parts — which is no small feat in itself.

Gertrude Samuels

BAR MITZVAH STORY

> Gertrude Samuels is a journalist, world traveler and for
> the past eighteen years a staff writer for *The New York
> Times*. Known especially for her features in *The New
> York Times* magazine, Miss Samuels holds a citation from
> the Overseas Press Club for foreign correspondence and a
> Page One Award of the American Newspaper Guild for
> her series on Little Rock during the stormy events there.
> This story of a Bar Mitzvah in Israel is one of many
> pieces Miss Samuels has written with the Jewish city as
> background.

In the theater of this night—a darkly-quiet night, lit by an
orange moon that hangs like a jewel above our watchmen in
their ambushes, as well as above the mosque on the other side—I
want to make you this record, my son. Tomorrow, the village
will celebrate your birthday, the glorious thirteenth, when you
will be the Bar Mitzvah boy, the "son of the commandment"
who now becomes a man.

For this night, Joshua, I would spend it close to you. I think
the old scribes who handed down the Bible's legends probably
feel as I do tonight—as I put down the story of why you sleep
in peace and safety in the children's building, though thirteen
years ago this night all in this kibbutz had been destroyed.

As I write, I hear the prayerful chants of those who call
themselves our enemy coming from a few yards to the west in
the desert—floating down from the mosque with the same mournful, shrill importunings as our own prayers, theirs to Allah and
ours to God. I wonder that "the whole earth is full of His glory"—
their earth as well as our earth.

Our land now throbs with the music of new creation. The
orange moon hangs over nearly 10,000 dunams here planted to
wheat and barley, apple and pear orchards and a good banana
crop. We have 700 hives of bees, 60 milking cows and 150 cows

[315]

for meat, 8,000 laying chickens and incubators for 40,000 eggs that produce 400,000 chicks a year—a prosperous kibbutz, we are called. Thirteen years ago there was nothing left alive in these fields and no person left behind to write or ponder anything; all that remained were the twenty-six men and one woman who lay dead in these fields.

But I am going ahead of the story, and I want to tell it carefully, for many people were involved. Our friends popped up in the strangest places.

This is how it happened.

Our kibbutz, as you know, was named after a leader of the Warsaw Ghetto uprising. I have often wondered what the word ghetto conjures up in your mind—you who have only known freedom! Do you see a great wall damming in old Jews with flowing beards and earlocks, weighed down under their prayer-shawls with the grief of the ages? That would be partly true. More true would be the picture and spirit of the younger men, like your namesake, Joshua of Warsaw, who knew that they would have to die—there was no other way—but who refused to be stepped on like vegetables. Joshua had a very great idea, and though he and his little band of men had few guns and were quickly, even lazily, killed by the keepers of the ghetto, his idea never perished. It was that Jews must not tremble before those who would harm them. Even in the twentieth century, that is a new idea for the world.

We named the kibbutz for him because we believed in his idea. We had just started our kibbutz that year of 1943, the year of the Warsaw Ghetto uprising, and all our members had lost their families in Poland or the ghettos of other countries. We had to maneuver fast in order to get it built. The British, who held the Mandate over Palestine then, had forbidden the Jews to build here in the desert. We came at night, sometimes in terror—not of the British but of the jackals which infested the Arab fields nearby.

We threw up houses in a few hours and, most important, got roofs on them; the British had a law that when you built a house with a roof on, it could not be destroyed. In this way, our village —and many more like ours—got started on "forbidden land."

Some have compared our land, so strangely shaped, to an hour-glass where the sands of green and lovely Galilee in the north spill down to the Negev wilderness in the south. That description is poetic but incomplete. This land is a great heart that beat faintly for a long time, for thousands of years, so faintly that it seemed to be stopping altogether. But suddenly, not long ago, it began to pound with new health inside the old and frail body. The desert shall rejoice and blossom as the rose, said Isaiah, and that is what we set about doing here.

We put up our watch-tower, which also became our water-tower. From Tel Aviv and Haifa and far-off America there came tractors and live stock and seed to help us begin on the land. Technicians and water experts came to show us—shop-keepers, tailors, doctors, clerks—how to be farmers. Above all, though we did not need to be told this, they wanted us to make friends with our neighbors. The last was the easiest task to fulfil.

We were surrounded by Arab villages, so we had to be friends in order to develop. We wanted to in any case because—how can this be forgotten?—we are cousins. We felt the family ties very strongly.

Some Arabs were afraid at seeing a Jewish settlement so near to their villages in Migdal and Gaza. But before long they started to come. One very large village of more than 2,000 souls sent some of its members to us. In their flowing white robes and headdresses of many colors they might have stepped out of your Bible.

"We have watched your men in the field," they told us, "and we are curious. We must use sticks to scratch the earth. We like your tractor and would like to try it."

We let them borrow it. They brought us meat from Gaza, since Tel Aviv was too far off for us; we sold them guavas that were growing nicely, and gave them manure for their fields. They learned about our doctor and came to him. Their women were too bashful to come into the settlement; we built a wooden hut at the gate, and the doctor treated them there.

One of our members, Simeon, was an Iraqi Jew who taught us Arabic to help us understand our friends better. Whenever he met us in the fields or in the dining-room or library, he would insist on talking to us in Arabic. He was one of our shepherds, a rough, kindly man, not more than twenty-two, who hoped one day to be able to bring in his huge family who remained in Bagdad.

Simeon was happiest when he was out at the crack of dawn with the sheep, leading them to the hills, watching the day slowly ripen—that is, until Deborah came back from her studies at the University. She was the loveliest of our girls, as fair and blue-eyed as Simeon was dark and black-eyed. Soon he was teaching her Arabic so that she could be of help to the Moslem women in the medical hut.

All the *haverim,* the villagers, soon saw that nothing could separate these two, and they began to tease Simeon for teaching the teacher, instead of tending the sheep. He never minded the teasing; in fact, Deborah's presence seemed to make him work with the strength of a dozen men in the fields.

Amos was the secretary then—the *mukhtar,* the Arabs used to call him as they called their own village mayor—and some of us would go with Amos to visit our Arab neighbors in their villages, drink coffee together, and talk over farm problems.

In the spring, in just this time of year when the rain is over and gone, Simeon and Deborah were married by a rabbi who came from Tel Aviv. The mukhtars and their families came with many presents of sheep and fruit and a marvelous old coffee pot for the bride and groom. It was a big occasion, and we sang the songs of joy and of harvests.

For many years we were friends.

Then, in the fall of 1947 the United Nations wanted to divide Palestine and make it into two states—one for the Jews, one for the Arabs—and almost at once trouble broke out in our part of the country. It did not come from our friends, but from further west, from Arabs who did not know us or live among us. As a precaution, the Army sent up a few young soldiers from Tel Aviv. Some Arabs opened fire on them, which they returned. There were no casualties—but, though we did not realize it at once, the incident seemed to close a period of history.

Amos and another went on their horses next day to a neighboring village to talk it over, but the mukhtar refused to see them. When he returned, Amos told us quietly, "No one welcomed us or recognized us any more. Relations are finished."

He did not come to dinner that evening, but he doubled the watch at the fences, and stayed down at the gate with the soldiers.

There began a strange period of isolation and harassment. It could not have been created by our simple farm friends. It was ordered, or forced upon them, by some faceless higher-ups who knew nothing of us.

We were one Jewish village surrounded by many Arab villages. They put mines on the main road and in our fields. The haverim had to find ways to work the fields, while trying at the same time to cut the wires of the mines. Two members were killed while cutting the wires.

There was no question about our staying. We were Zionists who loved our homeland—so it was understood by New York and London as well as Tel Aviv that we would remain and we did not need instructions about this. We went on working our orchards and grazing our cattle and more men were killed by mines, but no one thought of leaving.

British officers who used to come through would ask in a not unfriendly way, "Why do you stay here? It is dangerous."

But they understood that we would not leave. Many of us had fought in the British Army against a common enemy during the war; we admired them for their pluck and stubborn resistance, and they knew that our people could be as stubborn. Some of the British wept when they came in to search for our arms; they told us that they were required to do this.

Just before you were born it was becoming clear that the British were really leaving the country, and that there might be war. The uppermost longing was to get the children out. There were seventy-five children here.

The doctor said that your mother must go to a hospital at once, but the way over the main road would be dangerous, and the way over the sands too difficult.

I had a friend in the British Army, a major stationed at Gaza, who had come to the kibbutz in the old days to talk and listen to the music. I went to the main road one day, stopped a British car and gave its driver a message to the major: "Please come at once. I need your help."

After an hour he came, and I told him that I wanted to take my wife to the hospital at Rehovoth. He said to hold on, he would ask permission of Cairo. As good as his word, he came back quickly with the answer—this time driving a Sherman tank for the journey! He was escorted by three other tanks. Your mother got into the major's tank and the convoy took off for Rehovoth. For ten tortuous days I did not know anything—until the good major returned with word that we had a son.

When the Egyptians encircled the camp that spring, our local commander came himself for the children. He drove in with his soldiers in armored cars, breaking through the line. They scooped up all the children, put them in the cars, and drove them out. From the water-tower, we could see that the children had penetrated the line in peace. When we saw that, everything seemed possible again.

By Passover, 1948, it was very tense. But some Arabs secretly remained our friends.

The mukhtar of one village helped to cut the wires of the mines to help the Israeli convoys go through. Another young Arab used to buy bullets in Gaza and bring them to us in a basket. He charged us high prices, but it was dangerous for him and we were willing to pay any price for them. We had no supplies.

The first night of Passover, we sat in the old dining-room, singing *Hatikvah*, with our soup and fruit and wine on the table. We kept on singing though the Arab village next to ours opened fire on us for the first time. We had guards outside and knew that the Arabs would not try to come in, but the machine-gun fire made a strange obbligato.

Later, at our radio, we heard that independence had been declared in the Museum of Tel Aviv, and that excitement in the streets and cafes was high. We could hear the Old Man's voice— and visualized him with his foaming white hair telling that distinguished gathering and the United Nations and the whole world the words that became engraved on our memory: "We, . . . assembled on the day of the termination of the British Mandate for Palestine . . . do hereby proclaim the establishment of a Jewish state in the Land of Israel."

There was no time for us to think about independence then or to drink to it. For two weeks we had been sleeping in our clothes. The mothers were worrying about their children. We had no water. We had a few arms and bullets. We could see the preparations for war around us.

When it was just breaking dawn, the Egyptian planes came over. They dropped their bombs and had an easy time of it. We had nothing to use back. At six o'clock the following morning, the Egyptian land forces started firing. They came with big guns, heavy artillery, tanks and machine guns. There was no heavy artillery at the kibbutz.

For eight days they fired over from the hills. It was not hard for them to shoot down everything that we had built for five years. Many of ours were killed.

I will tell only of one—Simeon.

He had been badly shattered with a grenade, his belly smashed to pieces. Deborah kept asking for him, and at last we told her and took her to Amos' house where he had been laid out. She looked at him without moving or crying, like a block of stone. Very quietly she took off his wrist watch. He was so drenched with blood that we had not had the heart to take off his belt of bullets. She reached over and loosened the belt for us, took it off herself, and handed it to us. Not until she left the room did she begin to shiver and break.

By the end of the eighth day we had orders from the Army to leave the kibbutz. We buried our dead in a common grave, and left everything behind except our rifles and signal wireless.

We were a silent group that left the settlement. But we did not feel the awful desperation that Joshua must have known in the Warsaw Ghetto—for there was no way that he could break out of the wall, while we were sure we were only withdrawing temporarily. He had been behind a wall; we were in our country. There had to be a difference. This could only be an interlude. We had not waited for this moment for two thousand years, only to give in because a round had been lost. Those were our thoughts, and our faith was justified.

The members spread around in various settlements. A few months later, the commander of the Northern Negev sent word by bicycle messenger that our kibbutz had been liberated. It was on the newscast from Jerusalem. Then everyone who had been in the kibbutz, for miles around, simply left their work and went to the road and hitched rides. They came back without even having to communicate with one another. Deborah came back, too.

"This is my only home," she said.

The destruction to the kibbutz was complete. We went first to stand at the grave of our comrades. Then we tried to find our rooms. Nothing was left. It was sad to see how people went looking for some belonging, a picture, a letter.

Everything in the music corner had been hacked to bits. This seemed hardest to believe. We had a rather large collection of records, all the good stuff—Beethoven, Chopin, Mozart—no dances. Every record had been broken and the bits piled in pails. The piano was smashed into small pieces. I remember feeling a strange anger at this senselessness. Why hadn't they taken the records with them instead of smashing everything?

Soon we were all reunited again—to start to build again, but this time ringed in by neighbors who now called themselves our enemy. Yet they are the same neighbors.

You asked me to look over your homework, my son, and I find that it makes a matchless postscript to what I have been writing.

Your teacher, Deborah, asks how you feel about living on the spot where history has been made, and whether you are afraid.

"*Lo*—no," you answer. "I am not afraid. This kibbutz is my country. All the years that we are living we are educated to live in such a place as this village, and I am not afraid. And the Arabs must not be afraid. We have to live with them in peace, because with war life can never be served here.

"We are Zionists and Socialists. We believe and we know that the poor people and the workers have no reason to fight, because the man working his fields must have peace to work to get his corn in and his milk in. I am sorry about the death of the Israeli soldiers and of the Arab soldiers, too. After all they are all sons of mothers who loved them and lost them forever."

My blessing for your Bar Mitzvah, my son, is that you retain this idealism and wisdom all the days of your life.

Rosanne Klass

THE JEWS
OF AFGHANISTAN — 1965

Miss Klass is the author of a novel *Land of the High Flags*. Her poetry and prose have appeared in a number of leading magazines. For three years she lived and taught in Afghanistan and recently, during another sojourn in the East, sent this report from the city of Kabul.

The sun slips down behind the mountain ridge of the Lion's Gate, the spiny backbone of the city of Kabul. As dusk spreads softly across this old capital city of a devout Moslem country, from minarets and over radio loudspeakers the voice of the *muezzin* calls the faithful to evening prayer. In the garden of my hotel, a servant turns toward Mecca and kneels to pray.

And in one wing of a rambling house in the modern section of the city, around the corner from a couple of embassies and hi-fi music shops, what remains of Kabul's Jewish community gathers together before the light has faded; for it is Rosh Hashanah.

I go along to the synagogue — two large rooms off the garden. They are simple, really rather shabby and bare. Along the walls, high narrow shelves hold the prayerbooks, neatly wrapped. The western wall, which faces Jerusalem (just as the *mehrabs* or prayer niches of the mosques face toward Mecca — but then of course educated Moslems will themselves point out how much Mohammed learned from the Jews), bears the ark and the eternal light; every other inch of it is covered with framed prayers, printed in the shape of the menorah.

Thirty or forty men are jammed in, standing, or sitting on crude wooden benches, or stepping forward to kiss the draperies of the ark. Some wear *yamulkas* which are really the soft Bokhara-style turban caps, embroidered with brilliant flowers. Others wear their dashing *karakul* caps or fedoras. In one corner sits a white-bearded old patriarch in flowering pantaloons and a long loose coat, his feet bare, an enormous turban wound about his head: he is visiting from Herat, where the Jews wear local dress more often than western business suits. Each man seems isolated, absorbed in his prayers. Little boys chew raisins, squirm restlessly, and pinch each other; their fathers suddenly emerge from prayer to pull them sharply to attention. The voices rise and fall, a babble and then, at one moment or another, a sighing, chanting chorus.

As a foreign guest, I am allowed to sit where I can look into the synagogue; but as a woman, of course, I must remain outside in the anteroom where a handful of women and girls are sitting about on carpets and cushions. Some of the young girls are thumbing through old copies of *Femme* and *Elle;* their hair is teased into towering beehives. The married women wear the traditional white dress of local Jewish women: high necks, tucked yokes, long sleeves tight at the ruffled cuffs, the gowns flowing full from the yoke to the floor, and scarves drawn about their heads and shoulders. They snatch at falling toddlers, and gossip cheerfully.

This is the remnant of Afghanistan's ancient Sephardic community. Although most of the Jews of Kabul are originally from Bokhara, Tashkent and Samarkand — families who fled and found refuge here when the Soviets took over in the 1920's — the community of Herat has existed, perhaps, since the time of Antiochus or near it. They have their own language, Gelaki, which is a mixture of Hebrew and Persian, and is written in Persian script.

When I was last in Afghanistan, more than ten years ago, there were several thousand Jews in the country; now there are about thirty-five families in Kabul and a similar number in Herat — about five hundred people altogether. The rest have gone.

Most of them went to Israel, simply because it is Israel. Others preferred India, because they are Middle Eastern merchants whose business is in money-changing and in quick-turnover transactions; and whose outlook differs from their grandfathers' insofar as now they ship cigarettes and pharmaceuticals by air freight instead of sending bales of wool by camel caravan. Israel is not good for such business, but in Asia it still thrives. A few have emigrated to New York, where their close-knit community lives unto itself in Queens, weaving the fabric of its life by shuttling back and forth between New York, Israel and the Orient, and almost entirely unconcerned with the larger patterns of the American community.

But those who are still in Afghanistan expect, for the most part, to remain here. They are prosperous, even wealthy. There is no persecution to drive them out, nor, within historical memory, has there ever been.

Afghans are predominantly of the Sunni sect, the broader and more tolerant of the two major branches of Islam. Moreover, the tensions between the Arab nations and Israel which have disrupted the historically tolerant relationships of Jews and Moslems elsewhere have had little effect here; for while the Afghans are Moslems, they are not Arabs. (Basically, they appear to be of European stock, with infusions of Turkic, Arab and Mongol peoples over the centuries.) Arab wars are not their wars, and Arab enmities are not their enmities. The government has, more or less as a matter of form, expressed sympathy with its fellow Moslem nations. But there has never been much active interest here in the issue of Israel, and the position of Afghan Jews has, in fact, been improving in recent years — reflecting a general improvement here for everyone.

But they have had problems. Afghanistan is 99 per cent Moslem, and Islam is the official national religion. There have always been some restrictions on non-Moslems, which affected the Jews, and these have been tighter in times of stress. They were especially troublesome during the years of repression which followed a series of chaotic upheavals in 1929-30, when the modernizing King Amanullah was overthrown, a brigand seized the throne, and the country was torn apart. The father of the present king restored order and mounted the throne, but his assassination in 1933 led to prolonged years of rigid and often harsh control. During that era, for example, Jews (and non-Jews, too) were sometimes harassed by local officials eager to extort a bribe. They were not allowed to own land, and at times it was difficult for their children to gain entry into the crowded public schools. On passports and draft cards, their nationality was often listed as Jewish, rather than as Afghan. (One must note, however, that the term "Afghan" still carried its original connotation of a particular ethnic group — the Afghans or Pathans — who gave their name to the country; and other groups such as Hazaras, Turkomans and Sikhs were labelled in the same way.)

[325]

In recent years this has been changed, as a new generation has begun a backbreaking drive to modernize the country and establish a genuine democracy (the first free national elections by universal secret ballot were held in September, 1965). The first article of the constitution adopted in 1964 pointedly states that the word "Afghan" applies to all citizens, and that non-Moslem citizens are free to practice their faiths. The Jews of Kabul have recently purchased land for a new synagogue, and many are property owners. While the draft cards still list religion, all such references have been removed from the passports.

An Afghan official (in the course of a chat about classical Hebrew, which he learned for his own pleasure) brought up the fact that some restrictions still exist, and need to be eliminated. So far as I can tell, the main one is a prohibition against Jews engaging in the import-export trade. (A number of them do, of course, using Moslem partners as front men.) This is a biased reflection of a real problem: Afghanistan desperately needs every dollar, franc and pound of its limited hard-currency foreign exchange for its efforts to develop and modernize. The local merchant — Moslem or Jew — rarely puts his money into capital investment here; instead he stashes it away in the modern equivalent of bags of gold: checking accounts in foreign banks. The Jewish merchants often invest in Israel. The total result is a steady drain on the resources of the country.

New laws are planned to encourage local investment and to bring businessmen to think in modern terms, but meanwhile it is an unsolved problem. The present laws are certainly slanted against Jewish merchants, and violate the spirit of the new constitution. In practical terms, though, it seems that they are more a theoretical handicap than a real one, although they do create understandable bitterness.

But if the Jews of Afghanistan are materially prosperous, they seem spiritually impoverished, their religious life shallow and thin. Tiny as it is, the community is split: in Kabul there are two synagogues, a larger one of Bokharian Jews, and a smaller one of Herati Jews. Some people hope that the two will unite in the new synagogue, but no one would bet on it.

The rabbi is locally trained, serves part-time, and devotes the rest of his time to business. Religious education amounts to learning enough Hebrew for prayers; the girls study just enough to become literate. The boys spend four hours a day at Hebrew school throughout their school years, but there is no talmudic tradition, and when they leave school, they are finished. The men devote no time to religious affairs.

Although they get their prayer books from Israel, they have no ties with religious institutions either there, in the United States, or in Europe. No one has shown any interest in them. A few years ago someone came to Kabul representing (they seem to recall) the Lubavitcher Rebbe. He tried, unsuccessfully, to raise funds and, more successfully, to collect ancient manuscripts; then he, too, vanished from their horizon.

Yet their sense of Jewishness is strong. For some, it leads to ghetto thinking. Yes, they are Afghans, but that is of no real importance, for they are Jews, as Jews are always Jews, and even if they never go to Israel, it is their home in their hearts. They live in and of two worlds at once.

On Rosh Hashanah I dined at the home of a wealthy merchant. The entry hall was a bare corridor with cheap cotton rugs. In the small parlor, a fine old Persian carpet hung on one wall, there was a hi-fi console and a rack of pop records, but the rest of the furniture was the stiff, ugly style which was once the only kind available here. The walls were sparsely decorated with family photos, colored calendars, picture postcards from Israel. In the center of one wall, a photograph of His Majesty King Zahir, framed with a bit of white tissue paper, was carefully pasted up. The family greeted me, sitting stiffly in their best clothes.

After bread and salt and good wine which they make for themselves, we have eight ritual foods: sheep's head and lungs with honey, apple and honey, cauliflower, beetroot, dates, squash, boiled beans, and sheep's tongue and feet. Then dinner itself: heaped plates of kabobs, pilaus and roast chicken, fruits and nuts. Over a glass of home-made vodka, green with herbs and the most violent liquid I have ever swallowed, I got into a discussion with the oldest son, a young man of about twenty, a student at the university of Kabul who hopes to study eventually in Germany. Why Germany? Because his father has much business there. Has he no qualms about studying in Germany? No. No, because, after all, a Jew is equally a stranger anywhere but Israel, so Germany is no different from any place else.

American Jews, he thinks, are foolish to think of themselves as Americans, and wrong not to want to emigrate to Israel. God told Moses to take the Jews to Israel.

But is he not an Afghan? Yes. Wouldn't he do in his army service here if he was drafted? Of course. Doesn't he have a picture of the king on his wall? Certainly; the king is his king, and a good man. Does he plan to move to Israel? No, because it is not a good place for business; he will stay here. But nevertheless he is a Jew, and we American Jews simply refuse to understand what that means.

Yet, I think I do know what *he* means: he means that though he may live his whole life in Afghanistan or elsewhere, he will be in Israel at least once, because if he can, he will *go home* to die.

But others are developing something closer to what we in America think of as Jewish life integrated into a non-Jewish community. For Sukot I went to the comfortable home of a merchant in his early forties. Exactly a dozen years ago I had spent the same holiday with the same family, who lived then for all eight days in a great carpet-hung *sukkoh* which filled their garden. There was none this year. My host made an apologetic gesture.

"In this climate," he said, "it's pretty cold at this time of year. So people here have given up trying to live in a *sukkoh*. Now we just have a symbolic one, at the synagogue. I think you do the same thing in America, don't you?"

His wife, a striking woman with a classic face, presided over an enormous dinner. I had seen her at the synagogue a few days before in her long white gown; tonight she wore a black sheath and pumps. Their two pretty, fawn-shy daughters giggled and shook their ponytails when their father urged them to try the English they study at school. He pointed to one of his sons; the boy was addicted to detective stories, translated into Persian. Did I think that was bad? Oh, well, he is going to Israel to live on a kibbutz for a while, and perhaps that will break the habit.

While we were in the midst of dinner, some Moslem friends dropped in unexpectedly to wish them a happy holiday: an official who had been a high school classmate, and his wife. We spent a pleasant evening in casual conversation, and after the others left, I stayed to talk a bit longer with my hosts. They plan to stay in Afghanistan, at least as far as they can foresee now.

"Life is good here now," he said, "and I think it will get better. We are citizens — we are Afghans. I think that all the Jews here voted in the elections — I know that we did."

Then why are they sending their son to Israel?

"Oh, the boys are squabbling all the time — you know how it is at that age. We thought this might help. My parents are in Israel, you know, and my sister and her husband too. I own a house there myself," he added, smiling thoughtfully. "I bought it fifteen years ago. I suppose that some day it is possible that I might use it myself but just now . . . no, just now I don't think so. As far as I can see now, our life is here."

"We are full citizens now," he repeated. Then his face lit up, and he leaned forward. "Do you know what happened when the Crown Prince got married?" he asked. "Well, of course everybody in the country sent a gift. The Jews did, too. Our representatives took it to the palace and presented it. And do you know what happened?"

He was beaming with pride.

"The king — the king himself — made a point of announcing that he personally especially appreciated the gift of the Jewish community of Afghanistan. He said that himself, in front of everybody! And then, do you know what he said to our delegation? He said, 'If the Jewish citizens here ever have any difficulties, please pick up the phone and call me directly — even if it is the middle of the night.' Yes, that's exactly what the king said to us — *even in the middle of the night!*"

So far as I know, His Majesty's sleep has not yet been disturbed; and it seems likely that, even if their numbers dwindle some Jews will remain, as they have for more than two thousand years, among the high mountains of the Hindu Kush.

[329]

Joel Lieber

LIFE CYCLE
OF AN ARAB VILLAGE

> Mr. Lieber lived in Israel for two years. How he did it
> he generously passed on to the readers of his book *Israel
> on $5 a Day*. His feature articles on travel and politics
> have appeared in more than fifty national publications,
> including *The Nation, Midstream, Saturday Review* and
> *Harper's Bazaar*.
>   This report on an interview with a Druze friend in the
> Arab village of Tira throws helpful light on a point of
> view not often expressed in such personal and human
> terms.

Our host said, "If you will tell me about America, I will tell you
about the Arab problem."

That seemed fair enough, and we sat down on cushions in a
large white-washed room, poorly lit by a single kerosene lamp.
In one corner there stood an immense refrigerator, a 13-cubic-
foot General Electric. Otherwise, the room was empty of orna-
ment, save for the three old men who lay on mats in the opposite
corner and listened but contributed nothing to the conversation
that followed.

Dusk had already fallen on the Arab village of Tira, in the
mid-Israel citrus belt region, where we had spent an afternoon
being subjected to the merciless hospitality of our hosts. We had
eaten too many times, and drunk too many cups of Turkish
coffee. By "we" I include Ali, a Druze friend who considers
himself considerably more civilized than the Arabs, but who
nonetheless accepted an invitation to visit the village that Shab-
bat from several of the villagers with whom he worked as a hired
hand at a nearby kibbutz. The Druze, Arabic-speaking and
Arabic-looking, have suffered long persecution at Arab hands,
fought on the Israeli side during the 1948 war, and following a
fairly secretive religion, can trace their forefathers clear back to
Jethro, Moses' father-in-law.

[330]

WILLIAM STEINEL

Our host, who assumed a position opposite me behind a tall bubble pipe, began to speak. He was sixtyish, and wore a beautifully embroidered gown. In the somewhat dismal setting, he gave off a certain dignity — sitting tall, prince-like and solemn, with his hands on his knees.

His first question was about the noises his refrigerator often made — terrible, racing sounds. He wanted to know if this was bad, Ali translated, because he paid a lot of money for this refrigerator. I discussed the subject of how refrigerator motors change speed, until, apparently dissatisfied with my lack of technical knowledge, he abruptly interrupted: "What do you know about Israel before 1948?"

I replied that I had read books and heard stories from people. He waved his hands excitedly and said something that made the old men in the corner break into cracking, barking laughs.

Ali said: "He says many things were different when the British were here. He says he liked it better then. He says he liked apricots — meesh-meesh-eem — and could eat as many as he wanted for very little money. But now he says he can't afford

[331]

them any more and that makes him sad. Apricots used to be cheap. Now the Jews have made them expensive."

"Is that the only difference between 1948 and now?" I asked.

My host proceeded to talk for five minutes, his cronies in the corner nodding vigorously, and concluded by telling Ali not to bother translating what he said. Ali picked up: "He wants to know about the buildings called skyscrapers in New York — which is the highest?"

I told them about the Empire State Building, that it was a hundred and two or a hundred and eight stages — something like that.

He lit the tobacco on top of the water pipe, sucked in a series of low, rumbling bubbles, and said: "How do the people eat near the top of the skyscrapers?"

"They could telephone down for food and have someone bring it up, or else go down on the elevator to a restaurant."

Then he directed a question to Ali, and I watched Ali explain, with motions that looked like he was drawing water from a well, the workings of an elevator.

"He says he has heard that in New York the trains go under the ground and over the buildings and skyscrapers."

"Under the ground, yes, but not over the skyscrapers."

Thumping bubble noises, like deep belches, preceded his reply. "But he says he has heard it."

I insisted it wasn't true, and I could see the skeptical look on the man opposite me.

"He says also that he has heard that planes come to give food to people who live high in the skyscrapers.

I refuted that also.

"He asks how do they grow things in New York, things for people to eat."

"The food comes from all over," I said, "but mostly from nearby places like New York State and the farms in New Jersey and Pennsylvania." Ali's translation gave Pennsylvania a particularly pleasant sound in Arabic.

Then my host hitched up his handsome gown over his shoulder and made a sweep of his arm, a somewhat pompous gesture as if banishing a subject from his kingdom. He spoke to Ali, who translated: "He wants to know your opinion of the Arab problem."

I asked Ali exactly which problem he referred to.

"He wants your opinion of the Arab problem, the problem of their minority in Israel, and the problem of the Arabs in the Middle East versus Israel."

Ali gave me a sympathetic look, but I could see from the anxious expression in my host's eyes that I was losing face with him each moment I hesitated. So I suggested that I thought peace should be the goal, and that I thought, from what I had seen, that Israel sincerely wanted peace. "Israel and the Jews have had too much war and killing to want anything but peace." I told him. I also said that cultural and medical and educational and commercial programs between the Middle Eastern countries and Israel would be to everyone's benefit. I mentioned, too, the stories I had heard about how the Cairo and Damascus radio broadcast hate programs against Israel, telling their listeners that they must drive Israel into the sea. I said that peace wouldn't come from radio programs like that.

Ali translated his reply: "He wants to know who will guarantee that there will be peace if the radio stops saying these things?"

"What does he mean — *who* will guarantee peace?"

After a brief exchange between Ali and our host, I was told, "Just what he said — *who?*"

It was a strange idea to grasp, the notion of two desert chiefs commanding great tribes, each declaring his word and his honor that the pledge of peace will be upheld; a word, a man's honor, and that is sufficient. It was so simple and romantic, so beautifully clear-cut, and the sad thing was that the real world doesn't work that way any more.

"No one man will guarantee peace," I said, adding that sincere displays of peace would be the best start and that it doesn't do any good for peace to shoot at farmers and children working in the fields. If there would be peace, I said, both sides must be truthful in wanting it, and willing to trust each other's intentions. (At this point I began to wonder how the people at the United Nations could continually talk about peace and such lofty matters without feeling uncomfortable and preachy, the way I felt now.)

"What would Syria and Jordan gain through peace with Israel?" my host shot back. "They are already civilized people. They are not primitive. They have cars and refrigerators and transistors. What more is there?"

I ticked them off: things like electricity, doctors, roads, building machinery, sanitary conditions, more schools, teachers.

Once again my haranguer hitched up his robes and made a waving motion of dismissal. "He says those things you mention have no — what would be the word? — no *style*. The Arabs still have style and tradition. The Westerners and these foreign Jews do not understand all the new things they make and use and do. He likes the world he can understand — build your own house, know who's teaching your children, following Allah's word."

After he had passed this along, Ali gave a great yawn. I had no answer immediately forthcoming, so my host added, "If Israel was sincere about peace why don't they let in the million Arabs in Gaza and Jordan who had their homes originally in Israel?"

I tried for a quick out by telling Ali that I was neither the United Nations nor the American Ambassador nor the Israel Foreign Ministry, that I wasn't qualified to answer a question like that. Without passing this on, Ali said, "Try to act as important as he thinks you are. Otherwise he won't value anything you've said. You are the first American he has ever met."

So I talked about the instability that a million Arab refugees in Israel would cause, the potential fifth column aspect, the fact that many of them had originally chosen to leave Israel, and that they were being held in idleness as political bait.

To this, he shot back: "They were tricked into leaving Israel. Egypt and Jordan isn't their home: Israel is."

His eyes had narrowed. He was so incensed that he neglected his pipe and it went out. Ali translated: "Do you know that before the war I was an important man with a house and land and that I lived in a village in Palestine where my ancestors had lived for many generations? And that the Haganah came and destroyed my village and took away my house and land?"

My silence seemed the cue for a more vigorous attack, and he thundered: "Do you know this?"

I said that I didn't, pointing out that I didn't know his situation, nor his village, nor the attitude of the people who lived there — whether they were friendly, neutral or hostile, and that from knowing these things, perhaps some explanation could be found.

Ali passed this along, looked at his watch, and yawned again. Before he could express his boredom any further, our host resumed: he said he lived in a village one mile from here and that he was the *mukhtar,* the headman, of this village. He said they had stayed out of the war but that the Syrians occupied the village and in an attack the Haganah pushed them out and then burned most of the village. He said many of his people fled into Jordan but that he stayed where he was, and that the Israelis confiscated his land and paid a very small price for it.

There was nothing I could think of saying to this, and during my silence a blue-gowned man set another tray of syrupy coffee in front of us.

My host hitched at his gowns, saying: "Now that you know about the Arab problem, you must tell people the truth about it. Tell it to the Israelis and to the Americans, and maybe one day we will have justice here. He wants you to guarantee that you will write the truth about these things."

I replied that I would certainly try to write the truth. Ali sent this along and our host replied, "Not *try* to write the truth. You must *guarantee* that you *will* write the truth."

I explained to Ali that I couldn't guarantee to write the truth because one man's truth is not another's, and that there was no absolute truth to satisfy everyone. I would write what seemed the truth to me, I promised him. "You should also tell him that he shouldn't ask for so many guarantees — guarantees for one man to keep the peace, guarantees that I'll tell the truth." I said that few honest men give guarantees and anyhow there weren't enough honest men around whom you could trust to give a guarantee. I asked Ali to please translate that as accurately as he could.

My haranguer nodded seriously, and I thought we were done. But, according to Ali, he replied: "Nevertheless, you must tell the truth."

He had worn me down, and not being able to overpower the desire, I said to Ali, "What is truth? Ask him if he knows, and that if he does, he should tell me." I had really hoped to stun him with a shockingly self-evident question, but I failed with my last card. His answer was simple and unimpeachable: "Truth is the word of Allah."

And on that note, I knew it was pointless to continue. I promised that I would write the truth, not try to write the truth, or guarantee him that I'd write the truth: just that I *would* write the truth.

My host cracked a broad smile across his big face. He stood

up, as did his cohorts in the corner. He gave my hand a vigorous handshake. He seemed satisfied at last.

"Ma'salaam," he said, and I echoed him, and he replied with "salaam aleikem" and heaped on me phrases of parting, peace, regret and hospitality: you have graced my house, until we meet again, may your way be peaceful.

I shook hands with the others. Ali, as anxious to go as I, was already at the car when I got outside. We lost no time getting started, although I had to navigate slowly along the sandy clay flats that led to the main road.

"Chavere," Ali said, "I will tell you something. . . . I don't know which village he was in, and I don't know whose side he took during the war of 1948. If he was good, as many others were good, then he should still have his land and house. If he was bad — and do not forget it was a war — *ka-cha*, thus what he deserves. But if he *was* good and still lost his land, then Israel has done an injustice." He paused for a moment and then went on. "But these Arabs, with their funny questions about skyscrapers and trains and elevators. . . ." His voice trailed off and he shook his head. "They sit around year after year in their cafes while their women and children work. And what do they ever know about anything? Nothing. They sit and they say the same things to each other over and over and in the end they know nothing."

We swung out onto the dark main road leading to the Hadera crossroad.

They know nothing, I thought, but they know a lot. They know they've been living in a place for a long, long time. They know who their fathers were for the last fifty generations. They know where they came from and how they must act and what has always been right and what has always been wrong. And that's knowing a lot. That's knowing more than I and a good many other people know. But after knowing that, perhaps Ali is right; after that, they don't know — they just don't know.

[336]

Georgia Litwack

SOUR NOTE
IN THE VENICE SERENADE

> Miss Litwack is a free-lance writer and photographer who
> has contributed stories and pictures to the *Christian
> Science Monitor, Better Homes & Gardens* and other
> publications.
>   To this report on the Jews of Venice, she brought not
> only a keen eye but a wit too often missing from this
> kind of journalism.

What does a Jewish tourist bring to Europe? Like his Gentile
counterpart, he trundles a variety of goals: to absorb the con-
tinent's culture, to partake of the diverse refreshments of travel,
and to bring back a few tangible reminders of his trip, some
"buys."

However, the Jew secretly carries in his luggage one additional
item—of no interest whatsoever to customs inspectors—and that
is a deep yearning to find in Europe . . . himself.

On his guide list for each city is certain to be, amongst the
museums and monuments, the must-eat-at restaurants, and the
must-patronize boutiques, directions on how to reach the synagogue, the Jewish cemetery, and that most eloquent tool of Jewish segregation the world has ever known, the ghetto.

This last he is sure to visit, even if a tight itinerary precludes
the others. He makes what the song writer has called "that
sentimental journey" to Rome's Ghetto on the Tiber, to the Jewish Quarter in London, to the Juderia in Madrid, to the Juiverie
in Paris.

In some he encounters hospitality, in some hostility, in all a
nameless depression. And yet he goes.

For what reason? Piety? Not likely. Scholarship? Hardly.
Curiosity? That's getting closer.

[337]

It is a curiosity that gropes inward, a searching after identity, a profound wish to find a brother in this distant land.

Let us therefore examine this phenomenon. Let us focus on the city which in the sixteenth century spawned the Ghetto Age. We speak of glittering, melodic Venice where, thanks to a peculiar geography, the children of Israel were more effectively isolated than ever before in their long history of persecution.

We enter a murky compound in the northern section of the city, a tiny, dismal island far from the spacious opulence of Piazza San Marco.

We wear the uniform that screams "tourist": guidebook in one hand, city map in the other, camera round the neck, enormous carry-all on the arm. From nowhere springs a self-styled guide. He greets us with an ingratiating "*Shalom!*" We respond in kind, whereupon he inquires, "*Synagoga?*"

Of course we wish to see the ancient structure, but having found a kinsman we attempt to engage him first in a brief interlude of camaraderie.

We search each other's faces cagily. He does not speak English, we cannot manage Italian. He is alien to Yiddish, we are bewildered by its Venetian equivalent, a conglomerate of Hebrew, Italian, and the regional dialect. Disappointed, we murmur, "*Si, synagoga.*"

He leads us to the huge carved doors of the Spanish Synagogue, richest in history of the five Jewish houses of worship still standing, unaltered, in the ghetto.

The *shamos* appears from thin air. Before guiding us into the dark interior, he glances significantly at our shabbily-clad "guide" to whom we had proferred a measly *grazia*. Regretfully, we accept the mores of the social structure and offer the gratuity, somehow saddened to degrade a fellow Jew with a tip for having given a helping-hand to a stranger.

We hurry inside to avoid having to witness his servile bow, consoling ourselves with the possibility that he might not even have been Jewish!

We marvel at the massive carved ceiling, the towering brass candlesticks and marble columns. The Spanish (S'fardic) Synagogue was designed by Longhena, architect of the famous Church of Santa Maria della Salute at the entrance to the Grand Canal. Elsewhere in the ghetto stands the oldest of the Ashk'nazi synagogues, housing an excellent Jewish Museum.

[338]

The Venetian ghetto is today only a loosely-defined area. Although Jews may live where they please in Venice, and do—still all the present-day residents of the ghetto are Jewish.

While postcard Venice perpetuates herself as a lacey, rosy rhapsody—all pink and white and blue and wedding-cake tracery—the ghetto moulders and crumbles. While the Venice of the pleasure-seeking tourist undulates to the gondoliers' serenade, a mournful quiet pervades the ghetto.

To reach the section from St. Mark's Square, the traveler takes a gondola or *vaporetto* (motor launch) along the Grand Canal to Ferrovia (railroad station) stop. He walks along the Fondamenta dei Scalzi past a bustle of stalls where everything from straw bags to fresh fish is displayed for sale. He passes the Campo (square) Saint Geremia, crosses the Ponte (bridge) de Cannaregio and finds himself in the Gheto Vechio, from which he enters the Gheto Novo.

Here is the main square, bleak and silent, where the magnificent sunsets on the pearly lagoon can only be imagined. Here is

A boy of the Venetian ghetto.

peeling stucco and crumbling brick, accented only occasionally by the delicate ironwork and elegant balustrades that made Venetian architecture a thing of artistic glory.

Around the graceful stone well-head at the center of the square is a cluster of handsome, obliging Jewish children. They have the exquisite, refined features typical of North Italians. They are austerely but immaculately dressed, the boys in the really "short" shorts of European youngsters, the girls in dresses, never in—horrors!—trousers of *any* length.

How did the ghetto of Venice come into being? How did it get its name? How did it function?

Paradoxically, the Venetian ghetto, an archetype of darkness and repression, was established at the peak of the Renaissance, a period of flowering and light.

If it is true, as philosopher Jean-Paule Sartre has said, that the anti-Semite is a man who is afraid, then the sixteenth century Venetian was well qualified for the role. His glorious city, after twelve centuries of splendor and dynamic growth, was entering a period of decline.

The Turks took her Byzantium, Christopher Columbus discovered America and new trade routes, and the Portuguese arrived at the Indies, all of which events destroyed Venice's domination of the commerce and politics of the Mediterranean.

The Most Serene Republic was wasting her substance on endless inconclusive wars. There were traitors within her precincts; elections were fraudulent; patrician status could be bought. The painter Titian's mythological nudes, while among the world's undisputed masterpieces, were pagan and carnal.

Rampant with corruption, filled with soldiers of fortune, Venice had sunk to the level of a playground for the world. All festivals, religious as well as civil, became occasions for amusement. Theaters and casinos multiplied. The mask and domino, a hooded masquerade costume pictured in so many of the narrative paintings of the period, hid the identities of the pleasure-seekers whose watchword was abandon.

The scintillating city of the lagoon, which had dominated with her power, now conquered with the impressive spectacle of her debauchery.

How advantageous a set of conditions for a pogrom! Might not the ruling Doges, seeking a scapegoat for the frustration of their ambitions—logical or not—find the Jews handy? It had been done before.

The ranks of the Jews in Venice were then being swelled by hundreds of refugees fleeing into the city from the Italian mainland towns during the anti-Semitic wars of the League of Cambrai. Hot on their heels were the friars, bringing with them the anti-Semitic feeling then running through Italy.

Once more the Venetians, innovators of the first order, drew on their fertile imaginations.

It is well known that Jews, stubbornly adhering to their belief in one God despite the constant victories of their enemies, had been segregated in the cities and towns of the world before. In 1179 the Third Lateran Council in Rome laid the foundations of strict control by prohibiting "true believers" from lodging amongst the Jewish "infidels."

But it remained for the inventive Venetians to give name and form to the institution of the ghetto as it has continued to this day.

When the city fathers proclaimed in 1516 that it was time for Christian citizens of Venice to be protected from contamination, several undesirable parts of the city were proposed for the Jews to occupy. The Doge decided to accept one councilman's suggestion that the *Gheto Nuovo* (*gheto* or *ghetto* being the Italian word for "foundry" and *nuovo* or *novo* meaning "new") be used. It was a grimy islet in the north of the city where cannons formerly had been cast.

On April 10, the day after the Eastertide Feast of Pentecost, the Jews were herded onto the dreary, miniscule island. Twenty-five years later, with the area impossibly crowded, it was expanded to include the abutting *Gheto Vechio*, "Old Foundry."

Thus did the word "ghetto" take on a new meaning, passing into the English language to designate the section of a city where Jews and—in broader use—other minority groups are segregated.

This recoining of a word was not the only new ingredient in the age-old stew known as "the Jewish problem." A yellow hat, forerunner perhaps of the Nazi yellow badge or star, was designed for Jews to wear at all times.

"The Italians have only to make a real effort in any direction," British writer Henry Colville once said, "and they go ahead of everybody else." The Venetians in creating their ghetto demonstrated such ingenuity.

Here were some of the restrictions, devised not to annihilate but to exploit, to segregate yet profit from the Jew:

1. No Jew could remain in Venice without a permit, expensive and needing renewal—for an additional fee—every few years.

2. At regular intervals the Jewish community had to renegotiate its contract to stay, with the price becoming progressively higher.

3. At sunset, all gates to the ghetto were locked, and the Jews were prevented by armed sentries (whom they were forced to pay) from leaving the enclosure till morning.

4. Forbidden to own land, the Jews rented the entire ghetto on a long lease, paying rent even when houses stood vacant. The day the Jews moved in, rents were raised one-third.

5. Profitable or not, Jewish loan banks were required to remain open.

To top it all, the Venetians, recognizing its picturesque possibilities, developed the area as a tourist attraction!

But the ghetto could not meet its obligations under the rapacious edicts. In 1735, the Senate was told the Jews were insolvent and the community was declared bankrupt. As one historian put it: "The Venetians, as realists, conceded there was no more to be got from them and crossed the account off their books."

When Napoleon Bonaparte in his conquest of the Republic opened the ghetto gates in 1797, the section was only a collection of alms-houses. At last the inhabitants of the miserable hovels were free to move.

But, says the legend, they did not have the strength to leave and are there still.

A New Song

The coalescence of thought and emotion in the single gesture of a poem, whether in terms of the rhyme and meter of traditional form, or the even stricter discipline of so-called free verse, is capable of extending the possibilities of language to its ultimate frontiers.

Religious poetry can no longer serve the needs of modern

[343]

man through simplistic devices and the tired vocabulary of the hymnal. The Psalms remain miraculously fresh, but the poet who seeks to deal with the theme of faith can no longer move us by mere parodies of biblical language. The poet who turns to Judaism for his theme faces a singularly difficult challenge. Like good Jewish music, good Jewish poetry must, first of all, be good poetry, where every word counts, where language must be compressed and arresting, and, at the same time, sing. The way of the poet is always hard. It is never enough for a poem to have good intentions. Lofty sentiments come crashing with a thud to earth when they are clumsily expressed. Yet some of the greatest poets of our age have dealt excitingly with religious themes and set giddily high standards.

Some days it seems as if every member of every synagogue in the land is trying his hand at poetry but most of it, alas, is hollow doggerel. It must be returned in the envelope that is so often thoughtfully provided. We have had the thrill, however, of discovering a few unpublished poets and the honor of receiving some stunning original work from poets of great reputation.

"A poem" said Archibald McLeisch, "should not mean but be." The thrill of poetic expression cannot be paraphrased. If the "meaning" were all, there would be no poetry — only prose. Sometimes in Jewish poetry the theme overshadows the poem. It is almost impossible to write successfully of generalized agony, which is perhaps why so few of the countless poems about the Hitler holocaust or the suffering of the concentration camp are successful achievements. The cargo becomes almost too heavy for the frail vessel of language, which drowns of its freight. The biblical theme calls for freshness of insight — here the poem becomes a kind of commentary. Prayers are the hardest to write, mingling, as they must, the fervor of profound belief with perfection of language. Yet the Jewish prayer book is an anthology of great prayer-poems accumulated over the centuries, and poets of our time may yet add to the store of this liturgical treasure.

Elias Lieberman

CABALIST AT MIDNIGHT

Now at the unholy stirring of night
with Ashmedai abroad whispering evil
into willing ears I stand fearful here
in the stillness before Thy ark.
Is it the sin of presumption driving me
or a sign from Thee, O Adonoi,
Who made man aspire beyond his reach?

I long to know what it is death to know:
secrets of creation, rituals to guard
sanctuaries of the mind from outcast demons
bringing confusion to dwellers of earth,
even levels on which Metatron and angels dwell.

My body has been starved until flesh
protests no longer its carnal craving.
I have stifled forbidden yearnings,
trembling to learn by the light of Thy 'Shechinah'
in one swift moment of revelation
the occult lore of Thy infinite spaces.

Let the Angel of Death shroud me
with the cerecloth of the Eternal Seeker.
I shall ever be thus, blinded, stumbling
but ever reaching . . . reaching . . .
before the ultimate darkness comes,
before my last searching breath shrivels
on Thy sacrificial altar fires.

JOHN GROTH

Paul Goodman

THE WELL
OF BETHLEHEM

Under the sun the reeking battle
in the barley-field the soaking blood
was sickening and frightful, by dusk
the warriors were no longer fascinated.
Their souls were empty and dubious.
The Philistines fled from Pasdamim
leaving many silent bodies
and some groaning that had been shrieking.
And David the young king the new
went hurrying to the cave his hold
as if he the victor were pursued.

His body-captains have preceded him:
"The King comes! for God's sake, water!
give us clothes without blood on them!
Thee God we praise, but—" They have lapsed
into a blank, being alive
but not much otherwise than those who lie
silent on the barley-field.

The woman and boys move busily
bringing the water and blowing up the fires
and now here spoke King David
in the gateway in a choking voice:
"I thirst. I am thirsty."

Instantaneously (like a picture)
two of the women are standing before him
with toward his lips a pitcher of water
and a pitcher of wine. Upon these pitchers,
not taking them, and past them at the women
looking for a long moment with glazed eyes,
David said, "From where is this water?"
She said it was the water from the well.

[347]

His eyebrows met. He said an awful oath
dangerous from the mouth of the anointed
and with a large arm struck
the pitchers from their hands.

The women's faces are white and open-mouthed.
It is still. The earthen pitchers
lie shattered in pieces on the stone floor
and the women are cowering in the shadows.
Nevertheless here is another damsel
standing before him with a pitcher raised,
"My lord, this is water from Adullam."
He did not strike her but he uttered a groan.
"I have fought hard—" he whimpered,
he did not sob but the tears of pity
rolled down his cheeks into his young beard,
"Will no one give me water
out of the Well of Bethlehem?"

Step back his soldiers from him! for that well
that well was in the camp of the Philistines
by the gate. A mother of grown sons
looks at him with wide eyes across her shoulder
seeing that he too was mad, like Saul.

Here he is standing silently flowing tears
because he had fought hard. There is an hour
in battle when the impetus is lost,
we have really been defeated and are dead,
there is nothing to do but strike another blow
and strike another blow and still another
wearier blow, there are not many more.
"Thee God we praise!" the shout is ours
but not from our throats and it penetrates
hardly, if at all, to our hearing.

Now I am thirsty but what is the good of water
not the water of my home where I was born?
I am already dead and what is the good
holding water toward my lips that is not the water of life?

Then the three captains of the King's body,
Eleazar, Jeshobeam, and Joab
—whom Joab was the first to scale Mt. Zion—
looked at their charge the body of the King.
Very wearily but not reluctantly
they girded on their swords and took up pitchers.
They brushed by King David in the gateway
not rudely but not considerately,
it was just how it was.
                                        It is no matter
for the King is not there where he seemed to be.
Was looking but he is not seeing anything.
It is too late. Now it is too late.
The King had already died of thirst
and therefore is inventing songs and verses:
'As the hart,' he singeth, 'panteth after water-brooks
—The voice of the Lord maketh the hinds to calve
and discovereth the forests!' See, his lip
his orange lip is curling with satisfaction.
'I laid me down and slept; I awaked!'
so he sang when he fled from his son.

Little spoke the three Mighties on their way
to fetch the water from the well of Bethlehem.
Jeshobeam—at whom the people look
askance because he slew three hundred men—
he said, "I go each time with no great joy,
but as I go I get deeper into it."
And Eleazar said, "He would do well
to quench his thirst with the available!
peevish and sullen not toward enemies
but just toward us who are his present help."
But Joab said, "It is the Lord's anointed,
hush. Hush!—" for even as he spoke it
they came on the first sentries.

The King has sat down, and the frightened women
still stunned get out their brooms
to sweep up the shards of the broken pitchers.
These shards of a brown glaze are still so soon
after the crash that they possess, each shard,

[349]

around it a bright outline, and hovering
close above them all a Violence.

As with their brooms the women sweep them up
the earthen shards turn rapidly to earth,
but the Violence on the newly cleaned floor
burns, if anything, colder in the broom-tracks
and in the room the echo of a shout.
But when the women wept, the Violence left us.

It was hard for the handmaidens of David
to please him, though they also did their best.

The three Mighties came back with one pitcher,
water from the well of Bethlehem.
They were bleeding darkly from old wounds
and bleeding brighter from new wounds.
The King sat half-reclined on a couch
looking around and seeing all things clear,
whom Joab came and offered him the water,
"Water from the well of Bethlehem."
Then David roused himself and bowed his head
deep in shame. Then up he stood at once
and took the pitcher from him, lest his Captain
might stand in front of him humiliated
by offering and not being accepted.
He accepted the gift with an obeisance
but he would not drink. In a deep voice he said:
"My God forbid it I should do this thing.
Shall I drink the blood of these men
that have put their lives in jeopardy?
for with their lives they brought it.
Therefore I will not drink it."
What shall I do with this water?
Embarrassed that I have it in my hands
and I am hot with shame.
Lack and loss may be consoled; but success
—only God can console.
                              So King David
poured out the water on the ground to the Lord.

[350]

And the women again brought him a pitcher of water:
"Here my lord, this is the common water."
But the King said, "Thank you; later.
I no longer thirst."

I no longer thirst! spiteful that I am!
Even so! Let me be magnanimous
and drink and try to slake my burning thirst.

Stanley Gottheimer

LOT'S WIFE

Lot's wife, remembered for her form, her final form,
Did she live for her cooking pots?
What was life like in Sodom for a respectable matron?
And her name, her name?
Looking back, she saw, she saw
Familiarity in the strange beast's jaw,
Met eye of the red basilisk
And suffered stonehood for her risk.
Contracting their heart-searing glance
Women knew her circumstance
Who lived faceless to die bloodless
Of war's hemophile homesickness.
Destroyer and His favorite
Chroniclers take time to sift,
Find flame and phoenix that they make
Diagrammed in the dust of wreck.
Lot's wife, nameless to a fault,
Shapes up silently in salt.
Disordered by the wind that wears,
Her form, our human way, are pairs.

[351]

Arthur Gregor

SPIRIT-LIKE BEFORE LIGHT

My parents are making the journey
they had hoped for long before
the migration that brought them
here. This time the destination
is Haifa. I went to see them off.
Their cabin was shockingly narrow.
An imposition of crude figuring.
My mother looked at first as if
this lack of regard had hurt her,
but not for long. My parents

have crossed many seas,
have been exposed
to more than one narrowness
dangerously close,
to walls too tall,
too near for human need,
to bars criss-crossing overhead,
the iron web of political ends.

At such times my parents have been accustomed
to construct in their minds the doors
that lead to stairs. To see themselves
pacing up and down on decks—
sea and sky falling away before them—
attending with their hearts
the names of their children
and of their children's children
announced and repeated behind clouds.

On this perhaps the last of their journeys
my parents are once more on the way

toward the fulfilment
their trapped and hunted fathers
and their fathers' fathers
had never doubted.
Beyond the roofs of the rooms that are narrow
the breeze that parts sea and sky
in endless succession—
for it rules there
and is at home there
in whatever it is comes after the parting—
my parents have had an instinct for.

They do not need to hear the voice
rattling on behind clouds
to know it is there
but have heeded the ancient prediction:
of Zion, the homeland, the holy dwelling.

This it is. Not a place.
It is not a place toward which they go.

They go, my parents,
whether they would admit to it or not
their whole being turned toward that
—spirit-like before light—
which no Jew will pronounce by name.

The place given as destination
is important and significant
but only in that it is the embodiment
of elsewhere—

elsewhere
where the breeze uplifts
where narrowness drifts
thin as a thin cloud
and is gone

elsewhere
where apparitions of sea and sky merging
vanish like mists in the sun

elsewhere
where the voice that is deeply
embedded in all tones
but does not speak in the world
speaks,
calls home its own

calls home its own

and the children enter.

Harry Roskolenko

PENITENCE

Everyday was not a holiday, but those days came
With silver brightness to engrave the tumbling air
Raging with singing cherubs in the holy places.
Before me all the worshipers echoed strangeness,
Their lilting, hushing, penitential voices
Inflecting a mystical, sudden sadness
That made their prayers heal my spiritual absences.

For I had yawned, as if the hum of voices
Was a pillow of God, making the child in me
Lie down and dream . . . and I was David
Smiting Goliath; and I was Saul, a King;
And I was a boy in holiness, waiting
For my father's hand to guide me to the loving lions.
Quietly, strangely, sadly, I lifted up my voice.

I sang aloud, shaking before this Majesty
Of faith and fear; my trembling inner accents
Glowing from my cherub's radiant face.
I was as one with all the worshipers, though yet a child
Confronting the past, acknowledging my future.
How well I see this scene for my world is hollow,
And I am filled with agony now, not purity.

Harriet Stolorow

HE SHALL LIVE A MAN FORBID

Graymalkin's Hecate spurns the toad,
The eye of newt, the pilot's thumb;
Her cobwebbed cauldron, out-of-mode,
Is left to moulder and corrode.

Still, poison bubbles, and the chant
Is even now being done and done:

"Beware the black man; eyes aslant;
The Stygian-bound non-Protestant!
Behold—the clause, good citizen,
When signed, protects your club, your home."

Hecate has filled the pen
With venom bled from gentlemen.

Rosanne Klass

EXODUS

There are laws concerning the conservation of matter:
Nothing is ever gained and nothing lost,
Exemplified in water.
It returns
Eternally to earth in varied forms.
Thus, the rain which dripped today along my pane
Flowed in Triassic oceans;
Thus, the sweat
Which fled the brow of Moses
Drowns me now.

[355]

Robert Greenberg

EICHMANN

The ghoul has gathered all the hands
In broken-crossed cartons to be shipped
To the fatherland.
Bootless feet are precisely packaged
One hundred per, trucked to move.
The spotlight barely glares on counted skulls
As dark sockets stare transfixed,
Yet something moves!
One unbroken skeleton scrapes movement
Flat against the neutral gravel,
Gathering its fingers to grasp false soap,
Stolen from the mass gas showers.
Ounces of sinew stretch and web the frame,
Veiled by dying cells of poisoned flesh,
Retreating breath spasms only in the hand;
Lesser men would miss the movement,
But the efficient whip-hand lashes
With lengths of wire barbed to cut,
Until the splintered fingers die
Open to release the stolen false soap,
Which the technician places
In marshalled order with the rest.
The false soap waits with perfect patience
For box-cars of those the state must wash.

Arnold Falleder

I SHALL NOT WALK
UNDER THE ARCH OF TITUS

On the walking
　　of the weakened
　　in the mountain
　　of all time—

Make me mild
　　to where I am,
　　where I am.

The newest son
　　of old children
　　by foot and foot
　　so strange a babe.

Men that are among me
　　sing in my hands.

Dawn fills me.

Night fills me.

Incredible towers light
　　when moons are down
　　the hill, and stars
　　go to the sky,
　　wander like mine.

Muriel Rukeyser

AKIBA

I

The Way Out

The night is covered with signs. The body and face of man,
  with signs, and his journeys. Where the rock is split
  and speaks to the water; the flame speaks to the cloud;
  the red splatter, abstraction, on the door
  speaks to the angel and the constellations.
The grains of sand on the sea-floor speak at last to the noon.
And the loud hammering of the land behind
  speaks ringing up the bones of our thighs, the hoofs,
  we hear the hoofs over the seethe of the sea.

All night down the centuries, have heard, music of passage.

Music of one child carried into the desert;
  firstborn forbidden by law of the pyramid.
Drawn through the water with the water-drawn people
  led by the water-drawn man to the smoke mountain.
The voice of the world speaking, the world covered by signs,
  the burning, the loving, the speaking, the opening.
Strong throat of sound from the smoking mountain.
Still flame, the spoken singing of a young child.
The meaning beginning to move, which is the song.

Music of those who have walked out of slavery.

Into that journey where all things speak to all things,
    refusing to accept the curse, and taking
    for signs, the signs of all things, the world, the body
    which is part of the soul, and speaks to the world,
    all creation being created in one image, creation.
This is not the past walking into the future,
    the walk is painful, into the present, the dance
    not visible as dance until much later.

These dancers are discoverers of God.

We knew we had all crossed over when we heard the song.

Out of a life of building lack on lack:
    the slaves refusing slavery, escaping into faith:
    an army who came to the ocean: the walkers
    who walked through the opposites, from I to opened Thou,
    city and cleave of the sea. Those at flaming Nauvoo,
    the ice on the great river: the escaping Negroes,
    swamp and wild city; the shivering children of Paris
    and the glass black hearses; those on the Long March:
    all those who together are the frontier, forehead of man.

Where the wilderness enters, the world, the song of the world.

Akiba rescued, secretly, in the coffin
    by his disciples carried from Jerusalem
    in blackness journeying to find his journey
    to whatever he was loving with his life.

RUDOLPH J. CARRASCO

The wilderness journey through which we move
    under the whirlwind truth into the new,
    the only accurate. A cluster of lights at night:
    faces before the pillar of fire. A child watching
    while the sea breaks open. This night. The way in.

Barbarian music, a new song.

Acknowledging opened water, possibility:
    open like a woman to this meaning.
In a time of building statues of the stars,
    valuing certain partial ferocious skills
    while past us the chill and immense wilderness
    spreads its one-color wings until we know
    rock, water, flame, cloud, or the floor of the sea,
    the world is a sign, a way of speaking. To find.
What shall we find? Energies, rhythms, a journey.

Ways to discover. The song of the way in.

II

For the Song of Songs

However the voices rise
They are the shepherd, the king,
The woman; dreams,
Holy desire.

Whether the voices
Be many the dance around
Or body led by one body
Whose bed is green,

I defend the desire
Lightning and poetry
Alone in the dark city
Or breast to breast.

Champion of light I am
The wounded holy light,
The woman in her dreams
And the man answering.

You who answer their dreams
Are the ruler of wine
Emperor of clouds
And the riches of men.

This song
Is the creation
The day of this song
The day of the birth of the world.

Whether a thousand years
Forget this woman, this king,
Whether two thousand years
Forget the shepherd of dreams.

If none remember
Who is lover, who the beloved,
Whether the poet be
Woman or man,

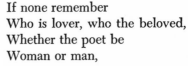

The desire will make
A way through the wilderness
The leopard mountains
And the lips of the sleepers.

Holy way of desire,
King, lion, the mouth of the poet,
The woman who dreams
And the answerer of dreams.

In these delights
Is eternity of seed,
The verge of life,
Body of dreaming.

PENROD SCOFIELD

PENROD SCOFIELD

III

The Bonds

In the wine country, poverty, they drink no wine—
In the endless night of love he lies, apart from love—
In the landscape of the Word he stares, he has no word.

He hates and hungers for his immense need.

He is young. This is a shepherd who rages at learning,
Having no words. Looks past green grass and sees a woman.
She, Rachel, who is come to recognize.
In the huge wordless shepherd she finds Akiba.

To find the burning Word. To learn to speak.

[362]

The body of Rachel says, the marriage says,
The eyes of Rachel say, and water upon rock
Cutting its groove all year says All things learn.
He learns with his new son whose eyes are wine.

To sing continually, to find the word.

He comes to teaching, greater than the deed
Because it begets the deed, he comes to the stone
Of long ordeal, and suddenly knows the brook
Offering water, the citron fragrance, the light of candles.

All given, and always the giver loses nothing.

In giving, praising, we move beneath clouds of honor,
In giving, in praise, we take gifts that are given,
The spark from one to the other leaping, a bond
Of light, and we come to recognize the rock;

We are the rock acknowledging water, and water

Fire, and woman man, all brought through wilderness;
And Rachel finding in the wordless shepherd
Akiba who can now come to his power and speak:
The need to give having found the need to become:

More than the calf wants to suck, the cow wants to give suck.

IV

Akiba Martyr

When his death confronted him, it had the face of his friend
Rufus the Roman general with his claws of pain,
His executioner. This was an old man under iron rakes
Tearing through to the bone. He made no cry.

After the failure of all missions. At ninety, going
To Hadrian in Egypt, the silver-helmed,
Named for a sea. To intercede. Do not build in the rebuilt
    Temple
Your statue, do not make it a shrine to you.
Antinous smiling. Interpreters. This is an old man, pleading.
Incense of fans. The emperor does not understand.

He accepts his harvest, failures. He accepts faithlessness,
Madness of friends, a failed life; and now the face of storm.

Does the old man during uprising speak for compromise?
In all but the last things. Not in the study itself.
For this religion is a system of knowledge;
Points may be one by one abandoned, but not the study.
Does he preach passion and non-violence?
Yes, and trees, crops, children honestly taught. He says:
Prepare yourselves for suffering.

Now the rule closes in, the last things are forbidden.
There is no real survival without these.
Now it is time for prison and the unknown.
The old man flowers into spiritual fire.

Streaking of agony across the sky.
Torn black. Red racing on blackness. Dawn.

[364]

PENROD SCOFIELD

Rufus looks at him over the rakes of death
Asking, "What is it?
Have you magic powers? Or do you feel no pain?"

The old man answers, "No. But there is a commandment saying
Thou shalt love the Lord thy God with all thy heart,
    with all thy soul and with all thy might.
I knew that I loved him with all my heart and my might.
Now I know that I love him with all my life."

The look of delight of the martyr
Among the colors of pain, at last knowing his own response
Total and unified.
To love God with all the heart, all passion,
Every desire called evil, turned toward unity,
All the opposites, all in the dialogue.
All the dark and light of the heart, of life made whole.

Surpassing the known life, days and ideas.
My hope, my life, my burst of consciousness:
To confirm my life in the time of confrontation.

  The old man saying *Shema*.
  The death of Akiba.

    [365]

PENROD SCOFIELD

V

The Witness

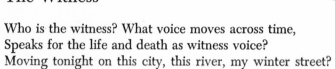

Who is the witness? What voice moves across time,
Speaks for the life and death as witness voice?
Moving tonight on this city, this river, my winter street?

He saw it, the one witness. Tonight the life as legend
Goes building a meeting for me in the veins of night
Adding its scenes and its songs. Here is the man transformed

The tall shepherd, the law, the false messiah, all;
You who come after me far from tonight finding
These lives that ask you always Who is the witness—

Take from us acts of encounter we at night
Wake to attempt, as signs, seeds of beginning,
Given from darkness and remembering darkness,

Take from our light given to you our meetings.
Time tells us men and women, tells us You
The witness, your moment covered with signs, your self.

Tells us this moment, saying You are the meeting.
You are made of signs, your eyes and your song.
Your dance the dance, the walk into the present.

All this we are and accept, being made of signs, speaking
To you, in time not yet born.

                              The witness is myself.
                                        And you,
The signs, the journeys of the night, survive.

[366]